The Civilization of the American Indian Series

The Apaches

For the Cuellos of San
Antonio, best wishes.
Don Worcester

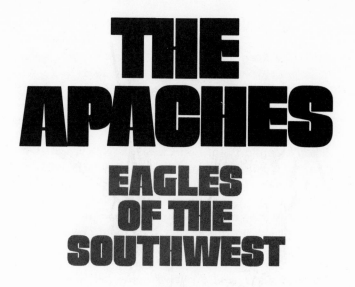

THE APACHES

EAGLES OF THE SOUTHWEST

By
Donald E. Worcester

University of Oklahoma Press: Norman

By Donald E. Worcester

Instructions for Governing the Interior Provinces of New Spain, 1786
(trans. and ed.) (Berkeley, 1951)
The Growth and Culture of Latin America (with Wendell G. Schaeffer)
(New York, 1956)
Sea Power and Chilean Independence (Gainesville, 1962)
(Spanish ed., 1971)
The Three Worlds of Latin America (New York, 1963)
American Civilization (with Maurice Boyd) (Boston, 1964)
Man and Civilization (with Robert Forster and Kent Forster)
(Chicago, 1965)
The Makers of Latin America (New York, 1966)
Contemporary America: Issues and Problems
(ed. with Maurice Boyd) (Boston, 1968)
Brazil: From Colony to World Power (New York, 1973)
Forked Tongues and Broken Treaties (ed. and contrib.)
(Caldwell, Idaho, 1975)
Bolívar (Boston, 1977)
The Apaches: Eagles of the Southwest (Norman, 1979)

Library of Congress Cataloging in Publication Data

Worcester, Donald Emmet, 1915–
  The Apaches.

  (The Civilization of the American Indian series;
v. 149)
  Bibliography: p. 359
  Includes index.
  1. Apache Indians—History. I. Title II. Series.
E99.A6W67   970'.004'97   78-21377

To the people called Apache

Contents

Illustrations

Maps

Preface

UNLIKE MANY PEOPLES who occupied marginal, undesirable lands, the Apaches roamed the mountains and deserts by choice and had no wish to abandon their nomadic way of life. Even when their incessant attacks caused some Pueblo villages to be abandoned, the Apaches did not occupy the sites. On numerous occasions they could have completed the depopulation of Sonora and Chihuahua,[1] but, as they candidly and somewhat boastfully remarked, they wanted the peoples of those provinces to continue raising horses and mules for them.

All Apaches spoke the same Athapascan language, but that did not mean there was always peace among the bands or even within them. The killing of an Apache called for retaliation. If one Apache killed another, the slain man's maternal relatives were obliged to avenge his death. If an Anglo or a Mexican killed an Apache, even though he might have been stealing horses, the chief of his clan or local group led a war party against the enemy. If possible, they killed the slayer; if not, any member of his race would do. If they captured an adult male, they turned him over to the deceased Apache's female relatives to torture and kill, as compensation for their loss.

Apaches had no tribal government, nor did they assemble as a tribe for any ceremony such as the Sun Dance of the Plains Indians. They were divided into bands, each with its own hunting and gathering territory and, in some cases, its own farming lands. What simple government they had was in the local group and its chief, though he lacked authority to punish his people. All chiefs of local groups were theoretically equal, although some, because of their character, "powers," or skill at war, had a wider influence than others.

The basic unit was the "family cluster" or extended family of several households who lived together because of blood, marital,

economic, or clan ties. In the rugged lands they roamed, cooperation among households was essential for both protection and obtaining food. It was unsafe for a man to hunt alone or for a woman to go far
from camp, except in the company of others, to gather seeds or
roots, and in any case the making of mescal entailed too much work
for one woman to manage by herself. It became customary, therefore, to share labors and their fruits with neighbors and related
households, so that all fared equally. "One must understand this to
understand Apache society. Out of all this has probably grown the
extremely gregarious nature of these people and their utter feeling
of loneliness and fear when compelled, through some exigency, to
live apart."[2]

John Rope, who served as a scout during the Apache wars of the
1880s explained the Apache attitude toward a family living apart
from others. "It may be all right for white people to live that way;
they seem to like it. But it would not do for us. We can't live off
alone. It isn't right. Other people would talk and say there was
something wrong with a family who did this; that they must be trying
to conceal something or that they were doing something bad."[3]

Morris E. Opler, a long-time student of the Apaches, observed
that "The close identification of the fate and fortunes of any individual with his entire body of relatives is one of the most important
conceptions which underlies Apache life. At every turn the Apache
child is guided and sponsored, not alone by his parents and immediate family, but by the larger body of blood kin. . . . At no time
do these relatives disappear from the background of the individual's
life."[4]

When a young Apache married he and his wife lived in her
family's camp. Thereafter he served her parents, though he did not
neglect his own. Because of the mother-in-law taboo, he and his wife
lived in their own separate dwelling, and he never spoke to his wife's
mother. The usual family cluster contained four or five
households—an older couple, a number of unmarried children, and
several married daughters and their families. Every family cluster
was under the leadership of a headman. Before sunrise each morning he harangued the families, and all were expected to listen and act
on his advice and his admonishment not to be lazy. The Apache
name for the headman meant "our smart one" or "he whom the camp
is under."

The next unit in size was the local group, comprising two to ten
family clusters and ten to thirty dwellings. The chief (nantan) of a
local group might inherit his title or win it by his ability to provide for

his people, and a capable chief was valued. Though he had no coercive powers, public disapproval was feared and avoided by the Apaches, and their children were made conscious of it at an early age.

Apache boys were toughened by strenuous exercise: they swam and ran before sunrise both summer and winter; sometimes they were made to roll nude in the snow. At sunrise, after they had dried themselves, they were told to run without stopping to the top of a hill and back. To make sure they breathed through their nostrils, they had to run both ways with a mouthful of water.

The girls also ran and swam, and some were as swift as the boys. Since Apaches considered body hair repulsive, young girls were warned that if they refused to swim early each morning they would have lots of pubic hair.[5]

Apache ceremonials were mainly concerned with healing the sick or, as in the puberty ceremonies, with preventing bad luck in the future. Apaches dreaded disease and fled in panic when pestilence struck their camps.[6] The most serious illnesses were believed to result from contact with certain birds or animals such as owls or coyotes. Illnesses caused by the various creatures had distinctive symptoms, and each could be cured only by a shaman or medicine man who possessed supernatural powers from the particular bird or animal.

The Apaches had a special fear of owls, and the presence of an owl around camp was a serious matter. There were no jokes or folk-tales about owls—it was bad luck even to talk about them. It was believed that the ghosts of dead people rose from their graves and entered the bodies of owls: the hooting of an owl was the voice of a ghost speaking in the Apache language and uttering threats against the living. Those who heard and understood the words were thereby exposed to "owl" or "ghost" or "darkness" sickness, which was likely to be fatal unless cured by a shaman whose powers came from owls.

Apaches scrupulously avoided the topic of death—the regular term for it, in fact, was seldom used. Instead of saying a person was dead, they used the phrase "he is gone." If death was mentioned during a war dance, the men stopped dancing; some would even quit the war party, convinced it would be destroyed. When an Apache died he was hastily interred so that the time in which living and dead were together was as short as possible. The haste reflects the Apache belief that a dire sickness could be contracted from the sight of the corpse or even from touching the deceased's possessions. Everything a man owned was buried with him or destroyed. His relatives disposed of all of his possessions, even though some might have been jointly owned with other members of the family. If this was not done promptly, Apaches believed, his ghost might return to recover the possessions, bringing "ghost" sickness and possibly death to his relatives.

Every effort was made to erase completely the memory of a dead relative. The dwelling in which he had lived was razed and the family moved at once. As few people as possible attended to the burial, then they burned their own clothes and bathed in sage smoke—"ghost medicine." The location of the grave was never mentioned. If it was absolutely necessary to speak of a dead relative they would refer to him as the "one who used to be called. . . ." Nothing was more certain to incite a deadly fight than to insult surviving relatives by calling out the name of the deceased in their presence. Children's names were usually changed after a death in the family because the deceased had called them by their names; continuing to use them, it was thought, would arouse painful memories.[7]

Apaches sought a variety of supernatural powers. For warfare, the most important of these was the "enemies-against power," which enabled them to surprise and defeat their enemies. Some men, like Geronimo, and some women were said to have the power to know what was happening far away. Other assets on raids or war parties were men with the "power" to make the wind blow hard, raising dust and offering concealment from the enemy, or to make the horses tractable.

Though never numerous, the Apaches successfully resisted all attempts to conquer them from the early seventeenth century until the last quarter of the nineteenth. They avoided pitched battles if possible, but when cornered fought to the death. As guerrilla fighters they were without peers; unlike the Plains tribes, they could not be starved into submission by extermination of the bison or any other animal.

These were the Apaches whose history is told in the following pages. From the coming of the Spaniards until they were finally run down by their own people and confined to reservations, the story of their relations with the newcomers was one of almost constant warfare. Weak in numbers but powerfully determined to preserve their cherished freedom, the Apaches were, and are, a remarkable people.

The Apaches

An Apache with a war club and feathered cap
Arizona Historical Society

I
The Apaches
and Their Neighbors

HARSH WAS THE LAND called Apachería, home of the Apache Indians, where every insect had its sting, every bush its thorns, every snake its fangs. Life was a daily battle for survival, a grim contest with a hostile environment and savage predators both animal and human. Rugged mountain and endless desert, this was Apacheland, and the Apaches were truly the products of their brutal environment. Although they preferred the mountains they were completely at home in any part of that tortured land: they suffered hunger and thirst and extremes of heat and cold without complaint. They saw an enemy in every stranger; they trusted no one outside the band; and there was occasionally bitter hostility between bands or even within them.

By hunting and gathering wild seeds and roots, Apaches could always find something edible; in time of need even lizards and pack rats were acceptable, but the Apaches shunned the flesh of bears, fish, and turkeys, This hand-to-mouth existence in a begrudging land forced them to separate into small, closely knit groups of a few families who were always on the move. The land could not support many of them in one place, and so they developed only the most rudimentary tribal organization. There were chiefs, but their authority stemmed largely from persuasion and personal prestige, for they had no sanctions over others. Apaches lived in absolute independence and were jealous of their freedom.

A warrior people, Apaches were born and reared for combat. From boyhood, a young man's training and games were designed to sharpen his senses, make him adept in the use of weapons, and develop to the maximum his physical stamina and fortitude. When an Apache youth was considered ready, he was allowed to serve his apprenticeship on raids. In these he was expected to fulfill a warrior's role, do all of the work at each camp, and learn from veterans. If he conducted himself properly, after four raids he was accepted as

3

a warrior. Many youths refused to go on raids, and others were rejected as unfit. Those who failed to qualify as warriors were treated with contempt. The hardy warrior produced by this exacting process was a relentless and pitiless foe, a master at stealth, surprise, and flight. His endurance was incredible; a warrior on foot could cover seventy miles in a day. Apaches scorned heroics: if they could not gain overwhelming advantage over an enemy by stealth, it was foolish to risk battle. There were too few men—none of the Apache divisions numbered more than a few thousand, including women and children—and Apache warriors could not afford to be cavalier with their lives. When cornered or protecting their women and children, however, they fought with reckless abandon, and it was a frontier adage that an Apache became more dangerous when he was wounded. Once out of range of enemy weapons, Apaches often slapped their buttocks and made other derisive gestures at their foes.

Both the Apaches and their kinsmen, the Navajos, belonged to the widespread Athapascan linguistic family, apparently the last migratory wave from Asia before the Eskimos reached this continent. Despite their late arrival in North America Athapascans were soon scattered from northwestern Canada to northern Mexico. It is not certain just when the ancestral groups of Apaches reached the Southwest, but they were well entrenched in some of their favorite ranges when Spaniards first visited their lands during the sixteenth century. Although anthropologists disagree on the approximate arrival time, many are convinced that the Athapascans were relative latecomers to the region. The Apaches were thoroughly at home, however, in the Southwest, and it seems unlikely that they could have become so acclimated to the rigorous desert and mountain environment in a short time. Apaches found life-sustaining food and water where others would have perished, and their intimate knowledge of a vast and uninviting terrain indicates that they had lived in the region long enough to become completely at home in it.

This study is concerned with the Apaches of New Mexico, Arizona, and northwestern Mexico. Over this vast desert and mountainous region roamed the Jicarillas, Mescaleros, Mimbrēnos, Mogollones, Chiricahuas, and Western Apaches—Tontos, Coyoteros, and Pinaleños. The names by which we know these bands were ones the Spaniards had applied to them by the late eighteenth century. Although the Navajos could be included and considered as Apaches along with the other southern Athapascans, they are customarily treated separately and will, therefore, be omitted here. The Kiowa Apaches and Lipans of the Southern Plains will also be excluded.

Jicarilla means "little basket" in Spanish and was the name given the Apache band skilled in making vessels of basketry. The Jicarillas, who roamed over northeastern New Mexico and southern Colorado, were never numerous, numbering less than one thousand. For much of the period since 1600 they were on friendly terms with the Mescaleros but not with the Navajos, though all spoke the same Athapascan language. The Jicarillas had periods of both hostility and friendship with the Spaniards, often joining them on expeditions against other tribes.[1]

The Mescaleros (literally, "mescal-makers") of central and southeastern New Mexico and western Texas were so called because of their custom of using mescal for food. Although the name was applied only to this group, most Apache bands used mescal. At one time the Mescaleros roamed on both sides of the Río Grande and eastward onto the plains, but their recognized hunting grounds came to be the Sierra Blanca, Sacramento, and Guadalupe Mountains east of that river and south into the Big Bend country and northern Chihuahua.

From at least 1630 on, near the headwaters of the Gila River in southwestern New Mexico were Indians called Gila Apaches or Gileños. The Mimbreños, Chihinne (or Red-Paint People), one of the Gila Apache divisions, lived in the Mimbres (Willow) Mountains and along the river of that name. Closely associated with them were the Bedonkohes or Mogollón Apaches, who lived in the Mogollón Mountains near the present Arizona–New Mexico border. Both were closely related to the Chiricahuas of southern Arizona—so closely, in fact, that they are frequently designated as Eastern Chiricahuas. But since each of these bands was known by the mountains it ranged, it seems more appropriate and less confusing to call them Mimbreños and Mogollónes. Culturally the Gileños and Chiricahuas were closer to the Mescaleros than to any other Apache band.

West of the Mimbreños were the Chiricahuas, who roamed the Chiricahua and Dragoon Mountains of southern Arizona. This was Cochise's band. South of them were the Nednhi (or Enemy People), frequently called the Southern Chiricahuas, who ranged the Sierra Madre and Hatchet Mountains of northern Mexico. Because all of

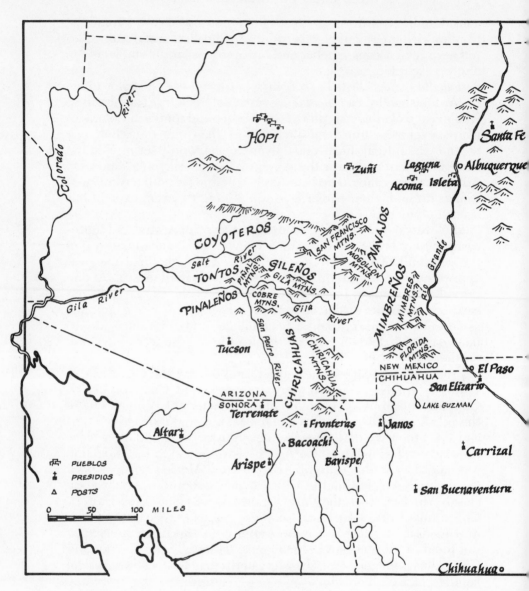

The Western Apaches

Based on Max L. Moorhead, *The Apache Frontier: Jacobo Ugarte and Spanish-Indian Relations in Northern New Spain, 1769-1791*
(Norman, University of Oklahoma Press, 1968).

these bands lived in rough, arid country, they did not attempt to plant crops but obtained food exclusively by hunting and gathering. Although all Apaches were nomads, each group had a favorite base, a refuge in which to store food for winter and from which to set out on raids.

Westernmost of the Apaches were the Tontos, Coyoteros, and Pinaleños, who lived in the Tonto Basin and around modern-day Flagstaff and the Little Colorado River, in the White Mountains around present-day Fort Apache, and in the Pinal Mountains. Because of their remoteness from Spanish settlements, these peoples and the regions they occupied were little known to the Spaniards before Jesuit missionaries moved north from Sonora late in the seventeenth century. The Western Apaches, as they are collectively called, raised some corn and other crops, and they were about twice as numerous as the Chiricahuas, Mogollones, and Mimbreños.

The various Apache divisions (they were not tribes in the usual sense) were known to Spaniards by a multitude of descriptive names before their modern designations were adopted. Because of this, and because some Apache bands changed locations, it is not always clear from Spanish accounts which band was involved in any particular incident.

In addition to the divisions and bands listed above, there were other warlike peoples who may also have been members of the Athapascan linguistic family, who were nearly always mentioned in conjunction with Apaches, and who were occasionally given that designation. These were the Janos, Jocomes, Mansos, and Sumas. The Janos and Jocomes were linked to the Chiricahuas and apparently had merged with them by 1700, for their names rarely appear after that date.[2] The Mansos and Sumas ranged farther east; they also disappeared as an independent people. The Tobosos of Nuevo León apparently were another Athapascan group with raiding practices similar to the Apaches, and eighteenth-century Spaniards regarded them as Apaches.[3]

Like many American Indian tribes the Apache bands and divisions became known by names others called them, for the Athapascans' term for themselves was *Diné*, meaning "The People." "Apache" is believed to be a corruption of the Zuñi *apachú* or "enemy," their name for their Athapascan neighbors, the Navajos. Because of their legendary fierceness, Apaches became known in Europe as well as America—in fact, a violent French dance was named after them. Their reputation for ferocity, earned in encounters with the Spanish, was still well deserved when Anglo-Americans clashed with them during the nineteenth century.

Apaches lived in *go-tahs* or camps, in groups of several families, and these were their primary political units. Young married men went to live with their wives' families, whom they served thereafter. In the early days raiding parties were usually formed from the members of a single camp, but on occasion men from several *go-tahs* might join for a raid. They left the women and children in a safe refuge with a supply of food and a few men to guard them, then set off.

Some Apaches, probably Jicarillas and Mescaleros, traded annually with the Río Grande Pueblos, exchanging hides, skins, tallow, and captives for Pueblo foodstuffs, tobacco, and cotton cloth. There is some evidence that Apaches camped in the vicinity of certain Pueblos during the winters. Relations between the two may have been generally peaceful, but had there not been interludes of warfare the Zuñis would likely have given the Navajos a friendlier designation than "enemy."

After Spaniards came permanently to New Mexico in the 1590s, the Apaches substantially increased their food supply by raiding the livestock herds kept at Spanish and Pueblo settlements. Since they knew nothing about raising cattle or horses and soon consumed those they stole, they came to depend more and more on raiding for food. Because they could rarely assemble a large number of warriors, raiding parties were small—usually four to twelve men. Raiders traveled on foot, concealing themselves for days if necessary, watching their intended victims until the opportune moment. Then they stealthily drove off the animals so that the loss might not be discovered for hours or days. They avoided fighting if possible, for it would jeopardize the purpose of the raid. If overtaken, they killed some of the animals in order to return and eat them later; then the Apaches scattered in all directions. If pursuit was prompt and determined, some animals might be recovered, but the raiders usually escaped. When the stolen animals had been consumed, the Apaches set out to raid once more. Groups of raiders might set out independently from camps hundreds of miles apart to raid ranches or settlements in New Mexico, Chihuahua, or Sonora, making it extremely difficult to organize an effective defense against them.

Apaches distinguished between raiding—for plunder—and warfare, which was primarily for revenge. Raids were organized when the meat supply was nearly exhausted. Usually an older woman of the group would call attention to the fact and suggest a plan for seizing enemy livestock. An experienced raider would shortly announce a raid and call for volunteers; any man who had served his apprenticeship with other raiding parties was eligible.

After selecting the enemy herd to be taken, a few raiders approached it in the early morning and shifted it quietly toward the others. These men surrounded the herd and drove it rapidly toward their country. On the return journey men and animals kept moving, often going without sleep for five days. Raiders had the right to give away the animals they had stolen—usually to maternal kinsmen, but also to women not related to them. According to custom, the stolen livestock was evenly distributed among the members of the camp, so that no family was excluded.

Although raiding parties usually drew all their members from a local group, war parties called on clan members over a wider area. If a warrior had been killed, it was up to his maternal kinsmen to avenge his death. The chief of the slain warrior's local group sent messages to clan chiefs of other groups, announcing a meeting. All who planned to take part assembled and joined in a "going-to-war" ceremony of dances and speeches designed to get them in the mood for combat. War parties, which might include as many as two hundred men, always included at least one medicine man, whose responsibility it was to encourage proper behavior and to predict the outcome. Captured children were usually adopted, but if adult enemies were taken alive, they were handed over to the slain warrior's female relatives to be tortured and killed. [4]

Apaches apparently first clashed with Spaniards in 1599, when they helped defend Ácoma Pueblo against Juan de Oñate, the first Spanish governor of New Mexico, who had brought a colony of settlers to the Río Grande valley the previous year. Whether these defenders were Chiricahuas, Western Apaches, or "Apaches de Navajó" is impossible to determine. In any event, Oñate's first settlement was soon the target of Apache and Navajo raids, although their object was Spanish livestock rather than destruction. Horses, mules, and cattle greatly enriched the Apaches' Spartan diet, and these Indians soon acquired a lingering taste for horse and mule meat, preferring it to beef or mutton. Apache raids became so costly that within a decade the New Mexico colonists petitioned the viceroy to allow them to abandon the colony. One of the Spanish priests, however, urged that New Mexico not be abandoned, for, he said, the Pueblo converts had lost the friendship of the Apaches. In 1609 the viceroy ordered the colonists to remain. [5]

After the coming of the Spaniards, Apaches continued trading with the Pueblos, as had been their custom. But Spanish governors, beginning with Oñate, aware of the steady market for labor in the mining camps to the south, began seizing Apaches and selling them as slaves. On occasion they even sold peaceful Apaches who had agreed to accept conversion, as well as others who came for friendly trade. It is not surprising that, as the sale of captives continued, Apaches developed an undying hatred for Spaniards. Apache families were close-knit, held together by powerful bonds of affection, and the loss of any close relative was the cause of genuine sorrow. Slave-raiding and the later practice of sending captives to Mexico City for disposition so intensified the Apaches' hatred of Spaniards and Mexicans that it never died.

By the 1620s Spaniards were well acquainted with the Apaches of New Mexico. Writing in 1630, Fray Alonso de Benavides was so impressed by them that he wildly estimated their numbers as greater than those of all the tribes of New Spain (Mexico). He made several observations about them, however, that were verified again and again during the centuries that followed. Apaches were, he wrote, "A people very fiery and bellicose, and very crafty in war." They valued chastity and punished a woman caught in adultery by cutting off the fleshy part of her nose. "They pride themselves much in speaking the truth," he added.[6]

When Apaches learned to use horses for something other than "belly-timber," both their mobility and their military power were greatly enhanced. There are no eyewitness accounts to tell us how or when Apaches first learned to ride horses, but a few documents do provide clues. Spanish authorities ordinarily prohibited Indians from owning or riding horses, but in 1621 the ranchers and missionaries of New Mexico were given special permission to employ Pueblo converts as herders.[7] During the 1630s there were frequent complaints that these converts, presumably disenchanted with their treatment by Spanish masters, had fled to seek asylum with Apaches or Navajos. It seems clear that Apaches were taught to ride horses by these Pueblo converts during the 1630s and 1640s. From about 1640 on there were many reports of conspiracies between Pueblo Indians and Apaches or Navajos against the Spaniards. In 1650, for example, some Pueblo herders turned over to Apache allies herds of Spanish horses.[8]

When they began using horses the Apaches patterned their riding gear after that of the Spaniards. They braided ropes of horsehair and rawhide and made saddles (with wooden frames), stirrups, and cinch rings. The first Apache saddle blankets were made of sheepskin,

buffalo robes, or deerskins. Later woven saddle blankets were acquired by trading with the Pueblos or by raiding. And to protect
their horses' hoofs on long rides the Apaches encased them in boots
of rawhide.[9]

Before 1680 Apache-Pueblo conspiracies were isolated, uncoor-
dinated, and ineffective, but even by 1650 Apache raids on Spanish
herds had become serious. Throughout the seventeenth century
governors continued capturing Apaches to sell as slaves. On their
slave-raiding expeditions the Spanish employed large numbers of
Pueblo Indians; this increased the enmity of some Apache bands for
certain Pueblo tribes, but it did not prevent cooperation between
others.

During the 1660s Apache hostility became so destructive and
widespread that no road was safe, for Apache warriors were constantly alert, ready to ambush unwary travelers. During the following decade Apache raids became even more devastating, and in 1672
the pueblo of Háwikuh was abandoned as a result. Jicarilla and
Mescalero raids caused the abandonment of the Tompiro pueblos
east of the Manzano Mountains by the early 1670s. In the Río
Grande valley Spanish herds were completely depleted, except for a
few carefully guarded flocks of sheep. In the meantime word of the
persistent sale of Apaches had reached the king, and in 1673 one of
several royal edicts commanded that Indian slaves be freed in New
Mexico and other northern provinces. But Spanish officials had long
followed a practice whereby unwanted or inconvenient royal edicts
could be circumvented without open disloyalty: they acknowledged
such decrees by saying, "I obey but do not comply." The slaves were
not freed, and the capture and sale of Apaches continued.

Apache raids left the cavalry unit at the presidio of Santa Fe
virtually horseless, powerless to punish enemy raiders. In the late
1670s, furthermore, a severe and prolonged drought, during which
hundreds of Pueblo Indians died, seriously weakened provincial
defenses. In 1677 Padre Francisco de Ayeta, the energetic Franciscan Superior of the missions of New Mexico, brought a wagon train
of provisions and one thousand horses for the troops. Convinced that
the province was still in grave peril, he returned to Mexico City to
petition for more provisions, troops, and horses. Heading north, he
had reached the Río Grande with wagons, a herd of horses, and fifty
soldiers recruited from Mexico City jails when he met Spaniards
fleeing south from New Mexico.

The Pueblo Revolt of 1680 had been carefully planned and coordinated by a Pueblo Indian named Popé; he had instructed the

leaders of the various Pueblos to count the days by means of knots in cords, so that all could attack on the same day. The rebel leaders also persuaded Apaches—apparently Jicarillas and Mescaleros—and some Navajos to join them in the uprising. This union proved decisive: the Spaniards decided to abandon New Mexico only after they were convinced that Apaches and Navajos were actually help- ing the rebels. And later, in contemplating reconquest of the area (which took sixteen years to complete), the Spaniards' main concern was the Apache and Navajo Indians. The Spaniards' first hope was that the Pueblo peoples would beg them for protection.

Comanche pressure pushed the Mescaleros westward toward the Río Grande during the reconquest of New Mexico. The Comanches also forced a band of Jicarillas out of their former range along the Arkansas River and into the Sierra Blanca. The southward push of the Comanches, primarily to acquire horses, cut both Mescaleros and Jicarillas off from their former buffalo-hunting grounds on the southern plains. In 1733 a Spanish priest established a mission among the Jicarillas near Taos pueblo, but it lasted only a few years. Apparently the Jicarillas accepted a missionary in the hope of secur- ing Spanish aid against the Comanches.

The Pueblo Revolt occurred at a time of shifting and extending Apache raids. The Mescaleros moved their raids to the northwest, into the Río Grande Valley. The Gila Apaches began striking at Spanish settlements to the south, in Chihuahua, forming an alliance with the Sumas, Janos, and Jocomes of western Chihuahua and eastern Sonora. During the 1690s Padre Eusebio Francisco Kino declared that these tribes and the Apaches had been raiding Sonora for "many years."[10]

Exactly when Apaches first entered southern Arizona is not known, but the early Jesuit missionaries in that region did not mention encountering Apaches until 1698, when Padre Kino met some in the San Pedro Valley near modern Fairbanks. The Apaches may have been pushed there by Spanish pressure or attracted by the prospect of sedentary peoples ripe for looting.

Between 1680 and the early 1700s the Western Apaches appar- ently were centered near the headwaters of the Gila. Along the Verde River of Arizona—in what was later Tonto Apache country —were the Yavapais, whose language was Yuman. Apaches were not mentioned in the San Francisco River region until 1747, nor in the White Mountains until 1808, but they may have been present and unreported earlier. Spanish campaigns from Zuñi in 1747 and 1754, as well as others from Chihuahua, may have forced some of the

Apaches of western New Mexico and southeastern Arizona to move farther west, thereby increasing Apache pressure on the Sobaípuris. Spanish expeditions from Janos and Fronteras may also have forced southern Apache bands to seek refuge in the Chiricahua Mountains and the San Francisco region.

Spanish Arizona was an extension of Sonora rather than of New Mexico, and Arizona remained part of Sonora until 1854. The Spaniards never occupied any part of Arizona beyond the Santa Cruz Valley and the Pima ranchería of Tucson. Jesuit missionaries had established missions among the Mayo and Yaqui Indians of Sonora early in the seventeenth century and soon afterward entered Ópata country. Pimería Alta, as northern Sonora was called because of the predominance of Piman tribes, was the home of Upper Pimas, Pápagos, Sobas, and Sobaípuris. These were sedentary, agricultural peoples, although the Pápagos of the southern Arizona desert subsisted mainly by hunting and gathering. Pimería Alta was bounded on the north by the lands of the Gileño Apaches, on the east by the San Pedro River, and on the west by the Colorado and the Gulf of California.

Jesuit missionaries, headed by Padre Kino, entered Pimería Alta during the 1680s.[11] The Piman peoples and Ópatas welcomed them and quickly accepted Christianity. The Sobaípuris of the Santa Cruz and San Pedro Valleys requested missionaries, but none was available until the eighteenth century. Jesuits were soon well aware of the growing Apache menace, and they came to rely on Ópata and Pima warriors to protect their missions and herds.

Of all the tribes the Spaniards encountered in North America none adopted the Spanish way of life more readily or more successfully than the Ópatas. They and the Pimas soon assumed major roles in the Sonora settlements. Because the Ópatas had forced their way into Pima territory as they moved along the Yaqui River, there had once been hostility between the two tribes. But as Apache attacks intensified, minor irritations were subordinated to the common problems of survival. Ópatas, because of their special relationship with the Spaniards, were called "the spoiled children of the Spanish crown" and "the most valiant, most noble and most loyal among all friendly tribes—the Tlascaltecas of the interior land."[12] They intermarried with Spaniards and later with Mexicans to the extent that they disappeared as a distinct tribe, and their language was ultimately replaced by Spanish.

The Ópata domain extended from the Huachuca Mountains of southern Arizona to central Sonora, but increasing Apache hostility forced the tribe gradually southward, leaving the northern part of its territory depopulated. Ópata villages were small and independent, for they were not politically organized at the tribal level. Fronteras, Bavispe, Baserac, and Arizpe were all in Ópata country; in 1778 Arizpe became the provincial capital of Sonora. Harmonious relations between Ópatas and Spaniards were marred only by an abortive plot in 1696 and by a few incidents in the eighteenth century.

Spanish officials considered the Pimas untrustworthy despite their notable services fighting against the Apaches, and several serious Pima uprisings reinforced Spanish doubts. Pima support of the Spaniards intensified Apache-Pima hostility, yet some Apaches still came to Pima villages to trade. Of all the Piman tribes the Sobaípuris were the most noted as warriors, for their lands bordered those of the Arivaipa Apaches and Chiricahuas, and they occasionally pursued raiders deep into the Chiricahua Mountains. A weak tribe would soon have been driven away or annihilated. Despite their courage and skill as fighters, however, the Sobaípuris could not hold out against Apache pressure indefinitely.

Apache troubles in Sonora paralleled those in New Mexico during the seventeenth century, for the raids increased in severity as the century passed and were especially troublesome throughout the 1680s. By the 1690s Apache depredations had almost depopulated the province. The Chiricahuas harassed not only outlying missions and ranches, but boldly penetrated the most populous parts of Sonora. The Spaniards called increasingly on Ópata and Pima allies to defend their towns and to participate in punitive expeditions.

Early in the 1690s, after the Chiricahuas and Gileños had driven the Ópatas from northern Sonora, Spaniards founded the presidio of Fronteras, which became a key post in the defense of the region against Apaches. In 1693 a *compañía volante* or "flying company" was also established to defend Sonora. One Apache band alone had stolen an estimated one hundred thousand horses, and the mobile unit was created to cope with such thefts by prompt and swift pursuit. But because Apache raids were sudden and widespread, the flying company could not accomplish all that was expected of it.

Although a combined Ópata-Pima force had successfully defended the Ópata mission and village at Cuchuta, Ópatas still looked on Pimas as culturally inferior—an attitude the Pimas naturally resented. Jesuits employed Christianized Ópatas as assistants at Pima missions, giving them authority over the neophytes and further straining relations. In 1695 resentful Pimas rose against the Spaniards, killing some Jesuits and their Ópata aides. The rebels then destroyed Altar and attacked Caborca, both mission settlements. Padre Kino arranged a peace meeting, and Pima chief El Tupo agreed to identify those who had killed Jesuits. But when the Pimas pointed out one guilty man, a Spanish officer unceremoniously beheaded him. The frightened Pimas fled, but soldiers and Seri allies followed in hot pursuit, killing El Tupo and fifty others. Those killed were innocent, and all had been promised protection. As a result of this betrayal, Pimas roamed the countryside, destroying Spanish towns and ranches until Padre Kino finally secured a general pardon for them several years later.

When Kino first visited the Santa Cruz and San Pedro Valleys of southern Arizona he found both areas fairly heavily populated, with ten or twelve villages of Sobaípuris in each valley, and a total population of perhaps forty-five hundred. Kino brought herds of cattle and horses to start ranches at Quíburi (near modern Fairbanks) and Bac (near the ranchería of Tucson). Quíburi was the village of Sobaípuri chief Coro, who had won fame in the wars against the Apaches by leading several successful punitive expeditions into their strongholds.

Because raiding had become virtually their sole livelihood, Apaches now relied almost entirely on stolen herds for their sustenance, and these herds enabled larger numbers of Apaches to congregate. As a consequence, raiding parties became much larger than before, sometimes numbering several hundred warriors and some women, and they often included Jocomes and Janos as well as Apaches. Depending on force rather than stealth, the raiding parties boldly attacked Spanish and Indian towns and even presidios. It was this change in tactics that made the incursions so destructive. Apaches were no longer content simply to run off livestock; their hatred for Spaniards impelled them to destroy everything possible. In 1693, for example, Apaches destroyed the mission at Cocóspera so thoroughly that it had to be abandoned.

Soon after this a unique encounter took place when several hundred Apaches, Janos, and Jocomes attacked the Sobaípuri mission of Santa Cruz de Quíburi. After terrorizing the inhabitants, the attackers ignored them and prepared to feast on barbecued horse meat. The Sobaípuris sent a runner to Coro with a plea for help.

The chief and about five hundred warriors, who had assembled for a campaign against the Apaches, hurried to the rescue from their village of Quíburi, about five miles away. El Capótcari, the Apache chief, seeing his warriors badly outnumbered, suggested that he and Coro each choose ten men to do battle and decide the outcome.

Coro accepted the challenge and selected his ten ablest warriors. El Capótcari chose his champions from among Apaches, Janos, and Jocomes. But the Pimas were skillful at parrying arrows, and they won the contest—last to fall was El Capótcari himself. The Apaches immediately fled, pursued by the Sobaípuris, and before the chase had ended more than fifty Apaches lay dead along the trail. The survivors split up, and different groups of them appeared at Janos, El Paso, and Santa Fe to ask for peace. Athough the victory was widely hailed, Spanish officials still doubted the dependability of the Upper Pimas. Padre Kino and other Jesuits who lived among them were more optimistic, but even they suffered several disappointments when Pimas suddenly abandoned their missions.

Despite occasional victories over Apaches, the balance was unfavorable to the Sobaípuris, and Coro moved his people out of the San Pedro Valley to Los Reyes, near modern Patagonia, soon after his triumph. They remained at Los Reyes until 1705, when they returned to Quíburi. After Padre Kino and Coro died in 1711, the Spanish did little to encourage or support the Sobaípuris for the next twenty years. Padre Luis Velarde, writing of Pimeriá Alta in 1716, complimented the tribe: "The Pimas are valiant and daring," he wrote, "as proven by the wars which the Sobaípuris and the rest of the Northern tribes have maintained against the Apaches. . . . "[13]

Although Spaniards had explored Arizona as far north as Casa Grande, no serious attempt was made to colonize the region during the seventeenth century. The discovery, however, of the famous *Bolas de plata*—huge lumps of silver—at Arizonac, a short distance south of the present Arizona-Sonora border, attracted a rush of miners and prospectors throughout the 1730s. The enormous lumps of silver were soon exhausted, and no veins were found. Although prospectors lost interest in the region and departed, other settlers remained.

During this same decade Jesuit priests began working among the Sobaípuris at Guevavi and Bac. Soon after, the Sobaípuris of the lower San Pedro Valley abandoned the area to merge with others along the Gila. In 1741 the viceroy of New Spain ordered a new presidio built between Guevavi and Soamca, to be garrisoned by Pimas, Sobaípuris, Pápagos, and Cocomaricopas. "Above all," he stated optimistically, "it will be able to defend the province from the frequent attacks of the Apaches and from their extortions and hostilities." The presidio of Terrenate, which was known by a variety of names, was built the following year.[14] It was at the head of the San Pedro Valley near the present Mexican border, a strategic location for checking Apache incursions. But although the troops were active, they were unable to fulfill the viceroy's expectations.

In 1750 Apaches destroyed the missions at Bac and Guevavi. The following year there was a general Pima uprising led by Luis Oacpicagigua of Saric, who had been named captain general of the Pimas for his help in subduing the Seris. The Pimas had rebelled, he said, because of oppressive treatment by the Jesuits, but they denied the charge, accusing him of seeking personal power. More than one hundred Spaniards were killed in the fighting, and it was several years before the Pimas were again at peace.[15]

One byproduct of the Pima rebellion was the establishment of the presidio of Tubac. In 1763, nevertheless, Tucson and San Xavier del Bac were both abandoned temporarily because of devastating Apache attacks; and four years later the Jesuits were expelled from all Spanish possessions, to be replaced by Franciscans in the missions of Pimería Alta.

The Apaches made a special effort to destroy the ranchería of Tucson, for it lay in the path of their raids to the south. Thanks to the efforts of Franciscan Padre Francisco Garcés, however, a walled village was built there. By the time the garrison of Tubac presidio was transferred to Tucson in the mid-1770s, the settlement was reasonably secure, though by no means free from Apache attacks.

The Sobaípuri population of the Santa Cruz Valley began declining about 1750, and the decline continued until the area was completely depopulated. Apache incursions were the principal cause of the population decline, but the ravages of disease were also partly responsible. Wary of the chronic war with the Apaches, the remaining Sobaípuris abandoned their villages in 1762, taking refuge at the missions of Soamca and San Xavier del Bac and at Tucson. Only in 1775, after all the Sobaípuris were gone from the lower San Pedro Valley, was a presidio established at Santa Cruz de Quíburi by the transfer of troops from Terrenate. After five years of constant warfare with Apaches, however, the troops were moved back to Terrenate. By 1800 the ranchería of Tucson and the mission of San Xavier were the only Spanish outposts in the lower Santa Cruz Valley.

In the rest of Sonora, Apache troubles were continuous throughout the first half of the eighteenth century, and the devastation became increasingly serious because of the larger numbers of Apaches in the raiding parties. Many Spanish campaigns to the Gila region and the Chiricahua Mountains originated in the presidios of Fronteras, Terrenate, and Tubac. The most ambitious of these was in 1747, a coordinated movement against the Gileños, with troops converging on them from several directions. But because of the difficult terrain and Apache elusiveness, the campaign was only moderately successful. It established a new pattern, nevertheless, and others like it would be more effective in the future.

The Gileños continued to raid New Mexico as well as Sonora and Chihuahua. In New Mexico military patrols were established, but the Gileños easily avoided them and frequently penetrated as far as Albuquerque and Laguna. Punitive expeditions sent sporadically from all of the nearby presidios did little to hinder the raiders.

During the 1750s Apache hostility was so damaging that many Spanish ranches and posts in Sonora were abandoned—some permanently—as far south as Altar. In 1756 a force of 140 Ópatas was organized to pursue Apache raiders to the Gila country, and three additional companies of Ópatas were recruited to reinforce the presidios. Since the Sobaípuris of the San Pedro Valley no longer absorbed the brunt of Apache attacks after 1762, the raids became intolerable. Throughout the 1760s Chihuahua ranchers lost thousands of horses, mules, and cattle to Apaches.[16]

Between incursions, Apaches frequently came to the presidios to negotiate the exchange of captives. Apaches selected the meeting places, confident that the Spaniards would not attack them while they held Spanish captives. After the exchanges were made the Apaches split up into small bands to steal horses and cattle on their way home. They also took advantage of the absence of troops who were on campaigns by raiding vulnerable settlements. In 1766, for example, while Captain Juan Bautista de Anza was off leading a force from Tubac against the Apaches, they ran off a herd of cattle from San Xavier del Bac. After 1765 the presidios of Fronteras, Terrenate, and Tubac each made monthly campaigns, but they brought no immediate relief.

Padre Ignaz Pfefferkorn, who served in Sonora from 1756 until the Jesuits were expelled in 1767, commented that Apache raiders drove off the stolen stock so swiftly that they were usually fifteen or twenty miles away before the loss was even discovered. And because Apaches killed and ate all the horses and mules except a few of the best kept for raiding, it was generally impossible to recover the lost herds. When the raiders attacked in large numbers they did not hurry, he noted, for a rear guard stood ready to ambush incautious pursuers. Apache boldness was such that they even attacked the soldiers guarding presidio horse herds.

Pfefferkorn blamed much of the trouble on the ineffectiveness of presidio troops. They had no training in the use of firearms, and though they were excellent horsemen and skilled with the lance, that weapon was rarely useful in battles with Apaches. The command of a presidio was, furthermore, a lucrative post. Pfefferkorn described the various ways by which presidio captains were able to profit by selling provisions, uniforms, and horses to their troops: "This is well known in Mexico City," he wryly remarked, "and the position of captain is not conferred on anyone who cannot prove his military worth with a cash payment of twelve or fourteen thousand pesos. He may or may not have a knowledge of warfare. . . . This is one reason why the savages play the master in Sonora." The troops pursued the Apaches occasionally, he added, but they usually returned empty-handed "because the Indians are too swift for them."[17] The situation was worsening, and to some Spaniards, Sonora seemed doomed to total depopulation. During the 1760s alone 48 settlements and 126 ranches north of the Yaqui River were abandoned. Despite Pfefferkorn's unfavorable view of them, some presidio captains, such as Juan Bautista de Anza, were excellent frontiersmen and Indian fighters.

In 1768 some 350 troops, among them veteran dragoons, all under the command of Colonel Domingo Elizondo, arrived at Guaymas for service in Sonora. Drawing upon the Sonora presidios and militias, Elizondo increased his force to 1100 men. They campaigned with some success against the Seris, but their efforts against the Apaches were unrewarded. It became increasingly apparent that it was useless to pursue Apaches at one point only, for they were active along the entire frontier. The Marquis of Rubí was sent to study the northern frontier defenses and make recommendations for improvement.

After an intensive three-year survey, during which he saw numerous burned-out ranches, Rubí recommended reorganizing the northern presidios into a single line, so that each controlled an Apache raiding trail. Grimly he urged making alliances with every other tribe and waging a war of extermination against the Apaches. Rubí blamed the troops' failure to deal effectively with Apaches on inept commanders and on the Apaches' amazing vigilance, speed, and endurance: "They use stratagems which always deceive our men."[18] Although presidios were relocated at various times thereafter, no amount of moving could make up for the lack of sufficient troops and adequate arms.

The military reforms of 1772 gradually improved the discipline and training of presidio troops, and their punitive expeditions became more effective.[19] In December 1773, nevertheless, as Anza prepared to march overland to establish a settlement at San Francisco Bay, Apaches ran off most of the horses and mules he had assembled at Tubac.

The non-Apache Indian population of southern Arizona had been greatly reduced by Apache hostility as well as by disease. Only twenty-three families remained at the mission of San José de Tumacácori; there were but eighteen families at Calabazas and nine at Guevavi, once the main mission. At Sonoita there were twenty-three families, but two years earlier Apaches had killed most of the women there. An insoluble problem for most of the mission villages was that their fields were along various streams, often several miles away and difficult to protect; those who worked the fields, therefore, were constantly exposed to danger.

Padre Bartolomé Ximeno, a Franciscan missionary at Tumacácori, urged consolidation of these little groups. "Otherwise," he predicted, "in a very few years the Apaches will finish off all of the small villages."[20] Only half a century earlier these villages had been fairly heavily populated, and the Tumacácori mission had owned twenty-five or thirty herds of horses as well as many cattle. By 1773 only ten horses—two of them mares—and fifty-six cattle remained.

In 1775 veteran Indian fighter Hugo Oconor assembled some fifteen hundred presidio and provincial troops and staged a coordinated campaign against the Gileño Apaches, driving them into a costly trap near the headwaters of the Gila, where 138 warriors were killed. More than one hundred women and children were captured, and nearly two thousand head of stolen livestock were recovered. A year later Oconor conducted another successful campaign, although he reported that the Apaches had destroyed nearly all of the remaining large haciendas in the north. When Anza returned to Sonora in 1777, he found Apaches again marauding freely over all parts of the province.[21] Anza inaugurated monthly campaigns against them, but without notable success.

According to Rubí's recommendations, presidios such as Fronteras, Terrenate, and Tubac were relocated at presumably more strategic sites. The Tubac garrison was transferred to Tucson, leaving the settlers of the former region undefended. Their pleas for troops were answered by the organization of a company of Pimas under Spanish officers. Both Pimas and Ópatas made effective infantrymen, and the Ópatas were successfully integrated with Spanish troops.

A new Ópata company was recruited to assist the Sonora presidios. It was the result of a suggestion by chief Juan Manuel Varela, who asked that his warriors be organized into a regular presidial company at Baserac or Bavispe. The Ópatas of this region had been hard hit and much reduced in numbers; establishing a presidio among them was a way of supporting faithful allies. A new presidio was also established at Buenavista, garrisoned by Ópatas and Pimas.

Although both Ópatas and Pimas bore a heavy share of provincial defense, the Spaniards continued to reserve their praise for the former, calling them the "most loyal vassals of our Lord the King . . . the most inclined to work, to till their lands, and to raise cattle; they are the truest and bravest in war. . . . "[22] By the 1780s Ópatas and Pimas filled the ranks of six Sonora presidio companies, and the Ópatas also maintained a picket of dragoons. What was even more unusual, they were allowed to supply some of the noncommissioned officers for their companies.

Despite the various improvements in military affairs, the Apaches had not yet been seriously weakened, and they continued to assault New Mexico, Chihuahua, and Sonora, attacking villages, mule trains, and even presidios. In 1781 the Sonora garrisons were increased in size and new firearms were distributed among the troops, greatly improving both morale and efficiency.

The Apache bands scattered throughout the mountains and deserts of the northern frontier were never numerous, but they effectively blocked Spanish advances northward at approximately the border between Mexico and the United States. The presence of the Río Grande Pueblos enabled the Spaniards to advance into and hold that region, except for the years immediately after the Pueblo Revolt in 1680. Spain's grasp there was never firm, however, and Jicarilla, Mescalero, and Gileño Apaches continued to run off herds from Albuquerque, Laguna, and Bernalillo. The presence of the Upper Pimas, and especially of the hardy Sobaípuris, had similarly enabled the Spaniards to cling to their tenuous footholds in the Santa Cruz and San Pedro Valleys of southern Arizona, but the Sobaípuris had been decimated in the process. Both valleys were constantly exposed to Apache incursions, with the result that the Spanish advance into Arizona progressed little between 1700 and 1800.

By the late eighteenth century Sonora's former prosperity had vanished under relentless Apache pressure. Mines, towns, and ranches had been abandoned as the population steadily declined. Cattle and horses, once plentiful, were scarce. The Apache problem was so serious and pervasive that in 1776 Spanish officials created a unique institution especially to deal with it—the Commandancy General of the Interior Provinces. This was a purely military administration, for the commander general would have military authority over the vast region between the gulfs of California and Mexico. He was not involved in civil affairs; his sole task was to protect frontier towns, mining camps, missions, and ranches.

The first commander general, Teodoro de Croix, recommended immediate action against the Western Apaches. Several Gileño bands had finally, by this time, been weakened by repeated Spanish campaigns and had settled peacefully near the presidio of Janos, where they planted crops. This was the first sign that the Spanish war of extermination was beginning to have an effect, but most of the Gileños fled within a year. The possibility of making peace with the Apaches by restoring those held as slaves apparently never occurred to Spanish officials; warfare with the Apaches and enslavement of Apache captives were accepted as unquestioned facts of life on the northern frontier.

When veteran Jacobo de Ugarte arrived at Arizpe to serve as governor of Sonora, he learned that his main problems were the rebellious Seris in the south and the unconquered Apaches in the north. Although the Seris and Gileños were probably never in league against the Spaniards, on a few occasions they do seem to have joined for attacks. Ugarte concluded that the solution to the Seri problem was to ship them off to Havana or elsewhere overseas. To deal with the Apaches he relocated a few presidios and established new ones.[23] In response, the Apaches simply selected new invasion routes. Some presidios began sending out fairly large forces on alternate months to hunt for Apache rancherías to attack. The tactics had been tried before without success, but the processes were repeated periodically because no better solution could be devised.

The improved military discipline and effectiveness and the increase in the number of troops and the supply of newer weapons, together with the constant killing or capture of small numbers of Apaches, however, gradually weakened the Gileños and Chiricahuas. By the end of the eighteenth century both bands, though fierce fighters, had only a few hundred warriors at most. During the 1780s Gileños had benefitted by an alliance with the more numerous Navajos, who joined them in force for invasions of Chihuahua. But Governor Juan Bautista de Anza of New Mexico exploited Comanche pressure on the Navajos as well as the Navajo desire for trade with the New Mexico settlements to induce some of them to take part in campaigns against their former allies. Navajo chief Antonio El Pinto, however, refused to be persuaded, and his followers also refrained from warring against Apaches.

Over the years the Spaniards had relied on extermination, a policy that offered no hope of eventual peace between Spaniards and Apaches if it should fail. In 1772 a new wrinkle was added, for a regulation of that year recommended sending unruly Indians from the Provincias Internas to Mexico City, where they could be distributed among worthy families as household slaves. Because some Apaches escaped from the Mexico City area and returned to their own people, greatly intensifying the hatred for Spaniards, Ugarte and other officials of the Provincias Internas favored sending such captives overseas.

In 1783 Teodoro de Croix sent ninety-five Apaches to Mexico City with instructions that they be taken to some place from which return was impossible. Commander General Pedro de Nava later recommended that all Indian prisoners of war be deported, regardless of sex or age, and this policy was gradually adopted.[24]

A few years later Viceroy Bernardo de Gálvez, who had served on the northern frontier, issued detailed instructions to Commander General Jacobo de Ugarte, introducing a new and more positive framework for relations with Apaches. They were to be allowed peace whenever they requested it and were to be punished relentlessly when they waged war. When peaceful the Apaches were to be furnished supplies and encouraged to live near presidios, where their movements could be observed. By giving them a taste for Spanish foods and for liquor (aguardiente), and by providing them with Spanish weapons, Gálvez believed Apaches could be made dependent on Spanish communities. He preferred to have them abandon the bow and arrow in favor of the Spanish musket, for guns required repairs as well as powder and lead. Holding back their supplies when they broke the peace would, he felt, surely dissuade them from committing hostilities. To keep them under pressure and in need of Spanish friendship, Gálvez favored encouraging other tribes to wage war against them.[25] For the first time in the long and costly wars with the Apaches, Spanish policy promised the possibility of a peaceful solution.

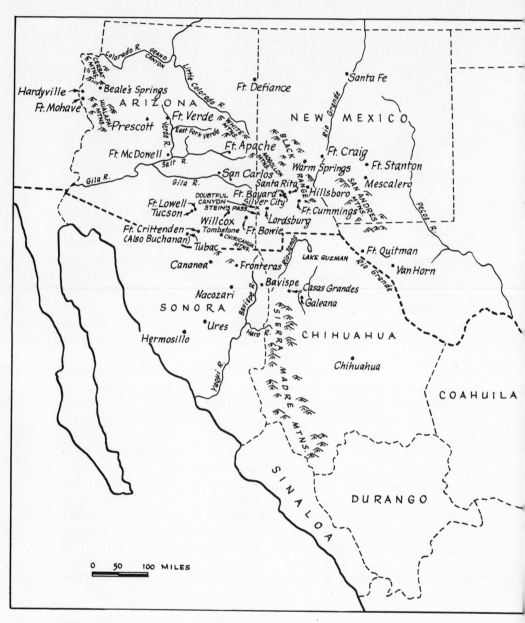

Western Apachería

Reproduced from Dan L. Thrapp, *The Conquest of Apachería*
(Norman, University of Oklahoma Press, 1967).

II
Apaches and Spaniards

THE GROWING EFFECTIVENESS of Spanish military campaigns was reflected in the increasing number of Apaches listed in Sonora baptismal records from about 1785 on. Most of these converts were undoubtedly captives taken in punitive expeditions, although some may have been from among those Apaches living near presidios as a result of the changes introduced by Bernardo de Gálvez. His policy of granting Apaches peace when requested, coupled with strenuous efforts to exterminate them when they waged war, quickly bore fruit.

In 1786 a band of Chiricahuas asked for peace in Sonora and agreed to live in an *establecimiento de paz* (literally, peace establishment, forerunner of the modern reservation) near the presidio of Bacoachi. Others, seeing their kinsmen protected and fed regularly, joined them. Having been constantly at war with Spaniards for so many years, however, the Chiricahuas were understandably apprehensive. When Colonel Jacobo Ugarte y Loyola and his troops passed through Bacoachi on their way to Arizpe, chief El Chiquito fled with his band. Those who remained offered to help Ugarte subdue the renegades and force them to return, but he declined. The Chiricahuas had fled out of fear, he said, not bad faith. He sent El Chiquito an invitation to return in peace, but warned him of the consequences of refusing. El Chiquito ignored both offer and threat.[1]

Viceroy Gálvez died in 1786, and his successor, Manuel Antonio Flores, was opposed to the policy of separate peace treaties with the Apaches in the various provinces, and with good reason. For although the Chiricahuas made peace with Sonora, they continued to raid New Mexico and Chihuahua, and other Apaches also found it convenient to remain at peace with one province while carrying on raids elsewhere. This practice gave them both a safe refuge and an opportunity to trade their loot. But it also gave the Spaniards of each province an opportunity to purchase peace at the expense of other provinces.[2]

Viceroy Flores, knowing of this Apache practice, ordered Ugarte to wage all-out war against the Gileños, using troops from Sonora and Chihuahua and employing Lipan and Chiricahua Apaches as scouts. If these bands refused to assist him, Ugarte was to attack them as well. There was to be no peace with any Apache band in Chihuahua despite the fact that Ugarte had convinced the Mimbreños and Mescaleros to settle down peacefully near Janos and other presidios. Flores ordered Ugarte to drive them from the province; as a result the Mescaleros resumed their raiding, adding substantially to Ugarte's problems. Campaigns against them intensified, and by 1790 the Mescaleros were again eager for peace, but it lasted only until 1796.[3]

In the fall of 1787 hard-pressed Spaniards in New Mexico persuaded some Comanches to join them in an expedition against the Western Apaches. The expedition met defeat but was reorganized and sent out a second time to convince the Comanche allies that Spaniards were not easily defeated. Although this second campaign was successful, Colonel Joseph Antonio Rengel considered Comanches more a liability than an asset. He ordered the Comanches to conduct campaigns against the Apaches by themselves in the future.

After Viceroy Flores resigned in 1789, his successor relaxed the orders regarding peace agreements, and eight or nine hundred Mimbreños were allowed to settle at San Buenaventura. But when another band on its way to join them was mistakenly attacked by the Ópata company from Bavispe, most of the Mimbreños, fearing treachery, returned to their own lands.[4]

A major campaign was now organized against the Mimbreños. Troops and Comanches from New Mexico swept south to drive them into the path of a force from Chihuahua that turned them west, where troops from Sonora, together with friendly Chiricahuas, closed the trap. The plan worked reasonably well, and sixty-one Mimbreños were killed or captured. But most evaded the trap and made swift raids into Chihuahua while Spanish troops were in the field and the garrisons weakened.

Those Chiricahuas still living at Bacoachi feared attacks by members of their band who had not surrendered, and early in 1788 El Chiquito justified their fears. In a sudden raid his warriors killed chief Isosé, who was known to be the most friendly to the Spaniards.

A subsequent campaign against El Chiquito failed, although a number of Chiricahuas accompanied the troops.[5]

Because of the vast distances involved and the multitude of Apache raiders, the Provincias Internas was divided into two commands. The Western Provincias Internas, Ugarte's domain, included the Californias, Sonora, New Mexico, and Chihuahua. When Ugarte assumed command Chihuahua was badly battered, for there simply had not been enough troops to defend it against Gileños and the Mescaleros driven out earlier by Viceroy Flores' order. The cumulative effect of the raids and killings was gradual but certain depopulation. Ranches, mines, and villages were abandoned as their owners or inhabitants were terrorized, robbed, and killed.

Between 1788 and 1795 several attempts were made to open a trade route through Apache country between Sonora and New Mexico by way of Tucson. The first effort, in 1788, led by Captain Manuel de Echeagaray of the Santa Cruz presidio, captured a few Apaches along the Gila. This induced several other chiefs, including Compá and El Chacho, to surrender and offer to help Echeagaray locate other Apache camps. He enlisted them as scouts and with their assistance was able to surprise several rancherías of Apaches. This was the strategy that would later lead to a final Anglo-American victory over the Apaches. It was, however, an unauthorized policy.

Governor Juan Bautista de Anza of New Mexico reprimanded Echeagaray for enlisting the Apaches as scouts: his orders were to kill or capture as many as possible; those with the captain could surrender as prisoners of war. But Commander General Ugarte approved the action, reminding Anza that Compá and the others were friends or relatives of the Chiricahuas and that it would be hazardous to alienate them. The achievements of the expedition were gratifying to Ugarte—54 Apaches killed, 125 captured, and 55 enlisted as allies—and a serious blow to the Gileños. The captives were sent to Mexico City for disposal by the viceroy.

By 1793 there were eight *establecimientos de paz* or reservations containing about two thousand Apaches. The Indian commissioners or agents were to prevent any of the Spaniards living in the area from cheating or annoying the Indians. Band chiefs served as judges and were expected to punish offenders among their own people. If any Indians fled, those remaining were to join the troops sent to bring them back. The commissioners held councils with the chiefs to remind them of the advantages of remaining at peace.

Peaceful Apaches were allowed to hunt off the reservations and to visit relatives living elsewhere. Those leaving the reservations had to carry passes to protect them from troops and to instill submission and respect for Spanish authority. Any who remained hostile were sent to Chihuahua for confinement.

The commissioners also selected informers to report on the actions and plans of others, and interpreters were also expected to act as spies. The agents issued weekly rations to those living within ten miles of the garrison, and they made head counts once a month. In order to help the Apaches become self-sufficient the agents assigned them farming plots and rewarded them for their efforts.[6] These reservation regulations foreshadowed those the United States would adopt during the nineteenth century.

The Conde de Revillagigedo, who succeeded Flores as viceroy, ordered that all Indians captured in war within the Provincias Internas were to be sent to Mexico City for transshipment to Veracruz or Havana to labor on the fortresses. Apache prisoners still in Mexico City were also to be sent to Havana, where they were shackled with leg irons to prevent escape. Some who were considered especially dangerous were cast into the dungeons of San Juan de Ulúa.

Since Apaches occasionally broke away from their guards, Revillagigedo ordered stricter security measures, which were somehow to be coupled with humane treatment and efforts to convert the captives. At times Apaches were deported before they had been proven guilty of waging war against the Spaniards. A young son of Ojos Colorados, an important Mimbreño chief, had been captured near Janos in 1788 and sent to Mexico City. Two years later, because his people were peaceful, Revillagigedo ordered him located and returned to his family, but he could not be found.

Most of the Apache captives were women and children, but on occasion there were a few warriors as well. Even the women and children managed to escape from time to time. In 1799, for example, fifty-one Apache women who were being escorted to Veracruz by dragoons, attacked their guards so furiously one night that most were able to escape.

Because Apache adults in Havana had made violent outbreaks, a royal order of 1800 declared that thereafter only Indian children were to be deported. Like so many royal orders, however, this one was ignored by colonial officials. Apache prisoners continued to be exiled to Havana until 1810, when the Mexican war for independence began.[7]

A diplomatic victory for the Spanish was achieved when Governor

Anza persuaded Navajo chief Antonio El Pinto to attack his Gileño friends after other Navajos had taken the same step. The Gileños recognized El Pinto and swore to kill him; in 1793 a Gileño war party entered Navajo country and made good the threat. The Spaniards rejoiced that the alliance between Gileños and Navajos had been ruptured; it had seriously aggravated the Apache menace in Sonora and Chihuahua because the Navajos were numerous and fierce fighters.[8]

In 1796 Colonel Antonio Cordero, a veteran of the Apache campaigns, summarized the results of a decade of warfare. The Apache wars, he admitted, might have been caused by the "trespasses, excesses and avarice of the colonists themselves. . . . " At the time he declared that the "wise provisions of a just, active, and pious government are bringing [the warfare] to a close. . . . " The government, he declared, did not want either to destroy or to enslave the Apaches.[9] But if the Spanish government had changed its desires concerning the Apaches, Spanish citizens had not, for they continued to sell Apache captives into slavery.

The Apaches, Cordero wrote, were extraordinarily robust and insensible to extremes of weather. Because of the scarcity of food they were constantly on the move, and in their speed and endurance were the equals of horses. In times of plenty they ate enormous amounts of food; in times of scarcity they bore incredible thirst and hunger without complaint. In general they lived in the most rugged mountains and were extremely jealous of their liberty and independence. Their dwellings (or wickiups) were circular, made of branches of trees covered with hides. They covered their heads with caps or hoods of leather, sometimes adorned with feathers or horns, and some decorated their clothing with porcupine-quill fringes.

The Tontos, Cordero continued, were the westernmost of the Apaches and therefore the least known. Most of them lived peacefully in their own lands, where they planted crops and supplied themselves by hunting burros and coyotes, "of which," Cordero commented, "there is such an abundance that they are likewise known by the name of Coyoteros."[10] The name Tonto was applied to the Apaches, Yavapais (or Apache-Mohaves), and Hualapais (or Apache-Yumas) living in the Tonto basin and roaming between the White Mountains and the Colorado River. Some Apaches had settled near the presidio of Tucson, where they were known as *Manso* or "tame" Apaches. The Western Apaches had not been exposed to punitive expeditions and were the most numerous of the Apache groups. The Coyoteros occupied the White Mountain region, and

An Apache with a feathered cap
Arizona Historical Society

although some Apaches ate coyotes, they did not. Those who roamed the Pinal Mountains were called Pinaleños.

At one time Chiricahuas had augmented their forces, Cordero pointed out, by uniting with the Navajos and some of the Western Apaches. But because of intensive campaigns against them, many Chiricahuas had settled near presidios in Sonora and Chihuahua. Continuous Apache hostility, however, had limited the Spanish occupation of Arizona to small communities near the presidios of Tubac and Tucson and to a few ranches in the Santa Cruz Valley. The only surviving missions were San Xavier del Bac and Tumacácori, near Tubac.

Cordero called the Gileños the most "warlike and sanguinary" of the Apaches. They had frequently raided Sonora and Chihuahua, but repeated campaigns against them had reduced their numbers by three-fourths. The Mimbreños had once been the most numerous and daring of the Gileños, but the band had suffered many defeats and had settled down at Janos and Carrizal, their numbers reduced by one-half. Cordero's estimates of Apache losses sound more wishful than accurate, for those allegedly decimated bands neither succumbed nor disappeared.

The Faroanes (from "pharoah"), probably a Mescalero band, ranged the mountains between the Río Grande and the Pecos. A small group of them were fed at the presidio of San Elizario below El Paso, but others raided New Mexico and Chihuahua. The Mescaleros had been hard hit by Spaniards and Comanches and were also much reduced in numbers. Cordero considered the Jicarillas a Mescalero band, although the two were not closely associated.

Commenting on Apache smoke signals, Cordero said, "In spite of the continuous movement in which these people live, and the great deserts of their country, they find each other easily when they desire to communicate. Understanding it is a science; but it is so well known by all of them that they are never mistaken in the meaning of its messages." A smoke signal on the slope of a mountain meant that Apaches were hunting their own people. A signal made on a high place and immediately put out meant for all to prepare to resist approaching enemies. There were many universal signals known to all bands, but some bands had, in addition, special signals of their own. Apaches always carried flint and steel or two prepared sticks for making fire, so they could send messages quickly at any time. They could relay messages two or three hundred miles in a few hours; this made it possible to assemble their scattered camps. Apaches were also excellent trackers, and could tell everything they needed to

Apache wickiups
Arizona Historical Society

know from animal or human tracks. They knew, for example, whether the tracks were made during the day or night, whether by a pack animal or a ridden horse, by animals being herded or simply grazing, "and a thousand particulars."[11]

By 1800 the Spaniards knew most of the various divisions living west of the Río Grande by their modern names. Easternmost were the bands that ranged along the headwaters of the Gila and southward along the Mimbres. They had been called Gileños or Apaches de Gila for two centuries, but after 1804, when Spaniards discovered or began working the copper deposits at Santa Rita del Cobre (near modern Silver City), these bands were called Mimbreños or Copper Mine Apaches. Their principal chief in this era was Juan José Compá, a man who could read and speak Spanish. The Mogollón band ranged the mountains of the same name near the present Arizona–New Mexico border; the mountains had been named for an early governor of New Mexico.

In the San Pedro Valley of eastern Arizona were the formidable Chiricahuas, close relatives of the Mimbreños. Their hunting grounds lay along some of the main plunder trails to Sonora, and when full-scale raiding was resumed, Chiricahuas would again be among the most active and destructive raiders.

A small band called Arivaipas lived in Arivaipa Canyon, beside a creek that emptied into the San Pedro. Like most other Apache bands the Arivaipas were called by the name of the region they occupied; although *arivaipa* means "girls" in the Pima language, there was nothing girlish about them. If, in fact, the Arivaipas actually carried out the devastating raids credited to them, they were, man for man, the most destructive band in Arizona. It was they who, in 1762, virtually forced the surviving Sobaípuris to abandon the San Pedro Valley. Arivaipas maintained close relations with the Pinaleños, merging with them when both were confined to San Carlos reservation.

The Tontos seem to have been a heterogeneous collection of linguistic families, united by common culture traits rather than by language. Included were the Hualapais, Yavapais, and possibly some Pinaleños. The first two spoke the same languages as the Yumas of the Colorado River area, but they differed from those sedentary kinsmen by living as nomads in the mountains of Arizona. They were so thoroughly associated with Apaches that they were generally called and considered to be Apaches. They were physically powerful and warlike, and their hatred of white intruders was unrivaled. During the seventeenth century Spaniards had called all warlike Indians north of Mexico City "Chichimecos." "Apache," too, became the generic term for enemy Indians, so in the case of the non-Athapascan Tontos, calling them Apaches was simply a return to earlier Spanish practice. Apaches, it should be remembered, did not call themselves Apaches.

When the nineteenth century opened there were many settlements of Manso Apaches at the various presidios as a result of the policy Bernardo de Gálvez had introduced in 1786. In 1807 Zebulon M. Pike saw "a great number" of them living around the presidio of San Elizario on the Río Grande.[12] Mansos were usually willing to serve as guides and to take part in battles against their own people. The result of the Gálvez policy was an unparalleled era of peace and prosperity for Sonora and southern Arizona, an era that lasted roughly from 1790 to 1830. It was not a time of absolute peace, however, for there were still bands of hostile Apaches in the mountains, and they occasionally did minor damage to settlements and missions. Between 1807 and 1812, for example, there were thirteen expeditions from the Tucson presidio and perhaps a similar number from Santa Cruz and other posts to the south. The Tucson campaigns resulted in the killing or capture of 137 Apaches.

Early in 1819 Captain Antonio Narbona led a large force from Fronteras to the Pinaleño lands to punish raiders who had harassed Tucson. Details of this major expedition are unknown, but soon afterward Pinaleño chief Chilitipage and 236 members of his band came to Tucson to surrender and settle down among the Mansos already farming there. This had been one of the most destructive of Pinaleño bands, and its desire to make peace was welcomed. It was always much less expensive for the Spaniards to feed peaceful Apaches than to wage war against them. Not long after Chilitipage surrendered, ten other Apache chiefs brought their bands to Tucson to surrender. These Apache actions came soon after Narbona's campaign, but what actually induced them to surrender is not certain. There is no doubt that some were weary of warfare and genuinely anxious to live in peace near the presidios, for they remained there many years.[13]

Although documentary evidence is fragmentary, at best, for the period from 1810 to 1821—the years during which Mexico struggled for independence—it appears that the Apaches did not resume full-scale raiding in Arizona or the rest of Sonora. They were, however, fairly active during this decade in New Mexico and Chihuahua. As funds for their rations became irregular, and as military morale visibly declined, some of those living near presidios began supplementing their rations by raiding distant settlements.

At the time of Mexican independence in 1821 the frontier presidios and settlements were little affected, although some garrisons were reduced in strength or temporarily abandoned. In many presidios the troops stayed on and continued patrols and punitive expeditions as usual. There were still Apaches living near the presidios, and in 1820 sixty-seven of those at Tucson were baptized; eventually the Mansos would be absorbed in Tucson's Mexican population.[14] Four years later Apaches living at Bacoachi took part in campaigns against hostile members of the band. Some time during the 1820s the Mescaleros fled from the *establecimientos de paz* in Chihuahua and returned to New Mexico, taking with them herds of horses and mules.

During the interlude of relative peace Spanish miners and ranchers in southern Arizona enjoyed their most prosperous years. Grants for large ranches were issued, and cattle-ranching became a major occupation of the region. Largest of the ranches was the San Bernardino grant in the heart of Chiricahua country. In 1822 Lieutenant Ignacio Pérez bought the grant, stocking it with cattle from the herd at Tumacácori. Over the next ten years his herd grew to an estimated one hundred thousand head, but resumption of Apache hostilities during the 1830s forced Pérez to abandon the ranch.

When Mexicans resumed mining copper at Santa Rita del Cobre in 1822, owner Francisco Manuel Elguea persuaded chief Juan José to keep his Mimbreños at peace with the miners and to permit pack trains (*conductas*) to carry provisions from Chihuahua and return with loads of ore. About half of the Mimbreños under Cuchillo Negro resented the arrangement and moved their camp to Ojo Caliente (Warm Spring but usually referred to as Warm Springs); they continued their raids into Mexico but did not disturb the miners. The two divisions were known as the Copper Mine and Warm Springs Apaches.

The valley of the Río Grande between Valverde and El Paso was the boundary between the hunting grounds of Mescaleros and Mimbreños, and travelers along this route were exposed to attacks from both. Spaniards aptly named this arid stretch of road *Jornada del Muerto*—"day's journey of the dead man." It was always difficult for the Spaniards, and later for the Mexicans, to keep this part of the road open. In 1825, because of incessant Apache and Navajo attacks, Valverde was abandoned.

The Mexican government was kept informed of Apache troubles in New Mexico. In 1831 Antonio Barreiro, legal adviser to the province, wrote an account of conditions there. He called Apaches the "most malignant and cruel" of all the wild tribes and the Gileños "certainly the most intrepid." On their raids they set up an ambush before running off herds, which was undoubtedly the reason that Mexican troops were not enthusiastic about hasty pursuit of Apache raiders. The speed with which they returned to their own lands with stolen livestock was remarkable. "Terrifying are the mountains which they ascend, and the waterless deserts which they traverse in order to wear out their pursuers, and the stratagems which they use to avoid the blows of those whom they have wronged," Barreiro wrote. They always left two or three men on the best horses to watch for pursuers. If followed swiftly by a superior force Apaches killed all but the horses they rode and then scattered, making pursuit hopeless. They showed the greatest courage when attacked. "They never lack calmness even when taken by surprise when they have not a chance for defense; they fight till breath fails them and usually prefer death to surrender." When enemies appeared they could break camp and flee with incredible speed. At such times they could travel one hundred miles without stopping. "They have an overwhelming dread of sickness and death. . . . Upon learning that any sickness is to be found near their rancherías, they flee to the most distant wilderness. . . . "[15]

Sonora's era of relative peace and prosperity ended abruptly in the 1830s when, for reasons that are not entirely clear, the Apaches resumed full-scale raiding. Hard-hit and shocked by the intensity of Apache fury, the people of Sonora and Chihuahua appealed to the government for help, but none was forthcoming.[16]

In an attempt to regain the lost peace, the commander of Chihuahua negotiated another treaty with the Mimbreños at Santa Rita del Cobre, dividing western Apachería into three zones and assigning a chief to keep the peace in each. Sonora was specifically excluded from the benefits of the treaty. Despite these efforts, however, failure to provide rations regularly led to renewed hostility. In 1833 Juan José and his people left Janos to resume their customary raiding, followed by the Coyoteros and Mogollones. The Mescaleros had concentrated their efforts on eastern Chihuahua, but in 1831 they routed troops and militia in Socorro, New Mexico, chasing them through the streets of the town.

Chihuahua and Sonora were once more exposed to frequent Apache attacks.[17] The failure of the 1831 treaties had demoralized the poorly armed people of Chihuahua, and Western Apaches penetrated boldly to the southern settlements of Sonora, killing more than two hundred people in 1833 alone. Most feared were the Coyoteros and Pinaleños of Arizona, who frequently joined the Chiricahuas and Mescaleros on large raids. On such occasions the Indians returned to their camps at a leisurely pace, for no troops dared follow them. In 1834, by a major effort, Sonora placed a small force in the field, but its accomplishments were insignificant in relation to its cost, despite the capture of the noted chief Tutije, who was executed at Arizpe. That same year Chihuahua bargained with the Comanches for help against the Apaches, but to no avail.

Sonora was torn by civil strife between federalists and centralists which aggravated an already deplorable situation. Ignacio Zúñiga, commander of the northern presidios, reported that between 1820 and 1835 at least five thousand persons had been killed and one hundred settlements abandoned along the northern frontier. And nearly as many persons had been forced to abandon their homes. There was, Zúñiga admitted ruefully, little left for Apaches to plunder.

The Western Apaches had their first contacts with Anglo-Americans during the 1820s, when trappers and traders entered Arizona from Taos and Santa Fe. In 1825 about one hundred Anglos obtained licenses to trap beaver along the Gila, and it was here that they first met the Apaches. Among the trappers were James O. Pattie and his father. After several skirmishes with Apaches they leased the Santa Rita copper mines and wisely made a treaty with Juan José, who had been much impressed by the superior weapons and fighting ability of the Anglos. The Apache chief gave the elder Pattie a tract of land for cultivation, even promising not to molest the Mexicans whom Pattie hired to farm it.

The Upper Pimas and Maricopas also had their first contacts with Anglos during the 1820s, when parties of trappers sought beaver pelts on the lower Gila. Relations between these Indians and Anglos were invariably friendly; both tribes, using irrigation, had produced a surplus of food they gladly traded for metal tools and implements. All who visited their villages commented on their honesty and prosperity as well as their helpfulness to travelers.

The Apaches, if wary of the Anglos, continued their forays against Mexicans. By 1835 much of northern Sonora had been deserted because of destructive raids. During the 1840s the population of Arizpe declined from about seven thousand to fifteen hundred as a result of Apache attacks as well as the transfer of the capital to Ures. Apaches roamed freely throughout Sonora, entering the presidio of Fronteras at will and repeatedly harassing Tucson. There were still, however, rancherías of Manso Apaches at both Tucson and Tubac during the 1840s.

Because presidio troops were poorly provisioned and often unpaid, and since some were criminals who had been sentenced to military service instead of hard labor, the garrisons were much less effective than they might have been. Unless the central government provided the means and direction for revitalizing the army, however, little could be expected of it. The people of Sonora and Chihuahua were obliged to seek other means of protecting themselves. Treaties and punitive expeditions had proved equally ineffective. In desperation the people of the two states turned to a third possibility: a war of extermination, promoted by the payment of bounties for Apache scalps. Chihuahua created new military units hopefully named "defenders of the state," and employed them in reinforcing Carrizal, Janos, and Casas Grandes, but Sonora took a more drastic step by offering 100 pesos for the scalp of any Apache warrior of fourteen years or older. An added inducement to scalp hunters was the provision that they could keep any stolen property they recovered. Later bounties of 50 pesos for women's scalps and 25 for those of children were offered. For a few months this policy placed the Apaches on the defensive; thereafter raids were resumed with redoubled fury. Again the desperate Sonorans petitioned the government in Mexico City to send them troops.

The scalp-bounty system attracted Anglos as well as Mexicans. In April 1837, James Johnson, who had gained the friendship of Mimbreño chief Juan José Compá, made a contract with the governor of Sonora after that state had established its scalp bounty in 1835. Johnson lured Juan José and his band to a feast in the Sierra de las Ánimas (modern Hidalgo County, New Mexico). While several hundred Apaches were crowded together Johnson fired a concealed cannon into their midst, killing and wounding scores. Before the bewildered survivors could organize their defense or flee, Johnson and his men attacked with guns, knives, and clubs. Johnson himself killed his "friend" Juan José. It was this brutal episode that turned Mangas Coloradas (Red Sleeves) into a bitter enemy of all Anglos. He reunited his Copper Mine people with the Warm Springs band and annihilated a party of trappers on the Gila. By cutting off the supply trains from Chihuahua the angry Mimbreños forced the Mexicans to abandon the copper mines. Johnson's massacre touched off a period of deadly warfare between Apaches and Anglos, and it aggravated the already bad relations between Apaches and Mexicans.

Johnson's instant success as a scalp-hunter won him fame and envy and induced Chihuahua to offer a similar bounty. The main effect of the bounty system, however, was to intensify the Apaches' hatred of Mexicans; it did nothing to solve the Apache problem in either Sonora or Chihuahua. As long as they had the strength Apaches were determined to wage pitiless and relentless war against bounty-offering Mexicans as well as bounty-collecting Anglos.

The most notorious scalp-hunter was not Johnson but James (Don Santiago) Kirker, who was known at the height of his scalping career as the "king of New Mexico." Entering the scalp-bounty business in 1838, he recruited a party of Delawares, Shawnees, Mexicans, and Anglos. Hunting in the upper Gila country, they surprised a rancheria of Apaches and killed fifty-five, in the process recovering some four hundred head of cattle and horses. The governor of Chihuahua had negotiated yet another treaty with the Mimbreños, but when he heard of Kirker's feat he invited him to Chihuahua City, where a contract was signed. Kirker increased his scalp-bounty army to two hundred men, promising the governor that for a fee of 100,000 pesos he would force the Apaches to accept a permanent treaty. Kirker paid each man a peso a day and half of any loot he found. A peso was then about equal in value to the dollar.

In September 1839, Kirker and his men found a band of Apaches in Taos, presumably there to sell plunder taken at other Mexican communities, and killed forty of them. In the following year, operating in Chihuahua, he took twenty prisoners in one raid. Kirker's fame spread throughout northern Mexico, much to the resentment of Mexican army officers. When General Francisco García Conde became governor of Chihuahua, therefore, he rejected Kirker's request for another scalping contract. Attempting to regain respect for the army, the commander at El Paso took several Mescaleros captive, including the wife of a chief. When the chief and sixty warriors came to demand the captives' release, the commander lured them into the garrison, where hidden men opened fire on them. The commander himself did not benefit by this trick, however, for when the firing began the chief stabbed him to death.

The year 1840 was disastrous for all of northern Mexico. Not only were Apaches raiding Sonora, but there were also Pápago uprisings along the Gila and Sonoita Rivers and many miners were slain. Farther east Comanches killed nearly seven hundred persons in Coahuila and perhaps as many more in Nuevo León. While Comanches ransacked San Luis Potosí and Tamaulipas, moving north with eighteen thousand head of livestock and one hundred captives, the Apaches were equally destructive in Chihuahua and Sonora. The Conchos River was the boundary between Apache and Comanche raiding areas; the Apaches usually remained west of the river, while the Comanches plundered everything east of it. Apaches and Comanches occasionally fought, as when the Mescalero chief Santa Anna warned the commander of the San Carlos garrison that Comanches were approaching. Together the troops and Mescaleros defeated the better-armed Comanches.

Apache raiding practice at this time was to strike in force; then, while the terrified inhabitants sought shelter, they scattered into small groups to round up cattle and horses. In November 1840, for example, four hundred Mogollones and other Gileños rode down the Sierra Madre, struck a few settlements, then broke up into small parties.

Anglo scalp-hunters concentrated their efforts on the Gileño Apaches, but the various bands apparently were not yet seriously injured. In 1841 they asserted that the only reason they had not .killed all of the Mexicans in the north was because the Mexicans raised livestock for Apaches. Their raids continued to be so damaging that Governor García Conde was forced to swallow his pride and negotiate with Kirker. Because it was well known that Don Santiago occasionally acquired "Apache" scalps from the heads of Mexican peons, the governor tried to protect his people by putting Kirker on a straight per diem (peso-a-day) contract. But the "king of New Mexico" was not to be bought for a pittance, and he retired to western Chihuahua, while Apache and Comanche raiders drove more and more people from their ranches and villages.

Kirker now worked with the Apaches, living among them and helping them dispose of stolen livestock profitably. One of his men claimed that Don Santiago was now "chief of the Apache nation," a claim not much more extravagant than that he was "king of New Mexico." Because of the activities of the scalp-hunters Apache raids had intensified: destruction of life and property was probably greater during the 1840s than any other decade of the century.

Between 1830 and 1841 Josiah Gregg made a number of trading expeditions from Independence to Chihuahua. He noted the Apache practice of maintaining peace with certain towns in order to have an outlet for loot and captives taken in Mexico. This practice continued regardless of what the state's official policy toward Apaches might be, for townspeople were always eager to purchase peace with the Apaches, even at the expense of their own neighbors. In 1840 Gregg saw a large trading party leaving Santa Fe to exchange whiskey and guns for mules and horses that Apache raiders were bringing from Mexico. Gregg remarked that this traffic with Apache raiders was encouraged by civil officials, including the governor.

When Apaches made truces with Chihuahua officials, they did so on their own terms—including the right to keep livestock stolen from citizens. The government even branded stolen livestock with a *venta* or quit-claim brand in a humiliating effort to secure peace. On his travels Gregg noted abandoned haciendas and towns all the way from New Mexico to northern Durango. The people clustered in towns and cities, for it was not safe to live away from them. The Apaches were so thoroughly the masters of Chihuahua that groups of three or four occasionally attacked herders within sight of Chihuahua City, driving off their stock without fear of reprisal. According to Gregg, the newspapers were full of accounts of the army's brave deeds in pursuing Apaches and of the extraordinary combination of circumstances that always compelled them reluctantly to "relinquish the pursuit."[18]

The Western Apaches entered Sonora and Chihuahua through a number of well-worn plunder trails. The westernmost of these, the "great stealing road" of the Coyoteros, originated in the Pinal and White Mountains of Arizona, crossed the Gila near modern San Carlos Lake, followed Arivaipa Creek, crossed the San Pedro Valley, passed the future site of Bisbee, and entered Sonora northwest of Fronteras. There the trail split into three branches: one went southwest to the mines and ranches of the Magdalena and Alisos River regions. Another went south toward Hermosillo, Arizpe, and Ures; the third followed the Nacozari River to the southeast.

The Chiricahua or Gileño trail was used by Chiricahuas, Mimbreños, Mogollones, and Tontos, who lived in the mountains south of the Verde River and east of the Santa Cruz. The trail crossed the Gila, followed San Simón Creek, and passed through the abandoned ranch of San Bernardino (near where the boundaries of Arizona, New Mexico, and Mexico meet) to the foothills of the mountains along the border between Sonora and Chihuahua. Another trail led from the region of Santa Rita del Cobre to Janos in Chihuahua, with a branch going to Sonora by way of Ánimas Peak. No region escaped the Apaches' attention, for raiding had become their way of life. Often various bands met at the Chile Cerro ranch on the Carmel River west of modern Ricardo Flores Magón, for it was a favorite rendezvous of Mimbreños, Mescaleros, and others.[19] Even though the Apaches were never numerous, their systematic methods of raiding enabled them to do enormous damage. Boys were trained from infancy, and by the time they reached fourteen they were ready to assume the role of warriors. Women, too, had their assigned duties guarding and herding stolen livestock, leaving the men free to fight off pursuers who might venture close. And when necessary women fought alongside the men.

Because the more numerous Comanches also intensified their raids during this period, all of northern Mexico suffered widespread devastation—the *tierra despoblado* ("unpopulated land"), it was called. Apaches killed Mexican men whenever possible, burned buildings, and carried off women and children to be adopted into the band or ransomed in New Mexico. Many of those who were adopted by Apaches, later refused to leave them when they had the opportunity, and some Mexican boys became Apache warriors. Sonora's problems were further aggravated in 1842, for while Apaches were active, the Yaquis rose in rebellion. The Mayos, Ópatas, and Pimas ceased fighting the Apaches and entered the uprising in support of the Yaquis, but the revolt was put down.

Officials of the northern states searched desperately for some way to bring peace to their troubled lands. The governor of Chihuahua again made treaties with the Mimbreños, Mogollones, and Mescaleros, promising to provide rations for them if they would surrender their captives and fight the Comanches in eastern Chihuahua. Other Mexican officials made similar treaties with the Comanches, promising them bounties for Apache scalps.

Because of these treaties with Chihuahua, the Mogollón and Mimbreño Apaches concentrated their raids on Sonora— Chihuahua now provided them with a refuge and provisions as well as opportunities for disposing of their loot. Although Chihuahua enjoyed a brief interlude of relative peace, Sonoran officials were understandably outraged. After Apaches camping near Janos in Chihuahua killed twenty-eight Sonoran soldiers and ran off the Fronteras presidio's herd of horses, Colonel Antonio Narbona raised a force of three hundred men and surprised three Apache rancherías near Janos; more than eighty Apaches were killed. Chihuahua City officials were furious, but there was little they could do except protest and await Gileño reprisals. But trouble came instead from the Comanches, who again swept over northern Mexico in the most destructive foray of the Indian wars. In 1845 a force of perhaps one thousand Comanches boldly pushed south as far as Zacatecas, little more than three hundred miles from the nation's capital.

In desperation the governors of Chihuahua and Sonora revived the scalp bounty; no other solution offered any hope. Governor Ángel Trías of Chihuahua also offered 9000 pesos for the scalp of Don Santiago Kirker, erstwhile chief of the Apache nation. Through an agent Kirker made Trías a counter offer to gather Apache scalps at the cut-rate price of 50 pesos each; Trías accepted. Kirker then assembled a force of 150 men and attacked the Apaches with whom he had been living, returning to Chihuahua City with 182 scalps as a result of this treachery. He did not mention it, but one of the scalps for which he was paid was that of his guide, who had gotten in the way of an Apache arrow. In addition to the scalps, Kirker brought back Apache captives, a large number of Mexican woman and chil-

dren who had been held by the Apaches, and much stolen livestock.
On another occasion his men followed Apache raiders into the Sierra
Madre Occidental, killing 200 and capturing 19.

By the time of the outbreak of war between the United States and
Mexico in 1846, conditions in northern Mexico were appalling; the
Apaches and Comanches had gravely weakened Mexico's capacity to
defend the region. While the war was going on Apaches destroyed a
number of towns in Sonora and forced Mexican troops to abandon
the presidio of Tubac. Kirker and other scalp-hunters had not improved the situation by killing Mexican peons for their scalps, yet
desperate governors overlooked these minor transgressions and
continued paying for all scalps submitted, for it seemed likely that
otherwise the Apaches would overrun all of northern Mexico. While
Mexican forces were moving toward the Río Grande to meet the
American threat, Kirker was hard at work. One day during July his
men killed Apache chief Reyes and 148 of his people.

Because of the war the hard-pressed governor had no funds to pay
for Apache scalps, and when Kirker refused to accept the rank of
colonel in the Mexican Army as payment he was declared an enemy.
With a 10,000-peso price on his own head Kirker fled toward the Río
Grande, where he met Colonel Doniphan's troops on their way to
capture Chihuahua City.[20]

In October 1846, General Stephen W. Kearny, who was marching
to California, met Mangas Coloradas and other Mimbreños near the
Santa Rita copper mines. The Apaches were friendly and seemed
anxious to be on good terms with the Anglos. In trading for mules the
Anglos found them "much shrewder" than they had expected. Captain A. R. Johnson, who was present at the meeting, described the
Apaches' clothing and weapons:

> They are partly clothed like the Spaniards, with wide drawers, mocca-
> sins, and leggings to the knee; they carry a knife frequently in the right
> legging, on the outside; their moccasins have turned up square toes;
> their hair is long, and mostly they have no headdress; some have hats,
> some have fantastic helmets; they have some guns but mostly are armed
> with lances and bows and arrows. . . . Just as we were leaving
> camp . . . an old Apache chief came in and harangued the General thus:
> "You have taken Santa Fe, let us go on and take Chihuahua and Sonora;
> we will go with you. You fight for the soil, we fight for plunder; so we will
> agree perfectly."[21]

Near the Río Grande the troops met two Mexicans returning from a
trading expedition to the Apaches.

Although the Apaches were cordial to the Anglo invaders at the outset, they soon had reason to wonder if this courtesy had been wise. Anglos had come to fight Mexicans; Apaches had been fighting Mexicans as long as they could remember. Those who had the same enemies, they reasoned, should be friends. It came as a considerable surprise, therefore, when the Anglos demanded that they cease their raids on the settlements of Mexico, New and Old. It was incredible—it simply made no sense, for within memory of man the Apaches knew no other living than by raiding. Did the Anglos expect them to starve? Both the Anglos and the Mexicans living in New Mexico were quite willing to purchase the cattle, horses, mules, and captives Apaches brought back from their raids into Chihuahua and Sonora. Why should they stop now?

When Anglo-Americans conquered New Mexico, they knew little of the Apaches. In November 1846 Governor Charles Bent, who had spent much of his life in the region, reported to Indian Commissioner William Medill on the Apaches. The Jicarillas, a band of about one hundred lodges and five hundred people, roamed northern New Mexico. Since there was little game left in the region the Jicarillas lived mainly by stealing livestock. They made pottery that was widely used for cooking, but they did not make enough of it to support themselves. The "Apaches proper" ranged through the southern part of the territory, Bent wrote, along the Río Grande and its tributaries westward to the headwaters of the Gila. He estimated their numbers at between five and six thousand. "For many years past they have been in the habit of committing constant depredations upon the lives and property of the inhabitants of this and the adjoining provinces, from which they have carried off an incredible amount of stock of all kinds. . . . " He mentioned that several bands were being fed by the state of Chihuahua to induce them to cease raiding, "but without having the desired effect."[22]

The Indian-fighting army of the United States had never campaigned against Indians as elusive as the Apaches, and it was totally unprepared for the swift movements necessary to bring them to bay. In 1848 detachments of the First Dragoons pursued Apache raiders occasionally but without overtaking them. During the following year many punitive expeditions were sent out, but few were even moderately successful. The raids continued without interruption, and between August 1846 and October 1850, Apaches and Navajos ran off more than twelve thousand mules, seven thousand horses, over thirty-one thousand cattle, and upwards of four hundred and fifty thousand sheep from New Mexico.

When James S. Calhoun arrived in New Mexico as Indian agent in 1849 he found that it was unsafe to travel more than ten miles from Santa Fe. "The wild Indians of this country," he reported, "have been so much more successful in their robberies since General Kearny took possession of the country, that they do not believe we have the power to chastise them." He recommended feeding the wandering bands so they would be able to give up their raids. They had in the past "supported themselves by depredations alone. This is the only labor known to them. The thought of annihilating these Indians cannot be entertained by an American public—nor can the Indians abandon their predatory incursions . . . for no earthly power can prevent robberies and murders, unless the hungry wants of these people are provided for. . . . " Calhoun was well aware of the potential troubles ahead if nothing was done to provide for the Apaches. Writing to the commissioner of Indian affairs, he emphasized that decisive action was imperative. "Expend your million now, if necessary," Calhoun urged, "that you may avoid the expenditures of millions hereafter. . . . The number of discontented Indians in this Territory is not small; and I regret to add, they are not the only evil people in it. The whole country requires a thorough purging. . . . " Calhoun also protested against the traders who visited the Apaches in complete safety because they traded guns and ammunition, and he mentioned regular meeting places where traders awaited Indians returning from raids into Mexico. Unless a new policy was adopted, he warned, troubles with the Indians would not end soon.[23] Calhoun's prophetic warnings went unheeded. In 1850 Gila Apache agent J. C. Hays resigned after only a year at the post because of his inability to accomplish anything "with the means furnished."[24]

For two years after 1846 American troops in northern Mexico kept Apaches and Comanches occupied, giving the region a much-needed respite. In 1848, nevertheless, Pinaleños who had made peace with Tucson forced the abandonment of Tubac and seized Fronteras, which they held for two years. When the Treaty of Guadalupe Hidalgo was signed by Mexico and the United States ending the war, American forces were withdrawn from Mexico, and Apache raiders again rode the plunder trails south to Sonora and Chihuahua. By the terms of the treaty the United States agreed to prevent Apaches and other tribes from crossing the border, but this soon proved impossible, at least without a major effort. The Mexican government created a number of military colonies in the north as part of the defense against Indians from the United States. The northern Mexican states also revived the scalp-bounty system: Chihuahua offered 150 pesos for a live woman or child, 250 for a live warrior, and 200 for the scalp of a warrior of fourteen years or more. Live warriors were much more dangerous to transport than bales of scalps, so the bounty for them was seldom collected. Other states passed similar laws, and parties of eager scalp-hunters returned to the mountains and deserts on both sides of the border; once more anyone with long black hair was in danger. Surprising an Indian camp, it was said, was like discovering a gold mine. The best season for scalp-hunting was from August to January, when Comanches camped in the Bolsón de Mapimí and Gileño Apaches wintered in the valleys of the Conchos River and its tributaries.

Some Anglo scouts and trappers were no more humane toward the Indians than were the scalp-hunters. Pauline Weaver, who served as guide for Philip St. George Cooke's troops on their 1846 march to California, pointed out a range of mountains where Tonto Apaches lived. "When I went over, once, from the Pimos," he said, "I met some lodges and had a fuss with them." When Cooke asked what sort of fuss, Weaver replied, "Oh, we killed two or three and burnt their lodges, and took all of the women and children and sold them." Cooke was shocked, but Weaver, without any sign or remorse, admitted that he had frequently sold Indian woman and children in New Mexico and Sonora. "They bring a hundred dollars," he explained.[25]

Hardly a day passed without reports of killings by Apaches and Comanches in Chihuahua and Sonora, and the officials of these states continued to search for remedies.[26] One governor persuaded Comanches to bring in Mescalero scalps. Another contracted with Seminoles, under Coacoochee (who had fled from Indian Territory in the United States), and runaway slaves, under John Horse, to gather Apache scalps. The Apaches knew about the bounties, for when Governor Trías offered 1000 pesos for the scalp of Mescalero chief Gómez, the chief responded by offering an equal amount for the scalp of any American or Mexican. The Mescaleros were particularly active in looting the wagon trains between El Paso and Chihuahua City.

Many Anglos made considerable wealth at the scalp trade, but there is no way of knowing how many of the scalps they turned in were actually those of Apaches. By the end of 1849, Chihuahua City, the "scalp capital of America," had paid out substantial sums for Apache hair, but Apaches still killed people on the outskirts of the city. The most properous year for the scalp purveyors was 1849–50.

Thereafter Kirker, John Joel Glanton, and other professionals of this grisly trade, finding Apache scalps increasingly difficult to collect, resorted openly to scalping friendly Indians. Alarmed at this practice, Governor Trías offered a reward for Glanton's scalp. Aware that the scalp boom was over, Glanton hastened to Sonora, where he received 6500 pesos for the hair of unfortunate Mexicans and Indians who had crossed his path along the way.

Many of the Anglo scalp merchants, including Kirker and Glanton, soon left for California and more prosaic pursuits. It should be noted, however, that in at least one case a form of poetic retribution overtook a scalp-hunter, for Glanton and his party were killed by Yuma Indians. Scalp bounties were still offered, but after 1850 only Mexican citizens could collect them. Kirker claimed that he and his men had killed 487 Apaches, but it might have been more accurate to say that they collected bounties for that many scalps.

The scalp bounty, although leading to the death or capture of a number of Apaches, provided no final solution to the Apache problem. By 1850 Apaches were raiding over larger areas than ever before. Tucson and many other towns were repeatedly struck, and raiders boldly ran off herds grazing near presidio walls. Other Apaches penetrated east of the Santa Cruz into the desert lands of the Pápagos, where they had rarely appeared before.

Some of the Apache bands had been considerably reduced in number by the indiscriminate killing of women and children for scalps. In 1850 the Warm Springs band that accepted rations from Mexican officials at Janos had only about two hundred warriors left. The total number of the band was estimated at about four hundred; in 1787 its members had been more than twice as numerous. Other Gileño bands had also suffered a decline in number.

In 1850 Colonel George Archibald McCall was sent to New Mexico to make a survey, especially of the U.S. military and the problems it confronted. There were, he reported, eight wild tribes in the territory, and of these the Navajos and Apaches were the most formidable enemies.[27] The raids they made on the Mexicans were prompted by the fact that they owned nothing and had to steal to survive. The Mescaleros, returning from raids into Mexico, were met on the Pecos, McCall noted, by traders from Santa Fe, who exchanged guns and ammunition for mules. The Apaches, who had a large number of captive women and children, would be more difficult to subdue than any other Indians, McCall predicted. The Jicarillas, on the north, were one of the smallest of Apache bands but one of the most troublesome, for they had killed more Anglos than any of the others. Although they had, McCall believed, no more than one hundred warriors and numbered no more than four hundred in all, he felt they must be exterminated. "I know of no means," he said, "that could be employed to reclaim them."[28]

McCall apparently considered the Sierra Blanca and Sacramento bands as separate from the Mescaleros—an error. Each had only about one hundred fifty warriors. What he considered as Mescaleros were the two southern bands, which ranged from the Guadalupe Mountains to El Paso. These two bands, under chiefs Marco and Gómez, had two hundred and four hundred warriors, respectively, and were the most powerful, but they rarely raided north of El Paso. They were friendly to the Anglos until 1849, when Glanton's scalp-hunters attacked them.

Like other Apaches, the Mescaleros could not understand the Anglo attitude toward raids into Mexico. Francis X. Aubrey, who was with a wagon train, met Marco and his band near Lympia Creek in west Texas. Aubrey told Marco that the Anglos wanted to be friends, but that the Mescaleros must not continue raiding in Mexico. Marco was astonished. "I had supposed that my Brother was a man of good sense," he said. "Has he, then, seen between the Pecos and the Lympia game enough to feed three thousand people? We have had for a long time no other food to eat than the meat of Mexican cattle and mules, and we must make use of it still, or perish. If you will give us cattle to feed our families, we will no longer take them from the Mexicans."[29]

One reason—initially perhaps the main reason—why U.S. troops were unable to cope with the Apaches, was that the dragoon horses could not keep up with those of the Apaches. On a number of occasions Apaches escaped at the last minute because their horses were superior in speed and endurance. After inspecting the military post at Rayado, in the Jicarilla country, McCall reported that all horses, whatever their condition, were routinely reported as serviceable, for better mounts simply could not be obtained. Part of the problem too was that dragoons carried seventy-eight pounds of arms and equipment, while Apaches carried only bows and arrows and lances. Horses brought from the northern states, McCall continued, took a year or longer to become acclimated and to be able to perform hard duty. He recommended purchasing three- and four-year-old horses in Tennessee and holding them on government farms in New Mexico for twelve or eighteen months before committing them to full duty.

The arrival of Anglo-Americans in force after the war with Mexico meant the end of one era and the beginning of another for the Apaches. Since both fought Mexicans, the Apaches assumed Anglos would be friends and allies. It was incomprehensible to them that they would be ordered to cease their raids into Mexican ranches and settlements. Against Mexicans, who were poorly armed at best, Apaches had little to fear. Now they were told they must stop raiding, or the heavily armed American troops would hunt them down. This dilemma may have caused the Warm Springs band to accept Chihuahua's offer of rations, and it certainly made the Apaches doubt the value of Anglo friendship. But this was only the beginning.

III
The Beginnings of Anglo-Apache Conflict in New Mexico

WHEN ANGLO-AMERICANS ASSUMED political control of New Mexico the Apaches were still carrying on their customary raids into Sonora and Chihuahua, although about two thousand of them were living peacefully near Janos. Toward Anglos, Apaches were initially deferential and friendly, for they assumed that anyone who waged war against the Mexicans must have other virtues. They had no idea in 1846 that Anglos were so numerous or so land-hungry, nor did they suspect that Anglos would swarm over Apachería at will. But when gold was discovered in California, the stream of Forty-niners traveling along the Gila made them apprehensive. The arrival of the Boundary Commission early in 1851 was even more worrisome, for it entered Mimbreño country with an escort of troops and without warning.

The first that the Mimbreños knew of the commission was when Cuchillo Negro and a small party of warriors encountered a lone horseman heading for Santa Rita del Cobre. The rider was John C. Cremony, scout and interpreter for the commission, who had ridden several miles ahead of the others. When he found himself surrounded, Cremony quickly covered Cuchillo Negro with his pistol and, in Spanish, ordered him to keep his warriors at a distance or be killed. Cuchillo Negro complied but refused to believe that other Anglos were near by, already in Mimbreño country. Cremony maintained the awkward position until his party appeared, when the astonished Apaches rode away.

Mimbreño lands had been unsafe for strangers since 1838, when Mexican miners were forced to abandon Santa Rita. The Boundary Commission, headed by John R. Bartlett, now began repairing the abandoned adobe buildings at the copper mines, while the military escort occupied the presidio, which was renamed Fort Webster. The presidio was triangular in shape, with towers at each corner.

50

The walls were adobe, three or four feet thick, and well preserved. Of the fifty or more adobe dwellings, however, many were in ruins.

The Mimbreños visited the intruders frequently, repeatedly asking how long they intended to remain. Although assured that the commission and its troops would move on as soon as the survey of that region was completed, the Mimbreños were skeptical. Why would anyone go to the trouble of repairing buildings for a short stay? They grew worried. They had driven the Mexicans out after the Johnson massacre of 1837 and did not want anyone else, even Anglos, taking their place.

Especially concerned over the intruders' presence was Mangas Coloradas, who had replaced Juan José as chief. The heavily armed Anglo force numbered over three hundred men, which made it too strong for the Mimbreños to attack with their bows and arrows and few guns. Mangas was the most influential Apache of his time, with friends and allies among other Apache bands as well as among the Navajos. He was a large, powerful man and a genuine statesman as well. On a raid to Sonora he had carried off a Mexican girl who, despite Apache opposition, became his wife. His two Apache wives would have accepted her as a slave, but not as an equal. Their brothers challenged Mangas, who met them in Apache-style duels with knives. When he had slain both of them there was nothing more for the Apaches to say or do—they accepted his decision. Mangas' Mexican wife bore him three attractive daughters. Like a medieval monarch he had arranged diplomatic marriages for them with the Chiricahua chief Cochise, with another Apache chief, and with a leading Navajo warrior. Now, with the Anglos in Mimbreño country, he called on the Navajos for aid, and four hundred warriors soon camped near Santa Rita. But because there was no opportunity for a surprise attack the Navajos departed.

In commenting on the Mimbreños, Bartlett concluded that they ranged on both sides of the Río Grande and as far west as the country of the Coyoteros and Pinaleños of Arizona. They lived part of each year in Sonora or Chihuahua, especially in the vicinity of Lago de Guzmán, west of El Paso. When he visited Sonora and Chihuahua in 1851 and 1852 Bartlett heard frequent mention of the chiefs he had met at Santa Rita, for their names were well known. According to information supplied by Mexicans who knew the Mimbreños at Janos, their numbers had been greatly reduced within the past five years. Although he admitted that certain Apaches were fine-looking physically, Bartlett saw no "mild or amiable" face among them. He estimated their total number at no more than five thousand.[1]

From his observations of the Apaches, Bartlett believed that it would be worthwhile to assign agents to them. "The pursuit most immediately adapted to their nature and habits," he wrote, "would be the raising of cattle and mules, a business which they could most profitably pursue, and which they fully understand already." He opposed the idea of concentrating the various Apaches on a single reservation, a policy adopted later with disastrous consequences. "The policy of concentration is a pernicious one," Bartlett astutely observed, "and can have but one result: it will stimulate their fondness for war. . . . "[2] This prediction came true during the 1870s.

Relations between Mimbreños and the Boundary Commission were outwardly friendly. The only friction that arose was over Mexican captives, whom the commission members were charged with rescuing when possible. They rescued a young girl from renegade traders who came to exchange guns for captives with the Mimbreños; then two Mexican boys escaped from the Apaches and sought asylum with the commission. The traders were frightened off, but the Mimbreños were incensed. Mangas Coloradas and other chiefs came to the commissioners' camp for a "big talk." An Apache warrior was raising the boys as his sons, Mangas explained, and he had become attached to them. He demanded their return, but reluctantly accepted payment instead. Chief Ponce reminded Bartlett that the Mexicans had many Apache captives, a fact that Anglos often overlooked.

In his book Cremony often referred to Apaches as "savages" and "barbaric," but he admired and respected them nonetheless. "In point of natural shrewdness, quick perception and keen animal instinct," he said, "they are unequaled by any other people. . . . To rob and not be robbed; to kill and not be killed; to take captive and not be captured, form the sum of the Apache's education and ambition, and he who can perform these acts with the greatest success is the greatest man in the tribe." Bravery alone was not highly respected; blind courage could get a man killed, and the Apaches saw nothing admirable in that. "They are far from cowardly," Cremony continued, "but are exceedingly prudent. . . . In no case will they incur risk of losing life, unless the plunder be the most enticing, and their numbers overpowering. . . . "[3]

Women, usually the wives of raiders, often accompanied Apache raiding parties. There was one notable exception of a single woman taking part in raids. This was Lozen, Victorio's sister, who was as adept as any man at stealing horses or handling a rifle. She was probably the woman Cremony recalled "who received particular honor from the other sex, but her Apache name has escaped from my memory. She was renowned as one of the most dextrous horse thieves and horse breakers in the tribe, and seldom permitted an expedition to go on a raid without her presence. The translation of her Apache title was 'Dextrous Horse Thief'."[4]

The Boundary Commission brought lasting troubles to the Mimbreños, for while it was working out of Santa Rita, prospectors discovered gold in nearby Pinos Altos, and some one hundred and fifty or two hundred miners set up camps in the area. Mangas Coloradas, who had offered to show Bartlett where there was more of the yellow metal that so fascinated Anglos, also told individual miners that he would take them to a place where gold was plentiful. As in the case of Bartlett, Mangas swore each of them to secrecy. But some of the miners discussed it and concluded that the offer was a trap. The next time the chief visited their mining camp they seized him, tied him to a tree, and whipped him severely. This was a capital mistake, for Mangas devoted most of the rest of his life to avenging this humiliation. Many a lone miner died slowly, head down over a fire or staked to an anthill, in atonement for the scars on Mangas Coloradas' back. Some years later, when a certain Dr. Thorne, a prisoner of Mangas', had saved the lives of wounded Mimbreños, he was taken, blindfolded, to a remote canyon where golden nuggets lay in profusion. As a reward he was allowed to have all he could carry. Mangas and other Mimbreños knew where there was more gold, but they did not disclose the locations.

There was no let-up of Apache hostility in Sonora. In January 1851, Ignacio Pesqueira, in command of 100 troops, intercepted and attacked a raiding party of 250 Apaches who were driving a large herd of stolen cattle. Though badly outnumbered, Pesqueira and his men fought until they had lost 26 dead and Pesqueira's horse had been killed. Certain that their commander was lost, the leaderless troops hastily withdrew. When Pesqueira walked into Arizpe a few days later he was welcomed as a hero and launched on a political career. The following month Apaches destroyed Mazatlán and defeated the troops sent to punish them.

On his way to Sonora Bartlett crossed the San Bernardino ranch, which had been abandoned during the 1830s by all except the wild cattle that still roamed there. He found the poorly armed people of Fronteras living in constant terror of the Apaches. The town had been abandoned in 1849, but General José María Carrasco, commander of Sonora, had reestablished it. In return for their raids in

Sonora (and their trading stolen livestock in Chihuahua), Carrasco had recently attacked the Apaches living at Janos. The captives taken were distributed among distant haciendas as servants (literally slaves), an old Spanish practice that had done much to sustain Apache hatred. Among Carrasco's troops, however, was an Apache sergeant who had been in the Mexican service many years. Evidently he had been captured as a child and had forgotten his own people.

Apaches were better armed than most of the people of Sonora and Chihuahua, and raiding was their lifetime occupation. Evidence of Apache devastation and Mexican demoralization was seen everywhere Bartlett traveled. The deserted villages and haciendas were too numerous to count. The old Ópata town of Bacoachi was destitute; its inhabitants were constantly on the defensive and unable to work their fields. The people of Arizpe, the former capital, also lived in fear of attack. While Bartlett's party was there Mexican troops brought in five Apache captives. That night other Apaches rode into town and demanded their release; the terrified guards hastily complied. On another occasion Apaches attacked a mule train within a few hundred yards of the town. The packers escaped by flight, but the entire train was lost. The people of Arizpe merely watched as the Apaches looted the packs and then leisurely rode away. To interfere with Apaches was to invite retaliation.

Constant harassment by Apaches continued to devastate northern Mexico. The people were so demoralized that they submitted to whatever the Apaches offered and did little to defend themselves. Shortly before Bartlett arrived at Santa Cruz in 1852, Apaches had made numerous attacks within a short distance of the town. The previous winter they had driven off a herd of mules from within musket shot of the presidio. The powerless troops watched, but made no effort to stop them. To show their contempt the raiders lanced a herd of cattle grazing outside the town walls, as if daring the troops and inhabitants to come out and be killed. Santa Cruz, which had once been a fairly prosperous community, had been reduced to a population of two hundred; and between Santa Cruz and Janos Bartlett saw nothing but deserted ranches and settlements. All of northern Mexico was becoming a wilderness.

Throughout the 1850s Mexican punitive expeditions against Apaches were rarely effective. On one occasion Bartlett saw some two hundred poorly armed and ragged troops from the Tucson presidio hunting Apaches. "These campaigns against the Indians," he commented, "are utterly useless, nor can they be attended with any success. During the last two years that the Mexicans have been operating against them on this frontier, not fifty have been killed."[5] In a skirmish a short time later, Mexican troops killed Coletto Amarillo, an important Mimbreño chief, but this had little effect on the raids.

Between 1851 and 1853 Apaches killed more than five hundred people in Sonora. The Ópatas were still the main bulwark of Mexican defense and were, in dress and appearance, much like their Mexican compatriots. They were especially noted for their courage, for they and the Pimas were always willing to fight Apaches. The Ópatas were frank, obedient, and cooperative with the Mexicans as they had been with the Spaniards earlier. There were still Ópata infantry companies at Bacoachi, Babispe, and Tubac.

While Bartlett was at Ures he learned that a party of about one hundred Apaches had driven off a herd of horses and mules from the vicinity of Hermosillo. Although the city had a population of more than thirteen thousand, only forty men could be persuaded to pursue the raiders. When they overtook the herd near Ures, the Apaches simply turned and charged them with lances, killing thirty. The Ópata chief Tanori led his people in pursuit, killed many of the raiders, and recovered 860 horses.

Bartlett found that Janos, like the Sonora presidios he had seen, was in poor condition, reflecting Chihuahua's critical Apache troubles. In 1826 its garrison had been composed of six officers and ninety troops. By 1852 there were only twenty soldiers, and the presidio buildings were in ruins. The town's population had shrunk to three hundred. Like the towns of Sonora, it appeared doomed to an early end.

In New Mexico Anglo-Apache relations were unfriendly despite the efforts of some officials. During the fall of 1850 a party of Jicarillas on their way to the military post at Abiquiu to ask permission to live there, stopped at a New Mexican's ranch near Ojo Caliente and asked for food, which was given them. When they were off guard their host had his men fire on them, killing a warrior and three boys. As a result the superintendent of Indian affairs for New Mexico, James Calhoun, allowed the survivors to live at Abiquiu and supplied them with provisions. The man responsible for the killings was arrested but soon released. "The demoralization of Society here," Calhoun wrote, "is such [that] it would be impolitic, if not altogether impracticable to administer justice in this case. A considerable sum of money has been subscribed to procure a gold medal to be presented to this cold-blooded murderer, and this is done, chiefly by Americans."[6]

Drunkenness was already common among the Apaches of New Mexico. Calhoun reported that the Mescaleros would sell every blanket or animal they owned or could steal in order to obtain "ardent spirits."[7] Dr. Michael Steck, agent to the Gileños, recommended issuing corn meal to Apaches instead of corn because they fermented the corn to make *tizwin*, an alcoholic drink. Indian agent John Greiner stated that the Jicarillas got drunk at every opportunity and then boasted of all the whites they had killed. He noted that settlers in northern New Mexico could not be prevented from trading "Taos Lightning" to them. Steck feared trouble with the Mimbreños because, thanks to the connivance of settlers trying to buy protection, the band could not be prevented from getting drunk.[8]

One of the problems concerning relations with the Apaches—a problem that would continue for two decades—was the lack of any consistent Anglo policy except extermination. Early in 1851 Calhoun wrote the commissioner of Indian affairs that "murders and depredations are almost daily occurring in this Territory, South and West of Santa Fe."[9] Calhoun had recommended confining the Apaches to restricted areas, but when Mescaleros and Jicarillas asked if he would make a peace treaty with them, he had no authority to do so.

Some Jicarillas were not only peaceful but actually helped citizens protect or recover their flocks from Navajo raiders. These were members of chief Francisco Chacón's band. On one occasion they pursued a party of Navajos and recovered three thousand sheep, which they returned to the owners. And the people of Manzana, sixty miles southeast of Albuquerque, reported that the Jicarillas had protected them and their flocks for many months.[10]

Despite the guarantee in the Treaty of Guadalupe Hidalgo that the United States would prevent Indians from raiding across the border into Mexico, Congress ignored the Apache problem, leaving both Mexico and the Anglo settlers in the Southwest largely on their own. Anglo authorities, moreover, were seldom united in their efforts to control the Apaches. The type of civil-military controversy that would complicate the Apache troubles into the 1880s was evident from the outset. Colonel Edward Vose Sumner, First Dragoons, who was named commander of the military district of New Mexico early in 1851, was instructed to cooperate with Calhoun in all matters relating to Indians. Calhoun was convinced after a chief came to Santa Fe to see him that the Gileños could be kept peaceful if Congress would make a modest appropriation for their support. He wanted to visit the Mimbreños at Santa Rita del Cobre, but Colonel Sumner refused to provide an escort, thus effectively cancelling the visit. "If," Calhoun wrote the commissioner, "this is in pursuance of instructions from Washington, our Indian Affairs must be conducted by the officers of the Army, or they must be neglected."[11]

Although miners remained in Mimbreño country after the Boundary Commission left, they had no military protection. Fort Webster had been merely a temporary installation to protect the commission while it was in the region. But the Mimbreños were convinced that they had driven the troops away and became bolder. Many members of the band who had been living at Janos returned to help drive the miners out of their lands. In January 1852, on the recommendation of Major Enoch Steen of the First Dragoons, Fort Webster was reoccupied by an infantry company. In September the garrison was moved to a site near the Mimbres River, where a new fort was built, also named Webster. Major Steen and two companies of dragoons were sent to strengthen the garrison. Late in 1853 Fort Webster was abandoned and the troops were transferred to Fort Thorn on the Río Grande, one of the posts General John Garland had ordered built to control the Mescaleros. A strong garrison at Fort Webster would have helped control the Mimbreños, but the policy of placing military posts in Apache country was slow to develop.

Treaties with various Apache bands were negotiated during the 1850s, but the Senate consistently rejected them. Major John Greiner, acting Indian agent during Calhoun's illness, invited the Mescaleros to Santa Fe for a council, and thirty chiefs and headmen accepted. In July 1851, they agreed to a treaty of "perpetual peace and amity." Greiner also arranged for a meeting with Gileño chiefs at Ácoma. Colonel Sumner decided to conduct the negotiations himself, but insisted that Greiner accompany him. Mangas Coloradas entered the camp and said to Sumner, "You are chief of the white men. I am chief of the red men. Now let us have a talk and treat."[12] Congress still refused to ratify the treaties, and relations between Anglos and Apaches worsened. In February 1852 Calhoun had reported military defeats and the interruption of travel by Apaches in many parts of the territory. "If the outrages continue," he wrote Daniel Webster, the territory will be left a "howling wilderness."[13] In his official report for 1852 Sumner strongly recommended returning New Mexico to the "Mexicans and Indians."

In 1853 Governor William Carr Lane negotiated a number of treaties with the wild tribes, promising to furnish corn, salt, beef, and breeding stock for the first year and "reasonable subsistence" for the next three years. Without waiting for the Senate to confirm the treaties, Lane assembled a large number of Mimbreños near Fort Webster and advanced them money from the territorial treasury so they could begin farming. As often happened in dealings with Indians, men who made promises in good faith were unable to keep them. Lane was soon replaced by David Meriwether, who found the territorial treasury nearly empty. Meriwether saw two ways of controlling the Indians, by feeding them and by force. "The former has been the policy of my predecessors; the latter" he concluded, "has not been effectually tried."[14] Since initially at least he preferred force to food, Meriwether was not disappointed when Congress declined to confirm the treaties of his predecessor. But when their supply of provisions was stopped the Mimbreños felt betrayed.

Lane had concluded a similar treaty with the Jicarillas, promising that the government would feed them for five years while assisting them to become self-supporting. The treaty was to go into effect only when approved by the Senate, but the Jicarillas, totally unfamiliar with constitutional requirements, assumed that it was already in effect. They went into camp near Abiquiu to wait for the promised supplies, and the army fed them in the interim.

When the Senate rejected the treaty, Governor Meriwether tried unsuccessfully to explain what had happened. The Jicarillas could not understand why, after they had been promised provisions if they would remain peaceful, the army suddenly quit feeding them. Faced with starvation, they returned to their old habits. Anglo settlers soon complained of thefts of livestock and called for the army to protect them against an expected Indian war. An attempt to settle the grievances of Apaches and Anglos failed, and dragoons fired into a group of Jicarillas, killing a number of women and children. Although armed mainly with bows and arrows, the Jicarillas quickly retaliated, killing twenty-four dragoons and wounding nearly as many. Open warfare followed. Meriwether concluded that no other band of Indians did more damage to New Mexico.[15]

Feeding the Apaches, as the Spanish and Mexicans had learned, was far less costly than fighting them, especially when they were willing to accept provisions and live in peace near an army post. Like the Jicarillas, the Mimbreños grew increasingly irate over what they considered Anglo treachery. For a year they directed their raids primarily against Anglo settlements, miners, and ranches. Property of immense value was destroyed or stolen, and many people were killed. When Fort Webster was reoccupied by troops the Mimbreños recognized that their lands were again in jeopardy, and their fury further increased.

Greiner's treaty with the Mescaleros had been with only the Sierra Blanca band, which made an effort to abide by the agreement and keep the peace. Other Mescaleros who roamed the Davis, Sacramento, and Guadalupe Mountains as well as the Big Bend country, probably did not know of the treaty and certainly did not consider themselves bound by it. While Josecito and other Sierra Blanca Mescaleros were visiting Santa Fe to report that their people had planted crops—the surest sign of virtue in Anglo eyes—and to remind the governor of his promise to build a fort in their lands, the southern groups were harassing traffic on the San Antonio–El Paso road. The Sierra Blanca band was wrongly blamed for these depredations.

Anglos were well aware that Apache raids into Mexico spared them from suffering even greater devastation. In discussing the Gila bands and the vast area over which they roamed, Meriwether commented, "The facility and impunity with which [Sonora and Chihuahua] are plundered and robbed, has measurably saved our own people from like visitations during the last and present years."[16] In July 1853 alone Apaches killed 170 people in Sonora, destroyed the towns of Chinapa and Santa Cruz, and raided southern Arizona.

E. A. Graves, agent to the Mimbreños, was at least somewhat hopeful that they could become self-supporting. He described the attempt to get them started planting crops along the Mimbres River near the copper mines. "This enterprise was attended with some little success," he wrote, "and it is believed, if this policy were persisted in, a change might be wrought in the condition of these degraded Indians."[17]

Concerning Apaches in general and their destructive raids into Mexico, Graves concluded that the government must see to it that the Apaches disappeared quietly and painlessly, for "to exterminate the aborigenes of the forest and mountains is a policy that no enlightened citizen or statesman will propose or advocate." He did not, however, hold out much long-range hope for any Indians. "That this race, the aborigenes of America, are destined to a speedy and final extinction, according to the laws now in force, either civil or divine, seems to admit of no doubt, as is equally beyond the control or management of any human agency. All that can be expected from an enlightened and Christian government, such as ours, is to graduate and smooth the passway for their final exit from the stage of human existence."[18]

In answer to his question, "How is this to be done?" Graves noted that the Apaches must obtain food peaceably or by force. "No animal creature, whether civilized or not, will perish for the want of food when the means of subsistence are within his reach."[19] But he admitted that "to feed and clothe those Indians, either wholly or partially, is an expensive operation. It is a policy that promises no results beyond the simple fact of keeping them quiet for the time being. As long as this policy is continued their peace can doubtless be purchased, and they will be kept quiet, but it only postpones the evil day." Graves suggested confining the tribes to reservations and teaching them to farm, giving them inducements to give up bow and arrow for ax and hoe. "If you make war upon them and conquer them the same question arises, What to do with them? You will either have to take care of them or destroy them."[20]

The Gadsden Purchase, negotiated in 1853 and ratified in June 1854, transferred all of Arizona and New Mexico south of the Gila to the United States. The U.S. government, after having made little effort to prevent Apaches from raiding into Mexico, now took advantage of Mexico's willingness to make concessions and abrogated the agreement to control the Indians.

The newly acquired territory was in the heart of Apachería, for it contained the lands of the Mimbreños, Mogollones, Pinaleños, and Chiricahuas. These bands subsisted almost exclusively by raiding, so the problem of controlling the Apaches was more complicated than before. The difficulties in dealing with increased numbers of hostile Apaches discouraged Governor Meriwether, even though Congress appropriated money for the purchase of goods to be given them in exchange for signing treaties. Meriwether did not immediately attempt to open negotiations with the Apaches.

Officials in Washington were frequently made aware of the Apaches' customary way of providing for their needs and of the necessity of offering them a less violent alternative. In his annual report for 1854 Commissioner of Indian Affairs George W. Manypenny echoed these warnings, admitting that Apaches "must steal or starve," and argued that they should be subsidized by the government until they could support themselves or else they would have to be exterminated. "That the obligations of Christianity, as well as the dictates of humanity," he piously concluded, "demand the efficient action of the government, must be too obvious to require discussion.

We have to some extent taken possession of the lands of those Indians, driven them from their only means of support. We should now teach them to live without this resource, or their destruction is inevitable."[21]

Early in 1854 Kit Carson assumed his duties as agent to the Jicarillas, Utes, and Pueblo tribes. Shortly thereafter the Jicarillas were accused of robberies, and Lieutenant Bell of the Second Dragoons set out to punish them. His troops located a party of Jicarillas, but they denied having stolen the missing animals. As usual in such instances it was deemed proper to punish one Indian for the misdeeds of another, so the troops opened fire, killing many, including a leading chief. Carson moved quickly to prevent a general war by visiting a large band of Jicarillas camped less than a day's ride from Taos. His efforts were not successful, however, and three days later there was a general Jicarilla uprising.

A detachment of sixty dragoons came on a large party of Jicarillas and fought a costly battle with them; only seventeen men survived.[22] Colonel Philip St. George Cooke of the Second Dragoons took the field with a large force, accompanied by Kit Carson as Indian agent and guide. "The Indians that are now committing depredations," Carson reported, "are those who have lost their families during the war. They consider they have nothing further to live for than revenge for the death of those of their families that were killed by the whites; they have become desperate. . . . "[23] He hoped to prevent further needless slaughter, but the Jicarillas had scattered so completely that it was impossible to confer with them. Carson believed that the government should invite them to negotiate a "fair and just" treaty, but Acting Governor W. S. Messervy did not deign to make the first gesture of peace.

Major James H. Carleton, accompanied by Kit Carson, trailed a party of Jicarillas to Fischer's Peak in the Ratón Mountains. They surprised the camp, killed a number of warriors, and scattered the rest. The fighting continued, but the Jicarillas, with only one hundred or one hundred and fifty warriors in all, were kept on the defensive. Two large forces were in the field against them in 1855—dragoons under Colonel Fauntleroy and New Mexico Volunteers under Ceran St. Vrain. The latter fought seven battles and took a heavy toll. In August of that year headmen of the Jicarillas and Utes went to Carson asking for peace. He arranged a council between them and Governor Meriwether on the Chama River; there peace treaties were concluded that established reservations for the two groups in northern New Mexico.

When news of Meriwether's treaties reached the people of Taos they were outraged. The reservations, they protested in letters to Washington, were too close to Taos and must be moved much farther away. Perhaps because of this protest Congress did not ratify the treaties. In 1856 agent Lorenzo Labadi wrote from Abiquiu that the Utes and Jicarillas were both abiding by the treaties but were destitute, waiting patiently for the arrival of the implements and seeds Meriwether had promised them. Labadi urged the government to provide food for the Jicarillas so they would not be "compelled through hunger to commence stealing and committing other outrages again."[24]

Because the Mescaleros were still harassing traffic on the San Antonio–El Paso road and along the Río Grande, in 1854–55 a number of columns crossed and recrossed their lands, inflicting costly defeats. Early in 1855 Captain R. S. Ewell of the First Dragoons marched through Mescalero country with a force of 180 men. He fought several skirmishes with them, killing, among others, their "great war chief Santa Anna" and one of his sons. But because it was mid-winter and bitterly cold the dragoons' horses gave out, and toward the end of the campaign they could not keep up with the infantry.[25]

While Ewell was camped on the Bonito a group of Mescaleros hurried to Dr. Steck asking for peace. He promised to protect them until he could give them an answer. General Garland, whose forces were trying to inflict total defeat on the Mescaleros, was understandably disappointed by the request. "This step was not a *little* annoying," he said, "when we were prepared to strike. . . ."[26]

Despite Garland's annoyance a reservation was set apart for the Mescaleros in their own country, with agency headquarters at Fort Stanton, built on the Bonito River early in 1855. Congress, as usual, did not approve the treaty, but the agency remained and provided the Mescaleros with trade goods and some tools. These Apaches were inclined toward peace, but Anglo policies made it difficult for them to remain peaceful. When they settled at Fort Stanton, for example, officials recognized a "principal chief" although the Mescaleros did not. He was expected to command the obedience of every member of the band and was held responsible for the actions of all. It was an impossible situation, completely contrary to Apache tradition, for no chief could command obedience.

Another injurious policy was that of severely restricting the Mescaleros' movements without providing them more than partial rations. The restriction was intended to prevent them from stealing livestock or going on raids to Mexico, but it also kept them from hunting or making mescal. The partial rations were not enough to sustain life, and the Mescaleros were not allowed to organize hunts. As they saw their women and children starving, the warriors became desperate.

In a letter to Governor Meriwether, Lieutenant Colonel L. J. Miles urged him to provide more food for the Mescaleros—it was obvious that they must steal or starve. He also recommended assigning them an agent of their own, noting that "Dr. Steck, one of the best I ever knew, being identified by them, with the Gila Apaches, can never acquire their confidence or control them; and if he succeeds, would lose his influence over the Gilanians; for there is considerable jealousy between these tribes."[27]

Despite this warning Dr. Steck, whose headquarters were at Doña Ana, was appointed agent for the Mescaleros as well as the Gileños; he was determined to keep them out of trouble and start them farming. In this he had the cooperation of Gian-nah-tah (Always Ready), an influential Mescalero chief whom the Mexicans called Cadete (Cadet). When settlers reported livestock missing, Cadete was frequently able to recover the stolen animals. But when he could not—sometimes the famished Mescaleros had already eaten them—Dr. Steck cut off their meager rations and they fled into the mountains. Depriving them of food simply aggravated a bad situation, making it more necessary than ever for them to steal or die of hunger. Fortunately for the Mescaleros, the governor disapproved Steck's policy and ordered him to feed them. In November 1856 Steck made contact with the Mescaleros and distributed blankets, clothing, and food, promising to issue beef and corn to them once a month.[28]

Not all Mescaleros, however, were willing to farm or remain peaceful. The Agua Nuevo band under Mateo and Venancia stayed in Dog Canyon in the Sacramento Mountains. Another band under Marcus remained in the Guadalupes, from which its war parties slipped out to attack unwary travelers between San Antonio and El Paso.

Cadete's efforts to keep his people out of trouble were relatively successful and were recognized and acknowledged by some officials. Others continued to blame the Sierra Blanca band for every theft reported, although horse stealing and cattle-rustling were by no means confined to Indians. On one occasion Major Thomas H. Holmes, commander at Fort Stanton, investigated charges that the Sierra Blanca people were involved in the attacks on the San

Antonio–El Paso road. After careful investigation he reported that this band was in no way connected with the raids. "This abstinence on their part," he concluded, "is entirely to be ascribed to the small amount the acting assistant commissary of subsistence at this post was authorized by Dr. Steck to issue."[29]

Governor Meriwether had opened communications with the Gileños during the summer of 1855, following victories over the Mescaleros and Jicarillas. Mimbreños and Mescaleros were both temporarily awed by U.S. military power, and their chiefs were willing to take up farming under the direction of their agent. Both, Meriwether reported, were in the most destitute condition. The Mimbreños knew and trusted Dr. Steck and welcomed him to their camps. He found them genuinely eager to start farming again and immediately set them to planting. Their crops were fairly successful, and by the end of the second year they had raised enough corn and vegetables to provide for their needs. Self-sufficiency was the eventual goal at all reservations, but one rarely reached in a short time. The Mimbreños, however, appeared capable of achieving this goal quickly if they were fed and furnished the necessary tools and seeds. In fact they seemed to be well on the way to success, even though they were not provided food as promised and nearly half of them had died of diseases introduced among them by Anglos. In the end the Mimbreños were frightened off by Colonel Bonneville's Gila Expedition of 1857.

Typical of the attitude of Anglo officials toward Apaches was Indian Commissioner J. L. Collins' recommendation that the Mescaleros, Mimbreños, and Mogollones be placed on a reservation near the Gila and that Jicarillas and Utes be placed on another. "It may be asked," he wrote, "will the Indians agree to this arrangement? I believe they will; but whether they agree to it or not, they should be *compelled* to submit to it. They have no more right to live in the way they have been living for the last few years than the thief has to pursue his calling, and to receive presents to keep him in a good humor with those whom he is robbing."[30]

The Mogollones remained troublesome, and in March 1855 Colonel Daniel Chandler campaigned against them, with only moderate success. On his return he passed the peaceful camp of Mimbreño chief Delgadito; the Indians gathered to watch the command march by, for they were expecting a council with Dr. Steck. When the troops were within musket range they fired into the camp without warning. One woman was killed and another and several children were wounded. When Delgadito was finally able to confer with him

Colonel Chandler explained that he thought they were Mogollones and agreed to pay for their losses. General Garland accepted Chandler's explanation, adding that "officers of the army have too much intelligence and humanity of feeling to make a ruthless attack upon even savage foes."[31]

Chandler's campaign led to reprisals, and one of the victims was Navajo agent Henry Dodge, who disappeared while on his way to Zuñi. Captain Thomas Claiborne of Fort Thorn sent a message to Mangas Coloradas asking him to locate Dodge's captors and negotiate for his release. Mangas sent Delgadito to warn Dr. Steck that the Mogollones and Coyoteros had united for a war against the Anglos, later reporting that a party of those two bands had killed Dodge.

In October Mogollones stole 150 mules from Bernalillo County. Troops pursued them and recovered most of the mules. "This band of Gilanians," wrote Acting Governor W. W. H. Davis, "have [sic] been in the habit of making annual robbing excursions into the same section of the country in the fall of the year, to procure food to last them through the winter."[32]

Colonel B. L. Bonneville, temporary commander of the department, had taken no action against Apaches, but the killing of agent Dodge inspired him to order the Gila Expedition of 1857; its purpose was to exterminate the Gileños. Three large columns converged on the Gila and Mimbres Rivers—Colonel W. W. Loring from Albuquerque, Major Enoch Steen from Tucson, and Colonel Dixon S. Miles from Fort Thorn. Miles entered the upper Gila country and cornered a large band of Mogollones and Coyoteros near Mount Graham, killing forty-two and capturing thirty-six. Loring and his Mounted Riflemen struck Cuchillo Negro and his band in the Cañon de los Muertos Carneros (Canyon of the Dead Sheep), killing the Mimbreño chief and others and taking a number of captives. After this campaign the Gileños abstained from raiding New Mexico for a time, but continued their raids into Sonora. The Mogollones asked for a conference with Colonel Bonneville and Steck, offering to give land in exchange for peace. As neither the agent nor the department commander had the authority to make peace the offer was declined, but the Apaches were warned that they would be annihilated if they continued raiding. This campaign frightened away the peaceful Mimbreños who had taken up farming at Santa Rita del Cobre.

Coyoteros protested to Steck that they had been unjustly attacked by Bonneville. They had always regarded Americans as their

friends, they said, and they wanted to continue as friends. Steck
explained that the attack was punishment for the death of agent
Dodge. One Coyotero chief admitted that Dodge's killer had indeed
been slain in the attack. The killer's presence, Steck explained,
justified the military attack on them. The chief then asked Steck to
intercede with the commander at Fort Defiance for the release of
Coyoteros captured in the battle; six of them had already died in
prison.

Most of the Mimbreños and Mogollones remained for some time
in Mexico, where they had fled from the Gila Expedition. Steck sent
runners to them, urging them to return. Many came back to Santa
Rita but their confidence was badly shaken. Although the copper
mines lay within the unofficial reservation that Meriwether had set
apart for the Mimbreños in 1855, Steck persuaded them to allow
Anglo miners to work in peace. The Mogollones, however,
threatened to drive the miners out, prompting Steck to urge Indian
Commissioner Collins to distribute gifts among them as pacifiers.
Steck estimated the number of Mimbreños remaining at seventy
men and about four hundred and fifty women and children, and the
Mogollones at one hundred twenty five men and five hundred
women and children (although about an equal number of Mogollones were still in Mexico).[33]

Because the Apaches and Navajos were well-known for their
penchant for stealing livestock, it was easy to blame them for all
thefts, real or imagined. The fact that they were not always guilty
was pointed out in a letter from Colonel Thomas T. Fauntleroy to
General Winfield Scott. "The greatest embarrassment arises," he
wrote, "from the fact that many of the claims set up against the
Indians of New Mexico for plundering, stealing the stock and the
like, are either fabricated, or to a considerable degree exaggerated,
and if war is to be commenced upon the simple presentation of these
claims, the causes for war become interminable, or the Indians must
be extirpated."[34]

A number of officials supported the idea of furnishing rations to
the Apaches, for it was obvious that they could not possibly give up
raiding otherwise. Among these was Dr. Steck, who informed the
commissioner of Indian affairs that defenses in the region were
inadequate and that the best hope for peace was a friendly policy and
a liberal supply of rations. He pointed out that the Mescaleros and
Mimbreños had been peaceful since the policy of feeding them was
adopted and noted that both had extensive fields under cultivation.
Colonel James L. Collins, superintendent of Indian affairs for New

Mexico, supported Steck's view, saying that the only choice was between supporting them and exterminating them. He recommended the establishment of a reservation near the Gila, far from all settlements, and a large military garrison to supervise it. It is unlikely that many disagreed with the view that the Apaches must be fed or exterminated; unfortunately, too many favored the latter policy.

Dr. Steck was well aware that the Gileños had been treated unjustly and that disease had greatly weakened them. They had shown forbearance, however, and he was generally optimistic about them. "The Mimbres and Mogollón bands seem willing to be controlled by the advice of their agent," he wrote, "and have confidence in the kind intentions of the Government toward them. In their intercourse with the citizens they have suffered many impositions; have been made drunk; have been swindled out of their horses, and [had] many of them stolen by Mexicans, at or near the agency. They have also been murdered in cold blood. . . . "[35]

Steck's other charges, the Mescaleros, also had had many provocations to resume hostilities. In February 1858 a party of New Mexicans from Mesilla, calling themselves the Mesilla Guard, attacked the Mescaleros camping near Steck's headquarters at Doña Ana. In April other New Mexicans surprised a Mescalero camp near Fort Thorn and killed a number of men, women, and children.[36] Angered by this civilian interference with peaceable Indians, General Garland sent troops to capture the murderers and threatened to withdraw all soldiers, leaving the citizens to defend themselves. But because of the ensuing outcry the post was not abandoned. Garland warned them, nevertheless, that those who perpetrated acts of violence and outrage had no claim to protection and would receive none. White settlers replied that the Mescaleros should be removed from New Mexico or exterminated.

Early in 1860 Steck visited the Mimbreños again and found them still peaceful though destitute. Anglos and New Mexicans at the stage stations, at settlements along the Mimbres River, and at the copper mines had driven away all the game. The Mimbreños complained bitterly about encroachments on their best lands. If no permanent reservation were set apart for them soon, Steck warned the commissioner, Mimbreños would have no land left.

In 1861 the threat of a Confederate invasion from Texas caused the withdrawal of troops from all forts in the Apache country, for they were needed to defend New Mexico. The Confederates expected Southern sympathizers to assist them on entering the territory, but they were disappointed. Confederate troops temporarily occupied some of the abandoned forts, but were forced to withdraw from New Mexico in 1862, after their defeat at Apache Canyon.

When they saw the troops march away from the forts the Mescaleros and Gileños were convinced that they had driven them out. Here was a welcome and unexpected opportunity to rid their land of intruders. The Apaches would make the most of it.

IV
The Beginnings of Anglo-Apache Conflict in Arizona

WHILE NEW MEXICO SUFFERED constant Apache raids, other Apaches continued to harass Tucson during the early 1850s, attacking the Mexican presidio and occasionally killing unwary travelers. In February 1851 Royce Oatman and his family left the Pima villages on the Gila to cross the desert to Yuma. The Oatmans had been with an immigrant party that split up in Tucson. They and several other families were short of provisions and money, and so had driven on. The Pimas were always helpful to travelers, but their harvest had been poor and they had little food to spare. Oatman was desperate; his oxen were weak, and his food almost gone.

A traveler who had just arrived from Fort Yuma on the Colorado reported that the route was safe, for he had seen no Indians. Oatman decided to go on alone with his family. They traveled for seven days with great difficulty; the oxen were barely able to draw the wagon. Dr. Lecount and several other travelers overtook them. Seeing that Oatman's oxen were too weak to continue, Dr. Lecount promised to push on as rapidly as possible and send the Oatmans help from Fort Yuma.

The next night Indians attacked Lecount's camp and ran off his animals. On foot, with little food, he had no choice but to continue, for it was at least thirty miles back to the Oatman camp. He left a note on a tree, warning Oatman that Indians were in the area. Several nights later the Oatmans camped at the same place, but failed to see the doctor's note. The following day they went only a short distance before the oxen gave out and then camped near the Gila. Indians believed to have been Tonto Apaches visited the camp and killed Oatman, his wife, and four of their children, carrying off Olive, who was sixteen, and Mary Ann, who was ten. Fourteen-year-old Lorenzo was left for dead but survived.

When he recovered consciousness Lorenzo Oatman painfully

made his way back to the Pima villages. His sisters were eventually traded to Mohaves. Mary Ann died, but Olive remained a Mohave slave until 1857 when she was ransomed. Their story was well known: the Reverend R. B. Stratton wrote a melodramatic account of the Oatman girls' captivity which was widely read.

Against Apaches the Pápagos of Arizona had come to play a role similar to that of the Ópatas in Sonora. Whenever Apaches attacked citizens or Manso Apaches of Tucson and ran off herds of livestock, troops from the Tucson presidio, citizens, Pápagos, and Manso Apaches usually pursued the raiders and tried to recover the stolen animals. In combatting Apaches in Arizona at this time Pápagos were often more effective than Mexican troops.

The Pápagos numbered about three thousand during the 1850s. Like the Pimas and Maricopas, they were uniformly friendly and helpful to Anglos. Because of Mexican encroachments on their lands in Sonora, from 1855 on many of them crossed into Arizona, until at least three-fourths of them lived there.

In 1858, special agent G. Bailey reported that the four thousand Pimas and five hundred Maricopas in Arizona had not been given the tools and seeds promised them. It was necessary, he warned, to give them certain possession of their lands. "Sound policy, therefore, would suggest the necessity of preventing any cause of complaint on this score, *and of doing so at once*," he wrote. The title to their land should be confirmed, and they should be furnished the tools, seeds, and clothing promised them, and an agent should be assigned them. Since their loyalty was unquestioned, Bailey also recommended supplying them with arms and ammunition.[1]

Special agent Sylvester Mowry took a colder, more impersonal view of the Pimas and Maricopas. "The end of these people, like that of all Indian tribes, is only a question of time," he wrote, applying the "vanishing red man theory" to them.

> It is the duty of the government to preserve them, if possible, in their friendly attitude; to encourage and stimulate their industry, and not to hurry them, as long as they are peaceful, to their doom. The idea of civilizing and Christianizing them, exposed as they are to all influences of a frontier people, is the idle dream of a pseudo-philanthropist. The rapid . . . settlement of the Territory will bring them soon enough in contact with "the humanizing and civilizing influence of the white man," and the result will be the inevitable one that has followed its contact with other tribes: the men will become drunkards, the women prostitutes, and disease will soon leave only the name of their race.[2]

In 1859 John Walker was appointed agent to the Pimas and Maricopas, but he remained in Tucson and at first did little for them. That same year Congress appropriated money for implements and clothing for the two tribes, and, more ominously, to conduct a survey of their lands. Since the Pimas and Maricopas were consistently peaceful, no treaty was made with them, a fact that worked to their disadvantage.

Anglo ranchers and miners entered southern Arizona soon after the Gadsden Purchase was ratified in June 1854. That year Pete Kitchen began ranching near modern-day Nogales, and three years later other Anglos took over the huge Canoa Ranch near Tumacácori. Kitchen brought thirty Ópata families from Sonora to work the land and guard the herds against Apaches. The "Stronghold," as his fort-like ranch house was called, was built on a prominent hill, and a lookout was stationed on the roof at all times to warn those working in the fields when Apaches approached. The ranch was attacked many times, but it was well defended and survived when other ranches in the area were destroyed or abandoned. According to legend, in 1873 Kitchen and Cochise ended their warfare after Kitchen had rescued Cochise's son Nachez from Mexican renegades.[3]

The United States government did not immediately send troops to Tucson or other parts of the newly acquired territory south of the Gila. The Mexican garrison withdrew from the Tucson presidio, and the citizens vociferously demanded protection. In 1856 the War Department finally sent four companies of the First Dragoons to take up a position near Tucson. However, Major Enoch Steen, commander of the dragoon detachment, was unwilling to establish a post near Tucson where, he said, there was no grain, no grass, and no public quarters.

Locating the new post proved to be complicated. Over the protests of Tucson citizens, Steen chose the old Calabasas Ranch on the Santa Cruz (near its confluence with the Sonoita), some sixty miles south of Tucson, too far to afford the town more than token protection. The dragoons camped there for a year without inflicting serious damage on the Apaches and without checking their raids into Sonora. In June 1857 the soldiers were ordered to move and built Fort Buchanan at the head of Sonoita Creek. It was never more than a collection of adobe huts without the protection of a wall or stockade, and its garrison was rarely strong enough to engage in serious offensive or punitive operations. The Apaches scorned it, passing boldly in sight of it on their raids into Mexico and stalking among its buildings after dark. No officer dared walk from one building to another at night without a cocked pistol in his hand. Fort Buchanan lasted only a few years before being set on fire and abandoned in 1861, when Union forces withdrew from Arizona to defend New Mexico.

Some of the miners of southern Arizona maintained a precarious peace with local bands of Apaches by supplying them with provisions and ammunition. These local treaties, many the work of Dr. Steck, were generally effective as long as Apaches were allowed to continue their raids into Mexico. In 1856 Charles D. Poston, who had mining interests in the Tubac region, asked Steck to arrange a meeting with several Apache chiefs at Santa Rita. He found them quite willing to make peace with Anglos as long as there was no interference with their "trade with Mexico." They made a treaty on that basis, one which the Apaches did not violate. Poston established his headquarters in the abandoned presidio of Tubac.[4]

Agent Sylvester Mowry, in a somber report to the commissioner of Indian affairs dated November 1857, held out no hope for Apaches. "My own impression," he wrote, "is that the Apaches cannot be *tamed*; civilization is out of the question."[5] Later, when Mowry represented mining interests in Arizona, he advocated a policy of outright extermination, arguing that "There is only one way to wage war against the Apaches. A steady, persistent campaign must be made, following them to their haunts. . . . They must be surrounded, starved into coming in, supervised, or put to death. If these ideas shock any weak-minded individual who thinks himself a philanthropist, I can only say I pity without respecting his mistaken sympathy. A man might as well have sympathy for a rattlesnake or a tiger. . . . "[6] He recommended, in the meantime, a string of forts to keep the Apaches north of the Gila.

Another settler with mining interests in southern Arizona was Raphael Pumpelly, who disagreed with Mowry's implication that all wrongs were committed by the Apaches. "It is said," he wrote, "that the Indians are treacherous and cruel scalping and torturing their prisoners, it may be answered that there is no treachery and no cruelty left unemployed by the whites. Poisoning with strichnine, the willful dissemination of smallpox . . . these are heroic facts among many of our frontiersmen."[7]

The Indian Bureau, convinced that a "decisive" policy was required, sent special agent George Bailey to study the Apache situation and make recommendations. He reported that most of the raiders came from north of the Gila. Although raiding parties might follow difficult and obscure trails on their way to Sonora and Chihuahua, making it impossible to intercept them, when returning with stolen animals they were obliged to follow available water. The establishment of a military post at the mouth of the Arivaipa, another at the crossing of the San Pedro, and a third where Fort Webster had been located would, Bailey believed, solve the Apache problem. In 1858, however, the number of troops in the southern part of the territory was reduced, precluding the garrisoning of additional forts.

The Indian Bureau also sent Dr. Steck and others to confer with the Chiricahuas at Apache Pass about travel. Cochise agreed to allow the Overland stage, which began running between El Paso and San Diego in 1858, to pass safely through Chiricahua country. He also promised that his people would not molest travelers who followed the same route in small parties. Steck next conferred with the Coyoteros, who made a similar agreement not to harass travelers. He was much impressed with the Coyoteros, calling them the most powerful and most reliable of all the Apache bands. They had, he reported, about six hundred warriors, large herds of cattle and horses, and well cultivated fields. They were, he added, less warlike than other Apaches.

Early in 1859 Steck also held council with the Pinaleños at Cañon del Oro, not far from Tucson. Like the Coyoteros, they planted extensively; and they also agreed to permit travelers to pass through their lands in peace.[8] Most of the Arizona Apaches, Steck concluded, seemed willing to remain at peace north of the Mexican border, but they had no intention of giving up their time-honored activities in Sonora and Chihuahua. In fact, even while Steck was conferring with them, Western Apaches were raiding far to the south, destroying haciendas, seizing women and children, and driving off herds of horses and mules.

Although they farmed more and seemed to Steck less warlike than other Apaches, Coyoteros were still among the most active raiders into Mexico. Coyotero chief Francisco asked the station agent at Apache Pass whether or not Apaches would be allowed to raid Sonora if United States troops were to take possession of that state from Mexico. The agent said no. Francisco angrily retorted that "as long as he lived and had a warrior to follow him, he would fight Sonora, and he did not care if the Americans did try to stop it, he would fight till he was killed."[9] There were frequent complaints of thefts of livestock in the Tucson and Fort Buchanan areas, and at least some of them were the work of Pinaleños and possibly

Coyoteros. Steck recommended the appointment of two additional Indian agents, one for each band. But the Coyoteros were added to Steck's own agency, although he could not possibly handle bands as widely separated as the Mescaleros, Gileños, and Coyoteros.[10]

Until 1858 Apaches did not molest Charles Poston's livestock or that of others in the Tubac region, although raiding parties were often seen there on their way to or from Mexico and could easily have run off the herds. Trouble came from an unexpected source, a group of Maine lumberjacks who had established a lumber camp on the Canoa Ranch of the Sopori Land and Cattle Company. A party of Sonora ranchers had stopped at Tubac and told Poston that some Apaches had run off a herd and were coming that way with it. In exchange for his help they offered to divide any of the animals recovered. Because of his own successful treaty with the Apaches, however, Poston refused.

The Sonorans then rode on to Canoa, where the lumberjacks joined them in ambushing the Apaches and recovering the herd. About the time of the next full moon a vaquero from Canoa galloped into Tubac, shouting that the ranch was being attacked by Apaches. By the time a rescue party reached Canoa every man had been killed, every building burned, and every animal run off, ruining the company financially. Apache vengeance was thorough, and the Anglos of Arizona quickly learned why the people of Sonora usually declined to challenge Apache raiders. Troops from Fort Buchanan were sent after the Apaches, but soon lost their trail.

Early in the summer of 1859 Colonel Bonneville toured Apache country. The Chiricahuas appeared peaceable, but were blamed for numerous thefts of livestock. On one occasion, however, they ran off eighty animals from the Sonora Mining and Exploring Company. Troops and miners pursued them, recovering fifty of the animals. Cochise sent the Anglos two Chiricahuas with eleven more animals, explaining that they had thought the livestock was the property of Mexicans. Stealing from Mexicans was not, to the Apaches' way of thinking, a violation of any treaty.

On another occasion a party of Pinaleños on their way to Sonora stopped at the Patagonia mine, where they were usually given flour and tobacco to keep them friendly. One of the miners, perhaps unaware of the local treaty, ordered them away, and was killed when firing broke out. Colonel Bonneville recognized the need for protecting settlers in the San Pedro and Santa Cruz Valleys, and recommended locating one fort in the mountains near Tucson and another on the San Pedro. "These Indians," he reported, "are becoming bold and rebellious from their successful depredations, and should be chastised."[11]

Colonel I. V. Reeve and two hundred men pursued a party of Pinaleño raiders for three hundred miles, ruining their horses without forcing the Apaches to give battle. This fruitless chase convinced Reeve that military posts should be established directly in Apache country, where punishment could be prompt and effective. As a result of the recommendations of Bonneville, Reeve, and others, in 1859 the War Department ordered Fort Breckinridge built at the junction of the Arivaipa and San Pedro.

After another visit to the Chiricahuas in 1859 Dr. Steck concluded that they should be united with their Mimbreño kinsmen in New Mexico. This suggestion, which was far from pleasing to the Chiricahuas, was a harbinger of the Apache concentration policy that was to bring war and bloodshed to Arizona and New Mexico during the 1870s and 1880s.

In 1860, perhaps sensing North-South tension within the army and noting the decreasing activity of the troops, Apaches intensified their hostilities, and little was done to check them. Many officers resigned their commissions to offer their services to the Confederacy. About this time an incident occurred at Apache Pass that has been blamed for touching off twenty-five years of the fiercest Apache warfare.

In October 1860 a band of Apaches, probably Coyoteros, stole some cattle and captured a boy from a ranch on the Sonoita. The ranch belonged to John Ward; the boy, known as Felix Ward, was half-Apache, the son of Ward's common law wife, Jesusa Martínez, who had been an Apache captive. A small force from Fort Buchanan searched for the boy for a short time and then gave up.

Some months later, near the end of January 1861, Lieutenant Colonel Pitcairn Morrison, commander of Fort Buchanan, sent Lieutenant George Nicholas Bascom and fifty-four men of the Seventh Infantry on the trail of stolen livestock. Bascom was also ordered to try to recover the Ward boy. If the Chiricahuas refused to cooperate, he was authorized to use force. When the detachment marched out Fort Buchanan was left with only twenty-five effective troops, hardly enough for its defense.

When he arrived at Apache Pass, convinced that the Chiricahuas held young Felix Ward, Bascom ordered six Chiricahuas seized as hostages. Cochise denied that his people had taken the boy, but promised to bring him from the Coyoteros if Bascom would wait ten days. Bascom agreed. A day or two later, however, Cochise returned under a flag of truce, accompanied by Coyotero chief Francisco and a large number of warriors. Bascom started to ride out to meet the two chiefs, but then began to suspect their intentions and stopped. At this moment two Overland Mail employees who had been on friendly terms with the Chiricahuas, left the stage station and walked toward them. Bascom ordered them back, saying he had no prisoners to exchange for them should they be captured. They ignored his order and continued. The Chiricahuas attempted to seize them; one escaped, but the other was killed. Chief Francisco lowered his white flag and pointed toward Bascom's troops, shouting to his warriors. Bascom lowered his own flag and ordered his men to fire. After an exchange of shots the Apaches withdrew.

A few days later Cochise returned, offering to trade a prisoner and sixteen government mules for the Chiricahua hostages. Bascom replied that he would exchange prisoners only if the Ward boy were returned. A note from James F. Wallace, a captive of the Chiricahuas, stated that the band had three other Anglo prisoners and would come the next day to exchange them. But the following morning, while the army mules were being watered under guard of a sergeant and fifteen men, about two hundred Apaches swooped down and stampeded them. Shortly after this, Apaches attacked a stagecoach a few miles from Apache Pass; others killed eight Mexican teamsters and burned their wagons between Apache Pass and Ewell's Station.

On February 10 Dr. B. J. D. Irwin and a small escort arrived from Fort Buchanan to care for the wounded. They brought with them a Coyotero chief and two warriors captured en route with stolen cattle. Four days later Lieutenants Isaiah Moore and Richard Lord arrived from Fort Breckinridge with seventy men of the First Dragoons. Since Moore was senior to Bascom, he assumed command. On February 16 Bascom and forty men joined the dragoons in a scouting patrol. They found the bodies of the four Anglo captives, but saw no Indians.

On February 19 Bascom started for Fort Buchanan, accompanied by Dr. Irwin and the dragoons under Lieutenant Moore. When they reached the place where the teamsters and captives had been slain, they hanged three Chiricahua hostages and the three Coyotero captives in retaliation. The remaining Chiricahua hostages, a woman and two boys, were taken to Fort Buchanan.[12]

A myth grew up about the Apache Pass incident, and it has never died. According to this legend, Bascom tried to seize Cochise under a flag of truce, but failed. Then Bascom presumably hanged his hostages, despite a violent protest from Sergeant Reuben Bernard, who allegedly was court-martialed for insubordination. After this Cochise retaliated by killing his white captives and then launched a campaign to kill all whites in Arizona.

There was a Sergeant Bernard in the First Dragoons at Fort Breckinridge, and he apparently did accompany the troops under Lieutenant Moore to Apache Pass, but no record of his court-martial has been found. He later rose to the rank of brigadier general, a most unlikely promotion if he had been tried for insubordination. The dragoon detachment did not reach Apache Pass until ten or eleven days after the supposed treachery to Cochise, so Bernard could not possibly have advised Bascom against what he considered improper conduct.

Although it is still customary to blame the intensification of Apache hostility on the Bascom Affair and on Bascom's "stupidity" at Apache Pass in February 1861, it appears that the 1858 Canoa incident, together with North-South tensions in the army and the withdrawal of troops from the Arizona forts, were actually responsible. Charles D. Poston blamed both the Canoa incident and Bascom, but he dated the events at Apache Pass in early 1858 rather than three years later. By 1861 Apache depredations were already serious. Then with the abandonment of the Arizona forts by Union troops, Apaches seized the welcome opportunity to eliminate all Anglos from southern Arizona.

The Apache Pass myth first appeared in 1870 with Raphael Pumpelly's account of the incident, and most writers have accepted his version even though he was not present. Pumpelly's first acquaintance with Apaches came when he and another young Easterner rashly pursued two Apaches who had stolen a horse. The fugitives disappeared beyond a dense thicket, which suddenly was alive with whooping Apaches, waving lances and bows. Pumpelly and his equally terrified companion dismounted, aimed their rifles, and pulled the triggers. Both guns misfired. The Apaches hooted and leaped about in amusement, slapping their backsides in their customary gesture of derision. The two youths fled, knowing that the Apaches could easily have killed them.[13] Pumpelly was no doubt sympathetic toward the Apaches and, like many citizens of the territory, critical of the army.

It was apparently Pumpelly who first accused Bascom of trying to seize Cochise under a flag of truce (presumably over the opposition of Sergeant Bernard) and of later rashly ordering the Chiricahua hostages and Coyotero captives hanged. Because of Pumpelly's

Chiricahua Chief Cochise
Western History Collection, University of Oklahoma

published account of the affair, Lieutenant Bascom has been severely castigated by scores of writers for his colossal "blunder" that
brought on a quarter of a century of devastating warfare. Those who
have berated him have ignored the fact that both Dr. Irwin and
Lieutenant Moore were Bascom's superiors, and that Lieutenant
Moore was actually in command of the combined forces at the time
of the hangings.

According to Bascom's own reports what actually happened was
that he conferred with Cochise, who told him that Coyoteros, not
Chiricahuas, had taken the Ward boy. Bascom then ordered six
Chiricahua hostages seized—three men, a woman, and two boys.
Cochise informed Bascom that if he would wait ten days, he would
get the boy from the Coyoteros. Bascom agreed, but Cochise apparently met chief Francisco and a large Coyotero raiding party and
decided instead to attack the troops.

In 1877 William S. Oury, Butterfield stage agent at Apache Pass,
refuted Pumpelly's version of the incident in an article entitled "A
True History of the Outbreak of the Noted Apache Chieftain Cochise in the Year 1861."[14] Oury took issue with Governor Safford,
who had criticized Bascom's actions.

Some years later Dr. Irwin wrote a similar article, "The Fight at
Apache Pass," to correct inaccuracies in T. E. Farish's *History of
Arizona* and to refute a statement by a veteran of the Seventh
Infantry who had served in Arizona and who had joined in the attack
on Bascom.[15] In his article, which was not published until 1928—
more than a decade after his death—Dr. Irwin pointed out that
although they allowed the stagecoach and well-armed parties to pass
through their country, the Arizona Apaches had been far from
peaceful in 1860. There were many reports of Apache hostilities that
year, including attacks on Fort Buchanan. Not all Apache forays
were directed against Mexico. Dr. Irwin forcefully cleared Bascom
of any responsibility for ordering the hangings, stating, "it was I who
suggested the summary execution, man for man. On Bascom ex-
pressing reluctance to resort to the extreme measure proposed, I
argued my right to dispose of the lives of the three prisoners captured by me, after which he acceded to the retaliatory proposition
and agreed that those three prisoners and three of the hostages taken
by him be brought there and executed." Lieutenant Moore also
accepted responsibility for the executions.[16]

Bascom never had to defend himself against the charges, for he
was killed at the battle of Valverde in New Mexico almost exactly one
year after the Apache Pass incident and eight years before Pumpel-

ly's book was published. Bascom's commander at Fort Buchanan approved of his conduct, and his actions were also emphatically endorsed by his superiors at Santa Fe.

During the spring of 1861 military operations in the Southwest were paralyzed by the coming conflict between North and South, and the troops did little more than defend their posts. Then orders came to destroy and abandon the Arizona forts and for the troops to march to the Río Grande to defend New Mexico against a threatened Confederate invasion from Texas. In June Apaches twice attacked Fort Buchanan, killing a few soldiers and running off horses and mules each time. In July the troops burned the stores, set fire to Forts Buchanan and Breckinridge, and then headed for Santa Fe.

Poston and other Anglos wisely concluded that without troops to protect them it would be unsafe to remain in southern Arizona. But before they could complete preparations for leaving, Apaches emptied the company's corrals of horses and mules. Others attacked the Santa Rita Mining Hacienda, and all Anglos fled from the eastern side of the Santa Cruz. Poston's Tubac headquarters was surrounded by menacing warriors, but the employees and their families were escorted safely to Tucson, where the few Anglos remaining in the territory had sought refuge.

Although it has frequently been said that Apache warfare entered its most intense phase immediately after the Bascom Affair, it was not until U.S. troops withdrew that warfare exploded all over the Gadsden Purchase region. "During the summer of 1861," J. Ross Browne wrote, "when federal troops were withdrawn, the Apaches renewed their depredations and the barbarous races of Sonora turned loose to complete the work of destruction."[17] South of Tucson only Pete Kitchen's ranch and Sylvester Mowry's mines remained in the possession of Anglos.

It is true that Cochise deeply resented the hangings at Apache Pass and that he labored long and hard to avenge them, but the major Apache outbreak of violence in southwestern New Mexico as well as in southern Arizona began when the Union troops withdrew from the garrisons in Apachería. Just as the Sioux and Cheyennes chose this same opportunity to rid their lands of white intruders, the Apaches seized the occasion to recover their lands. Emboldened by the thought that they had caused the troop retreat, they struck at mining camps, ranches, and settlements in a major campaign to drive all Anglos from Apachería. It was the best opportunity ever presented, and Apaches took full advantage of it.

V
The Mescaleros' Nemesis

DURING THE SUMMER OF 1861 Confederate troops from Texas entered southern New Mexico and took possession of the abandoned forts, immediately bringing them into conflict with Mescaleros and Mimbreños. On one occasion a Confederate detachment from Fort Davis was trailing Mescalero raiders and had the misfortune of overtaking them: the whole force was annihilated. In October Confederate Colonel John R. Baylor received a call for help from the miners at Pinos Altos. With the help of a detachment of "Arizona Guards" they had beaten off an attack by Mimbreños and Chiricahuas led by Mangas Coloradas and Cochise. Although the Arizona Guards had been organized to defend the miners in the area, they were soon called to serve the Confederacy for a year.[1] Baylor sent one hundred men to protect the miners, but Confederate authority in New Mexico was short-lived.

Union forces in New Mexico were equally exposed to Mescalero attacks. In December 1861 General E. R. S. Canby, commander of the department, wrote that Indian troubles were getting more costly each day. The only solution he could offer was to place them all on reservations, but that was a plan for the future, not the present.

When Colonel Baylor was named territorial governor of Confederate Arizona he established his headquarters at Mesilla, in southern New Mexico. Early in 1862 he sent a Confederate force to occupy Tucson. Baylor had already come to regard Apaches as a major problem, for they had frequently looted his supply trains. Learning that Captain Helms of the Arizona Guards had held a conference with some Apaches (probably Mimbreños), Baylor ordered him to lure them to another meeting, claiming that the Confederate government had passed a law ordering the extermination of all hostile Indians. Helms was, therefore, to kill all adult Indians and sell the children to pay for the cost of killing their

81

parents. "Leave nothing undone," Baylor advised, "to insure success, and have a sufficient number of men around to allow no Indian to escape. . . . "[2] The Confederate defeat at Glorieta or Apache Canyon in March 1862 ended Baylor's plans for exterminating the Apaches, and when Confederate officials learned of his orders to Helms, Baylor was relieved of all military duties. Confederate General H. H. Sibley favored a milder treatment for Apaches and Navajos—selling them as slaves.

Union plans for recovering Arizona and New Mexico were quickly under way, with Major James H. Carleton training California Volunteers for the task. Carleton, a veteran dragoon, had been stationed in New Mexico after the war with Mexico and had commanded several expeditions against the Jicarillas. John C. Cremony, who had served with the Boundary Commission, was a cavalry captain in the Volunteers. Carleton's training methods were effective, and he soon molded a capable fighting force. But by the time the first group of California Volunteers entered Tucson in May 1862 the Confederates had already withdrawn.

When he reached Arizona Carleton established Camp Lowell near Tucson. Forts Buchanan and Breckinridge were in ruins, so new sites were chosen, and Breckinridge was renamed Fort Stanford in honor of California's governor. Next Carleton sent Colonel Edward E. Eyre on a reconnaissance mission toward the Río Grande. At Apache Pass Eyre met a large number of Apaches, who swore eternal friendship and then fired a few shots into his camp. Before moving his force to the Río Grande Carleton sent an infantry company and a wagon train ahead to establish an outpost and supply depot on the Overland Trail. The infantry and a mountain howitzer battery under Captain Thomas L. Roberts marched ahead of the wagons, which were guarded by Cremony and his cavalry company. A few cavalrymen accompanied the infantry to serve as couriers. The route led through Apache Pass.

When his scouts reported that troops were coming toward Apache Pass, Chiricahua chief Cochise sent word to Mangas Coloradas asking for help; Mimbreños and Chiricahuas were lying in ambush when the infantry arrived. The troops had marched forty miles across the desert without water, and the Apaches blocked the way to the only spring within miles. From behind rocks high on the sides of the pass the Apaches opened fire. The troops pulled back a short distance and brought up the mountain howitzers, which sent shells screaming into the rocks and crags. The Apaches had never faced artillery before, and it soon drove them away.

Once the spring had been secured Captain Roberts sent a sergeant and five cavalrymen to warn Cremony. A short distance from the pass, however, an Apache war party swooped down on the messengers, separating John Teal from the others. Teal's horse was killed, but he fought desperately and wounded one of the Apaches. The fighting stopped immediately, for the wounded warrior was Mangas Coloradas. The Mimbreños carried him to Janos, where he received the best medical care available—unsmiling Mimbreño warriors warned the doctor that if Mangas died they would destroy the town and kill everyone in it. Mangas soon recovered and returned to the Santa Rita region.

At the base of Apache Pass, Carleton established Fort Bowie to protect the route and spring. Soon after arriving in New Mexico he was promoted and named to succeed General Canby as commander of the territory. The Confederates had by then withdrawn from New Mexico, following their defeat at Apache Canyon, and there seemed no likelihood of another invasion. But Carleton's California troops were restless, possibly mutinous, and needed to be kept active. The energetic and ruthless new general decided to occupy his men with the task of pacifying the Apaches and Navajos. His instrument in this undertaking would be the veteran Indian fighter Kit Carson, a colonel of the New Mexico Volunteers. In support of Carleton's decision to wage unrelenting war on the Indians, Cremony remarked, "What the Confederates failed to appropriate, the Apaches [have] destroyed." The inhabitants of New Mexico, he noted, were demoralized and starving.[3]

A man of determination and unshakable conviction, Carleton became the nemesis of the Mescaleros and Navajos, and to a lesser extent of the Mimbreños and Mogollones. Although the troops he had left in Arizona spent much of their time pursuing or fighting Apaches, they had no successes comparable to the defeats of Jicarillas, Mescaleros, and Navajos he orchestrated in New Mexico. To Carleton the situation was simple and uncomplicated—the Mescaleros had made peace earlier, but owing to the Confederate invasion they had broken the treaty and waged war on Anglo settlements. That they had also fought against the Confederates was irrelevant. The fact remained that they had broken a treaty. The remedy, as Carleton saw it, was equally simple—make them regret their rashness by killing as many as possible. If any men survived they would surely become treaty-worshippers.

In October 1862 Carleton ordered Colonel Carson to reoccupy Fort Stanton with five companies of his New Mexico Volunteers and to punish and control the Mescaleros. Carson was reluctant to take part in what he quite properly envisaged as a war of extermination, for he was no Indian-hater and he was convinced that the Apaches could be brought under control by less drastic measures. The Mescaleros, armed mainly with bows and arrows, were desperately poor, on the verge of starvation, and Carson knew it would be a terribly one-sided war. But once General Carleton had made a decision there was no possibility of compromise. He had decided that the Apaches and Navajos should be pursued and killed off until the survivors, if any, were ready to throw themselves on his mercy. His orders to Carson and to the other field commanders were merciless in tone and intent.

"The Indians are to be soundly whipped," he said, "without parleys or councils. . . . All Indian men of that tribe are to be killed whenever and wherever you can find them. The women and children will not be harmed, but you will take them prisoners, and feed them at Ft. Stanton until you receive other instructions about them." No one, under any circumstances, was to receive the Indians under a flag of truce or make peace with them. If they wanted peace the chiefs and principle men were to go to Santa Fe and confer with Carleton directly. "I think that this severity," he concluded philosophically, "in the long run will be the most humane course that could be pursued toward these Indians."[4]

Dr. Michael Steck, former agent to the Southern Apaches, became superintendent of Indian affairs for New Mexico in 1863, the same year that responsibility for the Indians was temporarily transferred from the army to civil authorities. Steck had originally agreed that the Mescaleros should be confined on a reservation, but he was shocked by Carleton's brutal orders and appalled by the number of Mescaleros killed. He pointed out that between 1854 and 1860, when Mescaleros and Gileños had been supplied provisions, they had remained relatively peaceful, cultivating their fields. Steck declared that it was cheaper to feed Indians than to fight them: "The latter course," he wrote, "we have pursued up to the present, at an outlay of three millions annually to the government; the former, it is confidently believed can be the more effective plan, at a cost of one-twentieth the expenditures heretofore defrayed, and without loss of life or property."[5] Steck added, "It needs no prophetic eye to see that, in a few years, the Indians of New Mexico must be exterminated, unless the government interposes its benevolent hand to protect and support them."[6] But the hand that was extended was to be far from benevolent.

No New Mexico Indians had officially been placed on reservations, but as military commander of the territory, Carleton decided to set aside a reservation for the Mescaleros. Although an earlier one had been established for them at Fort Stanton, in their own country, Congress had not ratified the treaty. While Carson was establishing his headquarters at Fort Stanton Captain McCleave and two companies of California Volunteers entered the Mescalero country from the southwest by way of Dog Canyon, a favorite refuge. The campaigns were to last from November 15 to December 31, 1862; their goal was the total annihilation or unconditional surrender of the Indians.

Carleton's inflexible orders, rigidly carried out, soon caused serious injustice to Mescaleros. Late in October Captain James Graydon and his cavalry troop met old Manuelito, the most influential Mescalero chief, and his band. Manuelito signaled for peace and a talk. Graydon, following his orders, attacked without warning, killing Manuelito and José Largo, along with a number of warriors and one woman. Too late Graydon learned that Manuelito was also following Carleton's orders and was on his way to Santa Fe to confer with the general.

When he learned of this attack, Kit Carson was dismayed. He protested to Carleton, who did not want to risk alienating his most valuable Indian fighter. "If you are satisfied [that] Graydon's attack on Manuelita and his people was not fair and open," he replied, "see that all the horses and mules . . . are returned to the survivors of Manuelita's band."[7] Carleton did not modify his orders for killing Mescaleros, however, and the return of a few horses and mules was small compensation indeed for the loss of able chiefs and warriors.

Soon after this Captain McCleave met a band of about one hundred Mescalero warriors in Dog Canyon and defeated them. The survivors fled across the mountains to Fort Stanton and surrendered to Kit Carson, for they knew him to be fair and humane. Contrary to orders Carson protected them, sending five of them under escort to Santa Fe, accompanied by agent Lorenzo Labadi. Cadete was now the principal spokesman for the Mescaleros after the death of Manuelito. When the conference with Carleton began, Cadete said:

You are stronger than we. We have fought you so long as we had rifles and powder; but your weapons are better than ours. Give us like weapons and turn us loose, we will fight you again; but [now] we are worn out; we have no more heart; we have no provisions, no means to live; your troops are everywhere; our springs and water-holes are either occupied or overlooked by your men. You have driven us from our last and best stronghold, and we have no more heart. Do with us as may seem good to you, but do not forget that we are men and braves. [8]

Carleton's terms were blunt. Those who wanted peace, he brusquely told them, must go to the Bosque Redondo (Round Wood) or be treated as hostiles. When the war was over, he promised, they would be settled on a reservation in their own country.

By the time Cadete surrendered, November 1862, Carleton had already ordered work begun on Fort Sumner, near the Bosque Redondo on the Pecos northeast of Fort Stanton. The region, Dr. Steck noted, was suitable for only a limited number of Indians. Carson was ordered to send Mescaleros to Fort Sumner as soon as they surrendered; they were to be kept in a camp near the fort. "These Indians," Carleton instructed the commander at Fort Sumner, "are to be fed by your commissary; are to be treated kindly; [and] are not to be annoyed by soldiers visiting their camp at improper times."[9] Soon there were 350 Mescaleros at Fort Sumner, and others on their way. An estimated 301 had been killed, and Carleton was satisfied that the band had been thoroughly chastised. That spring the Mescaleros planted two hundred acres and harvested their one good crop of their miserable stay at the Bosque Redondo.

The Mescaleros who had surrendered were under the command of agent Labadi and Captain Cremony. When Labadi informed Cremony that the Indians had nothing to eat and were not allowed to hunt, Cremony persuaded the fort commander to let him lead a hunting party. The hunt was successful, and thereafter the Mescaleros trusted Cremony.

After Cremony won their confidence the Mescaleros stopped his couriers only to inquire if they belonged to his company. Cadete promised that neither Cremony or his men would be harmed by Mescaleros, and he kept his word. The Mescaleros also willingly helped him compile an Apache dictionary, and others demonstrated many of their skills for him—something they would not have done for any other Anglo. Tatsahdasaygo (Quick Killer) showed him how thoroughly an Apache could conceal himself where the ground offered no special opportunities for cover. On a stretch of open prairie, where there was only one bush, Cremony looked away for a few minutes while Quick Killer hid, then searched for him. When

Cremony finally gave up and called for him to show himself, Quick Killer was only a few feet away, completely buried under gramma grass.

On another occasion Nah-kah-yen and Cremony were hunting antelopes. When they saw a herd Nah-kah-yen tied a piece of red cloth to a yucca stalk, handed Cremony his rifle, and told him to go a long way off. Then he hid in the sand near the yucca stalk, knowing that the cloth would arouse the antelopes' curiosity. Cremony went several hundred yards away and watched. The antelopes went up to the red cloth and raced away several times. When Cremony finally returned to the yucca stalk he found that Nah-kah-yen had killed four antelopes with his knife.[10]

The Apaches' skill at horse-stealing was, of course, legendary. On one occasion the horses of the First California Cavalry were taken to the San Xavier del Bac region to rest and recover.

Lieutenant Colonel Ferguson of the First California Cavalry had an excellent horse, and on the march to San Xavier he had refused to allow this valuable animal to be tied to the picket line with the cavalry mounts, for fear it would be injured. Instead, he tied it about twenty feet from the other horses. No one heard a sound that night, but in the morning the horse was gone, its rope cut.

The Pápagos of San Xavier, who had corraled their ponies at night because of the Apaches, felt safe knowing that the cavalry horses grazed at night under heavy guard. The Apaches later told Cremony that they had known the Pápagos would become careless, and they ran off nearly every animal.

Cremony also described the Apaches' love of gambling, especially the hoop and pole game, in which they often would wager their last possessions. Two men played it by rolling a hoop forward then throwing poles so as to make them fall on the hoop as close to the butt of the pole as possible. Three prominent warriors served as judges, and their word was final. When the betting was heavy the excitement often led to violent quarrels. For that reason no one was allowed to carry weapons, and women were not permitted to watch, for they might cause trouble.

At the time General Carleton sent Carson after the Mescaleros he also ordered Colonel John R. West to wage uninterrupted warfare against the Gileños, who had driven the miners and ranchers from southern New Mexico. Like Carson West was to give no quarter, show no mercy. "There must be no peace, or conference, with any Indians living in any of the tributaries of the Mimbres or headwaters of the Gila, down as far as Fort Stanford, until they are completely

Playing the hoop and pole game at San Carlos
Arizona Historical Society

subdued. . . . If possible, the present war against the Apaches . . .
will be continued without intermission. . . . "[11]

Before commencing the campaign West sought cooperation from
Mexican officials. He wrote to Prefect José María Uranga of El Paso
that he intended to wage vigorous warfare against the Apaches east
and west of the Río Grande and requested Uranga to seek the
cooperation of the governor of Chihuahua, pointing out that
Apaches were allowed to trade stolen property at Janos. In a similar
letter to Governor Ignacio Pesqueira of Sonora, West advised him
that he would attack Apaches along the border and warned him to be
alert for those seeking refuge in Sonora.

There were a series of swift campaigns against the Gileños during
the fall of 1862 and spring and summer of 1863. Fort Craig on the Río
Grande was strengthened for these expeditions. In February Cap-

tain McCleave and four companies marched to the site chosen for Fort West; there Gileños ran off sixty cavalry horses. McCleave went in pursuit with one hundred men on horses already nearly broken down. They had followed the trail for several days when all but thirty of the horses gave out. Still the pursuit continued, for although the troops had had but four hours sleep in four days, the trail was now fresh. They surprised the Indians' camp, killed twenty-five Apaches, and recovered most of the horses. The Gileños were better armed than the Mescaleros, but even they were no match for well-trained troops armed with late-model rifles, howitzers, and plenty of ammunition.

In January 1863 Mangas Coloradas was killed, reportedly while attempting to escape from Fort McLane. The story is a tangled one and several contradictions have never been satisfactorily resolved. Daniel Ellis Conner, a member of Joseph Reddeford Walker's party of prospectors, wrote later that his party had decided to capture Mangas Coloradas and hold him as a hostage, so that they could prospect safely in Gileño country. They met the advance patrol of California Volunteers under Captain E. D. Shirland and apparently camped with them while men of Walker's party went to Pinos Altos to seize Mangas.

The kidnappers raised a white flag and waited. When Mangas and several others came up they trained rifles on the chief, telling him to inform his people that his safety depended on their good conduct toward the Walker party. They took Mangas to the remains of old Fort McLane, fifteen miles south of Santa Rita del Cobre and about equal distance southwest of modern Silver City. This Union fort had been abandoned along with others in July 1861. The men arrived with Mangas about the time that Colonel West reached the ruined fort. The next day, according to Conner, Colonel West insisted on taking custody of Mangas until he had accounted for two government wagons plundered recently near the Río Grande. Two soldiers guarded Mangas by a fire during a bitterly cold night. Conner was on sentinel duty for the Walker party, and the area he patrolled brought him near Mangas and the two guards. Toward midnight Conner noticed that the guards were annoying their prisoner, but they desisted whenever he approached on his rounds. Conner watched from a distance; he saw them heat bayonets in the fire and then place them against Mangas Coloradas' legs and feet. When the chief drew back they shot him.

Army reports fail to mention the Walker party and state only that federal troops took Mangas prisoner. According to these reports

Mangas had tried to escape three times when his guards shot him. Later a soldier of the California Volunteers who claimed to have been present stated that "General, then Colonel West said to the guards, 'Men, that old murderer has got away from every soldier command and has left a trail of blood for 5000 miles on the old stage line. I want him dead or alive tomorrow morning, do you understand, I want him dead.' "[12]

Whatever the story, in the next day or two the troops shot down Mangas' unsuspecting family before any of them grew suspicious. Then they returned to Pinos Altos and surprised the Mimbreños who awaited their chief's return, killing many. General Carleton, whether aware of the circumstances or not, reported: "Mangas Colorado, doubtless the worst Indian within our boundaries, and one who has been the cause of more murders and more torturing and burning at the stake in this country than all others together, has been killed, and in one battle a few days since over 20 of his followers were captured. . . . Hostilities against the Gila Apaches are now being prosecuted with vigor and will be productive of lasting benefits."[13] The "lasting benefits" he mentioned were not intended for Apaches.

Rumors soon began circulating to the effect that the death of Mangas Coloradas had been an especially dirty business. It was not that people admired Mangas or wished him alive, but Carleton's high-handed actions had alienated many. Judge Joseph G. Knapp of Mesilla criticized Carleton's "black flag" policy of preventing Apaches from surrendering and driving them to continued violence. Carleton, whose military authority made him invulnerable as long as the Civil War continued, ignored most of the protests, though occasionally he answered critics with pent-up irritation. There would be no let up in the war against the Gileños, he declared; the alternatives, he told Colonel West, were the "Entire subjugation, or destruction, of all men. . . . "[14]

The Gileños were harassed so constantly that by 1865 they, like the Mescaleros, had seen the numbers of their fighting men greatly reduced. Hundreds of Gileños had been killed and an equal number had died of hunger and disease; many children had been sold into slavery. The Gileños had been driven from their country to seek refuge in the mountains of Arizona and Sonora; they had so few warriors left they were no longer considered a serious threat.

In March 1865 Dr. Steck asked Carleton for an escort to Fort West, for he had received information that the Mimbreños wanted peace. Carleton replied that as long as the Indians were at war the army must handle everything. The Mimbreños, he said, were still in the hands of the military, *"and will be, until the military commander makes peace with them on his own terms."*[15]

After his victories over the Mescaleros Kit Carson was pressured into taking command of an expedition sent to subjugate the Navajos. In the meantime, despite his earlier promise to return the Mescaleros to a reservation in their own lands, Carleton had decided to keep them permanently at the Bosque Redondo. They had harvested only one successful crop there, the water was alkaline and unfit to drink, wood was scarce, and the Mescaleros' outlook was bleak indeed, but Carleton had convinced himself that they were happy at the new home he had given them. Once Carleton had decided they were happy, the matter was settled. What made an intolerable situation impossible was Carleton's decision to send all Navajo prisoners to the Bosque, presumably to share in the Mescaleros' new-found happiness.

Dr. Steck, who was well aware that the Bosque was unsuitable for a large number of Indians and who knew that Mescaleros and Navajos were far from congenial, predicted trouble. In January 1864, before Navajo prisoners arrived, Navajo raiders ran off many Mescalero horses. The Mescaleros hurried to Fort Sumner and asked for help. Most of Cremony's company were off on patrol, but twelve who were available joined twenty-five Mescalero warriors led by Cadete. They caught up with the Navajos at daybreak and routed them in subzero weather, killing many and recovering most of the horses. On other occasions Mescaleros had aided troops against the Navajos. The prospect of sharing the reservation with upwards of eight thousand hostile Navajos, therefore, was as appalling to the Mescaleros as it was to Dr. Steck.

In vain Steck urged Carleton to keep the Navajos on a separate reservation in their own country. He considered the matter so serious that he traveled to Washington to try to convince officials of the error of placing the two groups on the same reservation, but with no more success. On returning to New Mexico Steck tried again, suggesting to Carleton that he hold a council with the Navajos to learn their views. Carleton was, however, adamant: "It is a mockery," he replied, "to hold councils with a people who are in our hands and have only to await our decisions."[16]

In rationalizing to himself that Mescaleros and Navajos would live peaceably together, Carleton ignored the fact that the former had been recruited to fight the latter on several occasions. Indeed, chiefs Cadete and Blanco had played prominent roles in defeats the Navajos could not easily forget or forgive. As more and more Navajos arrived at the Bosque during the spring and summer of 1864, the situation became increasingly unbearable for the Mescaleros. There were, finally, more than eight thousand Navajos on the reservation, and they treated the Mescaleros roughly, seizing their cornfields and occasionally attacking them. Food quickly gave out because of poor harvests all over New Mexico; the Indians at the Bosque were naked and starving, suffering intensely from the bitter cold. Carleton, whose diet was adequate, told them they should be too proud to murmur at what could not be avoided, but his words gave them little solace. The Santa Fe *New Mexican* was even less sympathetic than Carleton, noting only that he had gathered at the Bosque "eight thousand Indians whose untutored minds, don't know enough to cover their behinds. . . . "[17]

If Carleton had any respect or admiration for the Mescaleros before they surrendered, he concealed it well, for the only terms he used to describe them were pejorative. He said, nevertheless, that he was determined they should be happy. He noted that "my anxiety is so great to make this powerful nation, which has surrendered to us, as happy and well cared for as possible under all the adverse circumstances which encompass us. . . . "[18] On another occasion, he said, "For pity's sake, if not moved by any other consideration, let us as a great nation, for once treat the Indian as he deserves to be treated. . . . They have fought us gallantly for years. . . . and, as brave men entitled to our admiration and respect, have come to us with confidence in our magnanimity."[19] But on one occasion, when the agent in charge permitted the famished Mescaleros to leave the reservation to make mescal, Carleton instructed the commander at Fort Sumner to kill any male Apache who left the reservation for any reason.

On a visit to the Bosque Redondo late in 1864 Dr. Steck was shocked by the destitute condition of both Mescaleros and Navajos, and at the number dying daily of hunger and disease. The Mescaleros who were able to travel were leaving for their own country, and many Navajos were slipping away, preferring to starve to death anywhere but at the Bosque. Steck informed Carleton of the deplorable situation and urged him to change his policy. Carleton refused. The general did not, however, approve of cruelty to those Indians who had surrendered, especially cruelty inflicted by civilians.

Because he had decided that the Mescaleros and Navajos would be happy together at the Bosque, Carleton was outraged when Dr. Steck or other meddling, misguided civil officials suggested that the Navajos wanted to return to their own lands and should be allowed to go. It was irrelevant what the Navajos wanted to do; their duty was to remain at the Bosque and be happy. When small groups of Mescaleros or Navajos slipped away from the reservation, Carleton ordered the troops to apply his sovereign remedy—hunt them down and kill all the men.

Starving and convinced that their cause was hopeless, Mescalero chief Ojo Blanco and his band fled the reservation in March 1864. At the urging of agent Labadi, however, they returned a few months later. Others continued to leave the Bosque despite Carleton's threats. When informed of this, Carleton did not consider changing his policy. He simply repeated his order to kill the men.

The year 1865 was a bad one for New Mexico in general, for unfavorable weather, plant diseases, and insects destroyed the crops. There was suffering everywhere, but at the Bosque it was intensified, for when supplies were low the partial rations were reduced to almost nothing. On November 3 all of the Mescaleros who had the strength to drag themselves away left the reservation and headed for their mountain retreats, preferring to die in familiar surroundings. Cadete had informed the army officers that his people would not stay at the Bosque, but would come in when given a reservation that could support them.

Before launching a fall and winter campaign against the Mimbreños, Carleton sent Lieutenant Colonel N. H. Davis to Pinos Altos to confer with the headmen of Mangas Coloradas' band about moving peacefully to the Bosque. About one hundred Mimbreños—including Victorio, three sons of Mangas, and Nana—came to the council. All were destitute. Davis gave them a glowing account of the food and clothing they would receive at the Bosque. He had not come to make peace, he told them, but to tell them they could have peace if they went to the Bosque. If they refused the war would go on; it was their choice, but they must not wait until the door was closed. Davis told them they could send a delegation to see the Bosque if they wished.

Victorio replied. "I and my people want peace; we are tired of war; we are poor and have little for ourselves and our families to eat and wear . . . we want to make a peace, a lasting peace, one that will keep; we would like to live in our country, and will go onto a reservation where the government may put us, and those who do not come in (of our people) we will go and help fight them. . . . " They said they wanted to see the reservation first, but their delegation failed to appear; Victorio sent Davis word that their horses had been stolen and that they could not meet him. Davis decided, however,

Mimbrẽno chief Victorio
Western History Collection, University of Oklahoma

that they were acting in bad faith and gave his troops orders to kill every male. "Death to the Apache, and peace and prosperity to this land is my motto," he concluded.[20]

Carleton continued to block Steck's efforts to aid the Indians and refused to allow him to accompany Davis to the Mimbreños. They must, he said, surrender unconditionally. As a result of Carleton's instransigence hostilities continued. And because both Dr. Steck and Judge Knapp had gone to Washington in attempts to convince officials that Carleton's policies were ruinous and had failed, both were now obliged to resign "for the good of the service."

After the Mescaleros left the Bosque no troops were sent after them; by then Carleton had surrendered control of the Indians to civil officials, and the misery and mismanagement of the Indians under his rule had been exposed. The Mescaleros returned to their favorite refuges in the Sierra Blanca, Sacramento, and Davis Mountains as well as in the Big Bend country. Some went north to join the Comanches, while others went to live and fight with the Mimbreños. There were occasional Mescalero raids on Anglo ranches, but some chiefs, notably Cadete, continued to avoid hostilities with Anglos.

One result of Steck's visit to Washington to plead for the Mescaleros and Navajos was that Congress provided for a joint committee to investigate the condition of the Indians, particularly their treatment by civil and military officials. Senator James R. Doolittle of Wisconsin headed the subcommittee sent to investigate Indian affairs in New Mexico and Colorado. His hearings began in Santa Fe on July 5, 1865; the following day Carleton ended martial law in New Mexico.

As a committee witness Carleton recommended that the office of commissioner of Indian affairs be abolished and that the Indians be kept under army control. It was, he said, a waste of time to negotiate treaties with Indians. "To go through the forms of making a treaty with a party, when the government is determined to have matters its own way anyhow," he said with candor, "is a mockery beneath the dignity of the United States. We can do right without resorting to any theatricals simply for effect."[21] Carleton maintained that the Bosque Redondo was ample for both Navajos and Mescaleros, disagreeing with Labadi that the Mescaleros were unhappy after the Navajos were sent there.

Indian agent John Ward, writing to the congressional committee on Indian affairs, gave other reasons for not placing much reliance on treaties. "The very chief who signs a treaty knows but little about it," he wrote, "and as to the entire tribe, they know less." Chiefs, he continued, exercised much less influence over their bands than many people believed; their power was nominal, at most. Ward pointed out, furthermore, that interpreters often were not able to make clear to the Indians everything agreed on in a treaty even if they tried, and sometimes information had to go through more than one interpreter. "Nor is there any doubt," Ward added,

> that some interpreters will introduce their own notions and opinions in the interpretation rather than . . . express those of the Indians. For the most part the only clause of a treaty that is ordinarily understood by an Indian is the one containing a provision for the amount of gifts the Indians are to receive. The prevailing idea with most wild Indians in making a treaty is that the government is obligating itself to pay the Indians a certain amount to get them to keep the peace.[22]

The people of New Mexico opposed the reservation system because there would be no more tribes from which they could capture servants. Even worse, reservations meant that the military forces would be reduced and the money these people made on government contracts would shrink.

Kit Carson testified for the committee by letter. Many of the Apaches, he said, understood farming and should be put on reservations. He did not think that the Arizona Apaches would object to being placed on reservations, but he was sure that the Jicarillas would resent being sent to the Bosque Redondo with the Mescaleros. "Allow me," he said, "to suggest the necessity of extreme caution and circumspection in locating Indians, to prevent internal dissensions, upon reservations. Different tribes," he reminded the committee, "besides being of different degrees of advancement in civilization, have feuds of long standing to excite them, [the] ambition of chiefs to satisfy, and long cherished traditions of delayed revenge to gratify."[23]

Major Greiner testified before the committee, protesting the appointment of Indian agents for mere political reasons. "The general policy of selecting men as agents for political services, rather than fitness for the position, and frequently changing them, is a great cause" he said, "of all our Indian difficulties. . . . In my experience I have never known a serious difficulty in the Territory between the Indians and the citizens which did not originate mainly with the latter."[24] Greiner also mentioned the conflict between civil and military officials. "The Indian department was once under the War Department," he noted. "Some fifteen years since it was taken away and placed in the Interior Department. From that time, from the Indian department at Washington down to the subagents in New Mexico, there has been a constant struggle by the military department to get the control of Indian affairs, and that struggle has been one cause of the difficulties."[25]

Captain Cremony also felt that the difficulties involving the Indian Bureau were beyond remedy as long as that agency remained politically oriented. He noted that every few years new and untried agents were sent to take over reservations, and new policies were introduced, to the confusion and dissatisfaction of the Indians. Cremony recommended total and sweeping reform, merging the bureau with the War Department. As Indian agents the government should employ the large number of retired army officers, many of whom had acquired considerable insight into the Indian character. In this way a regular and systematic policy could be pursued. He felt that the Apaches in particular could be subdued by the army and moved to reservations outside their own lands.

During the years immediately following the Civil War congressmen were cautious about appropriating money except for the benefit of their own constituents, and the Apache problem was neglected. Because of sweeping reductions in appropriations, no effort was made to help the Apaches become self-supporting, and the danger of war increased. At the same time it was impossible to formulate an effective and consistent policy for solving the Apache problems of New Mexico and Arizona.

General Ulysses S. Grant took a personal interest in the condition of the Indians, asking General John H. Pope for a full report. Pope replied that the Indians' situation was difficult and could not be improved without a complete change of policy. He mentioned the inconsistencies in dealing with Indians. No one knew the extent of wrongs done to Indians by white men, Pope said, yet these same men blamed the government if they suffered any loss of life or property. "What the white man does to the Indian is never known," he wrote. "It is only what the Indian does to the white man (nine times out of ten in the way of retaliation) which reaches the public."[26]

The Indians, Pope continued, no longer had lands of their own, for everywhere these were invaded by whites. Losing their land and home and means of subsistence, they were driven to the "necessity of warring to the death upon the white man, whose inevitable and destructive progress threatens the total extermination . . . of the Indians." Desperate and starving, the Indians had commenced hostilities against the whites with fury and courage. "Until lately the U.S. troops, small in number and utterly incapable on that account of affording security to the whites, or the protection of the Indians, have been strictly on the defensive," Pope noted. "The difficulty lies in the fact that we can promise the Indian under our present system nothing that he will ask [for] with any hope that we can fulfill our promise."[27]

In June 1865, because of rumors and reports of Indian slavery in New Mexico, President Andrew Johnson ordered the heads of the various departments to notify their staffs to take all lawful means to suppress the trade. Felipe Delgado, the superintendent of Indian affairs for New Mexico, protested that the captives had been purchased by citizens out of "Christian piety" in order to civilize them. In accordance with his instructions, nevertheless, Delgado published a warning against the purchase or exchange of Indian captives. The chief justice of the New Mexico Supreme Court testified before the Doolittle committee on the widespread use of Indian slaves. "The prices," he said, "have lately ranged very high. A likely girl of not more than eight years old, healthy and intelligent, would be held at the value of four hundred dollars or more."[28]

In March 1867 Congress passed "An Act to Abolish and Forever Prohibit the System of Peonage in the Territory of New Mexico and Elsewhere," a sweeping and final law which should have taken care of the matter, for it provided severe penalties for violations. But Indian slavery continued, and most of the estimated two thousand Indian slaves in New Mexico were Apaches or Navajos.

Within a few months after General Carleton's transfer from New Mexico late in 1866 Secretary of War Grant turned control of the Navajos over to the Interior Department. In the meantime Lieutenant R. McDonald made a thorough survey of the Bosque Redondo project and reported what others had long known, that it was unsuitable for an Indian reservation. He recommended abandoning it and relocating the Navajos on more suitable land.

In May 1868 General William Tecumseh Sherman arrived at the Bosque Redondo with authority to negotiate a treaty. The Navajos were eager, and within a few days an agreement had been reached to return them to their own country. On June 15 the joyous Navajos began the Long Walk back to their own land. Carleton's Bosque Redondo experiment in happiness for Indians was ended.

By 1869, when control of the New Mexico Indians was restored to the War Department, the United States had been trying to control Apaches for two decades, but only a few hundred of the surviving Jicarillas had been settled on a reservation—and that was only temporary. After the Mescaleros had fled the Bosque Redondo they disappeared from view for several years except for small-scale raids on ranch herds and a few large-scale forays. On one occasion they ran off more than one thousand cattle that rancher John S. Chisum was sending to Fort Sumner and drove them into the Guadalupe Mountains. Troops occasionally tracked Mescalero raiding parties into the Guadalupes, but failed to overtake them.

When complaints were voiced about the Mescaleros, agent Lorenzo Labadi wrote from his deserted agency headquarters at Agua Negra that they had been peaceful and obedient until Navajos had been sent to the Bosque and that the Mescaleros had pleaded for a separate reservation. He proposed that the Mescaleros and Jicarillas be put together on a reservation at Fort Stanton, a solution that would not have pleased the Jicarillas. Labadi was certain the Mescaleros would never return to the Bosque reserve. Pleading for an intelligent approach to the Apache problem, he resigned.

The Mescalero and Gila Apache agencies were combined once more, and Lieutenant A. G. Hennisee sent runners from Fort Stanton to contact the Mescaleros. Fifty-one of them came in, with no chief among them, to see what treatment they might expect. Hennisee had little to offer in the way of food, clothing, or shelter, so they had to provide for themselves. Despite this, however, Hennisee was optimistic.

The Mimbreños and Mogollones had been hard hit and forced out of their lands by Carleton's troops, but now some returned and agreed to settle at Cañada Alamosa. A few Mescaleros who had joined them earlier accompanied them to the reservation. To an optimist like Hennisee it appeared that New Mexico's Apache problems were at last on the way to solution.

VI
Anglo-Apache
Conflict in Arizona

GEOGRAPHICAL OBSTACLES MADE campaigning against the Indians in Arizona even more difficult than in New Mexico, and it took a number of years for the troops to overcome them. As one officer wryly commented, "I defy any one to make his way over this country without the aid of profanity. Many and many a time . . . I have come to some confounded cañon of piled-up rocks and slippery precipices, which would have been utterly impassable for myself and men if we had not literally cursed ourselves over."[1]

Although Arizona became a territory separate from New Mexico in February 1863 Carleton retained military control over it until 1865, and troops there continued to carry out his orders. In May 1863 the commander at Tucson learned of a hostile Apache camp in Arivaipa Canyon. He ordered Lieutenant Thomas T. Tidball to attack the camp with a force of California Volunteers, Anglo and Mexican civilians, some Pápagos, and Manso Apaches as guides. They traveled five nights and surprised the camp at daybreak, killing fifty and wounding as many more.

When gold was discovered near where Prescott would soon be founded Carleton was determined to make the area safe for miners by holding off the fierce Tontos and Yavapais, whose hunting grounds were being invaded. He ordered Fort Whipple built in the Chino Valley. Its commander, Major Edward Willis, reached an agreement with several hundred Indians living in the vicinity. He warned territorial officials who were on their way to the region of the delicate situation and of the need to avoid stirring up the Indians. Despite this warning, when these officials met the peaceful band their escort attacked it, killing twenty. Overnight all of the Tonto and Yavapai bands of central Arizona were on the warpath.

Early in 1864 rancher King Woolsey led three punitive expeditions against the Tontos, Yavapais, and Pinaleños who had stolen nearly every animal from the Prescott region as well as the mule herd from Fort Whipple. Woolsey had fought Apaches before and shared the frontiersman's conviction that in Indian warfare there were no foul blows. On one occasion while he and some others were prospecting they found their camp surrounded by Apaches. Woolsey quickly mixed strychnine with pinole, a flour made of corn and mesquite beans; he placed the concoction in a pack on a burro and then turned the animal loose. Naturally, the Apaches caught it and ate the pinole. When some fell to the ground in agony the others fled. This was Woolsey's so-called Pinole Treaty.

Assembling twenty-eight men, Woolsey sent one to the Pima villages to ask the Pimas and Maricopas for a war party to meet him on the Verde. Many miners had already abandoned the Prescott region as unsafe, and Woolsey was aware that the Tontos and their allies must be checked if any ranchers or miners were to survive there. He was joined by Pimas, Maricopas, one Yuma warrior, and one Apache-Mohave named Tonto Jack, but when the trail led into unfamiliar country, the Pimas turned back.

Still following the trail of stolen stock, Woolsey's party made camp in a dry creek bed.[2] Soon the mountains echoed with war whoops, as Tontos and Yavapais encircled the camp. The Apache-Mohave with Woolsey served as interpreter. The Tontos told him that his party had no chance to escape—everyone would be killed. The Apache-Mohave insisted that Woolsey and the others were prospectors and would give them pinole and tobacco for sparing their lives if they came to the camp.

One of the enemy, recognizing the Apache-Mohave, entered the camp to receive the proffered tobacco and pinole. One by one others followed. When Woolsey drew his gun and killed the chief it was the signal to attack; a few minutes later twenty-four Yavapais, Tontos, and Pinaleños lay dead, while others escaped with wounds.

In two other campaigns Woolsey and his men killed thirty more Yavapais and Tontos, temporarily easing the pressure on the miners around Prescott. Danger was still present, however, and territorial Governor John N. Goodwin declared that "The Indian difficulties are becoming very serious, and unless vigorous measures are taken, the new mining regions will be deserted."[3]

Warfare against the Tontos and Yavapais continued. A company of Arizona rangers killed twenty-three late in 1865. The following spring the Arizona Volunteers killed thirty or forty more in a campaign from Camp Lincoln; troops and Pimas killed another forty-seven in the same region. The Indians and settlers of Skull Valley met for a "big talk." While it was going on, troops arrived and killed thirty-two.

J. Ross Browne, who had visited Arizona in 1864 on a tour with the newly appointed superintendent of Indian affairs, Charles D. Poston, commented on the state of affairs. The conditions Browne described were at least partly the result of Apache hostility: "Mines without miners and forts without soldiers are common. Politicians without policy, traders without trade, store-keepers without stores, teamsters without teams, and all without means, form the mass of the white population."[4] Poston requested more troops and better coordination between the military departments, adding that "it is almost equal to going to a foreign country to pass from one military department to another."[5]

Apaches continued to make southern Arizona unsafe. Browne found two companies of California Volunteers at Tucson, but even so Apaches boldly appeared within three miles of the town. The Pápagos, as usual, did good service against the Apaches, but the road between San Xavier and Tubac was marked by the graves of people killed over the past several years. The old Calabasas Ranch, six leagues of fertile land along the Santa Cruz Valley, belonged to Manuel María Gándara, the former governor of Sonora. Browne had met Gándara on his way to California. Although he owned one of the finest ranches in the area, Gándara was poor, for Apaches had made it uninhabitable. A squatter, an old-timer named Pennington, had lived there for several years with ten or twelve of his daughters. His cattle had been driven off and the corrals burned, but because the ranch buildings were of stone, he had managed to survive.

The Arivaca Ranch, when it was occupied, had also been plagued by Apaches. Great care had been taken to guard the horses and mules at night; they were enclosed in a stout corral with a heavy chain wound around the gate. Watch dogs prowled and the vaqueros slept nearby. Despite these precautions, four or five Apaches quietly unwound the chain, opened the heavy gate, and ran off every animal. Five vaqueros pursued them and were ambushed.

In passing through Cocóspera Canyon, Browne was apprehensive of an Apache ambush, but his Irish driver was unconcerned. Anyway, he assured Browne, they would scalp him first. Why? "Because," he replied, rubbing his thick mat of hair, "I don't *think* as much as other gentlemen that's always writin'."[6]

In 1864 General Carleton ordered the best planned and most comprehensive campaign thus far against the Arizona Apaches. As usual his orders included his favorite phrase—"kill all males." A new post, named for Governor Goodwin, was to be established on the Gila and garrisoned by five hundred infantry and cavalry. The troops were to be kept on patrol against the Apaches, combing the country in every direction. On marches of seven days or less each man was to carry his own rations, which were limited to meat, bread, coffee, sugar, and salt. Each man would carry only one blanket. "To be encumbered with more," Carleton concluded, "is not to find Indians."[7]

Even before the troops had taken the field a large band of Apaches ran off the cavalry herd at Cow Springs in southwestern New Mexico. Captain Whitlock went in pursuit with cavalry and infantry, although the trail was already a week old. From his camp on the Mimbres Whitlock followed the trail only long enough to learn its general direction. Then he turned north to the Gila and marched downriver for five days, occasionally sending scouts to check the trail. Finally they located the camp and attacked, killing thirty Apaches and recovering the stolen horses.

Carleton's two-month campaign was to begin on May 25, 1864. He asked the governor to send out parties of miners and bands of Pimas and Maricopas at the same time, alerting the governors of Sonora and Chihuahua and asking for their cooperation. Even before the campaign opened, Lieutenant Colonel Nelson H. Davis, marching north from Fort Bowie, discovered an Apache camp and killed 49. The overall results of the campaign were 216 Western Apaches killed and many more wounded. Thirty were captured and sent to Carleton's favorite Apache retreat, the Bosque Redondo, for he was certain that they would be willing to return to their own people and convince them to move there. Despite the numbers killed and captured, to many Carleton's Arizona campaign of 1864 was a disappointment, considering the cost and the number of men involved. Governor Goodwin explained that the principal reasons for the failure of the campaign were the troops' ignorance of the countryside and their lack of competent guides.

Years later, in 1889, the Walnut Grove Mining Company filed a claim for $292,000 against the government because its Bally Bueno mine, near Prescott, had been destroyed by Apaches. The government was responsible, the company claimed, because in July 1864 General Carleton had assured its officials that he had "already inaugurated a campaign against the Apache Indians that will result in their complete subjugation, and should you induce friends in the east to join you in erecting a quartz mill . . . near Fort Whipple, the enterprise will be fully protected by the military." In March 1890 the claim was approved by a House committee.[8]

In August 1865 the one-eyed Coyotero chief Miguel and three others visited Carleton in Santa Fe to ask permission to visit the Coyotero prisoners at the Bosque Redondo. After lecturing them on the reasons why Coyoteros should pack up and move to the Bosque, Carleton gave them passes to visit their friends and to return with them to their own country; he was convinced they would sing the praises of life on his favorite reservation. The Coyoteros promised to tell their people what he advised, but after visiting the Bosque it is doubtful that they seriously considered leaving the White Mountains of Arizona for it.

In speaking about Apache hostility to the First Legislative Assembly at Prescott, Governor Goodwin said that it was useless to speculate as to its origins or as to which party was right or wrong. "As to them, one policy only can be adopted. A war must be prosecuted until they are compelled to submit and go on a reservation."[9] But there were no reservations set apart for Apaches even when they were willing to submit.

At the end of the Civil War five military divisions, nineteen departments, and a number of districts were established throughout the United States. New Mexico was a department of the Division of the Missouri. Arizona became a district of the Department of California, which was in the Division of the Pacific. Apachería, once under a single command, was thus split into separate jurisdictions under two divisions; one had headquarters at Fort Leavenworth, Kansas, the other at San Francisco. This led to duplication, confusion, and a painful lack of coordination. At the same time the rivalry between the War and Interior Departments over control of the Indians was reflected in pettiness and bickering between officers and Indian agents. It had been difficult enough to cope with Apaches when the troops were under a unified command; dividing the command simply compounded the problems and delayed the solution. Even worse, there was still no "Apache policy" except extermination.

Soon after this jurisdictional change a regiment of Arizona Volunteers was authorized for service against the Apaches. By the fall of 1865 350 men had been organized into companies composed of men of Mexican ancestry or of Pápagos, Pimas, and Maricopas. After a year of hard service and government neglect they were mustered out. Their success was reflected in General Mason's remark that "native troops, Pápagos, Pimas, Mexicans, and also volunteers of our own race, were more effective in the Indian warfare than two or three times the number of regular troops."[10] In their year of service they had killed or captured 100 Apaches, despite the fact that the volunteers were sent from warm regions to high altitudes in severe winter weather, many of them barefooted and only half-clothed, and all poorly fed.

It was Apaches rather than humanitarians who finally caused the government to consider a policy other than extermination. In March 1865 half-starved Apaches came to Camp Goodwin and asked Major James Gorman to allow them to surrender, saying they could hold out no longer. Gorman was willing, but he had neither the necessary provisions to feed them nor sufficient wagons to carry them elsewhere; and he had no orders to do anything except fight them. The best he could do was to tell them they could go free until he received instructions. They remained at the post, nevertheless, and others came in, until there were nine hundred in all camped near by.

After the Civil War had ended the Arizona posts were built, moved, abandoned, and renamed as the Apache threat fluctuated and shifted from one region to another. In May 1865 General John S. Mason was named commander of the District of Arizona and toured the territory with Governor Goodwin. It seemed to Mason that every ranch south of the Gila had been deserted, and Tubac was still unoccupied. North of the Gila conditions were not much better: all but two ranches had been abandoned and few roads were safe. Mason saw at once that the twenty-eight hundred troops stationed in Arizona were too few for the enormous task. There was also a crucial shortage of officers, for some posts had only one.

As Mason saw it the only hope for peace was to occupy the regions where the Apaches had refuges for their women and children and where they hid their stores for winter. Destroying these camps and stores in mid-winter would force the Apaches to surrender. Mason was unable to put his plans into effect, however, because of delays in receiving supplies, the exceptional severity of the weather, and a multitude of other obstacles. He did order Fort McDowell built on the Verde near its juncture with the Salt, and reopened Fort Breckinridge (or Stanford) on the San Pedro, renaming it Camp Grant. Upriver he established Camp Wallen, but it was abandoned after Camp Crittenden was built on a hill overlooking the unhealthful miasma where Fort Buchanan had once stood. Camp Lincoln, on the Verde, was renamed Camp Verde in 1868, the same year Camp

Crittenden was built. The Arizona forts were garrisoned by California Volunteers until 1867, when they were replaced by troops of the First and Eighth Cavalry regiments and twenty companies of the Ninth, Fourteenth, and Thirty-Second Infantry Regiments.

Apaches came to Fort McDowell and Camp Lincoln in 1865 asking for peace, but neither post could accommodate them—they were told to go to Camp Goodwin. They refused, pointing out that the Indians at Camp Goodwin were their enemies. For want of instructions, they were allowed to remain at McDowell, but on the condition that they plant crops and refrain from warring against the Anglos, Pimas, and Maricopas. This was a critical time; the number of troops in Arizona could have been increased and reservations for the Apaches should have been established, but nothing of the sort was done. Instead, General Mason was transferred and the command was divided into a northern and southern district, further complicating things.

One of the few Anglos to establish friendly relations with Apaches during the 1860s was Thomas J. Jeffords, who had arrived in Arizona in 1862 bearing dispatches from General E. R. S. Canby to Carleton. Jeffords had remained in Arizona where, as a Butterfield stage driver, he was wounded in an Apache ambush. For a time he was in charge of mail between Fort Bowie and Tucson; during the sixteen months he held this post Apaches killed fourteen of his mail riders. Jeffords finally resigned because the government failed to protect his men. Next he turned to prospecting, which in Arizona was an extremely hazardous occupation.

Jeffords hoped to reduce the risks by a bold stroke, a face-to-face meeting with Cochise in his own country. He was acquainted with Apaches (not only the ones who had left him scarred), and spoke their language, though not fluently. A friendly Apache led him to the edge of Cochise's retreat in the Dragoon Mountains and sent up a smoke signal to inform the Chiricahuas that a single messenger was approaching on a peaceful mission.

Though some men may have considered it a foolhardy venture, Jeffords rode alone into the Chiricahua stronghold and informed Cochise that he wanted to leave his weapons with the chief while they talked. Astonished at seeing a white man with such courage, Cochise agreed. Jeffords remained with him for several days; he found Cochise to be a man of great intelligence and ability, and the two formed a firm friendship. Cochise, like Apaches generally, despised liars, and he was truthful and candid in all things. He promised Jeffords that no Chiricahua would ever molest him, and none did.

Continuing Apache troubles made it imperative for the Pápagos and Anglos to continue cooperating for survival. In 1865 the Pápagos agreed to maintain a force of 150 mounted men to join Anglos in campaigns against the Apaches. To most Anglos the Pápagos were the "best" Indians in Arizona; distinction was made, however, between the "civilized" Pápagos of San Xavier del Bac and the "nomadic" ones roaming the desert to the west.

Although the goverment began appointing agents to the Pimas and Maricopas in 1859, the men chosen were heavily involved in trade and did little to set up schools or to aid the Indians in other ways. In 1869, when Captain Grossman was named their agent, he made the first sincere effort to initiate a program to help these friendly Indians. He set up agency headquarters at Sacatón and began controlling traders. The Pimas had claimed the land along the Gila for one hundred miles west of where the town of Florence was later located, but the government intended to allow them a reservation of only 64,000 acres or less. Grossman supported the Pimas' claims for more land, and the reservation was extended to include 145,000 acres. It was a substantial increase but far short of what the Pimas could properly claim. There were already serious Anglo encroachments on Pima lands, but because the Pimas had always been friendly to Anglos, the government made no formal agreement with them; as a result they had no treaty to support their protests.

The northwest corner of Apachería was Hualapai or Apache-Yuma country. In 1866 William H. Hardy, who lived on the Colorado near Fort Mohave, made an agreement with the Hualapais so that they would not molest his freight wagons. In return he gave chief Wauba-Yuba a paper that would show other whites he was friendly. But when Wauba-Yuba presented this paper to Sam Miller, who was camped at Beale Springs (in the vicinity of modern Kingman) the result was not what the chief expected. His purpose was to trade for provisions and livestock, but Miller had heard that Hualapais had killed a prospector recently and was suspicious. Their brief discussion ended when Miller grabbed his rifle and killed Wauba-Yuba.

Miller later was arrested at Fort Whipple and charged with murder, but a Prescott grand jury discharged him with a "unanimous vote of thanks." Many a miner and prospector had little reason to give thanks, for dozens of them were killed in retaliation, and mining operations in the area virtually ceased. The sudden war enveloped

all of northwestern Arizona, but the atrocities were by no means
one-sided. As Charles Spencer later wrote, commenting on a battle
with Hualapais in 1868, "I do not blame the Indians so much as some
people think I ought. It was wartime for them, and their men,
women, and children had been killed by the whites; so why not
retaliate. . . . and besides, I have seen some of their children killed
after having been taken captive. . . . "[11]

Constant pressure on the Hualapais forced them to surrender in
August 1868. They gave up their weapons and agreed to move to the
Colorado River and to remain peaceful. The hot, disease-infested
river bottom, however, proved intolerable, and in 1875 they fled to
the mountains where they were finally given a permanent reservation.

The Anglos around Prescott gave the Yavapais and other Indians
little opportunity to live in peace. Even though some of them
worked for ranchers and settlers they were never safe from indiscriminate attacks by Indian-haters. The army also attacked peaceable bands, murdering women and children, until the Yavapais
became desperate. Then their raids on Anglos became so intense
that by the summer of 1865 it appeared that all of central Arizona
would soon be lost.

The superintendent of Indian affairs for Arizona, J. W. Leihy, saw
the need for removing the Apache bands nearest the central Arizona
settlements. With the help of friendly Yavapai and Mohave chiefs he
persuaded about eight hundred Yavapais to move to the Colorado
River Yuma reservation. This move greatly eased pressure on troops
and citizens alike, and commerce, which earlier had been cut off
completely, began to revive.

In 1866 conditions in western Arizona were as bad as ever, for the
Yavapais became dissatisfied on the Colorado River reservation and
returned to the mountains of central Arizona. They apparently
intended to refrain from raiding, but because citizens attacked them
at every opportunity—whether they were friendly or hostile—they
were forced to retaliate; and once more travel west of Prescott
ceased. Troops following their trails destroyed their camps and
provisions, increasing their need to raid and pillage. Finally, as a
result of the pursuit, about nine hundred Tonto Apaches and
Yavapais settled at Camp Goodwin.

In southern Arizona Colonel Guido Ilgles of Camp Grant, on
orders from Colonel Charles S. Lovell, made a peace treaty with the
Arivaipas and some Tontos and Pinals, who agreed to accept a
reservation. But General McDowell, commander of the Depart-

ment of California, who was determined to bring the Apaches to their knees before treating with them, found the treaty "irregular, injudicious and embarrassing" and reprimanded the two officers. The peace terms, he told them, must be strictly enforced—any Indian found off the reservation was to be considered hostile.[12]

Early in 1867 General J. I. Gregg was made commander of the District of Prescott and the Upper Colorado, with orders to prevent the recurrence of the hostilities of the previous year. McDowell instructed him to keep his troops moving through the area of conflict and to conduct an aggressive campaign. Gregg agreed and proclaimed that all Apaches or Colorado River Indians found off the reservation would be treated as hostiles, even if they carried passes from Indian agents. McDowell decided, however, that attacking friendly Indians who had been given permission to hunt because Congress had neglected to supply provisions, was carrying aggressive warfare too far. He rebuked Gregg for starting wars against Indians who clearly desired peace and instructed him to modify his orders. Once Gregg was authorized to feed those Indians who surrendered, he was converted to peaceful methods.

Major Roger Jones, who had served in Arizona in 1857-58, was sent to make a thorough investigation of conditions there. He found the situation much worse than it had been a decade earlier. He made a number of suggestions, among them making Arizona a separate department to eliminate costly delays in communicating with headquarters in San Francisco, concentrating troops at fewer posts, and mounting the infantry for greater mobility.

General McDowell disagreed. All of Jones' recommendations had been tried before, he said, and without success. McDowell argued that there were no alliances between bands and that all of the hostiles lived in remote and inaccessible places; large bodies of troops could not move swiftly or secretly enough to be effective against them. The territory was not, as Jones stated, more insecure than ever, for there were fewer hostilities and fewer points to guard. Nothing could be gained by mounting the infantry, and with the limited forces available, concentrating the troops at larger posts would mean leaving many small settlements unprotected. McDowell did recommend that an additional cavalry regiment and one or two of infantry be sent to Arizona, and that two hundred Indian scouts be enlisted. "Officers," he explained, "are unanimous as to the value and usefulness of these scouts in the field." The general considered it useless to negotiate with the Apaches—there was no alternative to active pursuit "till they are completely destroyed, or forced to surrender as prisoners of war." He concluded with a question that had not yet been answered at any level: "But what is to be done with these Indians when captured or surrendered as prisoners of war?"[13]

Early in 1868 General Thomas C. Devin became commander of the Prescott subdistrict, with orders from General Ord to "capture and root out the Apaches by every means, and to hunt them as they would wild animals."[14] Devin launched a number of campaigns against the Apaches, sending troops to drive them from the land along the eastern rim of the Tonto basin. He planned to invade the basin itself, for it was believed that raiders took stolen stock there before trading it to Anglos in the Fort McDowell and Camp Reno areas. At the same time he arranged a council with Tonto chief Delshay (Big Rump), offering the Tontos peace if they would remain within the area bounded by the Verde and Salt Rivers and Black Mesa. Delshay and his band went to live at Camp Reno, where they gathered hay for the post contractor and served as couriers and guides. Because his forty-six patrols had killed only thirty Apaches and had captured just seven, Devin became convinced that the only way to subdue the Apaches was by opening trails to the heart of their favorite refuges. When the Apaches living at Camp Goodwin refused to surrender known "murderers" and promise to settle down permanently, Devin broke up the temporary reservation there, an act that merely prolonged the war.

At Camp Grant, General T. L. Crittenden made a new agreement with the Apaches which was to supersede the one Colonel Ilgles had made with them in 1866. But his terms were harsh and unacceptable, and after drawing their rations the Apaches fled to the mountains.

In 1868 Captain Charles A. Whittier was sent to make yet another inspection of Arizona. He agreed that feeding the Apaches was essential if they were not to be exterminated, but he maintained that keeping them as "Indian prisoners" was illegal. He recognized that peaceful bands were unprotected and exposed to the vengeance of frontier people, and that the government had done nothing concrete to solve the Apache problem.

The military companies in Arizona were all under strength, but pleas for more troops went unanswered. Many patrols were sent out, but they appeared to be more on the defensive than the offensive. Late in 1868 Indian troubles again became serious when Acting Governor H. H. Heath called on citizens to provide locally for their own defenses. This request was calculated to encourage the indiscriminate killing of Indians, peaceful or otherwise. The policy was soon put into effect against the Yavapais, who had fled the Colorado to escape epidemics of whooping cough and scarlet fever. Ten friendly chiefs were lured into a council then slaughtered, an act that erased all pacific gestures. Federal Judge H. H. Carter refused to take any action against the slayers, but Yavapai raiding parties killed Anglos wherever they were found.

General Halleck, commander of the Division of the Pacific, informed the secretary of war that nothing could be done about the attacks without two additional regiments and a substantial increase in the number of Indian scouts. He also pointed out the need to make Arizona a separate department. The secretary of war took no immediate action.

The policy of inaction continued in 1869, when conditions were worse than ever. The Yavapais again cut off travel in western Arizona, killing one hundred or more Anglos. In the south nearly all the settlers of the San Pedro region were killed or driven out. Yet in his annual report for 1869 General Ord asserted that his orders to "capture and root out the Apaches . . . and to hunt them as . . . wild animals" had been carried out with "unrelenting vigor." After many days in the saddle the troops had burned some camps, destroyed provisions, recovered some horses and mules, and captured two men and some women and children. They had killed upwards of two hundred Indians, and though quite a few soldiers had been lost, Ord was optimistic. "I think," he wrote, "the Apaches have discovered they are getting the worst of it."[15]

Ord may have been satisfied, but Apache hostilities were not interrupted, and the Apaches were not yet convinced that they were "getting the worst of it." Between June 1868 and July 1869 they had killed more than fifty Anglos in Pima County alone, and they killed nearly as many the following year.

Because the United States had only one Apache policy—extermination—there was little for war-weary Apaches to look forward to but continued fighting. Their plight can be seen on a small scale in the expedition of Colonel John Green, First Cavalry, to the White Mountains in 1869, where his men killed a few Coyoteros and destroyed their camps and provisions. His primary purpose was to look for a suitable reservation site, but he learned of a camp of friendly Apaches thirty miles to the north and sent a detachment under Captain Barry to investigate. If the report proved false, Barry was to attack.

Chief Miguel, whose camp it was, led Barry and the troops to it.

White flags flew over every wickiup and the Apaches appeared eager for peace, cutting corn for the cavalry horses and showing pleasure at seeing the troops. They were so friendly, Barry reported, "that the officers were united in saying that if they had fired on them they would have been guilty of coldblooded murder." Miguel and his people begged for a reservation and protection. But Barry had no instructions applicable to peaceful Apaches; he could only tell them to go to Camp McDowell and surrender.[16] Colonel Green reported to his superiors that the Coyoteros, if properly managed and protected by a military post, could form the nucleus for civilizing all Apaches.

In his report General Ord indicated why Apache hostilities were kept alive even when the Indians were tired of fighting and wanted peace at any price. "Almost the only paying business the white inhabitants have in the territory," he wrote, "is supplying the troops . . . and I am informed . . . that if the quartermasters and paymasters of the army were to stop payment in Arizona, a great majority of the white settlers must be compelled to quit. Hostilities are, therefore, kept up with a view to supporting the inhabitants. . . ." Anglos continually stirred up the Indians and then demanded more troops. The settlers also encouraged soldiers to desert, for each man took with him a good horse and a repeating rifle, which he would sell to a civilian for about one-third of their value.[17]

Joseph Fish, an Arizona pioneer, confirmed Ord's assertions, saying that the contractors left the territory as soon as they accumulated enough money. "The people were taught to oppose agencies where the Apaches worked and were fed. They feared that it would reduce the military forces . . . and lead to an inactive state of war."[18] As any citizen knew, there was no money to be made in an "inactive" state of war.

For these reasons Ord favored a reduction of the number of troops in Arizona, though 1869 was not an appropriate year for decreasing the military force in Apachería. In conclusion, he expressed an understanding of the situation as well as some sympathy for the Indians:

> The Apaches have but few friends, and, I believe, no agent. Even the officers, when applied to by them for information, can not tell them what to do. There seems to be no settled policy, but [only] a general idea to kill them wherever found. I am a believer in that, if we go for extermination, but I think, and I am sustained in my opinion by most of the officers accompanying my expedition, that if Miguel and his band were placed

on a reservation properly managed, and had a military post to protect them, they would form a nucleus for the civilization of the Apaches. . . . I even believe that if the Apache is properly managed, he could be used against the Apache, and so end the war in a short time. Miguel said he had soldiers, and would place them at my disposal whenever I wanted them.[19]

Ord also had much to say concerning Anglo attitudes toward Indians in general—they were regarded as "vermin to be killed when met. . . . " As a result, "attacks upon and murder of quiet bands, who in some instances have come in to aid in pursuit of more hostile savages, is nothing unusual in Arizona." The civil authorities did nothing to these men. Accordingly, Ord concluded, "reservations to be at all safe from such attacks in that country must be forbidden grounds to all white men, save the troops sent there to watch the Indians and guard them and officers of the Indian Bureau."[20]

In October 1869 an Apache war party attacked the stagecoach near Dragoon Springs in southern Arizona, killing the passengers and the military escort. The same party then seized a trail herd on its way to California. Troops from Fort Bowie recovered the cattle and discovered an Apache stronghold, but failed to force their way into it. Captain Reuben F. Bernard,[21] commander at Bowie, received reinforcements from camps Crittenden and Goodwin and assaulted the stronghold again. The troops killed a number of Apaches each time, but these campaigns and many others during the year did little to check Apache raids.

Because no constructive policy for treatment of the Arizona Apaches had as yet been devised, army officers found themselves, almost by accident, feeding and protecting Apaches who surrendered at some of the military posts. Since they could not bring themselves to kill Apaches who threw themselves on their mercy, the officers issued them rations or half-rations and hastily wrote to their superiors for instructions.

About the time President Grant took office in 1868 many former abolitionists were taking up the issue of Indian rights, and Grant was willing to try less destructive methods of pacifying and controlling the wild tribes. In 1869 a delegation of Quakers presented a memorial urging him to introduce new and positive policies for protecting and civilizing the Indians through education. Grant, who was ever sympathetic toward Indians, was receptive and turned to the Quakers for guidance. What emerged was his Peace Policy. Under it religious groups nominated the Indian agents; the army was restricted to a passive role.

Earlier in 1869 Congress had authorized the creation of a Board of Indian Commissioners to exercise joint control with the secretary of the interior over disbursement of appropriations for Indians, an action that clearly reflected disillusionment with the conduct and record of the Bureau of Indian Affairs. The board was to be composed of distinguished citizens, "eminent for their intelligence and philanthropy," who would correct the abuses in the Indian service. Among the board's duties were to supervise the purchase and shipment of annuity goods and to audit the accounts of the Indian Office, for it was in these areas that many irregularities had occurred.

Soon after the board's creation its secretary, Quaker idealist Vincent Colyer, traveled to Arizona to confer with Navajo and Apache leaders. These meetings convinced Colyer that the Apaches genuinely desired peace but were being offered only war. Throughout the East people agreed that the Apache wars were both futile and costly; they were anxious to see Grant's Peace Policy given a fair trial. The policy of extermination had been followed too long and at too high a cost—in human lives as well as in government appropriation. It was time for a change. For his part, General Sherman concluded that the Anglo occupation of the Southwest had been premature. "The best advice I can offer," he told Secretary of War W. W. Belknap, "is to notify the settlers to withdraw and then to withdraw the troops and leave the country to the aboriginal inhabitants."[22]

VII
Apaches and the
Peace Policy

THE YEARS 1870 and 1871 marked a significant turning point for the Apaches of Arizona and, to a lesser extent, for those of New Mexico. In the first place President Grant's Peace Policy, created the previous year, was well publicized and at least temporarily interrupted the policy of extermination. Military control of the Indians, which had been restored in 1869, was ended. In April 1870 the War Department made Arizona and southern California a department within the Division of the Pacific, greatly facilitating coordination of military campaigns against the Apaches, even though New Mexico remained under the Division of the Missouri. During this same period, too, the Camp Grant massacre occurred, accelerating the move to extend the Peace Policy to the Apaches. And finally, in June 1871, Major General George Crook was given command of the Department of Arizona. Each of these developments would have an impact on the Apaches.

When the Department of Arizona was set up, General George Stoneman became departmental commander; headquarters were at Fort Whipple. This change was long overdue, but it came at a time when Congress was especially economy-minded and had reduced appropriations for the army, making it necessary to curtail military activity. Within a few months Arizona citizens bitterly denounced Stoneman for inactivity, for allowing military posts to serve as "feeding stations" for Apaches who surrendered, and for failing to exterminate the Apaches. Easterners, on the other hand, enthusiastic about the Peace Policy, damned Stoneman for excessive cruelty, saying that he attacked all Apaches for the misdeeds of a few. In Arizona Stoneman was also criticized for drastically reducing the number of civilian employees and for cancelling fraudulent or unsatisfactory contracts. It should be noted that Stoneman kept as many troops in the field as funds allowed, but they accomplished little.

The fighting against Cochise had gone badly; Lieutenant Howard B. Cushing of the Third Cavalry was determined to kill the Chiricahua chief, believing that this would end the Chiricahua war. Cushing's F Company was stationed at Camp Grant, the post established near where Arivaipa Creek entered the San Pedro. Esthetically Camp Grant had little to offer—the "most God-forsaken post" Captain John Bourke called it, and he had seen most of the others. Cushing was known as a "gallant" officer, which meant that he was fearless to the point of foolhardiness, and he did not hesitate to risk the lives of his men as well as his own. His F Company, according to Bourke, had killed more Apaches than any other; and he called Cushing one of America's bravest. [1]

In May 1870 a wagon train on the road between Tucson and Camp Grant was looted by Apaches, and Cushing was ordered to pursue and punish them. With a German-born scout, Joe Felmer (who was married to an Apache woman), and Durán, a Manso Apache, to lead the way they followed the raiders' trail up Arivaipa Creek and the head of the San Carlos, where it disappeared. Durán knew the ways of the Apaches, however, and soon found it, leading back toward the junction of the San Pedro and Gila Rivers, passing within ten or twelve miles of Camp Grant. It crossed the Gila and entered the Pinal Mountains. Cushing and his men marched all night and surrounded the Apache camp before dawn. When the Apaches began to stir the troops opened fire, killing thirty. This Pinaleño raiding party, returning from Mexico, had come upon the wagon train by chance. After looting it they had covered their trail well, confident that no Anglo could follow it, but they had not reckoned on an Apache trailing them.

As Apache hostilities became ever more serious in southern Arizona Lieutenant Cushing was transferred to Fort Lowell and ordered to take the field against the Apaches wherever he might find them. Here was his opportunity to go after Cochise. With sixteen privates, a sergeant, and a civilian packer, he headed south to Camp Crittenden, formerly Fort Buchanan. From there they went to Pete Kitchen's ranch, and Kitchen guided them through the mountains. After leaving Cushing and his men Kitchen saw an Apache war party following them and set fire to the grass as a warning.

But on they rode, into the Huachuca Mountains where they came upon the tracks of a woman and a pony leading toward Bear Springs. It was soon obvious that the woman had purposely made her tracks visible. Cushing quickly ordered his men out of the canyon, thereby escaping a party of Apache warriors preparing to cut off their retreat.

A large war party of Apaches armed with breech-loading rifles now attacked them, apparently in an attempt to capture them alive. Cushing sent three men back for his pack train and ordered the others forward. Sergeant John Mott, seeing so few men facing overwhelming odds, asked Cushing if he thought it prudent to go farther; the civilian packer strongly urged Cushing to withdraw. Cushing scoffed at their fears, and with the sergeant, the packer, and five privates, marched against an unknown number of well-armed Apaches.

They had not gone far when Apache bullets answered the sergeant's question, for Lieutenant Cushing and the civilian fell dead. Sergeant Mott took charge and managed to get the rest of the soldiers safely back to Camp Crittenden. The Apache who led the attack was thought to be Juh (sometimes spelled nearly phonetically as "Whoa"), chief of the Nednhi Apaches of the Sierra Madre.

In Washington, meanwhile, Commissioner of Indian Affairs Ely S. Parker, a Seneca engineer who had served as Grant's aide during the Civil War and who had drafted the surrender terms at Appomattox, had asked the Quakers for a list of men they considered qualified to serve as Indian agents. Grant's plan for carrying out his Peace Policy was to appoint army officers to all but two superintendencies and seven agencies in the Indian service. These would be filled by men the Quakers recommended.

Congress, urged on by those who hoped to profit by appointments as Indian agents, refused to allow Grant to use military men as agents. To counteract this move Grant turned to other religious denominations and gave them the right to nominate agents for particular reservations. The Dutch Reformed Church, for example, was authorized to choose agents for the Apache reservations in Arizona. The system soon proved less effective than had been expected, however, for few of the agents thus chosen knew anything about Indians. Furthermore, many of them were more interested in winning converts for their church than in educating Indians or in defending their rights.

In the fall of 1870 Lieutenant Royal E. Whitman reported to Camp Grant for duty with Troop H, Third Cavalry, and as post commander. Whitman was a New Englander with a conscience who had been a brevet colonel during the Civil War; he did not shrink from opposing either his military superiors or the citizens of Arizona Territory when he was convinced that he was right. Whitman would

Arivaipa chief Eskiminzin
Western History Collection, University of Oklahoma

play an important role in Apache affairs while he remained at Camp Grant.

In February 1871 five old Apache women came to Camp Grant under a flag of truce to ask for the return of a boy who had been captured some months before. Whitman received them courteously and treated them with consideration, but the boy had become accustomed to life at the post and did not want to leave. The women left after a few days but returned a week later to trade, informing Whitman that the chief of their band wanted to come for a peace talk. Whitman encouraged them, and a few days later Eskiminzin and twenty-five warriors appeared. They were, the chief said, tired of fighting and wanted only to live in peace on their own lands. Eskiminzin's name was well-known in the territory, for he had both accusers and defenders. Some charged him with responsibility for many killings in southern Arizona; others believed he was innocent of the misdeeds attributed to him.

Delighted, but without orders to fit the situation, Whitman wrote to General Stoneman for instructions. In the meantime he saw that the Apaches were fed. While he waited for a reply two more bands asked permission to surrender. Whitman wrote again, saying that there seemed to be a good possibility that a large part of the Apache nation would surrender willingly. What did Stoneman advise?

Unfortunately, in his haste Whitman had neglected to brief his letter on the outside of the envelope as army regulations required. After six weeks the letter was returned to him with a curt notation calling attention to the missing brief. There was no acknowledgment that a significant number of Apaches had surrendered, no instructions for receiving others, no evidence that the letter had even been read. It was as if an angry god held the Apaches in limbo until his ceremonial rites had been properly observed.

By early March there were three hundred Apaches at Camp Grant. Whitman issued rations and counted them every other day. He arranged with the local contractor to put them to work gathering hay for the post, and nearby ranchers agreed to hire them for harvesting barley. All this time the Apaches were obedient and cooperative, obviously happy that the war was over. They even sent runners to other bands, urging them to surrender.

Tucson citizens at first praised Lieutenant Whitman and applauded the Apache surrender. But as raids and killings continued in the Santa Cruz and San Pedro Valleys, they began to suspect that Whitman was harboring a nest of murderers. Voices now rose in protest, mildly at first, but with increasing shrillness. Although they did not mention it some citizens bitterly resented the practice of buying hay from the Apaches, for this jeopardized one of the few dependable sources of their own income in the territory. They watched for an opportunity to destroy the feeding station experiment. Hostile Apaches soon provided them with an excuse.

In March Indians attacked a wagon train from Camp Grant and killed a rancher near Tubac. The Tucson *Citizen* heightened fears by reporting that there was a large number of Indians on the prowl in the Santa Cruz Valley. "Will the Department Commander longer permit the murderers to be fed supplies purchased with the people's money?" the editor asked.[2] Tucson citizens held a series of protest meetings during which the speeches grew increasingly inflammatory. Much of the talk concerned an extended citizens' campaign against the Apaches, but other plans were also quietly discussed.

A Committee of Public Safety was appointed, and it sent William S. Oury as leader of a delegation to General Stoneman. Their purpose was to request that greater attention be paid to "the continual depredations of the Apaches in the southern part of the Territory."[3] The meeting with Stoneman was unsatisfactory. He told them that President Grant and General Sherman had ordered him to modify his tactics to correspond to the administration's Indian policy of "moral suasion and kindness, looking to their Christianization." The reaction of the Tucson delegates was profane.

Stoneman was in an unenviable, impossible situation. In Arizona he was reviled for his supposed inactivity, while in the East he was attacked for brutality. He told the delegates he could do nothing for them under the circumstances. According to Oury's later account, the general advised them to protect themselves. This suggestion, if indeed it was made, certainly did not mean, as Oury interpreted it, that Tucson citizens should go on the offensive against peaceable Apaches. At any rate Oury convinced enough people of this view to raise a war party.

Apaches had continued arriving at Camp Grant until they numbered more than five hundred. They asked permission to move upstream, where there was still water in the Arivaipa. Whitman agreed, and they built wickiups in the valley about five miles above the post.

Early in April Captain Frank Stanwood reported for duty at Camp Grant and, since he outranked Whitman, assumed command. On his way to Grant Stanwood had conferred with General Stoneman, who finally issued verbal orders to continue feeding the Apaches as prisoners of war and to keep cavalry patrols constantly in the field searching out hostile bands. After inspecting the camp Stanwood expressed satisfaction with Whitman's arrangements and did not modify them in any way. The Apaches, he found, were obedient and not at all eager to purchase arms and ammunition. Many, in fact, had sold their bows and arrows. C. B. Briesly, the assistant surgeon at Camp Grant, was full of praise for the Apaches he met there. "I have been among nearly all the various tribes, on the Pacific coast," he wrote, "and . . . I have never seen any Indians who showed the intelligence, honesty, and desire to learn, manifested by these Indians."[4]

On April 10 an Apache raiding party struck San Xavier del Bac and drove off some of the Pápagos' cattle and horses. A group of citizens joined the Pápagos in pursuit; after a fifty-mile chase they recovered most of the animals and killed one Indian. Three days later Indians attacked the settlement of San Pedro, which was about thirty miles upriver from Camp Grant. One settler was killed. Those who pursued the raiders ran into a large war party, and during the ensuing skirmish three more Anglos were killed. The citizens of Tucson were irate, and the *Citizen* egged them on.

"Encouragement for Murder! The Camp Grant Truce a Cruel Farce," headlines proclaimed. There was, the newspaper asserted, "no reasonable doubt but that Camp Grant–fed Indians made the raid on San Xavier last Monday and because they were followed, punished and deprived of their plunder, they went to Grant, rested on Wednesday, and in stronger force on Thursday attacked the San Pedro settlement."[5] Lieutenant Whitman emphatically denied that any Camp Grant Apaches were involved, and others at the post confirmed his statements.

The Tucson citizens held a meeting at which Juan Elías represented the Mexicans and William S. Oury the Anglos. Together the two men approached Francisco, chief of the Pápagos. The Pápagos were always willing to fight Apaches; ninety-four of them volunteered to serve in the proposed expedition.

On April 24 Captain Stanwood turned over command of Camp Grant to Lieutenant Whitman and left on an extended patrol. Four days later a number of men slipped out of Tucson in small groups so as not to attract attention, assembling at Rillito. Forty-eight Mexicans joined Juan Elías, but of the eighty-two Anglos who had promised to come, only Oury and five others showed up. Oury had procured a canvas-covered wagon loaded with arms and ammunition supplied by the territorial adjutant general. Soon ninety-four Pápagos arrived, and the whole party proceeded cautiously toward Camp Grant by a circuitous route not usually traveled.

As an afterthought Oury had arranged for a strong force to be stationed at Cañada del Oro on the main road from Tucson to Grant, to stop anyone riding in that direction until the morning of April 30. This precaution proved crucial to his plans, for Captain Dunn of Camp Lowell noticed the absence of a considerable number of men from Tucson. Surmising what might be happening, he sent two couriers to alert Whitman of the possible trouble for his Indians. The two messengers were stopped by Oury's guard until the morning of April 30.

Early on that morning the war party reached Camp Grant and split into two groups. Elías, who had been elected leader, sent the Pápagos up the right bank of the Arivaipa, while he and the others proceeded up the opposite side of the creek. It was daybreak when they reached the Apache ranchería. Two lookouts, a man and a woman, sat on a hill playing cards. Pápagos stealthily slipped up on them and clubbed them to death before they could give the alarm. Then the Pápagos rushed the wickiups with clubs and knives, so as not to arouse the rest of the camp. Screams warned others, who fled up the canyon, and the slaughter was soon over. Some of the Pápagos paused long enough to rape Apache women before killing them. They herded the surviving Apache children together, set fire to the wickiups, and departed. The exact number of those murdered is not known—estimates range between 85 and 135. Of the known dead, only 8 were men.

A courier finally reached Camp Grant and delivered Captain Dunn's warning to Whitman. He sent two interpreters to warn the Apaches and to bring them to the post. But when the interpreters reached the camp they found no survivors. Whitman sent the post surgeon and a wagon loaded with medicines. The doctor found one woman alive and unwounded, but she was afraid to accompany him.

No Mexican or Anglo dared accept Whitman's offer of one hundred dollars to anyone who would seek out the Apaches in the mountains and urge them to return. The next day Whitman took a party of men to the ruined camp to bury the dead. By nightfall Apaches who had survived the raid began coming in. Eskiminzin returned, carrying his daughter.

"I no longer want to live . . . ," he told Whitman, "but I will live to show those people who have done this to us, that all they have done and all they can do, shall not make me break faith with you so long as you stand by us and defend us."[6] He asked Whitman to try to recover the children the Pápagos had carried off. Whitman was deeply moved by the Apaches' continued trust in him and their understanding of what had happened to them.

In the East reaction to the Camp Grant massacre was outrage. President Grant called it "murder" and denounced this setback to the Peace Policy. He informed Governor Anson P. K. Safford that the men who took part in the "indiscriminate slaughter" must stand trial or he would declare martial law in the territory. Grant also ordered U.S. District Attorney C. W. C. Rowell to leave Arizona City and take charge of the prosecution in Tucson. Wendell Phillips declared that "These ruffians of Arizona and these murderers of Apaches shall be hung just as certainly as if they committed murders in the yard of the State House, or upon the very steps of the capitol."[7] But Phillips was not familiar with frontier attitudes toward the slayers of Indians.

Even before news of the massacre had reached Washington the War Department had issued orders for the transfer of General Stoneman and the Twenty-first Infantry from Arizona, to be replaced in June by Major General George Crook and his Twenty-third Infantry Regiment. In his campaigns against the Paiutes Crook had gained fame while developing pursuit techniques that would serve him well in Arizona. He arrived without fanfare, and after conferring with his friend Governor Safford, he was convinced that the citizens were right and Whitman wrong. In fact he developed a strong dislike for Whitman even before they met.

Crook was already a widely respected officer, a genuine "soldiers' soldier." He seldom wore a uniform, preferring a corduroy or canvas suit when on campaign. He had tremendous self-control; he never drank or smoked or swore—at man or mule. There was nothing flamboyant about him; he made no dramatic gestures. He did not bombard his officers with detailed instructions—he simply told them what the goals were and how he planned to attain them. Probably no officer in the army was ever better served by his subordinates.

Immediately after his arrival Crook ordered every officer in the department to report to him and began preparing for a relentless campaign against the Apaches. He also issued instructions prohibiting the feeding of Indians at military posts except as prisoners of war in "close confinement." Although Crook had used Indian scouts on his Paiute campaigns, most were from other tribes, and it is possible that the idea of using Apaches to fight Apaches was suggested to him

General Crook with scout "Dutchy"
and the White Mountain warrior Alchesay
Arizona Historical Society

by Arizona pioneer Albert Franklin Banta. Crook should, Banta told
him, "fight fire with fire." When Crook asked what he meant, Banta
said, "Fight Indians with Indians; it is the only method to pursue in a
country so mountainous as Arizona; that infantry was practically
useless, and the cavalry was not much better. . . . " According to
Banta, Crook said the idea was good, as an experiment.[8] Using
Indians as scouts was one thing—using them as troops to fight other
Indians was quite another.

In Tucson during the weeks following the massacre no word of remorse was heard. Instead, all statements were calculated to justify what had been done. This meant proving beyond any doubt what had only been suspected before, that some of the Camp Grant Apaches had been involved in the raids and killings. It was said, for example, that the Apache killed after the raid on San Xavier had a front tooth missing, and men swore they had seen him at Camp Grant: this was taken to be positive evidence.

After the dead Indians had been buried, Eskiminzin went to the mountains for a few days, then the Apaches began rebuilding their wickiups. Some time later, toward the end of May, a cavalry detachment from Fort Apache rode through Arivaipa Canyon and came unexpectedly on Eskiminzin and other Apaches. Startled, the troopers opened fire, but the Apaches scattered swiftly, and none was wounded. Eskiminzin was now certain that there was no hope for peace with the Anglos. He said goodbye to Whitman, adding, "The one who breaks the peace is the one to blame." On his way to the mountains he visited a friend of many years, Charles McKinney, who had a farm near Grant. They ate a meal and smoked together. When it was time to leave Eskiminzin drew a pistol and killed McKinney. Later, when questioned about the killing, he admitted that he had done it to convince his people that there could be no friendship with Anglos. "Any coward can kill his enemy," he said, "but it takes a brave man to kill his friend."[9]

In July a wagon train escorted by an infantry company left Camp Lowell for Fort Bowie at Apache Pass. Eskiminzin led a war party to take the wagons, for the Arivaipas needed the arms, ammunition, and provisions. They cut the wagons off in Cienega Wash, at a time when the infantry column was a mile ahead of them. The plan misfired, however, for there were some soldiers concealed in the wagons, who fought off the Apaches until the infantry could return on the double. Eskiminzin lost thirteen warriors. He and his people retreated to the mountains and remained there until a runner from Colyer summoned them to Camp Grant in September.

Early in 1871 Congress had appropriated $70,000 to be used for gathering the Arizona and New Mexico Apaches on reservations and for promoting peace and civilization among them. The Board of Indian Commissioners directed Vincent Colyer to visit the Apaches again, to prevent an outbreak of warfare by establishing reservations for them. Before setting out Colyer met with President Grant, who greatly enlarged his authority to select and create reservations. At the same time Grant instructed Secretary of War Belknap to ensure that the army supported any agreement Colyer might make with Apaches. Colyer's instructions were to locate the nomadic tribes on suitable reservations, bringing them under control of the proper officials of the Indian service and supplying them with food, clothing, and whatever else might be needed. When Crook learned of Colyer's mission, he immediately suspended his Apache campaign.

In Santa Fe Colyer learned that settlers near the Cañada Alamosa agency had organized to destroy it. With the superintendent of Indian affairs for New Mexico, Nathaniel Pope, he hurried to Cañada Alamosa, only to discover that the Indians had fled to the mountains. When Colyer tried to arrange a meeting with them, the chiefs were unwilling to leave their refuge.

The situation of the Southern Apaches was volatile. Late in 1869 Lieutenant Charles E. Drew had been sent to take charge of them. He had found Loco and his band weary of war and eager for peace. They wanted to grow crops on the old reservation fields, but they also needed to hunt over a wide area. Drew forwarded these requests to his superiors with the hope that "judicious arrangements" would be made with the Indians, who were destitute as winter approached. Drew met in council with Loco, Victorio, and other Mimbreños as well as some Mescalero warriors at Cañada Alamosa. He persuaded them to wait there while he tried to convince government officials to supply food and clothing.

The Apaches waited while winter came on. Drew was just about to give up in despair when the Indian Bureau allowed him $2800 for the Southern Apaches. This was early in January, barely in time to prevent an outbreak. Although they had only an agency but no definite reservation, the Southern Apaches remained at Cañada Alamosa. By the fall of 1870 there were 790 at the agency, including Cochise and some Chiricahuas.

In October 1870 special agent W. F. M. Arny visited the Cañada Alamosa agency. He sent runners to inform the Apaches of his impending visit, but few were there to meet him. Arny went in search of them and, by persistence, was finally able to arrange a council with twenty-two chiefs, including Cochise, Victorio, Nana, and Loco.

Cochise informed him that since the hanging of the Apache hostages at Apache Pass in 1861 he had killed whites at every opportunity. He acknowledged that the Chiricahuas had lost many warriors and now had too many women and children to feed and protect. But, he said, since he had found that white men rarely talked "straight" or kept their promises, his people had no choice but to go on fighting.

To Arny's plea that the Chiricahuas settle down on a reservation and become "civilized," Cochise replied that his people wanted to be free to roam. They did not want to be confined to a reservation, and above all they had no wish to be like white men.[10] He agreed, however, to talk to the headmen of his band and inform Arny of their decision. Arny waited but Cochise did not return.

Even though Cochise had not agreed to live on a reservation Arny recommended establishing one for the Chiricahuas in southwestern New Mexico, far from any settlement. He also recommended the Fort Stanton region as a reservation for the Mescaleros. Eventually, on the recommendations of others, the government would take action, but Arny's suggestions seem to have been ignored.

Shortly before Colyer reached Santa Fe the people of Grant County had met at Mimbres and resolved to follow their stolen livestock wherever it had been taken and to recover it by force—"even at the sacrifice of every Indian man, woman, and child of the tribe." They would, they declared, treat as an enemy anyone who opposed them.[11]

The determination of the Grant County residents was expressed in a set of resolutions that Judge B. Hudson sent to Apache agent O. F. Piper. The residents resolved to deal "accordingly" with anyone who opposed them, whether Indians or their "accomplices"—Indian agents or army officers. "What we want to know is, whether our stock can be recovered or not from Indians on your reservation, when fully proved and identified, or if we are to be forever at the mercy of these thieving murderous Apaches, who have a 'house of refuge' at Alamosa; if so, the sooner we know it the better, because the citizens of this county are determined to put a stop to it, and if they carry out their programme *the Camp Grant massacre will be thrown entirely in the shade, and Alamosa will rank next to Sand Creek.*"[12]

Judge Hudson mentioned that missing stock had been tracked to the Cañada Alamosa reservation before, but he did not admit that agent Piper had recovered some animals Apaches had stolen. When he received the threatening letter Piper sent to Fort McRae for military protection, and a detachment of troops arrived the following day. Learning from Piper of the threatened massacre and seeing troops approaching was too much for the Apaches. They fled to the mountains and stayed there. Colyer sent runners to urge them to come in for a conference, but they suspected treachery and refused to meet him.

Much of Cañada Alamosa had been occupied by Mexican families who had encroached on the best lands until they held much of the reservation. Colyer decided that Cañada Alamosa was too exposed to settlers to be suitable for an Apache reservation. He inspected Ojo Caliente (Warm Spring), twenty miles north of the agency, but found there was not enough land there suitable for farming. The Tularosa Valley seemed ideal to Colyer, and he declared it the Southern Apache reservation, instructing Pope to have the Indians moved there.

Two warriors from Cochise's band arrived and told Colyer that they had suffered a defeat in Sonora. Pope sent a Mexican scout to invite Cochise to bring his band to Tularosa, but Crook's men intercepted the messenger in Arizona; Crook reprimanded him and sent him back empty-handed. The conflict between army and civilian authorities over control of the Apaches had by no means ended.

Colyer's visit to Arizona attracted much unfavorable attention even before he reached the territory. He was widely abused in the press and frequently threatened with violence. Citizens were especially aroused whenever Colyer conferred with an army officer who shared his views of Apaches. Contemporary historians also derided Colyer, although Hubert Howe Bancroft was somewhat apologetic. "Notwithstanding my slighting allusions to Colyer's mission," he wrote, "it must be understood that I do not deny the truth of his allegations that the Apache had often been grossly wronged. . . . A white man's reservation, under Apache control, would be somewhat more in accordance with the eternal principles of justice than the present state of affairs. I do not blame the Apaches for defending their homes and liberties in their own way." Bancroft added, however, that there was also no reason for Arizona settlers to submit to plunder and murder. "There was ample room for the application of our limited supply of benevolence and fair treatment," he concluded cynically, "after forcing the Indians to submission."[13]

At Fort McDowell the Tontos told Colyer they wanted peace, for even rabbits were safer than they, and they were starving. A chief told Colyer that soldiers had killed four of his children. "I have been present at a great many talks with Indians on the plains [during] the last seventeen years," Colyer wrote, "but I have to acknowledge that I have never seen more feeling or good sense exhibited by an Indian. . . . "[14] Yavapais also conferred with Colyer, but they vanished suddenly a few nights later. It was suspected that Mexican guides knowing this would stampede them, had told them Pimas were coming. Guides, like contractors, lost work and money when there was general peace.

At Camp Apache, which had been established as Camp Mogollón in 1870, Major John Green was optimistic about the Peace Policy and reported that the Coyoteros had cut 130 tons of hay, for which they had been paid in flour. Green made a special effort to keep them employed, but, as he told Colyer,

> The difficulty is, they furnish the wood so fast that in a few days we shall have enough for the winter; they bring it in at the rate of thirty cords per day. When they furnished hay they brought in as high as fifteen tons in one day; and it must be remembered that the former is broken off by hand or cut with worn-out axes, and the latter cut by knives, and all is carried on their backs. It is wonderful with what alacrity they go to work. It is true, nearly all is done by women and children, but a few men also work—more than at first. . . . [15]

This was all well and good for "Apache-lovers," who wanted to keep them peaceful and contented, but those who had profited from army contracts were outraged. Green came in for his share of abuse. Before leaving Colyer approved the reservation General Stoneman had established, and it was confirmed by an executive order that added a large tract south of the Gila. This new tract became the San Carlos agency.

Immediately after the Camp Grant massacre the White Mountain Apaches were frightened and disappeared into the mountains. Only chief Miguel and his band remained at the agency. Later in the year Crook enlisted some of Miguel's warriors as scouts, causing some resentment.

From Camp Apache Colyer and his military escort rode through Apache country to Camp Grant. Two young Apaches accompanied them; they made smoke signals at intervals along the way to inform Apaches of the party passing peacefully through their lands. Wild Apaches came to watch and to visit with them, but there was no disturbance.

At Camp Grant Colyer learned that a large party of armed civilians from Tucson was within twelve miles of the post and it was rumored that they planned to break up the Apache feeding station. Captain Nelson, post commander, sent a corporal and a few troopers to warn them off. They were prospectors, the civilians said, and had a right to cross the reserve, which they intended to do. Presumably they were on their way to the mountains, but there was no road or trail crossing the reserve that would have led them anywhere. The prospecting story seemed clearly a fabrication.

Colyer informed Captain Nelson that if he allowed the party to come within ten miles of the reserve he would remove all of the Indians to Camp Apache and would require Nelson to furnish an escort strong enough to protect them. Since President Grant had given Colyer unusual authority over the military, Nelson immediately complied. He sent Lieutenant Whitman to warn the citizens that if they came closer troops would fire on them. Because Tucson citizens already regarded Whitman as an outright enemy, they now blamed him for the order and vilified him more than ever.

Runners brought in Eskiminzin and his band, and Colyer tried to persuade them to move to Camp Apache because Grant was too close to white settlements for their safety. They refused to go to Camp Apache, however, saying that the Coyoteros were not their people and the region was not their land. Although he knew it must be only temporary, Colyer then agreed to designate Grant as an official reservation and allowed the Arivaipas and some Pinals to remain there. He warned them never to go beyond the reservation boundaries. Colyer promised to try to recover the children taken during the Camp Grant massacre by the Pápagos, but he was unable to locate them.

From Camp Grant Colyer went to Camp Verde, where he found the Yavapais destitute, seriously weakened by hunger and disease. They refused to move to Camp Date Creek but agreed to accept a reservation at Verde. Colyer set apart a reserve for them, extending it forty-five miles up the river from the post.

Colyer learned from them of many instances of mistreatment. One of the band had been killed by three white men who wanted his Henry rifle. The next day some of the same band were walking along the road in search of employment. Farmers saw them coming and surmised that they were out to avenge the one who had been killed. In their fright they opened fire on the Indians, killing several. Colyer saw a large band of Yavapais begging for food at a way station on the desert near Ehrenberg. They informed him that they had been driven away from both the Colorado and Date Creek agencies because the officers there did not want them around.

When he finally met Tonto chief Delshay, Colyer found him and his people nearly naked and anxious for peace. "I want to make a big treaty," Delshay told him:

> I will live with the soldiers if they will come to Sunflower Valley or Camp Carroll, if the Government will establish a camp there; I will make a peace that will last. . . . If the big captain at Camp McDowell doesn't put a post where I say, I can do nothing more, for God made the white

man and God made the Apache, and the Apache has just as much right to the country as the white man. . . . I am not afraid of the white man or the Mexican, but I am afraid of the Pimas and Maricopas, who steal into my camps at night and kill my women and children with clubs.[16]

Delshay refused, however, to take his people to live on half-rations at Camp McDowell. Soldiers, he said, had no right to expect Indians to live on less food than white men. The Tontos left suddenly one night, leaving meat cooking over camp fires. Colyer discovered later that a party of Pimas and Maricopas, knowing that the Tonto warriors were in McDowell to see him, had gone to their camp in Reno Valley and killed thirty-two Tonto women and children.

On a visit to the Pimas and Maricopas on the Gila, Colyer found them prosperous and independent but threatened with ruin. Whites who settled along the Gila above them had diverted so much of the water that none reached the Pimas' fields. The chief of one of the lower villages asked the agent for permission to take some of his men and drive the whites away. On another occasion the usually peaceful Pimas faced the commander of Camp McDowell, who threatened them with punishment for some suspected misdeed. Five hundred Pima fighting men lined up and told him they were ready. Since he had only one cavalry company, however, the commander decided that the punishment should be postponed or forgotten. Colyer recommended enlarging the Pimas' reserve because they had convincing claims to much more land along the Gila than had been allowed them.

In November 1871 an attack on a stage coach near Wickenburg, Arizona, had resulted in five deaths, including that of Frederick W. Loring, a prominent young Eastern scientist and writer. Everyone blamed the Tontos and Yavapais for the attack, but Colonel Dudley informed Colyer that he was convinced that bandits, not Indians, had been involved. Apaches, he said, would have taken the horses, blankets, and curtains, but none of these had been removed. "I do not believe there was an Apache near the scene of the murder," he concluded. "All honest men have the same opinion, if they dared express it."[17] But the publicity over Loring's death caused a wave of revulsion against the Peace Policy in the East. In Arizona, of course, almost no one had ever approved of it. Although Colonel Dudley was correct in his belief that Apaches ordinarily would have taken the horses and blankets, any who planned to return to one of the agencies probably would not have taken such evidence with them.

At Fort Whipple Colyer conferred with Crook. Relations between the two were correct but cool—Colyer had already complained to Secretary of the Interior Delano that Crook's policies as departmental commander jeopardized the success of the Peace Policy. It did not help matters that Colyer also ignored Crook's advice not to move the western Arizona Yavapais to the reserve at Camp Verde during the coming winter, but to establish a temporary reserve for them at Camp Date Creek.

Crook's well-concealed resentment boiled over into a personal letter to General J. M. Schofield, commander of the Division of the Pacific. He had understood, he said, that he was to be allowed to settle the entire Apache question. Now Colyer considered himself to be representing the president in carrying out his "pet theory." Crook complained that the Peace-Policy proponents were using Colyer as their instrument to make it appear that a lasting peace could indeed be made with the "much abused and injured Apaches." They were, Crook asserted, eager for him to wage war so he could be vilified as the "great North American Butcher." Colyer's peace with the Apaches, he concluded, was "humbug."[18]

When he completed his tour in October Colyer left Crook in charge of the Arizona Indians, an arrangement which satisfied the army. By the end of 1871, Apaches were drawing rations at Cañada Alamosa (nine hundred) and at camps Apache (thirteen hundred), Grant (nine hundred), Verde (five hundred), and McDowell (one hundred). More than half of the Apaches were now at peace, and reports indicated that more were coming in. It appeared to Colyer that he had solved the Apache problem, but it was not to be that simple. There were still the hostile bands to be dealt with, and the government was slow to provide needed funds so that those on the reservations could become self-supporting.

After a visit with General Schofield in San Francisco Colyer returned to Washington, where Secretary of War Belknap angrily accused him of interfering with the army. Colyer used his influence, nevertheless, to persuade Grant to prevent all-out war on the Apaches. The president's policy emerging from the pressures applied by Colyer and Belknap, was to designate as official reservations those sites selected by Colyer and to use the army to keep the roving bands on them. There Apaches would be fed and protected. The superintendent of Indian affairs for Arizona would have his headquarters at Fort Whipple, Crook's headquarters, and the War Department would select "suitable and discreet" officers to serve as Indian agents until civilian officials took over control.

General Sherman was instructed to put Grant's program into

effect. He ordered the commanders of the divisions of the Missouri and the Pacific to comply, adding that since the Indian Bureau was rarely able to feed the Indians the army's commissary department would provide rations so that the surrendered Indians would not starve. Sherman also soothed Crook, promising him that after a reasonable time the War Department would support whatever "measures of severity" he might adopt.[19]

In the meantime a campaign of calumny had been directed at Lieutenant Whitman from all over the territory. The "royal Whitman" was pictured as a drunkard, on duty as well as off, and one who protected Apaches only because of his peculiar interest in "dusky maidens."[20] After Crook had replaced Stoneman as departmental commander he was urged to relieve Whitman of duty at Camp Grant. Crook regarded the Peace Policy as a waste of time, and he was quite willing to remove Whitman when the opportunity arose. He bluntly told Whitman to modify his stand, but Whitman stubbornly refused.

When the citizens' party was turned back from crossing the Camp Grant reservation Crook supported the citizens against the "appeasers." He sharply reprimanded Captain Nelson, who under orders from Colyer, actually had no choice in the matter, and soon afterward transferred him out of Arizona. Crook would have sent Whitman packing as well but for the fact that Colyer had named Whitman acting agent at Camp Grant, partly in an effort to protect him from Crook.

U.S. District Attorney Rowell arrived in Tucson in mid-September 1871. The grand jury met in October, but it ignored his requests to take action against the men who had made the raid on Camp Grant Apaches. Rowell spread the rumor that unless the men responsible were indicted within three days the president would declare martial law. If the men were tried by court-martial they would surely be found guilty, for most army officers did not approve of citizens taking things into their own hands, especially in committing atrocities against peaceful Indians.

Reluctantly the grand jury returned the indictments, but most of its report concerned other matters (the relevance of which was not explained)—Apache hostilities and the sins of army officers, such as drunkenness, defrauding the government, and using their military positions to deflower Indian maidens. The citizen jurors had been aroused over Apache depredations before, but their concern for the chastity of Apache women reflected a new moral sensibility not characteristic earlier.

The grand jury indicted 108 men for murder, then added another name, that of Eskiminzin, for the death of Charles McKinney. Within a few hours after the indictments were known Rowell and his clerk were burned in effigy. Because of repeated threats against the two men the commander of Camp Lowell scattered soldiers through the crowd at the court house, with orders to protect them from mob violence.

During the trial the defendants remained calm, for the defense attorney skillfully justified the massacre instead of denying that it had occurred. He almost made it appear that Lieutenant Whitman was on trial. On one occasion he got Whitman to admit that the Apaches had agreed to serve as scouts against hostiles only if the army would help them on an expedition against Sonora. The most surprising aspect of the trial was not the jury's exonerating verdict but the fact that its deliberations lasted all of nineteen minutes.

Because of the vitriolic charges against Whitman that continually appeared in the press and because of his own feelings, Crook decided that a court-martial was necessary to clear Whitman's name or to remove him if he was found unfit for duty. A court was convened early in December, composed mainly of officers of the Third Cavalry. Most of the charges against Whitman were of drunkenness. The court, through a technicality, adjourned without examining the charges. Crook disapproved of the court's actions, but the Third Cavalry was ready for transfer to the Department of the Platte, so nothing more could be done at the moment. Whitman faced two more courts-martial the following year, and the last one found him guilty of "using disgraceful language toward his commanding officer and conduct unbecoming to an officer and a gentleman."[21]

A fresh outbreak of Apache raiding and killing caused the newly established Peace Policy to be quietly shelved late in 1871. The War Department authorized Crook to begin an energetic campaign against the Apaches, and in order to ensure his control of those on reservations, he was allowed to appoint acting Indian agents of his own choice. This gave him the welcome opportunity to remove Whitman from Camp Grant.

General Schofield's orders to Crook were detailed and specific. All roving bands were to go to the reservations at once—any Apaches found off the reservations would be punished as hostiles. Army officers were to serve as Indian agents on the reserves. Descriptive lists were to be made of all males old enough for war, and these men were to carry identification at all times and were to be counted at least once a day. No band that surrendered, unless it gave aid to hostiles, was to be punished for its previous actions. Families of absent warriors were to be held in custody until the men surrendered or were captured. No whites except officials were to be allowed on reservations without permission. Each Indian would receive specific amounts of food, the issue of which was to be supervised by army officers. Vigorous operations against hostiles would continue, and incorrigibles were to be hunted down with the aid of friendly scouts. Schofield conferred on Crook full authority to adopt such measures as might be needed "to give effect to the policy of the government."[22] Crook sent a message to the various Apache bands that they must be on reservations by February 1872 or suffer severe punishment. Hundreds of Apaches hastily obeyed.

Perhaps because of the unsatisfactory outcome of the Tucson trial, however, President Grant insisted on giving his Peace Policy another chance in Arizona. He sent General O. O. Howard, who had been successful in many negotiations with Indians, to investigate the Apache situation and, especially, to contact Cochise and the Chiricahuas who had waged unrelenting war for ten years. Once more, just as he was ready to launch a full-scale offensive, Crook was obliged to postpone it.

Howard, the "praying general," was a well-known friend of the Indians and, as a major general, outranked every officer on duty in the Southwest. With this advantage he could command military cooperation at any post. Complaints were coming in from all parts of Apachería, and the Mimbreños who had recently moved to the Tularosa reservation Colyer had created were restless and seemed likely to bolt at any time. Howard was charged with solving all of these problems, but his major goal was to negotiate with the elusive Cochise.

At Camp Grant Howard made arrangements for a great council with the Arivaipas at a later date, then he left for Prescott and a meeting with Crook. Because he felt that Lieutenant Whitman's pacific influence was essential, Howard had him transferred temporarily back to Camp Grant. But after his conference with Crook, Howard found himself inclining more to Crook's views of Apache problems than to those of Colyer and Whitman. The Reverend E. P. Smith, who accompanied General Howard, declared that Whitman's downfall was the work of groups who feared that his success with the Apaches would gain support for the peace policy. Crook, on the other hand, told Howard that Whitman's administration of the reservation was "criminally rotten" and barely concealed his resentment of Howard's action reinstating Whitman.

At the Date Creek feeding station Howard visited Lieutenant Frederick E. Ebstein, Twenty-first Infantry, who had been in charge of the camp since 1869, when the Hualapais and Yavapais had been hostile and no road was safe to travel. In 1870 a small group of Indians had approached the Date Creek station under a flag of truce. Ebstein fed them and allowed them to camp there; before long their number had risen to 650. Ebstein, issuing a pound of beef and another of flour to each Indian daily, encouraged them to work at gathering wood and hay by paying them a pound of flour for each load. Pleased with Ebstein's effective handling of the Indians, Howard gave him money to buy vegetable seeds so that Ebstein could instruct them in planting.

In May 1872 Howard returned to Camp Grant for his conference with the Arivaipas, Tontos, Pimas, and Pápagos. He persuaded Tucson's Mexican residents who had captive Apache children to attend the meeting, bringing the children with them. A large number of Anglos were also present, among them civilian and military officials.

Eskiminzin and his band arrived late and took their places for the council. As he approached them the general suddenly fell to his knees and began praying loudly. Before Howard had gotten far in his prayers every Apache had vanished. Eskiminzin was outraged at Howard for "making medicine" against them.[23] When the council reconvened Eskiminzin and others voiced their grievances and pleaded for a return of the Apache children, even though their parents were absent or dead. Howard favored returning the children to the Arivaipas, but because of strong objections he arranged for them to be cared for at the post until President Grant decided the issue. The Mexican families protested, because they had become fond of the children and regarded them as their own. Grant ultimately ruled that the children should be returned to their Apache relatives.

The Apaches made other requests: to be moved to a region where the land was better, the water supply adequate, and the climate more healthful. They wanted peace treaties with neighboring tribes to prevent another massacre, and they asked that Whitman be restored as their agent. Howard arranged the treaties, abolished the Camp Grant reserve, and created another at San Carlos, but he denied the request for Whitman's return as permanent agent because partisan feelings about the lieutenant were too strong.[24]

After the council Howard tried to convince Eskiminzin of his friendship. He asked, "could I not come into your lodges at any time—even when you are on the war-path?" Expressionless, Es-kiminzin replied, "Not unless you want to get killed." When Howard asked if any white man could visit them safely at any time, the answer was that only one could—Lieutenant Whitman.[25]

From Camp Grant Howard went to Camp Apache to hear the complaints of the Coyoteros. Learning that their rations were to be cut off, he had the order suspended and thereby prevented an outbreak. Seeing no immediate opportunity to confer with Cochise, he then took a party of ten prominent Apaches to Washington, where they were housed in the dormitories of Howard University. After an audience with President Grant the Apaches visited the College of Deaf Mutes; their knowledge of sign language enabled them to communicate with the students whom they referred to thereafter as "the boys who talked with their hands and arms."[26]

Because it was clear that the peace policy could not succeed among the Apaches unless Cochise was included, Howard was sent on another mission. Returning to Santa Fe late in 1872, he rode to the Tularosa agency in western New Mexico, accompanied by a Major Pope. Victorio's Warm Springs band of Mimbreños was there, but they were unhappy over having to leave Cañada Alamosa. Most of them talked of returning to their old lands at Warm Springs.

While Howard was at Tularosa a cavalry troop came in from a patrol. The troop guide was a "singular character" known to Howard by name—Tom Jeffords, the friend of Cochise and the Chiricahuas. Here was the opportunity Howard had sought. When introduced to Jeffords he immediately came to the point. "Can you take me to the camp of the Indian Cochise?" he asked. Jeffords looked "steadily and inquiringly" into Howard's eyes and asked, "Will you go there with me, General, without soldiers?" "Yes, if necessary," Howard replied. "Then I will take you to him" agreed Jeffords.[27]

Jeffords asked Chie, a son of Mangas Coloradas and a friend of Cochise, to accompany them, but he also felt he needed to find Ponce, whose father was also a close friend of the Chiricahua chief. Ponce had been sent to the Mescalero reservation at Fort Stanton sometime earlier, but he had left and now was raiding in the Cañada Alamosa region. After a short search, with Chie's help Howard and Jeffords found Ponce's camp.

When Jeffords suggested that he accompany them, Ponce asked, "Who will take care of these Indians?" General Howard answered that question by taking Ponce's entire band to the nearest Mexican village that had a general store. He bought them a thirty-day supply of food on the condition that they would remain where they were and neither raid nor steal. And since Ponce had no horse, Howard bought him one.

But when the small party started the long trip to Cochise's country Howard noticed that Ponce was on foot. Knowing that troops were looking for his band, Ponce had given the horse to his wife. It was too late to buy him another one, so General Howard shared his horse with him, a courtesy that pleased Ponce greatly. They stopped briefly at Fort Bayard, then at Silver City, where the reception was hostile. There were no Peace-Policy advocates in the mining town, and open threats were made against the Apaches.

When they reached the trail to Cochise's land, Chie made a smoke signal and then barked like a coyote. A reply came from nearby, for they had reached one of Cochise's outposts, one hundred miles from his stronghold. There were sixty Apaches—men, women, and children—camped at the outpost. Cochise's scout told Howard that before continuing he must reduce the size of his party. Howard sent three men to wait for him at Camp Bowie; his party was now reduced to Jeffords, Captain Sladen, and the two Apaches. Sladen was much concerned that Howard was exposing himself—and the rest—to great danger, but Howard had confidence in Jeffords and the Apaches.

They crossed the Chiricahua Mountains and the San Simón Valley to the foothills of the Dragoons. Several times during the day Chie and Ponce built five fires in a circle, to indicate that five men came in peace.

They came to a party of Apaches in a natural fort, a wide canyon with perpendicular walls, about forty acres of good grass, and several springs. There Tygee, a subchief, paid Howard's party a short visit. He was polite but appeared gloomy, and Howard noted that Chie and Ponce appeared troubled. "Will it be peace?" Howard asked. Ponce shook his head and replied in Spanish "Who knows?" When Howard lay down on his blanket to rest, some of the Apache children came and curled up by him, resting their heads on his blanket. The general was reassured. Turning to Sladen, he said, "This does not mean war."[28] Still no one knew whether or not Cochise would come.

The next morning a horseman approached, a short, thick-set man whose face was painted with black and vermillion stripes. Despite his fierce appearance, he dismounted and embraced Jeffords. This was Juan, a leading Chiricahua warrior.

Soon Cochise and his party arrived; among them was his son Nachez. "Buenos dias, señor," said Cochise. He was about six feet in height, with a pleasant countenance. As they sat in a semicircle, he asked Howard the purpose of his visit. President Grant had sent him, Howard answered, to make peace between Cochise and his people and the white men. "Nobody wants peace more than I do," was Cochise's reply. Howard suggested a reservation for all of the Apaches along the Río Grande. Cochise had been there and knew the country. "Rather than not have peace," Cochise said, "I will go there and take such of my people as I can, but that move will break up my tribe. Why not give me Apache Pass? Give me that and I will protect all the roads. I will see that nobody's property is taken by Indians."[29]

Howard agreed that what Cochise requested might be possible, but he thought the Río Grande region would be better, for there were five rivers in the area and good grazing for cattle. Cochise then asked, "How long, General, will you stay? Will you wait for my captains to come in and have a talk?"

Although it would take ten days to assemble the others, Howard was quite willing to wait. "We were once a large people covering these mountains," Cochise told him; "we lived well; we were at peace. One day my best friend was seized by an officer of the white men and treacherously killed. . . . The worst place of all is Apache Pass. There, five Indians, one my brother, were murdered. Their bodies were hung up and kept there till they were skeletons," he continued, referring to the hanging of captives and hostages at Apache Pass in 1861. "Now Americans and Mexicans kill an Apache on sight," Cochise continued. "I have retaliated with all my might. My people have killed Americans and Mexicans and taken their property. Their losses have been greater than mine. I have killed ten white men for every Indian slain, but I know that the whites are many and the Indians are few. Apaches are growing less every day. . . . Why shut me up on a reservation? We will make peace; we will keep it faithfully. But let us go around free as Americans do. Let us go wherever we please."[30]

While waiting for Cochise to assemble his headmen, Howard and Chie rode to Camp Bowie to inform the post commander that peace had been made with the Chiricahuas and to instruct him to issue the band rations; then the two returned. General Howard abandoned the plan to move them to Cañada Alamosa or Tularosa, instead assigning them their own land as a reservation, as Cochise had requested. The new Chiricahua reservation included part of the Chiricahua Mountains and valley on the west, and it lay along the Mexican border, a source of future difficulty. Also in keeping with Cochise's wishes, Howard named Jeffords as their agent. All of the

Chiricahuas kept the treaty as long as the government kept its promises. It was only when an attempt was made in 1876 to move them to San Carlos that trouble would develop.

With the Chiricahuas at peace, all the Apache bands were nominally under the Peace Policy by 1872, although certain questions concerning the control of those on the reservations had not been settled except in the case of Cochise's people. At most of the agencies, rations were issued every ten days, giving Apache raiding parties ample time to make swift strikes and return. Raiding continued in both northern and southern Arizona, while criticism of the Peace Policy mounted.

The Tontos and Yavapais at Camp Verde were restless and suspicious. When Crook established military control of the reservation a large number of them had fled, and others soon followed. Many returned, but when an important Tonto prisoner was killed, all fled. Crook ordered their recapture and daily muster, which ended any likelihood of a lasting peace without more warfare.

The Yavapais at Date Creek had been especially submissive to army control, and a civilian agent there was able to increase discipline. An epidemic of fever in August 1872 induced him to allow the sick to go to the highlands; once in their familiar mountains, however, they refused to return. Crook sent troops after them; when seventy of their men had been killed the Yavapais flocked back to Date Creek in greater numbers than before. To convince them that only peaceful Indians could find safety on the reservations, Crook arrested those suspected of having taken part in the 1872 killing of Frederick W. Loring near Wickenburg.

The Coyoteros at Camp Apache had readily accepted reservation life and control, and in their first planting season they raised and sold eighty thousand pounds of corn. Late in 1872, in preparation for the campaign he expected to commence shortly, Crook ordered all of them to move to within one mile of the Camp Apache agency and to submit to a daily head count. His purpose was to prevent them from being exposed to visits from the hostiles, but Howard had promised them safety anywhere on the reservation. Because their fields and livestock were left unprotected the Coyoteros were upset, especially when Major W. H. Brown arrived to enforce Crook's orders and to enlist Coyotero scouts. They remained cooperative, nevertheless, and soon the restrictions were relaxed.

In New Mexico the Mescalero and Southern Apache agencies had been combined in 1870. Lieutenant A. G. Hennisee at Fort Stanton was trying to control the Mescaleros, but only fifty-one had come in, with no chief among them, to see what treatment they might expect. Although he had little to offer them in the way of food, clothing, or shelter, Hennisee remained optimistic.

That same year, when the War Department transferred control of the Indians back to the Interior Department, the American Unitarian Association nominated A. J. Curtis as Mescalero agent. At Fort Stanton Curtis found only chief José de la Paz and twenty-seven of his band, who had been run down by troops. Curtis sent runners to others of the band, although some had gone to Comanche country. Cadete came in and was promised protection, land for cultivation, and a school if he and his people would remain at peace on the reservation. Soon there were 325 Mescaleros at Fort Stanton, and a party of them went to the Comanche country in search of others. A man was also sent under contract to Mexico, to persuade the Mescaleros there to return.

In 1871, partly because the House resented the Senate's authority to conclude treaties, all treaty-making with Indians was terminated. Thereafter no tribe would be regarded as an independent nation— all Indians were now "wards" of the United States government, and both houses of Congress would decide their fate.

As other Apaches surrendered in New Mexico many were sent to the Mescalero reservation. By 1872 there were 350 Lipan Apaches from Texas and 310 Gileños at Mescalero, although the Gileños' own reservation was at Tularosa. They had simply refused to go there.

The Mescaleros protested the settling of others on their lands, for there was open hostility between them and some of the other Apache bands. Cadete, who had persuaded many of the Mescaleros to surrender, was killed in La Luz Canyon while returning from Mesilla, where he had gone to testify against New Mexicans for selling whiskey to the Indians. His killer was never apprehended, but many believed that the whiskey traders had avenged themselves.

Although the Mescaleros again made an effort to remain peaceful and abide by the treaty, their troubles were not over. Part of the difficulty was that the boundaries of their reservation were vague, and neither Apaches nor others were sure exactly where its limits were. As a result Mescaleros were accused of stealing cattle when they had only killed strays found on the reservation. Because of complaints from ranchers and others, Major W. R. Rice arrested Santa Ana, brother of chief Roman. Holding Santa Ana as hostage, Rice demanded the return of some stolen horses he suspected were on the reservation. The Mescaleros panicked, and all but two hundred of them fled to the mountains. Most, however, returned a few months later.

Because of Mescalero dissatisfaction with the lack of adequate hunting grounds on the reservation, in February 1874 an executive order increased both the farming lands east of the mountains and hunting grounds on the west slope of the Sacramentos. Mescaleros were still accused of stealing livestock despite the fact that there were a multitude of non-Indian horse thieves and cattle rustlers operating in New Mexico.

On several occasions white groups attacked Mescalero camps on the reservation, killing men, women, and children and running off the pony herds. These attacks occurred within a short distance of the fort, but the troops claimed that they thought the Indians were fighting among themselves and made no effort to learn what was happening. Knowing that they were totally unprotected and lacking adequate arms to defend themselves, many Mescaleros again fled to their favorite havens in the mountains. The military displayed even greater obtuseness than before—the army now regarded the Mescaleros' flight as a hostile act. Troops followed the trail of the frightened Indians, who fled again, leaving all of their possessions, to wander cold and hungry through the mountains.

Whites raided the Mescaleros from time to time over the next few years, and again they fled to the mountains, without food and with little clothing. When their agent finally found them they were starving and nearly naked. He persuaded them to return. By this time, however, their whole former way of life was gone: ranchers had begun fencing their lands with barbed wire, and the southern buffalo herds had been destroyed. Although their agent reported that they were "tractable" and "susceptible of kindness," they could not avoid trouble with whites who continued to steak their horses.[31]

Although the Peace Policy had been given a full opportunity in Arizona and New Mexico, Apache troubles continued. There were still Apache raids into Sonora in the time-honored fashion, and these, despite Jeffords' denials, were attributed to the Chiricahuas. Because of its proximity to Mexico, the Chiricahua reservation became the favorite haven of unregenerate hostiles from other bands, and it was also a convenient stopping place for raiders on their way to and from Mexico. Jeffords, who realized that the Apache peace was a precarious thing, issued rations to Apache visitors without asking embarrassing questions. He trusted Cochise implicitly and never had occasion to regret it.

By now it was Crook's turn to try a different policy on the Apaches, and he was certain of each move he would make. First, the hostile bands had to be taught that there was no safe refuge from the troops and that complete submission was their only hope of survival. In his brief experience with Apaches Crook had learned a valuable lesson, one that would enable him to succeed where his predecessors had failed—only an Apache could catch an Apache. He would rely on Apaches not only as scouts but as fighting men.[32]

VIII
Crook and the Conquest of the Tontos

As an Indian fighter Crook had no superior. He was patient, determined, and had extraordinary physical stamina, as his men learned to their sorrow. He understood Indians—he was, in the view of many, "more Indian than the Indians."[1] When Indians were hostile he was a relentless foe, but he was considerate and humane to those who gave up the warpath. In Arizona he often recruited scouts from among the hostile captives, and they served him well. In dealing with Indians Crook never lied or made promises he could not keep. With the Apaches, he said, "gentleness, patience, intelligence, truth and honesty" were essential.[2] His policy was successful; the Apaches trusted him as they trusted no other officer except Lieutenant Whitman.

Starting in June 1871 Crook planned his Apache campaign with care and precision, so that the early patrols would propel the hostiles toward the Tonto Basin. There, where the Apaches were sure they were safe, the final blows would be struck and the campaign concluded. When they found that there was no safe haven anywhere in Arizona, the Apaches would lose the will to fight.

In preparation for the strenuous campaigning to follow Crook made a practice march with five companies of cavalry, a pack train, and Indian scouts. The scouts represented nearly every tribe of the region: Ópatas, Yaquis, Navajos, Manso Apaches, and Pueblos as well as some Mexicans, Anglos, and halfbreeds. Crook's aide during most of his Arizona campaigns was Lieutenant John G. Bourke, who later wrote *On the Border with Crook.*

The force left Tucson in July 1871, little more than a month after Crook had reported for duty. It crossed 110 miles of the desert to Fort Bowie in Chiricahua country, a gesture of warning to Cochise. From there the men marched north through the mountains to Camp

Apache and across an unmapped region along the Mogollón range to Camp Verde and Prescott, a distance of 675 miles.

On the march Crook was always the first up and saddled each morning, ready to ride. He was curious about every plant, animal, and natural phenomenon seen along the way, continually asking his Indian guides a multitude of questions. He studied the country carefully and made mental notes of the hazards as well as the opportunities for advantage.

Although Crook relied initially on scouts and guides from other tribes and on Mexicans, he soon came to reply primarily on Apaches. At Camp Apache he persuaded some of the Coyoteros to enlist as scouts, for the same pay and allowances as soldiers received. The Coyoteros were disturbed at the time because of Crook's order for all of them to move to within a mile of the agency, a precaution intended to protect them from hostiles once the campaign started. They were upset at having to leave their fields and livestock unguarded, but they proved trustworthy, and the order was soon relaxed.

From Fort Apache Crook sent out three companies of the Third Cavalry and the newly recruited Apache scouts under Captain Guy V. Henry to comb the country toward Camp McDowell. Henry reported that the combination of Apache scouts and cavalry exceeded his "most sanguine expectations," for the Apaches were "invaluable." Because of them his column had killed seven warriors and captured some women, under extremely unfavorable conditions.

Before other moves could be made, however, word reached Crook that Vincent Colyer was coming to introduce President Grant's Peace Policy and that the army was to cooperate with him in every way. Crook had already issued his general order stating that all bands must go to reservations or be treated as hostiles and that active operations would be maintained against the hostiles until they submitted to government authority. But because of Colyer's visit Crook was forced to suspend operations and wait impatiently for Colyer to fail in the optimistic peace venture.

While ostensibly remaining idle, Crook continued active preparations for his major offensive, which he was certain could not be long postponed. He was convinced that the Apaches would never settle down permanently until they had been driven from their most secure refuges and decisively defeated. Colyer's efforts to pacify Apaches by setting apart reservations for them would simply delay the day of reckoning, Crook figured. The confirmed hostiles would never submit voluntarily, and their continued raids would keep others disturbed. It was in part because of this hatred for those living peacefully on reservations that Crook was able to recruit Apache scouts to fight their own people.

Although he was determined to thrash the Apaches, Crook admitted that there were two sides to the matter. "I think that the Apache is painted in darker colors than he deserves," he wrote, "and that his villainies arise more from a misconception of facts than from his being worse than other Indians." On the other hand, he added, "It must be remembered that . . . a large portion of the white population were [sic] as barbarous in their modes of warfare as the Apaches themselves; that Arizona was still a refuge for the criminal and lawless men of other states and territories; that war and pillage had been bred into the Apaches, until they were the most savage and intractable Indians in the country; [and] that large bands of their nation still infested Northern Mexico. . . . "[3]

It was impossible, of course, to keep reservation Indians under constant surveillance, and the hostiles were occasionally able to recruit warriors for their raids. The Yavapais, who had settled at Camp Date Creek, sixty-two miles southwest of Prescott, continued to send out raiding parties. One of these parties was believed responsible for the 1871 attack on a stagecoach near Wickenburg, the so-called Loring massacre: one of the survivors was certain that the raiders had been Yavapais. Crook was determined that the Indians must be taught that reservations were not asylums for those who committed hostile acts. He went to Beale Springs, where he persuaded Hualapai scouts to accompany him to Date Creek for a showdown with the Yavapais. The Hualapais warned him that if he went there the Yavapais would kill him, for they suspected he knew who the guilty ones were. Instead, the Hualapais would ask for a council and conceal rifles under their blankets.

Before he could carry out his design, Crook was ordered to suspend operations once more while General Howard attempted another peace mission. It was September 1872 before he could resume his plan to punish the Date Creek renegades. In the meantime he had sent white and Indian scouts to gather evidence, and they convinced him beyond a doubt that the Yavapais from Date Creek were responsible for the Loring massacre. Mohaves from the Colorado agency even knew the identity of the raiders and were willing to point them out.

Captain Philip Dwyer, Fifth Cavalry, commander at Date Creek, died suddenly on August 29, and Bourke, Crook's aide, had to hurry to the post to take temporary command. When Crook arrived a short time later the renegade followers of chief Ochocama prepared to carry out their plan to kill Crook while two-thirds of the agency Indians were absent. Crook, unarmed but accompanied by a few soldiers and a dozen packers all of whom were heavily armed, went to the council with Ochocama and his men. The Yavapais appeared suspicious, and some had ominously painted their faces for war. Mohaves under chief Iretaba had arrived from the Colorado reservation to identify the guilty Indians. By agreement they would go among the others, handing a twist of tobacco to each of the killers. As each was thus identified soldiers or packers would quietly move into position to seize him when Crook gave the signal. The first tobacco was offered to Ochocama himself; suspicious, the renegade chief at first refused the gift but was finally induced to accept it.

When the last of the tobacco had been handed out Crook gave the signal to seize the renegades. They countered with their own signal, and a warrior near Ochocama raised his rifle and fired at Crook. He was not hit; Lieutenant Ross and Dan O'Leary either pushed the general aside or knocked the rifle from the warrior's hands. While three packers seized Ochocama and hustled him off to the guardhouse, firing broke out despite Crook's efforts to stop it. Though wounded, the chief escaped. The skirmish was quickly over, for the renegades had vanished among the rocks.

The hostiles fled to the mountains, and although their own people ordered them to surrender or be killed, most refused. Those few who did return expressed bitter hatred for Iretaba and his Mohaves; they reported that Ochocama and others were planning to go to the Colorado reservation and kill Iretaba and his warriors. To prevent further bloodshed, Crook convinced the hostiles that he had learned the identity of the raiders from others, not from the Mohaves. Soon Hualapai scouts informed him of the location of the renegades' camp.

Crook waited a few weeks and then sent out Captain Julius Wilmot Mason, a cavalry detachment, and eighty-six Hualapai scouts under Al Sieber and Lieutenant Walter Schuyler. They hid their pack train and horses in a canyon and made a long arduous nighttime march. At a spot called Muchos Cañones, where five canyons merged to form the Santa María, they found the renegades in four camps. The force divided, and each camp was surrounded. The men crouched in the cold till daybreak; when the Yavapais began to stir the scouts and soldiers opened fire. Forty warriors were killed, a number of women and children were captured, and all of the camp equipment and provisions were destroyed. On his return Captain Mason reported to Crook that the "Officers and men behaved splendidly and I cannot speak too highly of our Walapais [sic] scouts. Their scouting was excellent, and when the fight came off they were not a bit behind the soldiers. . . . "[4]

The hostile Yavapais were now thoroughly pacified, except for one small band that headed for Mexico. Crook sent a Fifth Cavalry force under Captain Burns after it; Burns overtook the fleeing Indians and brought them back. Thereafter the Yavapais gave no more trouble; Indian resistance in western Arizona was over. Early the next year at Crook's suggestion, the Hualapai scouts sent Dan O'Leary and others to California to purchase horses for them for breeding stock.

As Crook had anticipated it was soon clear that Colyer's belief that all Apaches would voluntarily come to the reservations had been overly optimistic, for the raids and killings continued unabated. Hostilities were especially pronounced in southern Arizona, but Tontos were also troublesome in the north. By this time many of the hostiles had acquired guns that were as effective as those of the troops, and they were desperate.

The War Department authorized Crook to proceed with his campaign, but once again he was forced to suspend operations while General Howard made his second visit to Arizona and New Mexico. On this occasion Howard had made his famous treaty with Cochise, giving the Chiricahuas a reservation in their own lands and an agent of their own choice. This treaty placed the Chiricahuas outside Crook's jurisdiction.

The often-postponed campaign finally began in mid-November 1872. Crook knew that Apaches were more vulnerable in winter than summer because they had to subsist on provisions they had stored. He ordered three separate commands out of Camp Hualapai, each composed of one cavalry company and thirty to forty Indian scouts. They combed the country around the San Francisco peaks and the Upper Verde region. In two weeks they killed a number of warriors, captured some women and children, and destroyed winter camps and provisions. Immediately after sending out these columns Crook made a rapid march to Camp Apache by way of Camp Verde and the Little Colorado. The distance was 250 miles; the troops were aroused every morning at 2:00 A.M. and were in the saddle by 4:00. The summit of the Colorado plateau meant an elevation of ten thousand feet and intense cold.

At Camp Apache Crook again enlisted Coyotero scouts, for he had

had to dismiss those recruited earlier because of the Peace-Policy interlude. One of those enlisted was Nocadelklinny (Bobby Doklinny to the troopers), who would later be an important medicine man and figure prominently in a renewal of hostilities.

From Camp Apache to Camp Grant was more than one hundred miles, but because the country was cut up by canyons it seemed much farther than that to Crook's men. They rode from 6:00 P.M. one day to 8:00 the next night. While exhausted troopers lay groaning on their blankets, Crook went off to shoot birds for their breakfast. "It was," wrote Captain Bourke, "this insensibility to fatigue, coupled with a contempt for danger, or rather with a skill in evading all traps that might be set for him, which won for Crook the admiration of all who served with him. . . . "[5]

At old Camp Grant Crook sent other columns to sweep the Tonto Basin from different directions. In all there were nine independent commands in the field at once, crossing and recrossing the hostiles' country, often surprising bands of Indians fleeing from other detachments. The Apaches had never been confronted by so many separate forces at once, and the results were devastating. Crook kept at the head of affairs and exercised close supervision by rapid marches from one point to another. He did not, however, interfere with the various columns, leaving their movements up to the officers he had chosen. They did not disappoint him.

The orders he gave were simple but direct: induce the Apaches to surrender whenever possible; if they refuse, give them all the fighting they want, and all at once, with no time for rest and recuperation; hunt the hostiles without interruption until the last warrior has been killed or surrenders; avoid killing women and children, and guard prisoners against mistreatment; whenever captives are willing to serve as scouts, enlist them at once. To Crook there was no acceptable excuse for abandoning a hot trail. If the horses gave out the men were to follow on foot.

The Apache scouts, on foot, were sent about a day's march ahead of the troops, but they kept in constant communication with the chief of scouts. Their duty was to find the hostiles' camps and lead the troops there, but on occasion the scouts' desire for battle was too strong, and they attacked the hostiles without waiting for the troops. Gradually they became the key part of Crook's fighting force—often they were sent out with only a token detachment of troops—and they did the bulk of the fighting. Because of the essential role of the scouts, the chief of scouts and the officer in command of the scout company were key figures. Two of the most effective chiefs of scouts

Apache scouts at work
Arizona Historical Society

were Dan O'Leary and Al Sieber. The latter attributed his remarkable control of the Tontos to the fact that he always told them the truth. "When I tell them I am going to kill them," he said, "I do it, and when I tell them I am their friend, they know it."[6]

None of the wild Apaches placed guards around their camps at night, as was typical of Indians in general, for among Apaches no one had authority over others. For Crook's men, therefore, it was simply a matter of locating the Apache camps and approaching them stealthily in time to be in position at daybreak. Without their scouts, however, the troops would have found the well-concealed camps only by accident.

A typical scouting patrol was the one composed of eight troopers and twenty Apache scouts which made an arduous all-night march through difficult terrain to strike Delshay's camp on Bad Rock

Mountain, killing fourteen. On the same patrol, thanks to a dog's bark, they discovered another camp, surprised it, and killed eleven more. It was clear to the officers that they owed every success to the scouts, but the Indian Bureau objected strenuously to Crook's use of Apaches to fight Apaches. Some high-ranking army officers were also resentful, for they regarded his reliance on Apaches as a reflection on the army's ability to fight Indians. Success, however, was as much a matter of finding the hostile bands as of fighting them.

Most of the officers who served in the Indian campaigns of the West left the management of their pack trains entirely to civilian packers, but not Crook. Bourke and the others were astonished at the general's concern for his pack trains, for he made a scientific study of them. He inspected every mule, rejecting any that did not meet his demanding standards. A mule fording a stream that could not drink without stopping, for example, was discarded. Crook also ordered that an *aparejo* or pack be made especially for each animal and that every article used by pack trains be made of the best material available. Everything about pack trains, including much of the terminology, was of Arabic or Spanish origin. *Jalma* was the Arabic word for pack saddle; the saddle cover was called a "suvrin-hammer," an Anglo corruption of *sobre-el-jalma* ("over-the-pack saddle"). Most of the packers were Mexicans, and the whole basis for the system was borrowed from pack trains that miners brought from Chile, Peru, and western Mexico.

Each mule knew not only its proper place in line but also its own pack gear, and a mule would simply refuse to move if another's pack were placed on its back. Well-trained mules, when packed, fell into line behind the bell-mare (usually a white animal), while untrained mules wandered about and caused much trouble. To identify these trouble-makers, packers shaved their tails. Trained mules were called "bell-sharp;" untrained mules were "shave-tails." Packers irreverently applied these terms to army officers, with the result that new second lieutenants are still known as "shave-tails." Because of Crook's untiring attention to his pack trains, his mules carried 320-pound packs, although government regulations specified 175 pounds as the average maximum weight for packs. On long campaigns involving rapid pursuit Crook's pack trains kept up with the cavalry, so his troops always had food and ammunition at hand. The daily routine when not on a forced march was "unpack, feed and curry and examine the animal from 'snout to brush'."[7]

When the campaigns began every capable officer was pressed into service. Crook's aide, Lieutenant Bourke, was assigned to Major

Brown's column, which marched from Camp Grant. It was composed of two companies of the Fifth Cavalry and thirty Apache scouts. In the Superstition Mountains they joined forces with Captain James Burns' company and his Pima scouts. The objects of their search were the camps of Chuntz and Delshay, thought to be in the Matzatzals or Four Peaks range. In the Pinals they rode from warm canyons to summits, where they camped in waist-deep snow. The pack train followed over the difficult trails, and, thanks to Crook's precautions, kept close to the cavalry and remained in good condition.

Late in December 1872 they were in the Salt River region searching for a cave which the scouts knew was a favorite refuge of the Tontos and where a large number of them were believed to be hiding. The country was especially rough, and the men had to climb on foot, under cover of darkness, in extreme cold. Scout Nantaje warned that they must kill every warrior or they would have to fight their way out. Someone scoffed at the likelihood of a large number of hostiles hiding in that forbidding country. Nantaje smiled. "Wait and see," he said.

Nantaje led Lieutenant William J. Ross and a dozen of the best marksmen among the soldiers and packers ahead to a strategic position. When they opened fire it sounded to those following like a battery of six-pounders. Major Brown sent Bourke and forty men down the side of the canyon on the run. They came to an enormous cliff, which had a large but shallow cave on a shelf about four or five hundred feet from the top. In front of the cave was a natural rampart of huge blocks of fallen stones.

In the opening fire of the advance party, six warriors had fallen, several of them members of a party of raiders that had just returned from harassing whites and Pimas along the Gila. Through an interpreter Major Brown called on the Apaches to surrender. Their reply was jeering and the slapping of buttocks, for their position seemed impregnable. Brown urged them to send out their women and children. The reply was more jeers; they would fight, they told him, until they were killed.

Apaches at the entrance of the cave shot arrows high in the air to make them fall on the soldiers hiding behind the rocks, but the arrows did little damage. When all of the troops were in position they were ordered to fire at the roof of the cave so that the glancing bullets would strike those seeking shelter. This strategy was successful.

Again Brown called on them to surrender. A strange sound rose

Geronimo and his warriors as they appeared on the warpath before surrender to General Crook in 1886
Western History Collection, University of Oklahoma

from the cave, a weird half-wail, half-exultation, the frenzy of despair and wild cry of revenge. "Look out!" Apache scouts exclaimed. "There goes their death song; they are going to charge!"[8]

Twenty warriors, "superb-looking fellows all of them," leaped over the stone ramparts with bows and rifles in hands. Half-standing, they opened a furious fire while others tried to slip around and outflank the troops. Six or seven of them were killed and the others driven back. From the cave came yells and groans and wails of women. Meanwhile one warrior slipped past the first line of troops unseen. Unaware of the second line, which had not yet fired a shot, he crawled behind the soldiers but was riddled by a volley from the second line before he could raise his rifle.

Brown ordered rapid fire into the cave for a few minutes and then a charge. There was no resistance. Seventy-six men lay dead and nearly all of the thirty-five surviving women and children were wounded. The cave was found to be a perfect stronghold, well-supplied with food and ammunition taken on raids. Women captives told Brown there was another large camp in the Superstitions, on the south side of the canyon, and that the warriors would soon attack. The attack, however, did not materialize. Unknown to Brown and his troops a wounded warrior had escaped detection. Hearing the scouts talking, he knew that they would make a rapid march to the pack train. When the warriors from the other camp arrived, therefore, he warned them and turned them back.[9]

The cave defeat virtually annihilated one of the most destructive of the Tonto bands and demonstrated convincingly that troops led by Apache scouts could reach the hostiles' most inaccessible and obscure refuges. It did not, however, end all Tonto resistance; each band would have to learn the same lesson.

These campaigns ended all doubts as to the value of the Apache scouts, for without them the troops would never have found the hidden camps. "The longer we knew the Apache scouts," Bourke wrote, "the better we liked them. They were wilder and more suspicious than the Pimas and Maricopas, but far more reliable, and endowed with a greater amount of courage and daring."[10] Crook enlisted as many of the Apaches as possible, for it prevented them from joining the hostiles, and the scouts served as hostages, guaranteeing the conduct of their own people. In addition they saved the troops from many hours of exhausting and disagreeable work.

After the Salt River cave battle the troops took the captives to Camp McDowell, rested a few days, and then returned to the Superstitions. They came upon a small party of Tontos, killed a few, and captured some women and children while others fled. A few days later an Apache boy came to them and said his people wanted peace. He was fed and sent back with the message that they should send an adult to treat. An old woman came next, for the Apaches were still uncertain of what to expect and were not willing to risk losing a fighting man. She, too, was fed and sent back. Next an old man came. The band was scattered, he said, but he would gather them and meet the troops at the junction of the Gila and San Pedro Rivers.

He kept his word, and a small group of Tontos surrendered with him. On the march to Camp Grant others silently joined the column, so that there were 110 Tontos when they reached the post. Crook immediately enlisted 26 of them as scouts.

At this time Crook relocated Camp Grant at the foot of Mount Graham. As the columns came in from campaigning they were resupplied with food and ammunition and given a few days of rest. Then they were sent back into the Tonto Basin to search for Apache refuges in the higher parts of the Sierra Ancha, the Matzatzals, and the Mogollones, where snow lay deep. There were some forces harassing Apaches at all times, destroying their provisions and giving them no time for rest and no opportunity to replenish supplies and ammunition. Since the troops were guided by some of the most skillful Apache scouts, who knew every hideout, there was no escaping them.

While these patrols were scouring the mountains a large war party struck the town of Wickenburg in March 1873, killing a number of people and running off herds of horses and cattle. Their trail led across the rough country along the edge of Bradshaw Mountain toward the Tonto Basin. There were no troops in the vicinity of the attack, giving the raiders a twenty-four hour head start before Major George M. Randall, Lieutenant Bourke, and a detachment of scouts and cavalry took up the pursuit.

The scouts knew where the raiders were heading—to a hideout on the summit of Turret Mountain, a refuge that seemed as inaccessible and secure as the Salt River cave. They led the way at night, scrambling up the mountain; by midnight they could see the glow of campfires. Before daybreak the scouts had positioned Randall and his men around the hostiles' camp. When the Tontos began to stir the troops opened a devastating fire and then charged, spreading panic among the astonished Tontos. Some of those who were not brought down by rifle fire raced to the edge of the mountain and disappeared, whether escaping or throwing themselves to their destruction was not known. Although some men may have escaped, most were killed and all but a few of the women were captured.

This victory, following the shocking defeat in the Salt River cave, broke the resistance of the major hostile bands. Knowing that Apaches were leading the troops and that there was no place left to hide, they were thoroughly discouraged. Soon groups from the remaining hostile bands came to Camp Verde and other posts seeking peace. They were told to return with their headmen. A few days later Yavapai chief Cha-lipun (Charley Pan) and three hundred of his band surrendered.

His men were not afraid of the Anglos alone, Cha-lipun said —it was fighting their own people that made them surrender. They couldn't sleep at night because they were afraid they would be surrounded and killed at dawn. They no longer dared hunt or cook mescal. Crook informed them that if they promised to live in peace he would be their friend.

Toward the conclusion of the campaign the various columns came in to Camp Verde. Officers and men were long-haired and bearded, dirty and weary, but proud of their success against so formidable a foe. In congratulating them General Crook said that the hostiles had complained that every rock had turned into a soldier. He did not forget those who had made it all possible, calling the Apache scouts "invaluable."

The work was not over, however, as long as Delshay and his band had not surrendered. Randall's column soon resumed the search in the Matzatzals. Delshay was an old opponent of the army, for early in 1867 Camp Reno had been established to check his depredations. Soldiers from that post had killed his brother, asserting that he had attempted to escape, and Delshay himself had been wounded by an army doctor. He had managed to hold his band together and continue raiding along the Gila and Salt. But Randall's column now surrounded his camp near a stream flowing south from the Mogollón rim. When the troops opened fire Delshay raised a white flag, calling out that he wanted to surrender.

Randall replied that Delshay had surrendered before but had always broken his word. He would obey orders, Delshay said, for he wanted to save his people from starving. Six months ago he had 125 warriors; now he had only 26. Randall accepted the surrender and took Delshay and his people to Camp Apache. But they disliked the White Mountain region as much as they had Camp McDowell, and the whole band slipped away to Camp Verde, where they were allowed to remain.

By April 1873 the major bands of hostiles had surrendered, but there were still small parties hiding in secluded canyons. Most of the time they remained out of sight day and night, but when forced by hunger they stole cattle and horses from ranches. Crook attempted to get word to these small groups of Apaches that if they did not surrender within a short time they would be hunted down.

At Camp Verde the surrendered Tontos were immediately put to work digging a needed irrigation ditch on the reservation, under the supervision of Lieutenant Walter S. Schuyler and the civilian agent, Dr. Williams. The agent had requested $5000 for the project, but the Indian Bureau had refused because officials were considering moving the Tontos to San Carlos. Schuyler gathered up all available tools—whether new or old and worn-out—from the military posts at Verde, Whipple, and Hualpai. With these and fire-hardened pointed sticks the Apaches dug a ditch five miles long. The men did the digging while the women carried away the earth in baskets.

It was too late in the season for planting, so Dr. Williams was unable to do much more than care for the sick, whose numbers were alarming. He allowed many Tontos to move to higher ground to escape the fevers that struck those living in the river valley. When Dr. Williams suddenly became mentally ill, Lieutenant Schuyler took over his work. With money saved from the sale of cowhides collected after beef issues and using Indian labor, Schuyler began work on a dam on the Verde.

After the irrigation ditch was completed Crook assembled the Tonto chiefs at his Fort Whipple headquarters for a meeting with the headmen of all the other Arizona tribes—Pimas, Pápagos, Maricopas, Yumas, Mohaves, Hualapais, and Yavapais. His purpose was to negotiate a formal peace among all of the tribes that had been enemies in the past. Once the peace was agreed on, the Tontos returned to plant crops. They soon had nearly sixty acres of melons and vegetables growing, and a larger tract was prepared for barley and corn. A water wheel to turn a small mill was built out of packing boxes for an outlay of $36. The Tontos were industrious and coopera-tive, and the prospects for success were promising.

There were still some Apache problems in western Arizona, but they were minor. The Hualapais of the Grand Canyon region were fierce fighters, and although some of them had befriended Anglos, they were ill-paid for it and driven to hostility. Late in 1870 Indians had raided Willow Grove. Troops guided by a Hualapai scout searched for them but the trail disappeared. Two settlers offered to search for the raiders if they could take the Hualapai scout. They returned later with a scalp; under questioning they admitted that they had given up the search and killed their guide. Dan O'Leary, the famous scout who was married to a Hualapai woman, was furi-ous, but nothing was done to the two men.[11] To pioneer folk the killing of an Indian, even a friendly one, was no crime.

Most of the Hualapais settled at Camp Beale Springs under the care of an Irishman, Captain Thomas Byrne of the Twelfth Infantry. Although Byrne had little to offer them beyond a modest allowance for partial rations, he acquired surprising ascendancy over the chiefs and leading warriors by virtue of his Irish eloquence. When they were in a surly mood he cajoled them back to good humor by asking if there was ever anything they had wanted that he had not *promised* them. Byrne was well aware that if this small group of warriors were to go on the warpath, it would take most of the troops in Arizona to drive them out of the rocky canyons of their land.[12]

Byrne was replaced by a civilian agent, but remained at the post. Then suddenly the Hualapais went on the warpath for no apparent reason. Unarmed, Byrne rode hard on their trail. When he overtook them they opened fire at him but missed. He rode up to them and heard their complaints: the civilian agent, they said, was cheating them. Believing that Byrne was responsible for all things at the post, they blamed him.

The Hualapais agreed to return with Byrne. At the post he discovered that the scales used to weigh rations had been set to show double the weight put on them. He also learned that the agent had sold most of the Indians' flour and salt to miners. Byrne angrily seized control of the agency, and although there was a great outcry against him in the Indian Bureau, he did prevent the outbreak of a costly war. The Hualapais provided scouts for the army and did good service against the Tontos, but when hostilities ended, they were ignored and left to starve.

Early in 1873 Congress abolished the office of superintendent of Indian affairs for Arizona and several others, for the purpose of simplifying Indian management. To increase efficiency, each agency was to purchase its own supplies and to report directly to the Indian Bureau. To prevent abuses, inspectors were to visit each agency at least twice a year. This change, however, had little effect on agents and contractors who conspired to cheat the Indians and the government.

That same year a telegraph line was strung from San Diego to Fort Yuma and on to Maricopa Wells, with branch lines to Prescott, Fort Whipple, Tucson, San Carlos, and Camp Apache. The first message over the new line was from General Schofield to Crook, congratulating him on his promotion to brigadier general.[13] The promotion, which moved Crook ahead of a dozen or more other officers, was the reward for his successful campaign. Another message over the new line was from Apache chief Pitone to Yuma chief Pascual. Pitone had been present at the peace negotiations, and he reminded Pascual that if the Yumas failed to keep their promises the Apaches would come and wipe them out.[14]

General Crook remained in control of all the Arizona reservations except that of the Chiricahuas. He chose capable officers to command the military forces stationed at each agency and urged them to learn all they could about the Apaches. His instructions were to

Waiting for rations, San Carlos
Arizona Historical Society

"treat them as children in *ignorance*, not *innocence*."[15] Control of
the reservation Apaches, however, was a serious problem from the
outset; at first all that could be done was to issue rations, take
occasional head counts, and impose mild restrictions on their
movements. When large numbers were congregated, the danger of
epidemics was magnified. In the past Apaches had customarily fled
from the scene of disease; medicines were in short supply even at
army posts.

As might be expected of so warlike a people, many Apaches remained restless and turbulent on the reservations, and minor outbreaks and rumors of uprisings were frequent. Settling the Apaches on reservations, Crook knew, was only the beginning, for the first few years of reservation life were crucial. One of the many obstacles to a peaceful adjustment was the bringing together of different and unfriendly bands and confining them on the same reservations. Old feuds smoldered and new ones were kindled among chiefs and warriors competing for influence.

It seems likely that if Crook had remained in charge of the Apaches for ten years they would have made the adjustment to reservation life and become virtually self-supporting without any major uprisings—although even he might not have been able to surmount the obstacles raised by the Indian Bureau's concentration policy. He issued instructions to help prepare the Indians for a measure of self-government. Former scouts from the various bands were organized into an effective Indian police force, and these men were also the instruments for influencing others. They were expected to be models of cleanliness and proper behavior and were required to grow crops. Women were encouraged to dress neatly and to keep their dwellings clean.

In order to introduce the Apaches to a money economy, Crook saw to it that everything they produced was purchased for cash. The scouts had been paid in cash at the same rate as soldiers. At their first payday Crook watched them spending their money on trifles, but said nothing. A short time later, however, he asked them what they had acquired for their wives and families with their earnings. Money, he told them, was like an acorn: properly cared for it would grow into an oak tree; spending it foolishly was like trampling on an acorn. He suggested that if they bought California horses, sheep, and cattle, their money would increase. Convinced, the Apaches sent to California for small herds of horses and sheep.[16]

Officers and civilian agents were to instruct the Indians in civil government in its simplest form. Crook urged the officers and civilian officials to maintain "perfect harmony" in everything concerning the Indians. In case of disputes they should refrain from taking any action until he had issued instructions. The inspector-general had already stated that when civilian and military officials failed to cooperate, "the Indian Department must succumb to the military to insure peace and prevent bloodshed."[17]

The so-called Indian Ring of government officials, contractors, and others who profited illegally through government contracts to furnish supplies, had no desire to see Apaches become self-supporting. Through their connections they were able to exert sufficient influence in Washington to have the Tontos moved from the Verde reserve, which had been promised them permanently, and where they were reasonably contented, to the desolate, un-healthful San Carlos reservation. The move, however, was delayed until early in 1875.

Trouble between civilian and military officials had arisen at Camp Grant even before Crook's Apache campaigns began. Agent George H. Stevens, who was married to an Apache woman, was regarded by many as one of the ablest Indian agents. But when a sergeant of the First Cavalry wrote a crude letter criticizing General Howard, who had appointed Stevens, and made it appear that Stevens was the author, Stevens was unceremoniously replaced. The interim agent, Dr. L. D. E. Wilbur of Tucson, was a willing tool of the Tucson contractors. When the Arivaipas and Pinals were moved from Grant to San Carlos, it was Wilbur who accompanied them.

The "sinister and greedy" Dr. Wilbur, in Crook's words, nearly succeeded in bringing on another Apache war in his efforts to undermine his replacement and to maintain both his influence over the Apaches and his lucrative relationship with the contractors. According to a board of inquiry, when Charles F. Larrabee arrived in December 1872 to take over as permanent agent, Wilbur did "all that a throughly bad man could do. . . . "[18] He tried to incite the Apaches to drive Larrabee away or even to kill him so that he could recover control of the profitable post. Once when the interpreter warned Wilbur that an Apache had come to kill the reservation's farming instructor, Wilbur had made no effort to prevent it, saying only, "Tell him to wait until I get out of here then he can do as he pleases."[19]

When Lieutenant Jacob Almy was placed in charge of the troops at San Carlos he was warned to expect trouble, but he was not pre-pared for it. It came as a result of a contest over leadership. The Apaches on the reservation were divided into hostile bands: one faction was headed by Eskiminzin and Capitán Chiquito, the other by Chuntz, Cochinay, and Tomás. One of Chuntz' warriors seduced Chiquito's favorite wife; an Eskiminzin warrior retaliated by killing one of Chuntz' followers. To prevent the explosion that seemed certain, Larrabee asked for a cavalry company at the agency. The arrival of troops prevented a general exodus, but Dr. Wilbur con-tinued to plot against Larrabee. On ration day late in May 1873 one of Cochinay's warriors tried to kill the agent, and in the melee that ensued, Lieutenant Almy was killed. The army immediately assumed control at San Carlos, and Larrabee resigned.

The civil-military conflict was now out in the open, and the "perfect harmony" Crook had requested was forgotten by both sides. Captain W. H. Brown, now in command, charged that the Indians had been tampered with, which was true, and that the agents were rascals and the interpreters liars, which was occasionally true. Crook declared that Wilbur's "criminal conduct" was simply the "outcropping of the old rottenness at Camp Grant," an oblique reference to the unpopular Lieutenant Whitman. Crook resolved to dispense with the "weak and vacillating" policy of the Indian Bureau, ordering Brown to introduce firm and impartial justice to all who behaved well and certain punishment to wrongdoers.[20] The regime of rigid discipline quickly restored order.

Finding some chiefs and others interested in growing crops, Captain Brown resumed work on an irrigation ditch Larrabee had begun. He observed, too, that the Apaches were taking good care of the cattle they had received. But in October 1873 the commissioner of Indian affairs ordered Brown to surrender control of the agency to James E. Roberts, agent at Camp Apache.

Major Randall replaced Brown as post commander at San Carlos and inaugurated an even more severe disciplinary regime. In January 1874 he ordered Eskiminzin arrested, but the chief fled to the mountains, followed by several bands. Most returned to the reservation in a short time, but because a violent storm had raised the Gila to flood stage they were obliged to camp across the river from the agency. Chuntz and others persuaded some freighters, who were also delayed by high water, to give them whiskey. When the freighters refused to give more the Indians killed them. Most of the Apaches, fearing they would be punished, fled to remote parts of the reservation. One group went off on a raid as far as Tempe, killing six citizens along the way.

The troops sent after these raiders were ordered to take no prisoners, but when the contrite renegades begged to be allowed to surrender, they were permitted to return to San Carlos. Their mood was now chastened, and their desire to cooperate was considerably strengthened—they were even willing to help the troops run down other renegades. The Apaches' willingness to punish members of their own bands made it clear that they now saw their only hope for survival was to adjust to conditions over which they had no control.

At Camp Apache Dr. Soule, a military surgeon, served for two years as agent and helped the Coyoteros make a successful start. They were Indians of "unusual intelligence, and the progress made was exceptionally rapid," Bourke reported.[21] James E. Roberts, who succeeded Dr. Soule in 1872, managed to obtain for them the fifteen head of cattle that President Grant had promised chief Miguel in June 1872 during his stay with General Howard in Washington; to these the commissioner of Indian affairs added fourteen more cattle and one hundred sheep. The Coyoteros showed great pride in the animals and took excellent care of them. Despite the promising start, Roberts had to cope with epidemics and drinking among the Indians. Tizwin, made by fermenting sprouted corn, was a serious problem. It was fairly potent, and tizwin bouts often ended in fatal brawls. To discourage its brewing, Roberts requested corn meal instead of whole corn for rations.

Roberts proved capable of maintaining discipline, but during his second year he faced increasing military interference in reservation affairs. Major Randall ordered the punishment of Indians who carried passes issued by the agent, held secret councils with their chiefs and headmen, or interfered with farming operations. Randall also ordered his own subordinates to supervise the issue of rations. Agent Roberts' career, however, was not without blemish. Before long prospectors discovered minerals on reservation land, and soon there was a clamor to return parts of it to the national domain. Roberts, whether through innocence, ignorance, or greed, became involved in some of the schemes for reducing the reservation.

The conflict between civilian and military officials at Camp Apache reached the critical stage early in 1875, when Roberts arranged for a head count of the various bands. The army then announced that it would hold a count on a different day. A snowstorm made the count difficult, but Roberts attempted to assuage the disgruntled Indians by issuing rations on the basis of his latest count. When some chiefs complained, Captain F. D. Ogilby seized the agency, claiming that it was necessary to prevent an outbreak, Faced with this action, the commissioner of Indian affairs ordered the Coyoteros transferred to San Carlos agency. Their removal was in keeping with the Indian Bureau's concentration policy, but there was another reason for the decision. At San Carlos the new civilian agent, John P. Clum, had demonstrated a surprising ability to prevent military interference.

It was only among the Chiricahuas that the Peace Policy was carried to its logical conclusion, for only there was a civilian agent,

Jeffords, in sole charge. He soon discovered that he could expect little support from his superiors in the Indian Service. Beef was supplied to his agency, but little else. Being no bureaucrat by nature or experience, Jeffords did not hesitate to break or ignore government rules, and he made unauthorized purchases when he deemed it necessary to preserve the peace. Although the commissioner and the other officials were elated over Jeffords' success in controlling the fierce Chiricahuas without even a hint of military support, they did not refrain from reprimanding him for his unorthodox procedures. They were, after all, accustomed to subordinates who followed the rules. It did not matter that Jeffords' actions were forced by their own neglect and were necessary to prevent trouble that would have led to military control of the Chiricahuas.

Cochise continued to cooperate fully with Jeffords, and when stolen livestock appeared on the reservation he ordered it turned over to the agent. For his part Jeffords obtained medicines for the Chiricahuas, paying for them out of his own pocket. In this way, and by exchanging surplus flour for corn, he kept the Chiricahuas from suffering the epidemics and dietary troubles that occurred on other reservations. Eventually Indian Bureau officials thawed and began to comprehend and appreciate his problems and, while still admonishing him occasionally for his unconventional practices, became considerably more liberal in providing supplies.

Jeffords faced unique problems, first, because the Chiricahua reserve lay along the Mexican border, and second, because neither Cochise nor his people regarded hostilities against the Sonorans as a violation of their peace agreement. Not only did renegades from Tularosa and other agencies stop off at the Chiricahua reservation on their way to and from Sonora, it is likely that Chiricahua warriors accompanied them on raids into Mexico. Jeffords was aware of the renegade visitors, but as long as most of the Chiricahuas behaved according to the agreement, he diplomatically provided the strangers with rations to keep the peace. Since the only military force in the area was at Fort Bowie, the Chiricahua reservation became the favorite refuge for malcontents from all of the other Apache agencies.

Although conditions had remained unsettled at San Carlos, there were even more problems at Camp Verde, where Tontos, Hualapais, and Yavapais were thrown together. The last two were on friendly terms with each other, but not with the Tontos. There were still small parties of Tontos in the Tonto Basin country, and Hualapai and Yavapai scouts were used against them, which did not lessen the hostility. During the summer of 1873 a few small parties bolted the reservation, but despite intense heat and lack of water, the troops and Indian scouts brought them back.

Lieutenant Schuyler and the civilian agent on the reservation were occasionally at odds, and Schuyler felt obliged on a number of occasions to take action to avoid trouble. Most agents, the lieutenant said, were afraid of Indians and willing to do anything to conciliate them, which caused the Indians to lose respect for them. "I am afraid of them myself," he admitted, "but have seen enough of them to know that the only way to insure my safety and their future civilization and prosperity is to make them afraid of me. An Indian . . . only knows two emotions, fear and hate, and unless they fear a person they despise him, and show in every way they can their contempt for his authority."[22]

Dr. William H. Corbusier was assigned to Camp Verde as agent in September 1873, and he was soon on friendly terms with the Hualapais and Yavapais, whom he found to be alert, intelligent, and great practical jokers. They were especially fond of puns that combined their own language and English. In helping the boys learn to speak English and to count, Corbusier taught ten of them to sing "John Brown Had a Little Indian" and soon this song was heard all over the reservation, day and night.[23]

Since there were still small groups that had not surrendered, chief of scouts Al Sieber made frequent patrols. Sieber and his scouts captured some women in the Red Rock country and persuaded them to tell where the renegade men were hiding. It was a secluded place in the rocks that could be reached only through a passageway wide enough for one man at a time to enter. Sieber and his Tonto scouts slipped through it during the night and captured the renegades. But General Crook was disappointed, for none had been killed. "Nothing short of some severe examples will thoroughly settle your Indians," he wrote Schuyler.[24]

In August 1873, when Crook learned that Delshay and a group of Tontos had escaped from Camp Verde, fearing that they were to be taken to San Carlos or that the Coyoteros were coming to attack them, the general hurried to Verde. Although several hundred Tontos had fled, by that time, most—including Delshay—had already returned. But tensions mounted at Camp Verde, and by September Schuyler was convinced that Delshay, who was surrounded by the most troublesome, irreconcilable of the Tontos, was the cause. Schuyler informed Crook of his suspicions, and Crook ordered the lieutenant to arrest Delshay and take him immediately to the post's guardhouse. Schuyler was to take enough men to avoid difficulties and not to attempt the arrest unless success seemed certain. And as a precaution, Crook ordered the lieutenant to assign men to kill any conspirators.

Head counts, Schuyler reasoned, were frequent events and should cause no alarm; the arrest could be carried out then. But Schuyler's Tonto interpreter was one of Delshay's followers, and shortly before the Tontos were summoned to the parade ground to be counted, he unloaded the lieutenant's rifle. When the Tonto malcontents were told they were under arrest, Delshay replied that he was not a prisoner and would not go to Camp Verde. His warriors sprang to their feet and drew rifles from under their blankets. It was then that Schuyler discovered that his own rifle was empty, and it was clear that Delshay had been tipped off. Schuyler and his squad of soldiers were surrounded by several hundred angry Tontos. At this critical moment Mohave Charley came to the rescue. He spoke to his warriors, telling them that Delshay and the Tonto renegades were bad men who should be killed. He called on the Yumas to stand by him, and they responded willingly. They decided that Delshay should be taken to his own camp as a prisoner, to remain there until Schuyler wanted him at the post. But Delshay eluded his captors and was soon off on another raid.

Schuyler and Sieber, with Tonto, Hualapai, and Yavapai scouts as well as a few troops, conducted a search for hostile camps near Turret Mountain. Schuyler sent Sieber and his Tontos to scout in one direction; Corporal Snook, a Hualapai chief, and Schuyler took the remaining scouts in another. Snook and his party found a camp of renegade Tontos and killed every man. The next night they marched through snow in weather so cold that they had to walk in circles till morning to keep from freezing to death. At daybreak they attacked Natotel's camp, killing fifteen.

After more scouting they found a camp in a hidden cave, though no renegades were present. Convinced that they would return, Schuyler and a few scouts hid and watched while the pack train returned to Camp MacDowell. The ruse worked, for soon the scouts saw women carrying water to the cave. That night Schuyler placed his scouts around the mouth of the cave, and at daybreak they killed the renegades, including Nanotz, one of the most feared. They also destroyed several tons of mescal. A short time later they killed Natotel, who ranked next to Delshay in prestige. Because Delshay, Chuntz, Cochinay, and Chandesi were still active in the Tonto

Basin, however, Schuyler launched a new campaign to bring them in or destroy them.

The Verde Indians were eager to accompany Schuyler, and he took 122 Hualapais, Yavapais, and Tontos. They came upon a camp in which all of the Tontos had been clubbed to death; the scouts knew this was the work of Pimas. During the campaign, scouts killed more than fifty men and captured a large number of women. Back at Camp Verde they asked the women where they wanted to go; about fifty of them chose to accompany the scouts. Since the scouts were willing, Al Sieber lined them all up and, in a ceremony that may have been lacking in proper ritual, declared them married.

Chuntz, Cochinay, and Chandesi were eventually tracked down and killed, but Delshay somehow survived. Crook reiterated his orders to Schuyler to run him and his band into the earth. "The more prompt[ly] those heads are brought in," he wrote, "the less liable other Indians . . . will be to jeopardize their heads."[25] Schuyler sent out three Tonto scouts who knew where Delshay was hiding. They returned in July 1874 with his head and claimed the reward Crook had offered. Mike Burns, a Yavapai orphan raised by Captain James Burns, Fifth Cavalry, said of Delshay, "He was not the only man who had taken up arms to fight and protect himself, his family, his people, his home, his property and the country of his ancestors, hoping that he might conquer his enemies and be left alone with his people to enjoy the freedom they were used to."[26]

The most troublesome of the hostile leaders were now gone, but there were still a number of small bands that stubbornly clung to their freedom, resisting all pressure to confine them to reservations. The Indian scouts kept on the trail of these renegades. Crook was convinced that some of the minor chiefs, such as Eschetlepan and Chapo, were not hopelessly unredeemable. He instructed Schuyler to induce them to surrender if possible; he would then confine them far from Camp Verde "until all the Indian is worn out of them."[27]

When he learned that the Indian Bureau was considering implementing the concentration policy, collecting large numbers of different bands on a single reservation, Crook wrote, "There are now on the Verde reservation about fifteen hundred Indians; they have been among the worst in Arizona; but if the government keeps its promise to them that it shall be their home for all time, there will be no difficulty in keeping them at peace, and engaged in peaceful pursuits. I sincerely hope that the interests that are now at work to deprive these Indians of this reservation will be defeated; but if they succeed, the responsibility for turning these fifteen hundred Apaches loose upon the settlers of Arizona should rest where it belongs." What was true of the Verde Indians, Crook added, was true of others, for they were all at peace on reservations that suited them, "and the responsibility of driving them to desperation by taking them from their native homes and placing them among enemies, in unhealthy and unpleasant localities, must rest where it belongs. We must turn our eyes to the Indian Bureau—our humanitarian, sympathetic, religious, peace and civilization [sic] Indian Bureau."[28] It was this same year, 1874, that authority for the Arizona reservations was transferred from the War Department to the Indian Bureau.

As rumors of a government plan to move them to San Carlos continued to circulate, the Verde Indians grew increasingly restless. They had cleared land and placed it under cultivation, and they had repeatedly expressed strong objections to moving. But Anglos now greedily eyed the fertile fields and began clamoring for removal of the Indians. It was a refrain that had been repeated countless times as Anglos spread across the West. When newspapers began predicting the closing of the Camp Verde reservation, the *Arizona Miner* of Prescott promised that if this occurred there would be serious trouble with the Indians.[29] A week or two before he was killed in July 1874, Delshay had secretly returned to the reservation to arouse the Tontos by telling them their land would be taken from them and they would be held on the desert where all would die. His information was largely correct, but his source remains a mystery.

Among those eager for the concentration of all Apaches on the San Carlos reservation were Tucson contractors, who stood to profit from government contracts. San Carlos was within easy reach of Tucson, and there was little likelihood that the Indians in that desolate spot could become even partially self-supporting in the near future. Crook continued to voice strong opposition to the move which violated the government's promises.

In February 1875 the Verde Indians were preparing their land for planting, but the seeds and tools promised them were long overdue, and the Indians showed none of the enthusiasm they had displayed before. Pakakiva (Shaking Body), Delshay's son-in-law, expressed the feelings of many: "Somebody," he said, "make bad medicine." Soon there were minor quarrels among the Indians, and strange white men were seen prowling about the reservation. When two Apaches arrived from San Carlos and told them that agent Clum was preparing to receive more Apaches there, the Verde Indians knew that their worst fears were realized. There was a great commotion and the wailing of women was heard in all of the camps.

The Indian Bureau sent Levi Edwin Dudley, former superintendent of Indian affairs for New Mexico, to Camp Verde to supervise the removal. Dudley conferred with Crook, who informed him that no troops would be used to force the Indians to move. Even before Dudley reached Camp Verde to tell them of their fate, the Indians knew he was coming and met him with shouts of "Kill him! Kill him!" Snook, one of the most trusted scouts, told Dudley that the Verde was their country and had been promised them forever. They would not go, he said, where their enemies outnumbered them. In the end, however, they reluctantly agreed.

Lieutenant Eaton commanded the small cavalry escort that accompanied the 1426 Indians who began the journey in February 1875, calling it "about as ugly a job as [was] ever laid on the shoulders of a subaltern in the days of our service in old Arizona."[30] Dr. Corbusier, who also accompanied them, urged Dudley to take them by the wagon road around the mountains to avoid unnecessary suffering. But Dudley insisted on taking them by the shortest route, which was 180 miles over the mountains. "They are Indians," he said. "Let the beggars walk."[31] A few of the old people were taken by the wagon road, but one man carried his disabled wife on his back the entire distance. Moved by compassion for the unfortunate Indians, most of the cavalrymen walked so that children and others could ride their horses. Because of feuding among the bands, scout Sieber put the Tontos in the lead, although they greatly disliked having their enemies behind them.

All lacked adequate clothing, and many were barefoot. Travel was interrupted by snowstorms, and the Indians were discouraged and sullen. The medicine men saw evil omens everywhere and were chanting constantly, while women and children wailed from hunger. They had an especially difficult time crossing a storm-swollen creek, for although Lieutenant Eaton urged a delay until the flood had subsided, Dudley insisted on crossing it immediately. Soldiers shuttled Indians across the raging stream on their horses, but the crossing took an entire night. Wet and cold and miserable, they camped a day to rest. "Ten days had passed since we left the agency," Dr. Corbusier wrote, "—10 days of untold and unnecessary suffering and privation—10 days which left their scars on whites and Indians alike, never to be healed."[32]

An Apache medicine man with the badge of his profession
Arizona Historical Society

The Hualapais and Yavapais had kept well apart from the Tontos, but Corbusier and Eaton, who knew Indians and their feuds, anticipated trouble. The day after crossing the Verde River boys from both groups began playing in an open space between the camps. Soon they began calling names, and adults on both sides joined in. Suddenly someone shouted "Kill the Tontos! *Kill* the Tontos!" and wild shooting broke out all over. Dudley, who feebly tried to stop the dash toward the Tontos, was brushed aside. Sieber and the cavalrymen rushed between the two hostile groups, and their action succeeded in stopping the shooting. They prevented a massacre, but at least five were dead and many wounded.

Dudley had been unable to obtain a pack train large enough to carry provisions for the entire journey, but he had sent a message to Clum at San Carlos, asking him to meet the expedition with supplies. Dudley had not waited for an answer and was not even sure his message had been received. When the food gave out he continued to push the Indians hard all day, so they would be too tired to fight. When they were forced to wade through the icy waters of the Salt River, Dudley was actually moved to pity them, "even though they were Indians."[33] They spent yet another cold, wet, and hungry night, which proved more than the Yavapais could bear. The next morning they and some Hualapais appeared with their faces painted as if for war. Dr. Corbusier hurried to warn Dudley, but too late, for a bullet whined over their heads. Corbusier shouted to the interpreter to tell them that Dudley was riding ahead to bring food. Sullenly they let him depart.

Fortunately Dudley's message had reached San Carlos, and he soon met a party that agent Clum had sent with a herd of cattle and a thousand pounds of flour. Although the Verde group had to travel in a light snowfall, the remainder of their difficult, month-long journey was made without incident. A final head count showed that 1361 of the 1426 Verde Indians who had started the trip reached San Carlos. Some had slipped away to go to the Colorado River reservation, while others had returned to their former havens in Rattlesnake and Hell Canyons. The whole story of this unnecessarily inhumane move can never be known, for Dr. Corbusier's notes were destroyed in the 1906 San Francisco fire.

Because of the long-standing hostilities among the various Apache, Yavapai, and Hualapai bands, the addition of the Verde Indians aggravated an already serious situation at San Carlos. The concentration policy would undo all that Crook had accomplished and postpone the day when Apaches would live peacefully on reservations.

After the vast majority of Apaches were settled on reservations the military mopping up operations continued almost without interruption. Many small groups had never surrendered, and they were joined from time to time by others who slipped away from one of the reservations for a nostalgic attempt to revive the old ways. It was a dangerous game, for if any patrol discovered them, the penalty for being away from the reservation without a pass was instant death. On some campaigns furthermore, the scouts were ordered to kill all renegades, to take no prisoners. On such occasions the scouts often slipped women captives back into the reservation. During the summer of 1875 Captain G. M. Brayton, with Sieber and his Tonto scouts, followed the trail of stolen mules and surprised a camp in the middle of a mule-meat feast and killed twenty-five Indians. Occasionally those killed were carrying passes permitting them to hunt in some other region, but even when the Apaches hunted only in the areas prescribed, many Anglos were so fearful of them that they opened fire without inquiring about passes. Whenever Indians retaliated for such attacks, their punishment was severe.

From the hard campaigning in Arizona and New Mexico during the 1860s and 1870s the cavalry learned that range-bred horses from California were superior to any others available. In appearance, however, they were much less impressive than the well-bred mounts from Missouri and the East. When General Sheridan inspected the Sixth Cavalry Regiment at Fort Hayes in 1875 he called it the finest he had ever seen in mounts, equipment, and appearance. The following year the Sixth was ordered to Arizona to replace the Fifth Cavalry, and at Santa Fe the two regiments were instructed to exchange horses and equipment. The men of the Sixth complained loudly about having to give up their splendid animals for the rough-looking range horses. The men of the Fifth, who knew that their trusted mounts were the best in the world for service in Arizona and New Mexico, resented these aspersions, and the two regiments came close to exchanging more than words. Once on the trail of hostiles, however, the Sixth Cavalry realized that the exchange had been to their advantage.

The cavalry horses from the East made a fine appearance on the parade grounds, but on the trail they soon weakened. The Ninth Cavalry at Fort Bayard was mounted on Missouri horses, but after four months of hard campaigning with little grain or hay, half of the animals were unfit for service. The Sixth Cavalry, according to

White Mountain Apache scouts, about 1875
Arizona Historical Society

Lieutenant Thomas Cruse, did not lose a single horse or mule.[34]

The pursuit of small parties of renegades continued throughout 1876, and some of the campaigning was as arduous as that of earlier years. Late in the year a few scouts cornered a party of renegades in a cave in the Four Peaks region and held them there during a night of snow and freezing rain, although none of the scouts was dressed in more than "shirts and drawers." The renegades were led by Es-keltseltle, an old chief who had persuaded many to leave the reservation and join him for raids. The cave was easy to defend, and the besieged had plenty of ammunition. When they were called on to

surrender and return to San Carlos, they jeered and slapped their
buttocks. But when a random bullet struck down Eskeltseltle, his
chastened followers surrendered. By such actions as this, repeated
hundreds of times, the renegade population in Arizona was eventually eliminated.

IX
John P. Clum and the Civil-Military Struggle for Control

IN AUGUST 1874 John P. Clum became agent at San Carlos after being nominated by the Dutch Reformed Church. He was twenty-three years old and inexperienced with Indians, but he was intelligent and fearless—some would say brash. He concluded that Apache troubles in the past had been caused by the dual civil-military rule, and he determined to avoid such troubles in the future by establishing firm personal control over the Apaches. When he was with Apaches, Clum was tactful and persuasive; with army officers he was usually abrasive.

On his way to San Carlos Clum visited Camp Grant, where a number of Apache prisoners were employed in construction. There he met Arivaipa chief Eskiminzin, who was being held a prisoner for no particular misdeed. Through interpreter George H. Stevens Clum promised to try to obtain the chief's release; Eskiminzin swore to cooperate with him fully at San Carlos. After Eskiminzin arrived at San Carlos a short time later, the two became the most faithful of friends, and "Skimmy" proved to be Clum's most effective ally among the Apaches.

The San Carlos agency was disorganized and confused, because of the alternating civilian and military rule. After a careful study of his charges Clum was convinced that he could, indeed, control them satisfactorily without help from the army. Within three days after arriving Clum inspected the camps of the various bands without a military escort. His conduct surprised the Apaches but shocked the army.

Lieutenant J. B. Babcock, commander of the cavalry detachment at San Carlos, pointed out gently to Clum that the army had been in control of the reservation ever since an outbreak that past January. The army's goal, Babcock said, was a permanent peace with the Apaches; he suggested that, to promote harmony, future councils

175

with the Indians should be held jointly. The troops would uphold civilian authority, he added, if Clum would simply endorse the orders given under General Crook's instructions.

Clum acknowledged that the civil and military officials should maintain harmony, but he made it clear that he would not share control over nonmilitary affairs. He would appoint Apache police and an Apache court to try offenders. Babcock continued to press for full cooperation between them, especially "where duties touch closely at the edges."[1] He maintained a cordial and proper attitude toward Clum, but informed Crook that the new agent resented the slightest indication of military interference. Temporarily, at least, Clum did admit the wisdom of military supervision of passes and of head counts and the military's punishment of offenders. The presence of troops prevented renegades from stirring up trouble and may also have been useful in inducing the Indians to farm and to work on reservation projects.

When he received the lieutenant's report, Crook ordered Babcock to ignore Clum's actions if they interfered with or jeopardized the safety of the reservation. Thus supported, Babcock was determined to maintain the military's role regardless of Clum's feelings on the matter. But that same day Clum withdrew from Babcock the right to issue passes and make counts. If Babcock needed information, he said, all facts of record would be available at the agency office.

Babcock notified Crook, who sent Major Randall from Fort Apache to resolve the differences. Clum was adamant—military interference must end. Any coercive measures by the army would be fully reported. Major Randall had seen stubborn agents before and was confident that in time Clum would be calling frantically on the troops to preserve or restore order on the reservation. He made no effort, therefore, to interfere.

Just as Babcock had been emboldened by Crook's support, Clum grew bolder when he learned that Indian Bureau officials were delighted by his stand against the army. As the personal feuding between agents and officers continued and was reflected in a similar contest between the War and Interior Departments, the objects of the battle—the Apaches—were occasionally forgotten.

Once he was sure he had won the Apaches' confidence Clum introduced a simple plan for self-government. Each band would select four men to serve as police. Clum was immediately gratified by the effectiveness of his Indian police, for all the bands meekly submitted to being disarmed, although they were still able to check

An Apache scout and his wife
Arizona Historical Society

out guns for hunting. They also promised to brew no more tulepai, or tizwin, an Apache favorite.

Soon, however, Esknospas, one of the Indian police, warned Clum that a large tizwin brewing operation was going on in a remote canyon north of the Gila. With his four Indian police Clum led a midnight raid on a camp of twenty-five or more Apache brewers. When the five men were settled in place around the camp Esknospas gave a warwhoop; it was repeated loudly by the others, so that within the canyon walls it sounded as if the attackers were many. The women fled and the men stood meekly by while Clum and Esknospas emptied the kettles. The eleven men were marched to the guardhouse, tried before the Apache court, and sentenced to fifteen days at hard labor. This raid cemented a feeling of mutual confidence between Clum and his police and at the same time convinced the Apaches that brewing tizwin was risky.

Because agency buildings were nothing more than shacks and facilities were generally lacking, Clum requested $5000 to begin a building program; its purpose in part was to keep the Apaches gainfully occupied. Now that he had become the Indian Bureau's champion in its struggle for control, the commissioner, in a burst of enthusiasm, gave him $12,000. Clum was certain that work was the best civilizing agent, and he kept the Apaches as busy as possible. The first building project was an office and quarters for the civilian personnel. He intended to stretch the building program out for several years, in order to extend its beneficial aspects. In all of his work he was greatly aided by his chief clerk, a retired cavalry sergeant named Sweeney, who served as assistant agent, assistant chief of police, and assistant supervisor of construction.

For their labor Clum paid the Apaches fifty cents a day in scrip, which the agency exchanged for food and clothing. He found them eager to work and was often hard-pressed to provide employment for all who desired it. Clum recommended to the Indian commissioner that payment continue to be in goods rather than in cash, believing that this arrangement would have a greater civilizing effect than money wages. He also requested scales, blacksmith and carpenter tools, wagons, harness, and everything needed for farming.

His plan for reorganizing the farming program included alloting a portion of arable land to each band and moving their camps near to their fields. The Apaches readily accepted Clum's programs, among them a daily count of all men and a weekly count of the women and children. Getting thoroughly acquainted with the Apaches and their beliefs, breaking up the tizwin operations, presiding at the Apache court, and supervising construction of a whole complex of agency buildings kept the youthful Clum fully occupied.

In October 1874 inspector Daniels, noting that all of the bands appeared satisfied, was impressed by the changed attitude of the San Carlos Apaches. Their successful farming operations had placed them well ahead of other Apaches he had visited. He recommended giving them some sheep as another inducement to work and thrift. He lauded Clum for his early success and strongly supported him in his conviction that civilian authority alone could—and should— control all reservation affairs.

Before leaving inspector Daniels held a council with some of the chiefs. One asked him to arrange for the return of the San Carlos Apaches who had been held at Fort Apache since the January uprising; Daniels agreed to try. As requested, agent Roberts did release the San Carlos Apaches and sent them on their way. They had not gone far, however, when Major Ogilby and a troop of cavalry arrested them and escorted them to the military guardhouse. Although he admitted that his actions were partly the result of personal feelings toward Roberts, Ogilby maintained, nevertheless, that he was following Crook's orders to arrest all Indians found off a reservation.

At this point Dutch Reformed Church officials spoke out against military interference on the Apache reservations and threatened to end their cooperation with the Indian Bureau if it failed to uphold its agents satisfactorily. The commissioner of Indian affairs immediately informed Secretary of the Interior Delano that the Indians at San Carlos and Camp Apache were sufficiently under civilian control to permit removal of troops from the reservations, but the commissioner took no immediate action. It was always easier and less likely to cause trouble to take an unfavorable action toward agents and Indians than to try to curtail the activities of the army.

The San Carlos Apaches appeared content with Clum's administration, for he kept them well fed and occupied with construction work and farming. Their health was considerably improved by the issue of twenty-five hundred pounds of soap every three months and by vaccination against smallpox. Clum managed the Apaches so smoothly and effectively that even the governor praised him.

Among other things that Clum learned about the Apaches was their contempt for liars. They loved to gamble, using crude cards made of horsehide, or play the hoop and pole game. Infidelity was rare among Apache women, and it was still punished by cutting off the fleshy part of the nose. Apache men were fond of both tizwin bouts and occasional wife-beating. Another Apache custom which others had noted earlier was to point with their noses rather than with their hands. Clum was never able to learn anything about Apache burial customs, for they were conducted in great secrecy. The name of the deceased was never mentioned, though it might be bestowed on a child a generation later.

The arrival of nearly fourteen hundred Tontos, Hualapais, and Yavapais from Camp Verde in March 1875 added enormously to Clum's responsibilities, for the number of unfriendly bands was increased and the possibilities for trouble multiplied. He kept the newcomers separated from the others for a short time and then introduced them to his regular disciplinary regime. When they appeared to be settling into the reservation routine and began building wickiups, he appointed four of them as police, thereby including them in his system of self-government.

The Tontos numbered around seven hundred, and the combined Hualapai and Yavapai bands were about the same. Knowing of the hostility between the two groups, Clum had them camp separately. Bringing fourteen hundred well-armed Verde Indians among one thousand unarmed San Carlos Apaches raised ticklish problems. The Verdes had to be disarmed before trouble occurred, but they were arrogant and suspicious and were likely to bolt if asked to surrender their guns.

Clum's Apache police were well aware of this problem. "How soon we take their guns?" Tauelclyee asked Clum. Goodah-Goodah and the other police also protested the Tontos' guns. The four policemen were ready to take on the fourteen hundred Verde Indians, but Clum decided to postpone the showdown for a few days and devise a less hazardous method. He called a council with the Verde Indians and placed Eskiminzin in charge of the San Carlos reserves, who were armed for the occasion.

When Clum announced that they must surrender their guns the Verde Indians leaped to their feet shouting angry protests and raced to their camps. These were scenes of the wildest confusion, with horsemen dashing about giving orders, women tearing down the wickiups and packing their belongings.

The Verde Indians did not stampede, but they were ready to fight or flee if their guns were demanded. When all were ready, they crossed to the south bank of the Gila and stopped. The emergency had brought Tontos, Yavapais, and Hualapais together, but they were not ready to risk leaving the reservation. For two days they

An Apache mother with her son and daughter
Western History Collection, University of Oklahoma

camped across the river from the agency. Clum insisted on compliance; they repeated their intention to fight.

Clum remained outwardly calm through the crisis. He held a count of the San Carlos Indians on Friday instead of Saturday, so that ration tickets could be issued in advance of ration distribution. The Verde Indians were told that they would receive no tickets until they voluntarily submitted to agency discipline. They argued all day, but at sundown they sent seventy-five rifles to the agency. It was by no means all of their guns, but it was a painful concession, a gesture of surrender, and Clum accepted it. Early next morning he and clerk Sweeney boldly rode into the Verde camp and ordered the Indians to line up for a head count and distribution of ration tickets. They promptly—if sullenly—complied. In a series of councils held thereafter, Clum and the Verdes reached an understanding, and they named four of their number to serve as police.

A special commissioner from the Indian Bureau complicated proceedings considerably by telling Clum that his attempt to force the Verdes to surrender their guns meant that he was assuming responsibility for a serious outbreak. It happened that a Hualapai warrior who understood English had overheard the conversation and repeated it to others. To the Apaches it seemed that Clum's action was unauthorized.

Clum bluntly told the special commissioner that the agency stagecoach would leave for Camp Grant in the morning and that he—the commissioner—would be on it. From Camp Grant the commissioner went to Tucson, where he caused an alarm by describing Clum's rash act and predicting a bloody outbreak to follow. But Clum knew his Apaches and the next day was able to inform Governor Safford that the Verdes had surrendered their guns—the commissioner's Apache war had been averted. When it was over Clum learned that Eskiminzin had tactfully and diplomatically counseled the Verdes, convincing them of the wisdom of yielding.

Eskiminzin had also organized an armed secret service among his warriors and on several occasions, when trouble seemed imminent, had stationed them unobtrusively around Clum to protect him. When Clum became suspicious, Eskiminzin admitted it. There were, he said, some bad men among the Verdes, and he was taking no chances on their killing Clum.

About this time the open breach between civilians and military officers at Fort Apache culminated in Major Ogilby's seizure of the Camp Apache agency, on the grounds that military control was necessary to prevent an outbreak. Roberts informed the Indian

An Apache cradleboard and baby tied to the mother's back
Western History Collection, University of Oklahoma

commissioner and then rode to San Carlos. It was at this point that Commissioner Smith ordered Clum to take charge of the Camp Apache agency, although his headquarters would remain at San Carlos.

Accompanied by Eskiminzin and fifty reliable warriors, Clum started for Camp Apache. On the trail he met Major Ogilby, who was on his way to San Carlos. Clum showed him the order, announcing that he would take charge that same day. Ogilby frowned, returned to Camp Apache, and placed Dr. Mickley temporarily in charge of the agency. Then Clum, using his authority as an ex officio U.S. marshal on the reservation, arrested Mickley for opening Roberts' mail. Clum informed the Coyoteros that he was now in charge and that their orders would come from him alone.

Giving Eskiminzin and the others time to counsel with the Coyoteros, Clum visited Fort Apache to pay his respects to the commanding officer. Although he was cordially received several of the officers made it clear that the army was still in charge of the reservation Indians. Clum ignored them and on the third day held a head count, the first ever at Camp Apache that was not supervised by the army. Major Ogilby was irate. The army would not relinquish control, he told Clum, and he would count the Indians on the following day, even if it was necessary to use all four companies against Clum and the Apaches at the ration issue Clum had scheduled. Clum warned the major, who had enough troops to start serious trouble, that he must take the responsibility for any problems that occured. And, Clum continued, there would be plenty if Ogilby attacked the agency, for Clum and the Apaches would defend themselves.

Returning to Camp Apache, Clum sent word to the Apaches to come to the agency—not to the post—in the morning. Ogilby ordered and threatened in vain, but then gave up and searched for other ways to harass the upstart agent. A few days later he ordered the Apache recalcitrants being held in the army guardhouses at Fort Apache and San Carlos released. Since discipline had already been undermined by the civil-military disputes, he reasoned, it should not take these trouble-makers long to incite others, and Clum would soon be obliged to call for help and surrender control. Clum's Indian police brought back two of the men released who were charged with murder, and Clum requested that they be confined again. The request was coldly refused.

Ogilby's next stroke was even more ominous. He issued an order which might well have brought him before a court-martial: in case of insubordination or hostility on the part of the Apaches the officers at Camp Apache and San Carlos were to disregard any request for assistance. Their only duty, Ogilby declared, was to protect government property and the lives of civilians. The Apaches were also informed of this order; it was an open invitation to start trouble. Soon there were tizwin brawls and fighting in some Coyotero camps, and the situation became menacing. Clum asked if he could rely on the troops should they be needed. He was bluntly informed that the troops would not take any action, even to guard prisoners.

Clum reacted immediately, charging the army officers with instigating insubordination and hostility. The commissioner of Indian affairs finally recalled him to Washington for a conference to settle the matter. Clum urged him to order the army post moved off the Camp Apache reservation, but the commissioner was reluctant to buck the War Department, for that might lead to political retaliation in Congress. The Coyoteros, on the other hand, would object strenuously to leaving lands General Howard had promised them forever, but their objections were not likely to affect appropriations. Clum pointed out various drawbacks to such a move. The commissioner listened, but his mind was made up: move them, he said. Clum returned to San Carlos. He was not the only one who objected to the move. General Schofield, commander of the Division of the Pacific, countered that the army had pacified the Coyoteros and moving them to San Carlos would be a serious setback to their progress.

In mid-July 1875 Clum, the Indian trader and interpreter George H. Stevens (whose wife was a Coyotero), Eskiminzin, and sixty trusted warriors rode to Camp Apache and held a number of councils with Coyotero chiefs and headmen. Clum soon learned that three of the eighteen bands could not be moved because some of the chiefs and headmen had enlisted as scouts for the army. About five hundred of the eighteen hundred Apaches were eager to move, because they had once lived near old Camp Goodwin on the Gila, but the others did not want to leave the White Mountains. Some were hesitant because the army had spread rumors that they were to be taken far away and killed. Clum gave passes to about six hundred, so they could remain at Camp Apache and harvest their crops; eight hundred went with him to San Carlos. Two weeks later the commanding general ordered Ogilby to provide an escort for Clum's protection during the removal, though troops were not to be used to force the Apaches to move.[2]

At this juncture W. E. Morford arrived at San Carlos with an appointment as agent for the Camp Apache reservation. Although Clum's authority over Camp Apache had been temporary, pending the appointment of an agent to replace Roberts, he was irritated and tried to dissuade Morford from continuing. The agency no longer existed, he said, for a fire had destroyed the agency buildings shortly after the removal. It was true that seven buildings at Camp Apache went up in flames, apparently set on fire by subagent L. C. Jenkins, presumably on Clum's orders.[3]

Morford immediately wired the commissioner, who ordered Clum to deliver the Camp Apache Indians to the new agent. There were still between eight hundred and nine hundred Coyoteros at the agency, but Clum refused to transfer authority over them to Morford, on the pretext that his orders specified only the agency property. Morford went on to Camp Apache, where he allied himself with the army against Clum. He reopened the agency, and soon learned that many Coyoteros had returned from San Carlos.

The battle over concentration was renewed, with Morford charging that the only reason for removal was to benefit the contractors of Tucson and San Francisco at the expense of those of New Mexico. Inspector Kemble, a Clum supporter, declared that Morford's assertion that Camp Apache was a better place for the Coyoteros than San Carlos was simply echoing the army officers' position. Morford and the army officers did indeed have a common interest in preventing the removal of all Coyoteros, and the military supported the new agent. General August Kautz, who had recently replaced General Crook as departmental commander, claimed that if the concentration policy were continued, it would make a four-company post at San Carlos mandatory in order to maintain control of the diverse bands. General Schofield agreed, adding that the Indian Bureau should be placed in the War Department so that graft could be eliminated. He was willing, he said, to carry out the Peace Policy, and he would not permit troops to wage war against peaceful Indians simply because some Indian agent demanded it.

With supplies furnished him by the army, Morford kept his agency open and functioning, and the number of Coyoteros at Camp Apache continued to rise. Chiefs who represented more than one thousand Indians declared that they would become self-sufficient within six years if permitted to remain on their own lands. Morford urged the commissioner to order the agency rebuilt to avoid the desperate resistance likely to occur if removal were attempted.

Finding this argument of questionable merit, the commissioner informed Morford that if his "perversity" continued, his post would be abolished. Shaken, Morford asked the post commander if the army would help move the Coyoteros. The answer was no. It soon came to light that the reason for Morford's intense opposition to removal was so he could keep his son on as chief clerk and get his daughter appointed as a teacher at a reservation school. Finally President Grant ordered the secretary of the interior to abolish the Camp Apache agency, returning the Indians there to the authority of the San Carlos agent. This did not mean the end of Morford's career as Indian agent, however, for his political influence enabled him to secure an appointment as agent to the Colorado River agency, where presumably his son and daughter were also gainfully employed.[4]

The civil-military conflict continued unabated when Clum informed the Board of Indian Commissioners that his Apache police force made it unnecessary to maintain a military post on the Camp Apache reservation. General Kautz, knowing that the difficulties between Morford and Clum had damaged discipline among the Apaches, leaving them restless and insubordinate, thought Clum was bluffing and asked Clum if he also wanted the troops removed from the San Carlos agency. If Clum refused, as Kautz expected, he would appear foolish. But instead Clum agreed to the removal, and late in October 1875 the garrison at San Carlos was transferred off the reservation.

Several companies of troops remained at Fort Apache, and there were still Coyotero scouts serving with them. Knowing that all of the Coyoteros could not be removed as long as the scouts were in the army, Clum requested Kautz to discharge them. Kautz refused and then added a barb of his own. He was apprehensive, he said, that the agent would soon lose control of the Apaches; and when that happened, the scouts would be essential. He did agree to discharge certain chiefs, however, saying that they might facilitate the removal.

Again Clum rode to Camp Apache to close the agency. He made no attempt to persuade the Coyoteros to move, but he reported to the Indian Bureau that the remaining Coyoteros had sold their crops and were returning to San Carlos. Apparently some of them were, for Kautz seemed to fear that Clum was succeeding.

Kautz appealed directly to President Grant by pointing out the evils of the concentration policy. For one thing, he said, it was a blatant violation of General Howard's promise to the Coyoteros. For another, in an area so thinly populated, concentrating bands as warlike as the Apaches was folly; if concentration must continue, he said, it should be in some isolated region such as the Fort Apache area. Kautz was certain that behind this policy were the contractors of Tucson and California, who had found it difficult to compete with those of New Mexico in supplying Camp Apache.

More than half of the Coyoteros were still at Camp Apache, where all but one band wished to remain. Kautz was certain that the Coyoteros would soon be self-sufficient if they were permitted to remain in their own country. The Indian Bureau vacillated, and the removal was never completed. The bureau again sent Inspector Kemble to Camp Apache late in November. He noted that a number of Apaches were moving to San Carlos, although there were nearly nine hundred remaining at Camp Apache. He was sure that the others, except for the enlisted scouts and their families, would move soon if the army did not prevent it. Because of Clum's imprudence and the plotting of the officers, however, the civil-military feud had reached such proportions that it had to be settled in Washington. Even though the Indians had made considerable progress as a result of Clum's program, the military's interference had delayed achievement of all the goals he had set.

Clum was still keeping the Apaches busy at building, farming, or digging irrigation ditches, and he continued to hold them responsible for enforcing the laws and regulations. In his building program and by clearing land for planting, he was able to employ hundreds.

The San Carlos Apaches were especially pleased with the results of farming. Eskiminzin and Disalin and their bands moved to remote parts of the reservation and began raising crops in earnest. Although it apparently did not occur to Clum, it seems that Eskiminzin wanted to grow corn so that he could brew and sell tizwin. At any rate, it was rumored that he had established a profitable tizwin trade.

The key to Clum's successful management of the Apaches was maintaining order and discipline by means of his Indian police and court. He believed that it was better for them to control their own behavior, and the Apaches proved him correct. When he was given control of the Camp Apache agency, he introduced that same system there. The men selected to serve as police were always respected members of the bands under their jurisdiction, which strengthened their authority. If Clum had placed police from one band over the people of another, or if he had appointed men who were disliked, his system would have produced resentment and violence. His police were armed with the latest model Springfield needle guns, and they

A group of Apache policemen
Arizona Historical Society

did not hesitate to use them against wrongdoers of their own bands, even of their own families.

The Indian police passed the most crucial test of their reliability in December 1875 when chief Disalin went on a one-man rampage. One of Disalin's two wives complained to Clum that he had a habit of beating her. Wife-beating was, in fact, a cherished Apache custom, and although warriors might submit to being disarmed, there was a limit, as Clum learned, beyond which they could not be driven.

Summoning Disalin to the agency, Clum lectured him on the agent's duty of protecting all Indians on the reservation, women as well as men. Disalin listened, his face expressionless, his thoughts well hidden. Satisfied that he had pushed this former renegade another step toward the white man's way of life, Clum dismissed him.

Disalin returned later, with a blanket over his shoulder, and went to Clum's office, A janitor entered at that moment, and Disalin quickly walked into Sweeney's office. A moment later Clum heard two shots. Sweeney ran from his office, and together they went outside. They saw Disalin, a smoking pistol in his hand, running toward the guardhouse, where chief of Indian police Clay Beauford had an office.

Disalin disappeared around the corner of the guardhouse. One shot rang out, followed by rapid rifle fire. By the time Clum and Sweeney arrived, Disalin lay dead on the ground. Tauelclyee and another Apache policeman had heard the pistol shots and had instinctively gone into action, without waiting for orders. Disalin had planned to kill Clum, Sweeney, and Beauford, then lead the Apaches off the reservation. Tauelclyee shook hands with Clum. "*Enjuh* (It is well)," he said, "I have killed *my own brother*. But he was trying to kill you, and I am a policeman. It was my duty."[5]

When Inspector Kemble visited San Carlos in December, he was astonished at the cheerfulness evident among the Apaches. They were, he noted, obedient and obviously satisfied, a condition he regarded as a thorough confirmation of Clum's reservation management. A month later four thousand sheep were distributed among the San Carlos Apaches.

Even though most of the Apaches remained on the reservation, small groups still bolted occasionally, to roam again unrestrained by boundaries. Late in February 1876, Clum sent Clay Beauford with fifteen Indian police to chastise renegades who had fled to the Tonto Basin. The punishment was severe; sixteen were killed before the others surrendered.

In May 1876 the concentration policy was again invoked, this time with regard to the Chiricahuas. On a trip to Tucson Clum learned that Pionsenay and a small party were on the warpath; the citizens of southern Arizona were terrified. On his return to San Carlos, Clum called the chiefs together and told them the news and of the Anglos' fear that some of them would join the Chiricahuas. The chiefs were excited, all trying to speak at the same time. Eskiminzin quieted them and then spoke. They would not join the Chiricahuas, he assured Clum, but they would go after them if he wished. The other chiefs agreed. Clum called for volunteers; within a few hours 250 had offered to serve, and others were coming to the agency from all over the reservation to volunteer.

Clum sent a message to Governor Safford, offering to join a civil or military force against the Chiricahuas with five hundred reliable scouts, or to take on the task with them alone. He and the Apaches waited anxiously for a reply, but none came. Two weeks later the commissioner of Indian affairs, on Safford's recommendation, ordered Clum to proceed to the Chiricahua agency, suspend agent Jeffords, and take control. If feasible, Clum was to move the Chiricahuas to San Carlos. Except for Pionsenay's outbreak, the Chiricahuas had been relatively peaceful, but in the eyes of Indian Bureau officials they had made little "progress toward civilization" under Jeffords' loose control. He had permitted them to retain their arms and horses, placing only mild restrictions on their freedom of movement.

The Chiricahuas' frequent visitors from other reservations, who averaged about two hundred a month, were a constant source of concern. Jeffords had continued to feed them, although he knew that a few Chiricahuas occasionally accompanied them on raids to Sonora. But because the reservation lay along the Mexican border, all raids were blamed on the Chiricahuas. Most of the raiders apparently came from Warm Springs, although after the Coyoteros were moved from Camp Apache to San Carlos, a number of disgruntled warriors also followed the old plunder trails south. A number of tizwin brawls and the killing of a noted Chiricahua warrior made visitors less welcome than before. As a result, the raids into Mexico had decreased sharply in 1875.

Another volatile element in the Chiricahua situation was the Nednhi band still in Mexico; it lived by raiding Mexican towns and ranches. Jeffords was convinced that this band carried on a trade in stolen property with those living on the reservation and also used the reservation as a refuge when being pursued by Mexican troops. Occasionally Mexican officials reported that herds of stolen livestock had been tracked to the Chiricahua reservation.

General Kautz, irritated by the army's exclusion from the Chiricahua reservation, blamed Jeffords for all wrongs. Jeffords' head counts, he declared, were too irregular and incomplete to keep effective control of his charges. Presumably Kautz wanted the army to take over that responsibility although, as Jeffords well knew, it would cause a stampede from the reservation.

After Cochise died in 1874 his son Taza replaced him, but Taza lacked the prestige and influence necessary to sway his people. He cooperated with Jeffords, who did everything in his power to aid the Chiricahuas while protecting the lives and property of whites. While he was alive, Cochise had also been successful in recovering stolen livestock.

Taza, son of Cochise, who replaced his father as chief
of the Chiricahuas in 1874
Arizona Historical Society

Another problem for Jeffords was a byproduct of the numerous freight-wagon caravans following the Overland Trail through Apache Pass. The freighters, the Chiricahuas discovered, were always willing to trade whiskey for horses and mules. Because of the fights that occurred whenever any of the Chiricahuas got hold of some whiskey, Jeffords requested permission to move his agency headquarters to Apache Pass, where he would be in a better position to prevent the whiskey trade.

Commissioner Smith, pressured no doubt by New Mexico officials, decided that for all these reasons the Chiricahuas should be moved to Warm Springs. There, he concluded, their management would be more economical and less complicated. He did not add what was a more cogent reason—that the contractors of New Mexico would benefit substantially by the change. He sent Inspector Dudley to secure the Chiricahuas' consent to the move.

Dudley visited the Chiricahua agency in April 1875. When they found out what he had in mind the Chiricahuas were furious. They warned Dudley that if he molested them it would mean war. After receiving Dudley's unfavorable report the commissioner allowed Jeffords to move the agency to Apache Pass.

Perhaps because Inspector Kemble saw little hope for making the Chiricahuas self-supporting while Jeffords remained in control, the Indian Bureau reduced the agency's beef allotment. As a result Jeffords was obliged to allow several bands to go to the Dragoon Mountains to hunt for game. While they were there a fight broke out and three were killed. Most returned to the agency, but Skinyea and a dozen families remained in the Dragoons.

In May 1876 some of the warriors with Skinyea joined a party of Coyoteros on a raid into Sonora and returned with a bag of gold and silver. They purchased whiskey from Indian trader Rogers and had a drunken brawl. Pionsenay, a brother of Skinyea, killed two of his sisters while drunk. A few days later he did penance by killing Rogers and his cook. Then, joined by others, he set out on a raid through the San Pedro Valley, killing a number of ranchers and running off livestock.

All of the Chiricahuas were aroused and apprehensive, and when troops from Fort Bowie pursued raiders into the San José Mountains, a general uprising seemed imminent; only the persuasive powers of Jeffords and Taza prevented it. They sent word to those with Skinyea who had taken no part in the raid to return to the agency and allowed Pionsenay to find a refuge in the Chiricahua Mountains.

Because of this outbreak, Governor Safford began a campaign to have Jeffords dismissed as agent and the Chiricahuas moved to San Carlos. Congress allocated funds for the removal; the commissioner assigned Clum the delicate and hazardous task.

Clum was in no hurry to undertake the move, however, delaying several weeks until there were enough troops in the area to handle any emergency. Clum rode to Tucson with fifty-four Indian police and interpreter George H. Stevens to await the troops, thereby giving the apprehensive citizens a chance to observe the disciplined behavior of the Apache police. The citizens were so impressed that they raised a fund to purchase uniforms of white trousers, red shirts, and outmoded army hats for the police. This was, no doubt, an unofficial atonement for the Camp Grant massacre five years earlier. General Kautz arrived and placed twelve cavalry companies and two of Indian scouts around the Chiricahua reservation.

When Clum, his Apache police, and the troops approached the reservation in June 1876 the startled Chiricahuas met in council. Skinyea and Pionsenay called loudly for war, but Taza and Nachez, sons of Cochise, spoke for peace. They made their point by killing Skinyea and five of his leading warriors and wounding Pionsenay; the other chiefs then agreed to the move.

The Nednhis had always lived south of the border at least part of the year. The Nednhi band of Juh and Nolgee, which Geronimo had joined, asked Clum to allow them to accompany the others to San Carlos. Geronimo, a Bedonkohe medicine man, became an important Nednhi war leader because of his "power" to know what went on elsewhere. Clum gave them three days to gather their people, but he also had his scouts oversee their preparations. The Nednhis killed their dogs, hastily packed their possessions, abandoned their old people, and headed south, rapidly outdistancing the cavalry force sent after them. At the same time some Chiricahuas fled to Warm Springs.

One of Pionsenay's men approached Clum to ask what terms the renegade chief might expect. Clum ordered Tauelclyee and twenty police to accompany him and to return with Pionsenay, "*alive if convenient.*" He added that if the messenger was a good guide, he should be brought back as well. If not, Clum didn't want to see him again. Tauelclyee grinned. "*Shebukensee,*" he said, meaning "understood."[6] The scouts brought in Pionsenay and thirty-eight others. Clum wired Governor Safford that he would turn Pionsenay over to federal officers in Tucson. But on the road to Tucson a sheriff and his deputy met Clum at Point-of-the-Mountain with a warrant

Chiricahua leader Nosey with his wife, 1881
Western History Collection, University of Oklahoma

for Pionsenay, and Clum was forced to surrender him. That same night Pionsenay escaped from the two officers.

Only 325 Chiricahuas made the move to San Carlos. The number of those who escaped was not known. Clum shrugged it off as about 100. Jeffords, who was best qualified to make an estimate, reported that 140 had gone to Warm Springs and that 400 others were on the loose. General Kautz was of the opinion that Jeffords padded the figures to clear himself of charges of fraud in the numbers he claimed to have fed. Among those who escaped were Taza's relatives, who remained in the Sierra Madre until the twentieth century.[7]

Control of the Chiricahua reservation was then transferred to Kautz, but he was not to allow any Apaches to remain there—any who appeared were to be treated as hostile. Soon there were reports of miners killed by Indians and of livestock missing. Troops found trails leading into Sonora, but no Indians. Kautz established Camp Thomas in the area of hostility, but without effect. When troops from New Mexico trailed raiders into the Florida Mountains and killed twenty, Arizona territorial officials attacked Kautz for inefficiency, and Governor Safford threatened to call out the militia—a slap at the regular troops.

Aroused by these actions Kautz sent Captain T. C. Tupper to make a thorough search of the troubled region. When Tupper reported that he had not found a single Indian Kautz was convinced that the killings and thefts were the work of renegade whites from Mexico. But after a raid in the area of old Camp Crittenden, Lieutenant J. A. Rucker and a company of cavalry followed the trail for several days, and in the Liedendorf Mountains of New Mexico they surprised a camp of Apaches and killed ten. They found horses and supplies that had come from the Chiricahua reservation, and Rucker reported that the region was swarming with renegades.

Kautz was now convinced that Jeffords' estimate of the number of Chiricahuas at large had been more accurate than he had originally thought, but the renegades had also gained recruits from Warm Springs. The raids and killings continued into 1877 despite the military patrols and punitive expeditions. Some raiders when pursued headed for Sonora, while others went to Warm Springs.

It was Warm Springs, however, that was the main source of raiders, for the Mimbreños. Mogollones. and Chiricahua renegades had always been fierce fighters. The agent at Warm Springs reported that all but a few of them scorned farming, and that they were too wild and restless to risk forming an Indian police force. Adding to the agent's problems was a shortage of rations early in 1876. He had

Chiricahua warrior Nachez
Arizona Historical Society

requested permission to trade surplus sugar for flour and beef but was refused. With the help of the territorial delegate to Congress the agent secured provisions in time to prevent a general outbreak, but raiding parties still went out. A cavalry detachment stationed west of the reservation discouraged a general exodus, but small groups slipped out to visit the Chiricahuas. And when Clum moved the Chiricahuas to San Carlos, chief Gordo and some of his restless young warriors slipped away to join their friends at Warm Springs. Their presence greatly aggravated the agent's discipline problems, for the renegades were arrogant and unruly.

Inspector Kemble visited Warm Springs early in 1876. He noted not only the turbulent warriors, but also saw evidence of graft. Before agent Shaw had been appointed, 330 Indians had received rations. Now Shaw claimed that the count had risen to between 1100 and 1300, but he had no records to substantiate his claim. Kemble was convinced that Shaw had submitted false returns and that the Indians' supplies had been traded for whiskey. Kemble estimated that there were actually 600 or 700 on the reservation and that they controlled the agent. He recommended Shaw's dismissal; in August 1876 James Davis replaced him.

The concentration policy and his role in it had made agent Clum well known. In July 1876 he took a party of twenty-two Apache chiefs, headmen, and their wives to Washington, and because the Indian Bureau refused to provide funds for the trip, Clum tried to finance it by putting on "Wild Apache" shows along the way. But the Custer massacre had occurred the previous month and public reaction was unfavorable. The shows were financially disappointing and the performances were discontinued.

In Washington they had conferences with the commissioner of Indian affairs, but did not get a great deal of satisfaction from him. While there Taza died of pneumonia and was buried in Arlington Cemetery. When Clum returned to San Carlos he found the Chiricahuas unhappy over Taza's death, for they believed Clum had neglected him. Nachez and a large party of glum-looking Chiricahua warriors met Clum in a remote canyon and demanded an explanation. Clum tried vainly to convince them that Taza's death could not have been prevented, that everything possible had been done to save his life.

Eskiminzin came to the rescue, solemnly recounting the story of Taza's illness and death and of his funeral and the great men, such as General Howard, who came to pay tribute. In conclusion he said, "My friends, I have spoken long, and you have been patient, but I had to speak because the story is true. I know you feel as I do. A good man, a great chief, is no longer with us. We are sad, and yet to any family it is an honor to have had one of their members cared for in the grand city of the Great White Father, as Tahzay was while ill, and then buried among graves of paleface heroes."[8] Nachez accepted Eskiminzin's explanation.

The elusive Geronimo made destructive raids into southern Arizona and New Mexico after fleeing from the Chiricahua agency in 1876, and once more the army was under attack for its failure to capture him. Early in 1877 the Arizona legislature appropriated $10,000 and authorized the governor to enlist a militia company of sixty men to protect citizens. Governor Safford asked Clum for sixty of his Apache police to serve as the territorial militia; Clum agreed providing Beauford could serve as captain. Clum marched the police to Tucson and turned them over to the state to protect white citizens against renegade Chiricahuas, surely one of the marvels of the Apache wars.

Because of the continued raiding General Kautz sent Lieutenant Austin Heneley to Warm Springs to see if renegades were using that reservation as a haven. Heneley learned that Mimbreños joined Chiricahuas for raiding and that Chiricahua renegades did, indeed, use the reservation as a base. While Heneley was at Warm Springs Geronimo returned from a foray with stolen cattle and was outraged that he was refused rations for the days he had been absent.

Heneley did nothing to alert Geronimo but reported his findings to Kautz, who relayed the news to the War Department, which passed it along to the secretary of the interior, who handed it over to the commissioner of Indian affairs. More than three weeks after Heneley made his report the commissioner wired Clum to arrest the Chiricahua renegades with his Indian police, if possible, and take them to San Carlos.

In the meantime relations between Clum and the military continued on a collision course. Earlier that year some Coyoteros had killed an old Apache woman near Camp Apache. The army made no report of it; when he belatedly learned of it Clum suspected the army of protecting the killers to undermine his authority, a challenge he could not ignore. He sent some of his Apache police to Camp Apache with orders to arrest or kill the guilty ones. They killed one of them, but in the process fired shots in the direction of an Apache who was a scout for the army. Major Ogilby was ready— his troops chased the police most of the way back to San Carlos.

Clum reported this "outrage" to General Kautz, who replied by accusing Clum of trying to drive the women and children of chief Pedro's band to San Carlos while their men were away with troops searching for renegades. Clum's actions, Kautz intoned, created a dangerous situation, so dangerous, in fact, that he felt obliged to order the scouts back to the reservation in hopes of averting bloodshed. In this way Kautz tried to shift the onus for unchecked Apache depredations from the army to Clum.

Burning with anger, Clum accused Kautz of "criminal inactivity" for leaving the people of southern Arizona exposed to Apache raids. Since the general was already under heavy assault by territorial officials and the press, Clum's charge stung him as intended. He reported to the adjutant general of the army that many renegades had been driven from the reservation by mistreatment and insufficient rations, an oblique suggestion that graft and mismanagement were rife in the administration of the reservation. Clum heard about this accusation as he was leaving for Warm Springs.

A short time earlier Clum had requested Kautz to furnish a military escort to Warm Springs. Pointing out that Warm Springs was in the military Department of New Mexico and out of his jurisdiction, Kautz suggested that Clum contact Colonel Hatch, commander of the Department of New Mexico. On orders from the War Department Hatch put nine companies of troops in the Warm Springs area. This was the proper arrangement, for one departmental commander had no authority in another department, but to Clum it was simply further evidence that Kautz was trying to block his success with the Apaches.

In April 1877 Clum requested Governor Safford to release the Apache scouts who had been serving for several months as militia and ordered Beauford to meet him in Silver City with them. Taking forty of his Indian police, he set out on foot across the desert to Silver City, some four hundred miles away. To Clum it was a lark, for he thoroughly enjoyed campaigning with the Apaches. When he suggested that they march twenty-five miles a day the Apaches laughed and said forty miles would be better. On the way they teased him frequently. After one thirty-mile march through cactus, sand, and heat they held a vigorous, two-hour war dance. Looking solemnly at the dancers Eskiminzin explained almost apologetically to the weary Clum that the Apaches felt they weren't getting enough exercise. Another example of their humor was the Apache name they bestowed on Clum—*Nantan-betunnykahyeh*—"Boss with the high forehead." Clum appreciated the joke—he was bald.

Moccasins were a problem on the march for the soles gave out after four days of desert travel, so every fourth day each man had to resole his moccasins. Along the way a severe sandstorm held them up once for thirty hours.

At Ford Bayard Clum learned that Colonel Hatch had ordered Major Wade and three companies of the Ninth Cavalry to meet him at Warm Springs on April 21, the day Clum expected to arrive, to assist in the capture of Geronimo's band. Knowing that the Apache police would not willingly cooperate with troops Clum did not tell them until the second night out of Fort Bayard, when he assembled Eskiminzin and a few of the others he trusted most.

When he informed them of the plan, the Apaches said nothing, but sat looking at one another. Apaches had a mysterious way of silent communication, of exchanging thoughts through the eyes. Clum had noticed this earlier among Apaches serving as judges or juries. They would listen to the evidence, look at one another for a time, and then the presiding chief would announce that the accused was guilty or not guilty. They had reached a silent, unanimous agreement.

Eskiminzin now spoke for all. Clum, he said, was the white chief of the Apaches. He had never lied to them and they would always obey him, but they didn't want white soldiers to help them take Geronimo. They knew how to fight Apaches—the soldiers didn't. "If they try to help us," he concluded, "we will not get Geronimo and his people, because they will know we are coming, and will run away to Mexico." A chorus of "*Enjuhs*" signified that this was the unanimous view. The debate continued for two hours; in the end the Apaches agreed to continue.[9]

On April 20 they were forty miles from Warm Springs, having joined Beauford and company in Silver City, where Clum bought some horses. They camped that night in a secluded valley fifteen or twenty miles from the agency. With twenty-two of his police, now mounted, Clum rode to the agency, where he learned that Major Wade would not arrive until April 22. This posed both a problem and an opportunity. Geronimo was camped three miles away. He might either destroy Clum's small party or leave for Mexico. Prompt action was required.

After dark Clum sent word to Beauford to bring the others in cautiously. They arrived at four in the morning and hid in an empty commissary storehouse across the parade ground from the main agency building. At daybreak Clum sent a message to Geronimo, saying he wanted to talk to him and other chiefs.

Convinced that Clum had only twenty-two Apaches with him

Geronimo, Gordo, Ponce, and others came as the sun rose, painted for war and defiant. With six of his Apache police standing in a line beside him, rifles in hand, Clum waited on the porch of the main agency building. Beauford and sixteen others stood between the main building and the commissary, ready to relay Clum's signal to the waiting police.

Clum accused Geronimo of breaking the treaty between Cochise and General Howard and also of breaking his promise to go to San Carlos the previous year. He had come, Clum said, to take him to San Carlos. It was a long trip, and he did not want any trouble with Geronimo or his people. Geronimo replied that Clum's words were very brave, but he and his men were not going to San Carlos; and he warned Clum that if he wasn't careful, he and his Apaches wouldn't get back either—"Your bodies will stay here at Ojo Caliente to make feed for coyotes."[10]

This was the showdown. Clum had expected several hours of haranguing first, but Geronimo was in no mood for lengthy discourses. Clum raised his left hand and touched the brim of his hat. Beauford relayed the signal and the commissary doors swung open. Two lines of Apache police raced in opposite directions to surround Geronimo and his people. No sound was made. Clum kept his eyes on Geronimo's right hand and saw his thumb move toward the hammer of his .50 caliber army Springfield rifle. Clum touched the butt of his own Colt .45, his second signal—Beauford and the twenty-two police raised their rifles and leveled them at Geronimo and the other chiefs a few yards away.

At that moment a wild Apache yell shattered the silence. A large Apache woman, fearing that Beauford was going to shoot Geronimo or others, had flung her arms around him. It was the sort of half-mad, half-comical incident, coming at a tense moment, that had caused chaos and massacre on other occasions. The Apache police looked to Clum for a signal but held their fire while the powerful Beauford tossed the woman to the ground and again leveled his rifle. The crisis passed quickly.[11]

The Chiricahuas were disarmed and held in the agency's walled corral, for there was no guardhouse. As a further precaution the agency blacksmith riveted ankle irons on Geronimo and the other chiefs. When Major Wade and the cavalry arrived next day the Chiricahuas were quite subdued. The only remaining task was to escort them to San Carlos. Clum wired the commissioner that the Chiricahua renegades had been captured. Since there were only six hundred Indians at Warm Springs he advised transferring all of

Geronimo in his prime
Arizona Historical Society

them to San Carlos. The commissioner agreed with this unfortunate and inappropriate suggestion and ordered the Warm Springs Apaches moved.

Victorio and other Mimbreños came in the same day. Clum told the Warm Springs chief that he would make a count before sunset. The Indians returned at the time set for the count, for Eskiminzin and other Apache police had been active among Victorio's people, telling them of their fair treatment at San Carlos and urging them to obey the order to move there.

The next day Clum received a telegram from Tucson with the news that two parties of Chiricahuas under Ponce and Nolgee were raiding in Arizona. Since Ponce was shackled and guarded in the agency corral Clum was able to point out to the renegades the value of head counts—being present at the counts each day cleared them of such charges.

Victorio and his people were unhappy to be leaving their favorite region, but they agreed to go in peace. They had the foresight, however, to cache their best guns and a supply of ammunition.[12] This was an Apache practice, and they had similar caches of arms, ammunition, bolts of cloth, and food in caves in the Sierra Madre and other retreats in Mexico. The trip to San Carlos was made without incident, except for the outbreak of a few cases of smallpox among the Apaches. Once more Eskiminzin came to the rescue: Put the sick ones in the wagon with Cullah, he said—Cullah had survived smallpox earlier and was in no danger.

Before the return trip began Colonel Hatch asked General Kautz for a military escort to relieve his troops when they reached the border of the Department of Arizona. Clum praised the New Mexico military forces for their cooperation, adding ungraciously, that the "Arizona military are useless." Captain William M. Wallace, commander at Fort Bowie, wired Clum asking where he wanted the Arizona escort to meet him. Clum curtly replied that "no escort has been asked for from Arizona and none will be accepted."[13]

General Sherman regarded Clum's rejection of the escort as a breach of personal and official courtesy, saying Clum had "no business" refusing it. General Sherman, Clum retorted, had no business interfering with his business. Kautz lamely excused himself for not providing an escort earlier on the ground that Clum had refused to allow him to recruit scouts at San Carlos. He had, therefore, to send for Hualapais, and the delay had made it impossible to furnish an escort.

The Warm Springs reservation was now closed although an estimated two hundred Mimbreño and Mogollón Apaches were still on the loose, for not all had been willing to go to San Carlos. As long as any Mimbreños or Mogollones remained in the area those who had gone to San Carlos would harbor thoughts of rejoining their friends in their own lands.

While Clum was traveling to Warm Springs and back Kautz gained considerable ground on him in their feud. Kautz informed his superiors that the absence of troops on the reservation had made it impossible to control or punish renegade Apaches. He had, furthermore, no way of acquiring information as to conditions on the reservation. His subtle approach was effective, for his request for authority to station an officer at San Carlos to observe the movements of the Indians and to inspect their supplies was approved. The secretary of the interior, who lacked Clum's relish for feuding with the military, agreed to the stationing of an officer on each reservation. When Clum triumphantly returned to San Carlos with both the Chiricahua renegades and the Warm Springs Apaches, therefore, he was in for a bitter shock. An officer and his military escort were already at San Carlos to oversee Clum's administration.

Without waiting to see if the officer would be cooperative or obstructionist, Clum shot off a virtual ultimatum to the Indian commissioner—either relieve him at once or increase his pay and provide for two more companies of Indian police. In the latter case he would control all of the Apaches without any military assistance whatsoever. When the commissioner rejected the demand for more pay and increased authority, Clum resigned and left the agency on July 1, 1877, leaving Inspector Vandever in temporary control at San Carlos.

The Indian Bureau's concentration policy was a tragic error, for it failed to take into account the consequences of moving Apache bands from their favorite resorts or of confining unfriendly bands on the same reservation. Carleton had tried a similar arrangement with Mescaleros and Navajos at the Bosque Redondo, and it had failed miserably in every way. The plan would be no more successful at San Carlos.

Among the critics of concentration was General Kautz, who charged that Indian policy was being manipulated by contractors and politicians for their own advantage. It was, in short, not a program for civilizing wild Apaches, as the Eastern reformers called Friends of the Indian piously maintained, but a crude and cruel plot for exploitation and dishonest profit at the expense of both the government and the Indians. Kautz warned prophetically that concentration would inevitably result in bloody uprisings whenever renegade leaders were able to take advantage of discontent and of the hostility between bands. Inspector Kemble, though outwardly supporting the policies of his superiors, also predicted trouble if an inexperienced agent were placed in control.

General Crook, who at the time was campaigning against the Sioux, had stoutly maintained that permanent peace with the Apaches could not be achieved unless the Chiricahuas were thoroughly defeated and humbled. Their removal to San Carlos had simply freed renegades from restraint by their own people, and although troops and Indian scouts from both Arizona and New Mexico constantly scoured the country for them, they had not been able to subdue them.

General Kautz, who was far more dedicated than territorial officials gave him credit for, was convinced that there were less than a dozen renegades active in the Fort Bowie region. When Lieutenant T. A. Touey's command was soundly thrashed by Apaches in Las Ánimas Mountains, however, Kautz realized that his estimate was too low. Inspector Kemble increased the general's embarrassment by recommending that the Indian Bureau send Apache police to protect military posts. And Governor Safford added yet another insult by leading a command of Indian police on a three-week campaign.

Most of the Apaches at San Carlos continued working and avoiding trouble, but they were occasionally disturbed by the activities of the renegades, by agent Clum's frequent absences on missions elsewhere, and by the policy of forcing unrelated and unfriendly bands to live at the same agency. Taken all together these irritations made for an explosive situation. Despite the danger, Inspector Vandever predicted that the Apaches would become self-supporting in five years if the Indian Bureau would allocate $30,000 for an irrigation project. Such a modest expenditure, he believed, would prevent much more costly troubles.

About the time Clum resigned the army suspended scouting for renegades. Inspector Vandever, as interim agent at San Carlos, sent out a detachment of Indian police to drive back small parties of Apaches slipping away from the reservation.

Vandever was no happier with army inspection of issues than Clum had been, although the presence of an officer apparently had a noticeable and beneficial effect on the amount and condition of rations issued. Yet Vandever accused the army of usurping the Indian Bureau's authority. The army struck back by charging Vandever with negligence, inefficiency, fraud, and other misdemeanors. Nothing came of the charge except that Secretary of the Interior Carl Schurz reprimanded Vandever for his attacks on officers whose cooperation he needed. Soon after this A. H. L. Hart replaced Vandever as agent.

The civil-military feuding could not be concealed from the Apaches, and it added to the restlessness and dissatisfaction of various bands, especially those from Warm Springs, who hated San Carlos. They watched and waited for an opportunity to return to their own country. One night in September 1877 Pionsenay entered the reservation surreptitiously to remove women and children belonging to his band. The Warm Springs Apaches virtually stampeded that same night. Victorio and Loco left the reservation with more than three hundred Warm Springs Apaches, heading eastward toward their former range in southwestern New Mexico. A new phase of the Apache wars thus began.

X
Victorio, Nana, and the Mimbreños

ON HIS VISIT TO THE APACHES of Arizona and New Mexico in 1871 Vincent Colyer, President Grant's Peace-Policy emissary, had recommended that the army provide food for the Mimbreños and his recommendation was approved. The numbers of Mimbreños and Mogollones at the Cañada Alamosa agency continued to grow as the complaints against them multiplied, for they were suspected whenever any of the citizens' livestock was missing. The Southern Apaches may well have been guilty of some of the thefts, but Apaches from Arizona and Sonora also raided the same region, and Anglo and New Mexican rustlers and horse thieves were often the guilty parties. Bands of armed citizens roamed the country looking for Apaches to attack, and their presence was probably responsible for Cochise's decision that Cañada Alamosa was unhealthful for the Chiricahuas.

The superintendent of Indian affairs for New Mexico, Nathaniel Pope, also visited Victorio, Loco, Nana, and their people and found them still asking for a reservation of their own, preferably at Warm Springs. Some Chiricahuas were also present, naked, hungry, and fearful of attacks by Anglos. Cochise, they reported, was on a raid into Sonora. Pope, knowing that Colyer was anxious to confer with Cochise, sent messengers in search of him in a vain effort to bring him to Cañada Alamosa for a meeting.

Because there were many New Mexican squatters on the best land around Cañada Alamosa, Colyer decided that it would be easier to find a new home for the Apaches than to buy out the intruders. After a brief visit to Ojo Caliente, or Warm Springs, however, he decided that there was insufficient arable land there and instead designated Tularosa as the Southern Apache reservation. He ordered the Apaches moved there, but the transfer was not made immediately. Colyer may not have been aware that the Mimbreños would be discontented with any location but Warm Springs.

Several months later Cochise camped at Cuchillo Negro, near Cañada Alamosa. Because he had lost many men and his people were without food he badly wanted peace and a reservation, but like the Mimbreños and Mogollones he disliked Tularosa and refused to take his people there. The number of Indians at Cañada Alamosa continued to grow, for they were joined by two hundred Coyoteros who were unhappy at San Carlos. In March 1872 they were all moved to Tularosa.

On General Howard's visit to Tularosa in July he found Victorio and the Southern Apaches dissatisfied with the reservation Colyer had selected for them. Howard promised to move them to Warm Springs the following year; it would be their permanent home, he promised them, as long as they did not break the peace.

There continued to be many thefts of livestock charged to the Southern Apaches, but since there was constant visiting back and forth between Tularosa and the Chiricahuas, and since parties of Coyoteros and other bands were occasionally in the region, responsibility for the thefts was difficult to ascertain. The Mimbreño chiefs denied that their people had committed the thefts and blamed "bad Indians" from other agencies.

The splitting of military control of Apachería between the Division of the Missouri and that of the Pacific in 1866 had aggravated the problem of restraining the Apaches of southern Arizona and New Mexico. To ease this problem the secretary of the interior recommended that the Chiricahua, Camp Apache, and Camp Bowie agencies be transferred to the jurisdiction of the Department of New Mexico, but strong opposition by General Crook and others induced him to abandon the idea.

Soon after Levi Edwin Dudley became superintendent of Indian affairs for New Mexico he held a council with the Tularosa Indians early in 1873. Victorio, Nana, Loco, and the other chiefs were in a sullen mood, demanding that they be moved to another location. Dudley insisted that they could move only if Cochise and the Chiricahuas joined them. Cochise still refused to settle at Cañada Alamosa, and Victorio and his people were equally unwilling to be transferred to either the Chiricahua or the Mescalero agency. To satisfy the Apaches and gain their cooperation it was necessary to provide separate reservations for them in their own lands, but this was a concept that only Colyer, Howard, Crook, and a few others grasped. To Indian Bureau officials one place was as good as another, and they saw no reason to acquiesce and settle the Mimbreños at Warm Springs.

While the local citizens were blaming the Tularosa Apaches, and especially Sancho, for thefts, the post doctor spoke favorably of them. "The Apaches," he said, "are a hardy race, with good constitutions. . . .They are virtuous, and there is no taint of syphillis among them."[1] Benjamin M. Thomas, agent to the Southern Apaches, was convinced that Victorio's band wanted peace and would help capture any Apaches who committed thefts, for Victorio had once even offered to kill Sancho for breaking the peace. But when Thomas asked Victorio and Loco to arrest some Apaches who had been trailed to the reservation with stolen stock they grew angry, probably because one of Victorio's nephews was among those to be arrested. Thomas continued pressuring them until they rushed from his office and signaled their warriors to get their weapons and horses.

While the Mimbreño warriors rode menacingly back and forth in front of the agency headquarters Major William R. Price arrived with three companies of the Eighth Cavalry and another of Navajo scouts. Victorio agreed to confer with Price the following day at his own camp in a canyon some distance from agency headquarters, but when Price arrived for the meeting he found Victorio's camp deserted. At Thomas' request Price tried to arrest some women and children to hold as hostages, but all fled into the the mountains. Price's men did manage, however, to seize Victorio's nephew and one other warrior, both of whom were considered trouble-makers. The two were held as hostages until Victorio and other chiefs returned to the agency, and then they were released.

In 1874 the Indian Bureau again raised the question of removal and concentration, but Dudley declared that moving the Southern Apaches to Mescalero, beneficial as it might be, could not be accomplished peacefully. In the meantime Major Price had sent cavalry detachments to scout and map the Southern Apache country. His men reported that the Tularosa Apaches frequently visited the Chiricahuas and that together they went on raids into Mexico.

The Southern Apaches continued to insist on leaving Tularosa, and since the Indian Bureau believed that concentrating the Apache bands at one or two agencies would result in substantial savings to the government, it proposed settling both the Southern Apaches and the Chiricahuas at Warm Springs. Commissioner Smith ordered Dudley to visit Cochise and Chiricahua agent Jeffords to sound them out on the idea.

When Dudley reached the Chiricahua agency in the summer of 1874, Cochise was dying, and there was no other Chiricahua who had so great an influence over his people. Jeffords confirmed reports that Indians frequently came from Tularosa to join the Chiricahuas on raids into Sonora, leaving their families at his agency. When the warriors returned from raids and demanded rations, Jeffords said, he supplied them, for if he refused they would simply go raiding again. By feeding them he hoped to keep them near the agency, but he asked Commissioner Smith for instructions.

On his visit Dudley concluded that Jeffords could persuade the Chiricahuas to move to Warm Springs. "I have seen no man who has so complete control over his Indians as Agent Jeffords," he wrote the commissioner, recommending that Jeffords be named agent at the new reservation. Jeffords did not have all of the qualifications for being agent, he continued, but he did maintain control, and when Chiricahuas left the reservation, he usually knew where they had gone. "If the Apaches can be taught to work," Dudley concluded, "Jeffords is the man who can teach them."[2]

Since the Tularosa reservation was still unacceptable to the Southern Apaches Dudley recommended closing it, moving them to a new agency at Warm Springs, and sending Tularosa agent Thomas there to make preparations. Thomas requested that at Warm Springs the commissioner not apply a new order, inspired by the Friends of the Indian, requiring all Indians to work in exchange for food. Although he had reported some success in persuading Apaches to take up farming at Tularosa, he was sure that most of them would bolt the reservation if the new order were strictly applied.

Before the Apaches were moved to Warm Springs Thomas, who regarded the presence of a military force as beneficial, asked for a cavalry detachment to be stationed at the new agency, a request that was granted. The move was made in mid-summer 1874; by November, when John M. Shaw replaced Thomas as agent, there were about four hundred Indians on the agency rolls.

Throughout the next year the Southern Apaches were relatively quiet, for they were happy at Warm Springs, and they seem to have been well fed. The number of Indians reported to be at the agency soared to more than thirteen hundred. Doubts soon arose as to the accuracy of Shaw's head counts, and it was rumored that he estimated the number present by the amount of beef he dispensed.[3]

Rumors circulating during 1875 that they were to be moved to San Carlos in accordance with the concentration policy disturbed the Southern Apaches, for they disliked that region even more than Tularosa and they were on unfriendly terms with some of the Apache bands there. They had not forgotten, furthermore, that they had been promised a permanent home at Warm Springs. But the concentration policy had many active supporters outside the Indian Bureau—contractors and land-hungry settlers. They brought pressure to bear on Congress and the Indian Bureau, and bureau officials succumbed.

While the Verde Apaches were being moved to San Carlos in 1875 Anglo and New Mexican settlers began encroaching on reservation lands at Warm Springs in anticipation of a similar move. Agent Shaw attempted to keep the Apaches peaceful by excessive issues of rations, although he was also suspected of selling government supplies illegally for his own benefit. He was convinced that Victorio, Loco, and the other Mimbreño chiefs would keep their people out of trouble if they were well fed.

There was only a small detachment of troops stationed at Warm Springs, and when a large number of Chiricahuas arrived after their reservation had been closed, Shew feared trouble. Colonel Edward Hatch, commander of the District of New Mexico, quickly provided an adequate cavalry detachment, but the presence of the Chiricahuas kept the others stirred up, especially the young warriors.

In the spring of 1876 Colonel Hatch himself visited Warm Springs where he found the Apaches well armed with Springfield, Winchester, and Sharps rifles as well as with pistols. The Indians were in a surly mood, complaining that the government had not supplied them with meat for a month. Their young men were off raiding, they added, and it would be better to accompany them than to stay at Warm Springs and starve.

About the same time that Hatch reached Warm Springs some Chiricahua warriors also arrived, ready for a raid. Victorio, Loco, and the other chiefs informed Hatch that they planned to make a peace treaty with Sonora, so that they could live there and raid New Mexico. They would be better off, Victorio told the colonel, being at war with the Anglos, for then all of the other Apaches would join them. At this critical moment Hatch received orders from the army to feed the Apaches and keep them on the reservation regardless of what the Indian Bureau did.

The chiefs told Hatch bluntly that they could not prevent their young men from raiding and that they had no difficulty trading horses and mules for arms and ammunition. The chiefs said that if they wanted to retain their influence, they had no choice but to take part in the raids. In his report Hatch stated that both Mescaleros and Mimbreños were raiding widely and were more formidable than ever. He felt that the agents had no control over the Apaches; it would help greatly, he said, if the Southern Apaches could be disarmed, but he knew that was impossible without a costly fight.

The coming of the Chiricahuas to Warm Springs was unsettling, especially when Geronimo's band arrived. Agent Shaw's worries increased when Loco, who tried to help preserve the peace, was attacked during a fracas in which one warrior was killed. Applying the concentration policy, by causing the Chiricahuas to scatter had greatly aggravated the Apache problem at all of the agencies.

In September 1876 a company of Ninth Cavalry and Navajo scouts rode onto the reservation to attack and burn Victorio's camp, for reasons that were not stated. Other cavalry units crossed and re-crossed the country around the reservation. A party of citizens took advantage of the Apaches' preoccupation with the troops to run off a herd of their horses. Those Apaches who tried to remain peaceful became frustrated and angry.

There were many rumors that Geronimo, Pionsenay, and other Chiricahua renegades were using Warm Springs as a base for raids and as a refuge. In March 1877 Lieutenant Austin Heneley had seen Geronimo there just after returning from a raid into Mexico. It was Heneley's report that eventually led to Clum's daring arrest of Geronimo and his band and to the unfortunate removal of the Southern Apaches to San Carlos. Victorio protested in vain that General Howard had promised them that they could live perma-nently at Warm Springs and that their removal was clearly a viola-tion of his promise. Many Apaches slipped away and avoided re-moval; those warriors who did make the unwelcome journey hid their guns and ammunition in case of future need.

At San Carlos Victorio's people were located at the subagency at old Camp Goodwin on the south side of the Gila, nearly thirty miles from agency headquarters. Camp Goodwin had been established in 1868; the area was unhealthful, and in 1877 a severe form of malaria paralyzed the whole garrison, killing one-fourth of the men. The post was abandoned as unfit for use, but it was here that Victorio and his people were sent to live.[4] The Southern Apaches and Coyoteros were at odds, and there were many potentially explosive incidents. Many of the Warm Springs Apaches died of hunger and disease, and

Nana, one of the Mimbreño leaders who succeeded Victorio;
photographed in 1884
Western History Collection, University of Oklahoma

Victorio was determined to remove his people at the first opportunity.

In August 1877 Pionsenay, Nolgee, and some of the other Chiricahua renegades came to the subagency and declared that they wanted to surrender. The clerk replied that he had no authority to negotiate with them and could accept only unconditional surrender. Pionsenay and his men then stole some horses and carried off many of the renegades' relatives, following the Gila upstream into New Mexico. Victorio, Loco, Nana, and the Mimbreños, excited by this action and knowing that the cavalry would follow the Chiricahuas, stole some Coyotero horses and fled north. A force of San Carlos Apache police, scouts, and Coyotero volunteers followed hot on their trail and caught up with them the following morning, capturing some women and children, most of their horses, and all of their supplies. At the same time cavalry from Fort Bayard followed Pionsenay's trail far into Mexico before turning back empty-handed.

Victorio's people wanted only to return to their old home at Warm Springs. In October they sent word to the commander at Fort Wingate that they were ready to surrender. Although he had no idea what to do with them, he accepted the surrender of Victorio, Loco, and 187 others, while Nana and other Mimbreños headed for Mescalero.

Before going to the Mescalero agency at Blazer's Mill, Nana sent the young warriors and most of the horses to the Rinconada, an inaccessible and remote canyon. With sixty-two others he walked to the agency headquarters, whee agent Godfroy entered their names on the rolls. The young warriors were not mentioned, and because they had not been counted they could leave at any time without arousing suspicion.[5] Nana soon discovered that from time to time Godfroy sent wagonloads of Mescalero goods to traders in Las Cruces. On one occasion Nana and a small party relieved the freighters of the goods and took them to cache in the Rinconada.[6]

At Fort Wingate, meanwhile, Victorio stated emphatically that he and his people would not return to San Carlos under any circumstances. While officials in Washington debated whether to send all Mimbreños to Mescalero or allow them to return to Warm Springs, other members of the band continued to surrender. By November, when they were taken to Warm Springs to remain there while the bureau decided their fate, the number had risen to 250, but of these only 52 were warriors. The return to Warm Springs proved only temporary, for although army officers strongly recommended leaving them there and Colonel Hatch had assured them that they could remain if they behaved, the Indian Bureau had already decided to sell the government land and property at that agency. Bureau officials had been able to reverse their decisions on other occasions, but they refused to at this critical moment.

The Mimbreños asked for permission to send a delegation to Washington to explain their grievances to government officials but were refused. Others requested that their relatives who were still at San Carlos be sent to join them. The Indian Bureau, however, showed no desire to resume control of the Southern Apaches, leaving them in a virtual state of limbo. In the meantime they were obedient and cooperative, to prove that they deserved to remain at Warm Springs. General Sheridan, who had urged the bureau to leave them there, now bluntly warned the commissioner that unless the bureau took charge of the Mimbreños, he would recommend turning them loose. This threat, as might be expected brought on a flurry of activity.

Victorio had kept his people on friendly terms with the people of the nearby town of Monticello, protecting them from other Indians, so they could trade for guns and ammunition there. One day the trader informed him that a few days earlier he and his son were rounding up cattle when seven "outlaw" Apaches attacked them. He shouted to them in Spanish that he was a friend of Victorio, and they rode away. Nana and a party of warriors dashed after the troublemakers and, although the raiders had covered their trail, caught them three days later. The renegades boasted of their killings and of their powers of witchcraft and informed Nana that their ghosts would haunt him if he killed them. One was a boy who was obviously a captive. Nana took the boy with him and rode away, leaving his warriors to kill the six outlaws.[7]

Because they dreaded being taken back to San Carlos the Mimbres Apaches even offered to live on half-rations if they could stay at Warm Springs. The Indian Bureau stubbornly insisted, nevertheless, that they return to San Carlos. The Apaches waited nervously, keeping out of trouble and hoping that the bureau would relent. But they were determined to die fighting rather than return to slow death at San Carlos.

In mid-October 1878, a year after they had returned to Warm Springs, the Mimbreños learned by some mysterious way that in ten days two companies of the Ninth Cavalry were coming to escort them to San Carlos.[8] Victorio bitterly protested the move to San Carlos, but Captain Frank T. Bennett could only follow his instructions. A Mescalero woman asked Bennett for permission to return to

her own people, and he agreed. Instead of riding off toward Mescalero, however, she whipped her horse and headed up the canyon
toward the main camp, "hallooing at the top of her voice that the
soldiers were coming, and going to kill them all. . . . " Victorio and
about 80 others panicked and dashed for the mountains leaving most
of their possessions behind.[9] Bennett seized as a hostage Loco, the
Mimbreño chief who was most friendly to Anglos.

The troops were soon in pursuit of the fleeing Mimbreños, but
they scattered into the mountains and disappeared. Later chief
Sánchez returned to the agency and said that Victorio would come in
with the others if Captain Bennett promised to protect them. Bennett agreed, but Victorio was already on his way to Mexico, and
those who had come in with Sánchez slipped away to join him.
Bennett rounded up all who remained and escorted them to San
Carlos. They reached the agency late in November, after much
suffering from snow and cold weather while crossing the mountains.

Several weeks later Nana, Sánchez, and fifty others showed up at
Mescalero, naked and starving. An order to take them to San Carlos
was not carried out, for indecision was replacing determination
among Indian Bureau officials. Early in 1879, when Victorio and his
people finally surrendered to Lieutenant Merritt at Warm Springs,
he allowed them to send men to Mescalero to bring back Nana and
all of the others who wished to return. Ordered to explain this
unauthorized action, Merritt replied that Victorio had convinced
him that he and his people preferred to die fighting rather than to
return to San Carlos.

Hatch approved of Merritt's action and warned Superintendent
Pope that if an attempt was made to move the Apaches to San Carlos,
many of them would have to be killed. The Indian Bureau now
agreed that the Mimbreños could be moved to Mescalero instead of
to San Carlos, although Mescalero agent Samuel A. Russell stated
emphatically that he considered them trouble-makers and preferred
not to receive them. Commissioner of Indian Affairs Hayt assured
Russell that the Mimbres Apaches had been well behaved when
treated fairly, reminded him they were on friendly terms with the
Mescaleros, and ordered him to receive them.

When Lieutenant Merritt tried to explain to Victorio that his
people were to be transferred to Mescalero instead of San Carlos,
the interpreter may have garbled the message, for Victorio reacted
violently. Shouting that he would die first, he signaled to his people
and all dashed north into the San Mateo Mountains.

It was now Colonel Hatch's turn to react in anger. He dispatched cavalry and Indian scouts to the Warm Springs area with orders to capture the renegades and take them to San Carlos. But having convinced Indian Bureau officials that the proper course was to take the Indians to Mescalero, not to San Carlos, he could not persuade Washington to change the orders again. Hatch then sent Tomacito and other Mimbreños from Mescalero to hunt for Victorio and persuade him to come to that agency. But Victorio had already swung west and then south into Mexico, leaving a trail of death and devastation.

Some time during the spring of 1879 Victorio did learn, much to his surprise, that his people were to be sent to Mescalero rather than San Carlos, and he sent word to the Mescalero agent that he was willing to surrender. In June he and some of his warriors arrived, begging Russell to tell them immediately if they were to be taken to San Carlos. When he answered that they could remain at Mescalero as long as they behaved, they pleaded with him to have their families brought from San Carlos. Russell agreed to try. By late July 1879 there were nearly one hundred fifty Warm Springs Apaches at Mescalero, and Russell was confident that they would remain peaceful if their families were allowed to join them.

Both Hatch and Russell had promised to protect Victorio if he surrendered, but Russell soon faced a dilemma. Authorities in Grant County had issued indictments against Victorio for murder and horse-stealing and were likely to attempt his arrest. Russell wired the commissioner of Indian affairs for instructions as to what he should do if local officials came to arrest Victorio.

Somehow Victorio learned of the warrants for his arrest, and he surmised what was likely to happen to him; he had, furthermore, little confidence in the promises of protection. A few days later he and his people vanished, and with them went some disgruntled Mescaleros. Russell was astonished and irritated, for he could not imagine why they had left the reservation when their families were already on the way there from San Carlos.

It was several months before Russell learned the reason for the exodus. A few days after Victorio had learned of the indictments against him, Judge Warren Bristol, prosecuting attorney Albert J. Fountain, and several others crossed the reservation on a hunting and fishing trip. Victorio and his people knew or suspected who they were and were convinced that they were coming to arrest Victorio.

Thus it was that when it seemed that the Warm Springs Apaches were happily settled at Mescalero, soon to be joined by their families, they took what for many was their last warpath. The situation was even more tragic, for the Indian Bureau had finally agreed that when they were reunited with their families they could return to a reservation of their own at Warm Springs. Had this simple solution been reached a short time earlier, many a life—Anglo, Mexican, and Apache—would have been spared. Ninth Cavalry troops followed the fleeing Indians but failed to overtake them.

Agent Russell, who still had much to learn about the Apaches and their ways, appeared to be personally offended at their flight. He informed the commissioner that the Warm Springs Apaches had neither fear nor respect for the army, and that it would teach them a lesson to be severely "*thrashed*, if such a thing is possible."[10] As it turned out, such a thing was not possible, at least as envisaged by Russell.

Soon after their flight from Mescalero Victorio, Nana, and about forty warriors descended on the horse and mule herd of Company E, Ninth Cavalry, at Warm Springs, killed the eight men guarding it, and ran off the entire herd. A few days later Major Albert P. Morrow, commander at Ford Bayard, fought Victorio's warriors, killing ten and wounding others, but at a substantial cost. Morrow estimated that Victorio had about one hundred men, although he had only forty-three when he left Mescalero. "All our stock is gone," Morrow admitted. "I sent every available soldier out."[11]

Two of the Warm Springs Apaches on whom Victorio relied most heavily were his sister Lozen and old Nana. Lozen's "power" was in locating the enemy. When Victorio wanted to know in which direction the enemy was, she would stand with outstretched arms, palms up, praying to Ussen. She slowly turned, following the sun; her hands tingled and her palms changed color when they were pointed at the enemy. The intensity of the tingling in her hands indicated whether the enemy was near or far. Nana's "power" was locating and capturing ammunition trains, but he was also considered the shrewdest strategist of all the Warm Springs Apaches.[12] Both of these "powers" were essential to Victorio's success.

Although raiders' wives frequently accompanied them on raids, it was unusual for an unmarried woman to do so. But Lozen was an exception, for she fought as ably as any warrior and took part in much of the fighting. She was, furthermore, the only woman invited to sit in council, for she was also gifted as a strategist.[13]

James Kaywaykla, who was a child at this time, recalled later that "Until I was about ten years old I did not know that people died except by violence. That is because I was an Apache, a Warm Springs Apache, whose first vivid memories are of being driven from our reservation near Ojo Caliente with fire and sword."[14]

Following Victorio's attack troops from all over New Mexico converged on the Warm Springs country, and Lieutenant Charles B. Gatewood came from Arizona with his Apache scout company and three pack trains. "I must state right here," wrote Lieutenant Thomas Cruse, who accompanied Gatewood, "that it was the pack trains that finally defeated the Indians, this on the admission of all the noted chiefs with whom we talked later on. The troops were enabled to hold on the trail as long as the Indians left one, and as the Apache is a temperamental person in spite of his stoicism, this persistent following 'got on his nerves.' " When the troops caught up with the Apaches, the pack trains were there with ammunition and supplies. "The Apaches," Cruse said, "remarked that this was *very* discouraging."[15] Victorio reportedly was greatly disheartened and then furious when he learned that Coyotero scouts and pack trains were after him, for he knew the scouts and their fighting ability.[16] He sent them word that he intended to get revenge by raiding San Carlos and killing their families.[17]

One detachment caught up with Victorio in September 1879 near the head of Las Ánimas River and fought an all-day battle before having to withdraw. The fight took place in rough mountains, where the nimble Apaches were completely at home. Before the troops withdrew the Apaches had captured their pack train and supplies.

Soon Major Morrow's unit and Gatewood's scouts also came upon the hostiles and attacked their camp. The long battle ended in a draw, though the troops and scouts captured most of the Apaches' horses and mules. Such losses, however, were only a slight disadvantage to the Apaches, for they melted into the mountains where it was impossible to follow. And when they reached safety they stopped to wave their breechcloths and make other uncomplimentary gestures, daring the troops to follow.[18] As Morrow's troops withdrew from the mountains Victorio's men harassed them all the way. Victorio then headed for the Mogollón Mountains, followed at a distance by Morrow.

Victorio had to be alert for enemies wherever he went, for a number of columns of troops and parties of civilians were out after him. One party of civilians from Mesilla had the misfortune to come close; they were ambushed and annihilated. Morrow's black troopers, however, stayed doggedly on Victorio's trail over mountain and desert into Mexico, marching several days without water. At one spring there was enough water for only one half-pint for each man and animal; at another the hostiles had thrown the body of a coyote in the water; and one spring had water too muddy to drink because the Apaches had ridden their horses through it.

Finally the scouts saw dust ahead at the edge of the Guzmán Mountains and reported that the hostiles were there on the defensive. Although horses and mules were falling behind or dying at every mile Morrow and his troopers grimly pushed on, to attack on foot. They fought their way nearly to the top of the hills where the hostiles had thrown up rude barricades, but with boulders rolling down on them, the troops had to give up. They had been on the trail steadily for seventy hours without water and were in desperate need. The civilians who criticized the army for inactivity were badly misinformed, for any greater effort was physically impossible. The Apaches were, Gatewood reported, well armed with late model Winchesters and seemed to have plenty of ammunition.

Victorio had with him about one hundred fifty warriors, including some Navajos, Mescaleros, Lipan Apaches from Texas, and Comanches as well as Mimbreños and Mogollones. Major Morrow's force was down to eighty-one men and eighteen scouts, for half of his command had been left behind. Morrow gave all of the credit for driving Victorio into Mexico to Gatewood's Apache scouts, for he knew that without them his command would never have been able to follow Victorio's trail.[19] Their accomplishment is even more impressive when one realizes that at this time the Apache scouts still had not been given horses; they were, nevertheless, able to keep well in advance of the cavalry.[20]

Leaving the troops behind, Victorio led his band to the Candelaria Mountains near the El Paso–Chihuahua City road, camping at a waterhole known as the Tinaja de Victorio. His scouts noticed unusual activity in the town of Carrizal. Sánchez, who had been a Mexican captive and had been trained as a vaquero, dressed in the clothing of a vaquero he had killed and rode into Carrizal on a horse bearing the well-known Terrazas brand. He soon overhead discussions of a plan to invite Victorio's people to a fiesta, give them all the liquor they could drink, and then kill them. A few days later a Tarahumara Indian rode into Victorio's camp and invited the Apaches to the fiesta.[21]

In the past Victorio had maintained peace with certain Mexican towns, protecting them from raids so they would furnish his people with guns, ammunition, calico cloth, and other necessities. On this occasion, however, he sent a small raiding party to run off some horses from Carrizal. A party of eighteen Mexicans pursued them into a carefully laid trap where every man was killed. Thirty-five men came in search of the first party, and again the trap was set: fifteen more were killed. A few days later Victorio's men captured an entire pack train and were again well supplied. They kept caches of food, utensils, blankets, bales of cloth, guns, and ammunition in isolated caves. If they lost their possessions in a surprise attack, they soon replenished their supplies from the caches.[22]

Victorio's was not the only Apache band on the warpath, for Geronimo, Juh, Nolgee, and Chato still raided from their refuges in the Sierra Madre of Sonora. It is possible that some of the skirmishes reported between troops and Apaches were with Juh or Geronimo rather than Victorio, and for a time the three joined forces. Apache hostilities in Chihuahua were particularly destructive in 1879; during one six-week period nearly one hundred fifty people were killed.

Because Victorio had a mixed force, including renegades from a number of tribes, and because they often split up into small parties to search for horses and mules, one of his earlier policies had been abandoned. Victorio had always befriended the lonely Mexican sheepherders in their isolated camps, and they had gratefully shared their ammunition and food with him. But now on his recent rampage through New Mexico these herders were the most numerous of the civilian victims.[23]

Opinions as to the cause of Victorio's devastating outbreak differed among army officers and civil officials, but those who were most knowledgeable about the Apaches were generally sympathetic. Lieutenant Gatewood, one of the most successful Apache fighters of the Crook era in Arizona, stated candidly that any man of discretion empowered to adjust Victorio's well-founded claims could have prevented it.[24] General Willcox, commander of the Department of Arizona, remarked that "It is believed by many that Victorio was unjustly dealt with in the first instance, by the abrupt removal of his people from Ojo Caliente, New Mexico, to San Carlos, and that such removal, if not a breach of faith, was a harsh and cruel measure, from which the people of New Mexico have reaped bitter consequences."[25]

General John Pope, commander of the Division of the Missouri, though no admirer of Apaches, whom he called "idle vagabonds, utterly worthless and hopeless," was even more blunt. "This outbreak of Victorio," he wrote, and the severe campaign against him, still in progress, involving the loss of many of our men, and the murder by Indians of about seventy persons, mainly Mexican herders, were due to the determined purpose of the Interior Department to effect the removal of the band to the San Carlos agency in Arizona. There is already a large number of Indians collected at that agency, mainly Indians of Arizona. Victorio and his band have always bitterly objected to being placed there, one of the reasons given by him being the hostility of many of the Indians of the agency. He always asserted his willingness to live peacefully with his people at the Warm Springs (Ojo Caliente) agency, and so far as I am informed, gave no trouble to any one while there. I do not know the reasons of the Interior Department for insisting upon the removal to San Carlos agency, but certainly they should be cogent to justify the great trouble and severe losses occasioned by the attempts to coerce the removal. The present is the fourth time within five years that Victorio's band has broken out. Three times they have been brought in and turned over by the military to the Indian Bureau authorities. Both Victorio and his band are resolved to die rather than go to the San Carlos agency, and there is no doubt that it will be necessary to kill or capture the whole tribe before present military operations can be closed successfully. The capture is not very probable, but the killing (cruel as it will be) can, I suppose, be done in time.[26]

In 1879 Crook remarked that "During the twenty-seven years of my experience with this Indian question I have never known a band of Indians to make peace with our government and then break it, or leave their reservation, without some ground of complaint; but until their complaints are examined and adjusted, they will constantly give annoyance and trouble."[27] Sherman, in his annual report for 1881, also echoed Pope: "I do not know the reasons for the Interior Department insisting on the removal of these Indians to Arizona. They must have been very cogent to justify its cost to the settlers and to the government. Victorio's capture is not very probable, but his killing, however cruel it may be, will be done in time."[28]

Pope tried to induce those Mescaleros with Victorio to return to the reservation, for it seemed unlikely that Victorio would ever surrender. He also made the unwelcome suggestion to the secretary of the interior that the Indian Bureau ought to learn what promises had been made to the Warm Springs Apaches from the time of General Howard's visit on. "It is probable," he concluded, "that much would be developed by such an investigation to extenuate, at least, the feeling, if not the conduct, of the tribe."[29] The Mimbres had protested many times that General Howard had promised them that they would remain permanently at Warm Springs.

Recalling that all of the Chiricahuas had been removed because a drunken Chiricahua had killed two whiskey peddlers, Pope blamed that removal for subsequent troubles: renegade Chiricahuas had then gone to Warm Springs and stirred up the Mimbreños; when the renegades were captured by the San Carlos Apache police, the Warm Springs Indians were also moved to San Carlos; and, of course, some had fled to Mescalero and persuaded about half of that band to join them in war. The result of these errors had been five years of the most savage warfare in Arizona and New Mexico.[30]

Early in 1880 Mexico began massing troops for an all-out campaign against the Chiricahuas and Mimbreños, for the two bands had killed and robbed many Mexicans. For a time the two bands had united and were virtually invincible, but in January Juh and Geronimo separated from Victorio. Scout Archie McIntosh, Captain Harry L. Haskell, and Tom Jeffords, contacted Juh and Geronimo and persuaded them to go voluntarily to Camp Apache.[31]

Louis H. Scott, the American consul at Chihuahua City, suggested cooperation between U.S. and Mexican troops in a "war of extermination," with both sides agreeing that either army could cross the border freely in pursuit of Indians. Otherwise, he observed, they would hide in the mountains on one side of the border and raid on the other. Only if they were constantly harassed on both sides of the border was there any likelihood that they would surrender their arms and promise to remain on a reservation. "One may study the Indian character," Scott concluded, "and moralize over his lamentable condition, but his ideas are not firmly fixed on the Indian question until he has been chased by them, and then his mind is settled on the question forever." Scott was apprehensive over the possibility that the renegades would make peace with Mexico and then confine their raiding to the U.S.[32]

In January 1880 General Gerónimo Treviño, who commanded the Mexican forces in Chihuahua, warned U.S. officials that about one hundred Apaches and their families were heading toward Mesilla. Victorio had continued raiding and fighting battles with Mexican troops for several months and apparently hoped to recruit more men at Mescalero. He crossed into Texas below El Paso, but was twice driven back across the Río Grande.

General Pope was certain that Victorio acquired his recruits from among Apaches living in Mexico, but there were also renegades

VICTORIO, NANA, AND THE MIMBREÑOS 225

from many tribes with him. Pope's goal was to disarm the Apaches, for they were, in his words, "a miserable, brutal race, cruel, deceitful and wholly irreclaimable"; and since there was no game to hunt in their country, their only use for guns and horses was to rob and murder.[33] But before the Mimbreños could be disarmed they had to be captured, and that was another matter. Colonel Hatch, seeing so many well-armed Mescalero warriors, was convinced that they supplied Victorio with recruits, and he began planning to disarm and dismount them in order to weaken Victorio.

Although U.S. and Mexican troops were deployed along the whole border, Victorio and his people crossed the Río Grande undetected on a number of occasions. Early in January 1880 Major Morrow's scouts came across their trail, and the command caught up with them on Percha Creek and battled them until dark. Morrow's troops stayed on Victorio's trail along the eastern side of the Black Mountains, passing near the Warm Springs agency. They fought another indecisive battle in the San Mateos. With three columns of troops after him, Victorio divided his men into small parties to scour the country for horses and mules, grouping at Las Ánimas Creek. There the commands of Captain Carroll and Lieutenant Rucker found them and drove them back across the Río Grande into eastern New Mexico. Half of Victorio's men were now on foot, and the pursuers moved quickly to cut them off from either the Mescaleros or Mexico. From time to time one or another of the columns overtook the Apaches, but Victorio's skill in choosing defensive positions continued to baffle them; on occasion the Apaches turned and became the pursuers.

Colonel Hatch sent more cavalry companies to the region and suggested that the families of the Warm Springs Apaches be returned from San Carlos to that agency as bait, believing that this stratagem might make it possible to end the war. If Victorio's men did not fall into a trap trying to reach their families, they would surely join him and slow up his movements enough so that the troops could overtake and annihilate his band. But the Indian Bureau refused to comply, for this would mean reversing the concentration policy. It was up to the army to bring Victorio's band to San Carlos.

During the late winter and spring, while Victorio made his swift and destructive raids across southern New Mexico, the press was vitriolic in its criticisms of the army. "We are dreaming of a golden age—a future empire—and fifty dirty, lousy Indians have us in a state of siege," wrote the editor of the Silver City *Daily Southwest* in

March 1880. And in June the same paper blasted Colonel Hatch: "Hitchity Hatch-ity, here I come. Old Vic's after me, but you must keep mum."[34]

Hatch, whose hard-riding troops were under particular attack for failing to kill Victorio and his band, commented on the "exceeding roughness" of the mountain ranges where Victorio found refuge. "The well-known Modoc Lava beds are," he said, "a lawn— compared to them."[35] He took personal command of the campaign and reorganized his men into three battalions, each under a seasoned Indian fighter. The forces in Texas and Arizona were alerted and readied to help conclude what he hoped would be the final campaign. Hatch planned to subdue the Mimbreños and defang the Mescaleros at the same time.

Victorio was reported to be camped in the San Andrés Mountains, not far from Mescalero. Agent Russell sent Caballero and another Mescalero chief to urge Victorio to surrender at the agency, but neither chief returned. Russell soon learned that about thirty-five Mescalero families had also joined the Warm Springs band. Caballero eventually returned with Nana's promise to settle at Warm Springs if he could do so in peace, but Caballero and some of the other Mescaleros slipped away to rejoin Victorio.

Hatch ordered his three battalions to converge on Mescalero in April 1880 while a fourth column under Colonel Grierson marched west from Fort Concho in Texas to intercept any Mescaleros fleeing in that direction. Part of Captain Carroll's command, with men and animals weakened from drinking from a spring that contained gypsum, staggered into Membrillo Canyon badly in need of water. They found Victorio and his men in control of the springs there. The startled Apaches, perceiving that there was something wrong with the troops, quickly surrounded them and prepared to kill them one at a time. Ill or not the troops fought all night and were saved from annihilation only by the timely arrival of part of Hatch's battalion. It still required a day of hard fighting to dislodge the Apaches and gain control of the springs. When a courier brought him news of the battle Hatch changed his route and marched hastily to Membrillo Canyon, barely missing Victorio and his men. The Apaches hid as the troops marched by, and Hatch lost an opportunity to end the war.

Once safely out of reach of the troops Victorio divided his band; one party headed west for the Black Mountains, while the other turned toward Mescalero. The troops who had taken part in the battle were convinced that Victorio still had many Mescaleros and Comanches with him.

When he learned of the trail leading toward Mescalero Hatch decided to carry out his plan to disarm the Mescaleros and sequester their horses and mules. His troops were already in position around the reservation, and he had earlier demanded that Russell order the Mescaleros who were not involved with Victorio to move close to agency headquarters. He now informed Russell of his intentions. If they had known his purpose, Russell told him, the Mescaleros would not have come in—they came only because they trusted him, and now their trust was to be betrayed. At first he refused to cooperate, but when Hatch threatened to order his Apache scouts to attack the Mescaleros, Russell had no choice.[36] He believed that the Mescaleros would surrender their guns and horses peacefully if they were assured that their belongings would be returned when the troubles were over. Hatch agreed and also promised that those who obeyed would be well treated.

When the startled Mescaleros were lined up for a head count just over three hundred were present, for many had been frightened off by the sight of so many troops and Apache scouts. Gatewood's scouts, seeing the Mescaleros driving horses and perhaps unaware that they had been ordered to bring their animals to the agency, suspected that they were escaping and attacked. A number of Mescaleros were killed in this and other skirmishes but thirty or forty warriors did escape. All who had surrendered were herded into a corral which had long been used for cattle and horses and were kept there an unreasonably long time.

Hatch immediately ordered a search of those who had surrendered, confiscating a few guns and some ammunition and, Russell suspected, other property belonging to the Indians. He wrote a long report of the affair to the Indian Bureau, charging Hatch with unnecessary harshness and mistreatment of peaceful Indians. The secretary of the interior forwarded it to the War Department for an explanation; the secretary of war gave it to General Sherman to answer. Sherman, who had no one to pass the report along to, reminded the secretary of war that the Indian Bureau had agreed to the disarming of the Mescaleros and said he was confident that Colonel Hatch would not permit any unnecessary cruelty. He pointed out, furthermore, that "Undue sympathy for these savages amounts to aiding and abetting a common enemy." Russell agreed concerning undue sympathy toward a common enemy, adding, however, "I do feel and express sympathy for those that are at peace, and obedient to the requirements of the Government."[37]

The troops drove off all the Mescalero horses and mules that could be found. Some stolen animals were returned to their former owners, and the rest were sold or turned over to the army pack trains. The Mescaleros would never be compensated for their losses. Troops remained on the reservation until January 1881.[38]

The disarming of the Mescaleros and the way it was carried out raised a lingering storm of protest, and Hatch was subjected to much abuse. Probably his action was a necessary part of running Victorio into the earth, for there was no doubt that Mescaleros had joined his war parties on many occasions. In all of the fighting except for the battle with the Apache scouts Victorio gave more than he received; and although he withdrew from one mountain range to another he was not driven, and those who followed too closely on his trail were made to pay for their rashness. But even though he inflicted more casualties than he suffered, every loss was serious for Victorio, as his chances of finding new recruits who were already seasoned warriors steadily declined. The Mescalero reservation had been his best recruiting ground, and now he had lost that source of men and supplies.[39] He could only fight on with fewer and fewer men, knowing that in the end all would be killed or captured.

Most of the Mescaleros who escaped Hatch's net headed south toward the Guadalupes. By this time Hatch had learned what Crook had discovered earlier—that the only way to fight Apaches successfully was to use Apache scouts as fighting men. But when he asked for two more companies of Apache scouts, he was refused. Senior army officers were not prepared to admit that Apaches were more effective fighters than soldiers were.

The Apaches' hit-and-run raids continued to inflame the New Mexican citizenry throughout 1880 and the army continued to be bitterly attacked for its failure to contain or capture the raiders. But army detachments were campaigning after Victorio as hard as was physically possible, and in the process many officers and men were broken in health and dozens of horses were ruined. Colonel Henry Grierson, for example, made a hard fifteen-hundred-mile ride through the Sacramento and Guadalupe Mountains of eastern New Mexico without finding the elusive Victorio.

Unable to take his revenge on the Coyotero scouts, Victorio sent his son Washington and a small party to raid the band's camps around the San Carlos agency. At Ash Creek, when they were twenty miles from their goal, the raiders came unexpectedly on some hunters from San Carlos and were forced to fight. After dark the raiders rode on to the Gila and at daybreak fired into some of the camps at the subagency, killing several and running off some horses. Those attacked, however, were not Coyoteros but Nednhis, members of Juh's and Geronimo's bands. Arizona citizens soon had a moment of terror, for it was widely believed that Victorio and ninety men had cornered a company of the Sixth Cavalry in Rocky Canyon. It was nearly the other way around, however, for troops and scouts caught up with the raiders in the afternoon, but at night they escaped to rejoin Victorio in New Mexico. [40]

In May 1880 Hatch, his men and horses exhausted, camped on the Fresco River and requested fresh troops and scouts. Chief of scouts Henry K. Parker asked Major Morrow for permission to pursue the hostiles with his scout company. Morrow agreed, and Parker and his men found Victorio's camp in an isolated canyon near the headwaters of the Palomas River. Parker, knowing that a critical moment had arrived, sent his scouts out a few at a time to determine the best strategy. They reported that the camp was in a position that could be attacked. Parker sent a Mexican packer to Hatch informing him that he had Victorio pinned down, and requesting troops and more ammunition.

At dark Parker sent twenty scouts in one direction and thirty in another; with the remaining ten he cautiously took up a third position near the hostiles' camp. They moved slowly and silently all night and by daybreak all three groups were in their designated positions. The thirty scouts opened fire. The startled hostiles fled, some without their guns, toward the place where Parker and his scouts were hiding. A volley from them turned the survivors in another direction, where the twenty scouts were already looking down their rifle barrels.

Victorio's men quickly recovered their composure, took up defensive positions, and returned the fire. The fight continued all day while Victorio called on the scouts to join him against the white eyes. Since he received no reply from Hatch, Parker concluded that his messenger had been killed. Late in the day he and the scouts were dangerously low on ammunition, with only about five rounds apiece. They had killed at least thirty of Victorio's people and run off most of their horses and mules. But since Hatch had sent neither ammunition nor troops there was nothing they could do but withdraw. Completely out of provisions, they killed a horse for food.

For reasons that are still mysterious Hatch had simply assigned the packer to another pack train and then hurried off to Fort Craig, where he sent a telegram asserting that his column, with some help from the scouts, had struck Victorio's band. Parker never received a satisfactory answer as to why his request had been ignored, but he knew that the first real opportunity to force Victorio to surrender had been foolishly thrown away. The kindest words said in Colonel Hatch's defense was that he was an "imbecile."[41] This was Victorio's only defeat thus far, and it was by other Apaches, not army troops.

After Parker and the scouts withdrew, Victorio divided his band into three parties, and all headed for Mexico by different routes. From this time on, Victorio, who had previously been invincible, was plagued by misfortune, for among the slain were some of his ablest warriors, men who could not be replaced. Major Morrow quickly took the trail of one of the three parties, caught up with warriors herding stolen stock, and killed ten of them, including Victorio's son Washington.

Agent Russell asked some of the Mescalero headmen to send messengers to their people who were still with Victorio, informing them that this was their last chance to surrender. The Mescalero headmen refused, saying that they would not go to Victorio's camp and that those who were with him deserved to be killed. Victorio had frequently urged them to join him, but since he brought them only trouble they would not listen. Russell argued that the Mescaleros with Victorio were prisoners, but his pleas met a stony silence.

The defeat of Victorio's band at the hands of Parker's scouts excited hopes that the Apache war could be speedily concluded. Colonel Hatch insisted that the fugitives be followed across the border before they could rest and recover or join forces with Geronimo and Juh. On this occasion, however, Mexican officials refused permission, for they had a number of military units after the Apaches.

At San Carlos agent Joseph C. Tiffany suggested sending a group to persuade Victorio to surrender, adding that some of the San Carlos Apaches were willing to kill or capture him. Nothing came of this suggestion, however, probably because of the army's reluctance to rely on Apaches for fighting.

For a time Victorio camped in the mountains west of Eagle Springs, Texas. Possibly in an attempt to reach Mescalero, he crossed into Texas and cornered a small force under Colonel Grierson. Only the timely arrival of reinforcements saved Grierson's command and forced Victorio back into Mexico.

In August 1880 Victorio moved north again. Forewarned by his scouts, Grierson set a trap for him with two companies of the Tenth Cavalry. The wily old warrior refused to enter it and, when the troops opened fire prematurely, sent his warriors to the attack. Grierson had other troops concealed nearby, however, and they joined in the battle. Late in the afternoon an army supply train approached, escorted by black troops of the Twenty-fourth Infantry, who were concealed in the wagons. When the Apaches attempted to loot the train to replenish their ammunition, they met a devastating fire. Victorio retreated into Mexico once more, leaving his camp and supplies behind.

The Mescaleros under Caballero now tried to part company with the Warm Springs band, but Victorio killed Caballero, and the remaining Mescaleros had no choice but to remain or face the same fate. The knew that Victorio's time was running out, and they watched for a chance to leave him.

In October of 1880 veteran Indian fighter Joaquín Terrazas of Chihuahua was searching for Victorio with a large force of Mexican troops. His scouts came across Victorio's trail heading east, and Terrazas followed it. At Tres Castillos they cornered Victorio and most of his people, at a time when they were almost out of ammunition, and fought an all-night battle. Some of the Mescaleros were away on a hunt, and Nana had led a Mimbreño party in search of ammunition. Some of the women and children and a few warriors escaped, but many were captured. After his celebrated victory Terrazas informed Hatch that his troops had killed seventy-eight Apaches—Victorio and sixty warriors as well as some women and children. Victorio's career was ended, and most of his warriors had died with him, but the Apache war was not yet over. Nana and at least thirty warriors had escaped annihilation.

After the Tres Castillos fight Nana sent Kaetennae to search for survivors. He reported that Victorio and some others had taken their own lives after they ran out of ammunition. [42] A month after the Tres Castillos defeat a party of Apaches attacked Mexican troops south of Carrizal, killing nine including a sergeant who was riding in Victorio's saddle and who was hacked to pieces by the irate Apaches. Apache hostilities were widespread in Mexico, and many Mexicans were killed and mutilated. [43]

After Victorio's death every Apache attack or raid was attributed to Nana, although there were also Chiricahua, Nednhi, and other renegades in Mexico who crossed the border occasionally. Gordo, another Warm Springs Apache, also had a small band which joined

Nana occasionally. But even when attacks occurred in several places at the same time, it was concluded that Nana had divided his forces.[44]

Nana, who was perhaps seventy years old by this time, still wanted peace and a reservation at Warm Springs, but he preferred to die fighting than return to San Carlos. He was a guerrilla leader of the same qualities as Victorio, and he carried on the war as the slain chief would have done. Despite his age and infirmities, no Apache had greater endurance than Nana. Late in 1880 he crossed the Río Grande with a small party and was joined there by about twenty-five Mescaleros. They etched a bloody path across southern New Mexico, killing sheepherders, prospectors, and anyone else unfortunate enough to fall in their path. They came on a detachment of the Ninth Cavalry, skirmished with it, and then headed west; the cavalry stayed grimly on their trail, giving them no chance to rest. Troops caught up with the Apaches once more, but Nana's warriors soon outdistanced them on their way to southwestern New Mexico.

With cavalry and civilian parties constantly in search of them the Apaches moved from one mountain range to another. They stopped to fight only where there were large boulders to shield them and mountains at their backs. When they scattered into the mountains, pursuit had to be abandoned. It was a hard and exhausting life, but to Nana's people it was preferable to living at San Carlos. Half-starved and weary, with only the ammunition and guns they could capture or steal and handicapped by having to protect women and children, Nana and about seventy-five warriors outmaneuvered and outfought the cavalry forces that kept relentlessly on their trail. The renegades rode incredible distances, replacing their worn-out horses with fresh ones stolen from ranches.

Several groups of Anglos roamed the mountains of southwestern New Mexico and other Apache refuges. One party of thirty-six men had combed the San Mateos without seeing any sign of Apaches. One day during the spring of 1881—forgetting the old frontier adage that when one saw signs of Apaches he must be careful, but when he saw none he must be even more careful—they rested at noon, leaving several men to guard the horses. Nana's warriors swooped down on them, killing one, wounding others, and stampeding all of their horses.

Lieutenant John F. Guilfoyle and his black troopers stubbornly followed Nana's trail, overtaking the Apaches several times for brief battles. Finally, when his men and horses were exhausted and their equipment had worn out, Guilfoyle had to give up the chase and rebuild his company. Other forces followed the fast-moving Apaches, and in several skirmishes killed a few of them. The loss of a single warrior was a serious blow to Nana, for replacements could rarely be found. General John Pope acknowledged the difficulties in bringing the Apaches to bay. "There is no great trouble in dealing with them when found," he said. "The difficulty is to find them."[45]

In the Black Mountains, a favorite summer refuge of the Apaches in bygone days, Nana found no peace from the troops. He turned again toward Mexico but in Guerrillo Canyon ran head on into twenty troopers of the Ninth Cavalry under Lieutenant G. W. Smith. In the fierce fighting that followed Smith and five others were killed. Although Nana continued on to Mexico unmolested, the army reported that he had been defeated. The Apaches were happily unaware of their defeat and would have been astonished to learn of it. In about six weeks this aged warrior and a few dozen hardy Apaches had covered a thousand miles through enemy territory, fighting off pursuers and living off the country. They had killed fifty men or more, captured or stolen several hundred horses, and evaded at least one thousand troops as well as hundreds of civilians.

Hiding in the Sierra Madre refuges were the remnants of several bands—Juh's Nednhis; Chiricahuas under Nachez, Chato, and Chihuahua; the Chihinne or Warm Springs people under old Nana and the rising war leader Kaetennae; and the Bedonkohes of Geronimo. Because other Apaches were serving as scouts against them their cause was virtually hopeless, but most preferred to die fighting in the mountains than to perish from disease at San Carlos. Some were convinced that there was no escape from reservation life, but they knew others would kill them if they tried to leave. Most, including Nana and Geronimo, were convinced that they would receive better treatment from army officers then from civilian agents. They had feared General Crook, whom they called *Nantan Lupan* (Gray Wolf Chief), but they also knew him as a man of his word.

XI
The Cibecue
Outbreak

AFTER CLUM'S DEPARTURE from San Carlos on July 1, 1877 the Apaches had many reasons to be discontented. Because contractors were unable to supply beef cattle of the weight called for in the government contract the Indian Bureau would not allow the agent to accept any. The famished Indians prepared to flee the reservation in search of food, but General Orlando B. Willcox, commander of the Department of Arizona, interceded and supplied enough flour to feed them for a week. He briefly considered making the San Carlos Indians prisoners of war so the army could legally feed them. The Indian Bureau was finally stirred to action and supplies of food were provided with greater regularity for a time, but dishonest contractors and agents continued to defraud the Apaches.

At the time Victorio's band was brought back to San Carlos in December 1878 agent Hart was under suspicion of graft and fraud. Early in 1879 the Indian Bureau sent Inspector J. H. Hammond to investigate. He found that after Hart inspected the cattle purchased for the reservation, he left the animals with the contractor, who delivered smaller or inferior cattle when beef issues were actually made. Hammond closed this loophole by ordering that the cattle be marked with a special brand when purchased. Hart resigned shortly thereafter, leaving Hammond temporarily in charge at San Carlos.

Hammond proved no more capable of resisting temptation than his predecessor had been, for he was soon involved in a mining venture with Hart and others. He discontinued his investigation, assured Hart that he would not be prosecuted for any frauds discovered, and surveyed the reservation's western boundary in order to exclude a mine that Hart had sold to the son of Commissioner of Indian Affairs Hayt.

In April 1878 Geronimo, Ponce, and others slipped away to Mexico where they joined Juh and Nolgee at the former's refuge.

Later Lieutenant H. L. Haskell, scout Archie McIntosh, and Tom Jeffords made contact with them and urged them to return to San Carlos. Weary of the hard life and constant harassment by Mexican troops, they surrendered at Camp Rucker late in the year and returned to San Carlos.

In March 1879 McIntosh, angered at the corruption he had observed at San Carlos, wrote a confidential letter to the commander of Camp McDowell. To McIntosh's chagrin the letter was published in the Phoenix *Herald*.[1] The Board of Indian Commissioners, hearing these rumors of graft and collusion between Hart and Hammond, sent General Clinton B. Fisk, president of the board, to San Carlos to see for himself. Fisk was shocked to learn that the graft was condoned by Commissioner Hayt, who had kept reports of dishonesty from reaching Secretary of the Interior Carl Schurz. Thanks to General Fisk's visit and to McIntosh's letter, Schurz immediately relieved Hayt, giving him one hour to empty his desk and clear out.[2]

Captain Adna R. Chaffee was then ordered from Fort McDowell to San Carlos to restore order. Chaffee dismissed most of the civilian employees and reorganized the Apache police. Aware that many Coyoteros still longed for their own lands at Camp Apache, he allowed 355 of them to return. Chaffee's job was not easy. He discovered that the beef contractors had tampered with the scales used for weighing cattle. He also faced the usual problem of delayed deliveries; clothing and blankets needed for winter arrived only in mid-February, barely in time to prevent an outbreak.

Although both Clum and Jeffords, each an experienced and effective Apache agent, were interested in obtaining the San Carlos agency, on the recommendation of the Dutch Reformed Church the Indian Bureau appointed J. C. Tiffany of New York to the post. Tiffany arrived at San Carlos in June 1880 and immediately started construction of a school. He planned to open it in the spring of 1881, but in December a number of prominent Apaches insisted that their sons receive instruction immediately, and Tiffany agreed. He kept many Apaches employed on projects begun by Chaffee; even Juh and Geronimo agreed to work as long as they received full rations. New irrigation ditches opened fourteen hundred additional acres for cultivation, and in 1881 the Apaches had a successful harvest of corn, wheat, and barley.

By means of the Apache police under the direction of A. D. Sterling Tiffany maintained strict discipline, but his problems multiplied. Miners flocked into the McMillen District and Mormon farmers used the Gila for irrigating their farms, causing crop failures for the Apaches downriver. Others encroached on reservation lands near Fort Apache. And when coal deposits were discovered in the southern part of the San Carlos reservation miners ignored reservation boundaries until the army removed them. Part of the trouble was that the reservation's limits had not been marked by an official survey, and Congress refused to provide funds for one despite warnings that a serious conflict was brewing. The miners leased reservation lands and paid royalties on the minerals removed, which temporarily eased the problem although the constant intrusions on reservation lands drove some Apaches to desperation.[3]

In this potentially explosive situation two prominent Coyotero chiefs, Diablo and Eskiole, were killed in feuds between bands during the fall of 1880 and spring of 1881. Nocadelklinny, a Coyotero medicine man, began holding dances around the graves of the two chiefs. His claim that he could bring them back to life aroused intense excitement among the frustrated and desperate Apaches, just as the Ghost Dance would among the Sioux nearly a decade later. It was the first moment of hope for them.

Eight years earlier, Nocadelklinny had enlisted in Company A, Indian scouts, at Camp Apache for Crook's campaign against the Tontos. Company A was under chief of scouts Corydon Eliphalet Cooley, with Alchise as sergeant, and was attached to Company I, Twenty-third Infantry, under Captain George M. Randall. Late in November 1872 they scouted the area between Camp Apache and Camp McDowell, finding only a few hostiles. From McDowell they moved into the lower Verde country. It was this force that surprised and destroyed a large camp of Tonto Apaches on Turret Mountain late in March 1873 after following their trail from near Wickenburg.

The Coyotero scouts were discharged in June, when their six-months enlistments expired. A short time later Nocadelklinny accompanied a delegation of Apaches to Washington, where each was given a peace medal by President Grant. Some time after this Nocadelklinny attended an Indian school at Santa Fe where he learned a smattering of Christianity, especially of the prophets who meditated in isolation and of the Resurrection. On his return he resumed his activities as a medicine man, frequently going alone into the mountains to fast and meditate.

By 1875 Nocadelklinny had achieved enough prominence to merit comment by the Camp Apache post surgeon, L. Y. Loring, six years before the "Cibecue affair" brought him a moment of national prominence. Nocadelklinny, Loring wrote, "about fifty years of age, is an honest sober man. He is chief of the largest subtribe which may be accounted for by his generosity and mildness. He controls his people with a steady hand, and is impartial in his dealings with both white men and Indians. At one time he was hostile, but is now well affected towards the Government."[4]

His fame gradually spread to other Coyotero bands, and he began holding dances at which he prophesied the resurrection of dead warriors and the return of the former days of Apache freedom. He claimed, too, that the shirt he wore had magical powers to protect him against enemy bullets. The dances attracted increasing numbers of Apaches, for all were desperate and willing to grasp at any straw of hope.

Because of the growing notoriety of Nocadelklinny's dances, Lieutenant Thomas Cruse, Sixth Cavalry, who was in charge of scout Company A, sent his chief of scouts, Sam Bowman, to observe the dances and report on them. Bowman, who was half Choctaw, returned and, to Cruse's amazement, immediately resigned, saying that he wanted to go to Indian Territory. Cruse pressed him for a reason, but he would say only that he had been in Arizona for seven years and that it was time to visit his people. As soon as he was released he was on his way. Chief packer Nat Nobles later told Cruse why Bowman had left so suddenly. "He said that kind of dance always meant trouble with his people," Nobles explained. "He believed it would bring the same here and he didn't want to get mixed up in it. So he decided to go see his folks."[5]

In July 1881 Nocadelklinny visited Colonel Eugene A. Carr, Sixth Cavalry, who was temporarily in command at Fort Apache, and informed him that he was holding dances near Cibecue Creek in order to raise the spirits of dead warriors. Carr and agent Tiffany gave him permission to hold a dance near the north fork of the White River, not far from the post. Lieutenant Cruse, who with other officers observed the dance, noted that Nocadelklinny had a hypnotic influence over the Apaches. What astonished Cruse even more was the fraternizing between groups and bands that previously had been enemies; perhaps this was the most ominous sign of the medicine man's growing influence. Certainly it gave Cruse cause for "thought and speculation" to see Apaches whose own people had tried to kill them walking about as if among friends. Nocadelklinny's followers, Cruse concluded, were getting out of control.[6]

Nocadelklinny and his following returned to Carrizo Creek in the Cibecue area and continued the dances. Apache scouts at Fort Apache asked for passes in order to attend the dances; they frequently overstayed their leave and appeared physically exhausted and unfit for duty when they returned. Cruse observed too that they were becoming sullen and insubordinate, and some remarked that the country belonged to them, not to the white eyes. Something or someone, Cruse knew, was giving them new thoughts. The same attitude was becoming widespread among the general reservation population, for all of them seemed to have lost interest in work, as if expecting soon to be relieved of that onerous aspect of the white eyes' "civilization." When the post trader refused further credit to one warrior the Apache merely shrugged. "What difference does it make?" he asked himself. "Pretty quickly now, I'll have it all, anyway."[7]

The one Anglo who knew the Coyoteros and their country better than any other was the former scout Cooley, who with his wife (the daughter of Coyotero chief Pedro) was ranching near the reservation. But Colonel Carr, for personal reasons, declined to consult Cooley—the former scout was a friend of General Crook, and Carr had no great admiration for Crook.

The dead warriors Nocadelklinny had promised to bring back to life failed to appear, but Nocadelklinny's promises and performances nevertheless attracted growing numbers of Apaches to the dances. When his incantations failed to resurrect the dead chieftains, however, several disappointed Apaches threatened to kill him. Nocadelklinny saved himself by saying that the dead chiefs refused to return until all of the white eyes had been driven out of the country, and that day, he predicted, would soon come.

When he learned of this ominous forecast, Colonel Carr reported the matter to General Willcox. "It is now reported to me by Interpreter Hurle [sic]," Carr wrote, "that Nockaydetklinne is telling the Indians that the dead say they will not return because of the white people; that when the white people leave the dead will return and that the whites will be out of the country when the corn gets ripe. Hurle thinks his next move may be to hasten the departure of the whites, and that he may be working them up to a frame of mind suitable for that purpose." Carr added that he was not certain whether or not the rumors were serious, but he felt it was his duty to inform the departmental commander.[8]

Willcox instructed Carr to keep a close watch on the situation, to take any steps necessary to prevent trouble, and to keep in touch with the agent at San Carlos. Carr informed Tiffany that he did not consider Nocadelklinny dangerous, adding prophetically that to arrest him might start an uprising. Later, however, he reported that scout Sam Bowman expected an Apache outbreak after they had harvested their corn. This news worried Tiffany, and he was even more concerned when Carr forwarded Nocadelklinny's statement that the dead Apaches refused to return until the white eyes were gone from their land. Carr added that his interpreter "says that the Indians think this Doctor will be the head of all the Indians, that he says the ground will turn over, the dead will rise and the Indians be above the whites; that they will have possession of this Post, that the soldiers will have to give up their horses to them, etc."[9]

Tiffany sent a runner to Nocadelklinny, urging him to come to San Carlos for a talk and inviting him to hold his dances at San Carlos, but the medicine man did not reply. Tiffany then sent some San Carlos Apache police to escort him to the agency. Although they were regarded as virtually invincible, they returned after a few days in a sullen mood and without either their guns or Nocadelklinny. Apparently Nocadelklinny's followers had overpowered them and taken their weapons.

After one unusually frenzied dance an entranced Apache approached Nocadelklinny. He knew that those of his people who had died still lived but were invisible, he said, and he asked Nocadelklinny to call on the great leaders who had died to help the living: ask them, he begged, what we should do about the white eyes. Nocadelklinny and three of his closest followers went to a mesa top to fast. "Come to us! Show yourselves to us again," they called to the spirits. "Tell us, your people, what we must do."[10]

> "There appeared to us," one of the men told Cruse some years later, three of those great ones. They were like shadows at first, but we saw them rise out of the ground, very slowly, and coming no further than the knees. All about them they looked, then to us they said: "Why do you call upon us? Why do you disturb us? We do not wish to come back. The buffalo are gone. White people are everywhere in the land that was ours. We do not wish to come back."
>
> And we cried to them, saying, "But tell us what we must do!"
>
> And they answered us as they began to sink into the ground and to become shadows.
>
> "Live at peace with the white men and let us rest."

When the four men reported to the others, each group interpreted the vision in its own way. None, however, doubted it, for it was an article of faith that the dead still lived, invisible except at certain times. "To malcontents who had been preaching a war of extermination against the whites," Cruse wrote, "it was a solemn injunction to clear the Apache country of the enemy. To no more than a handful was it a command to remain at peace. Naturally, the war faction was our interest."[11]

The situation at both Camp Apache and San Carlos worsened, for the trusted scouts were increasingly insubordinate, grumbling that if the white eyes didn't leave they would be driven out. When the San Carlos agent refused to give passes, hundreds of Indians left the reservation anyway. Tiffany ordered the Apache police to stop them, but was told that was impossible. Now thoroughly frightened, Tiffany was more convinced than ever that Nocadelklinny was a serious threat to peace; he wrote Carr suggesting that he arrest or kill the medicine man. Colonel Carr did not, however, intend to take such hazardous action on his own authority; the army was restricted from acting unless the agent requested help.

Another message, this time from General Willcox, directed Carr to arrest Nocadelklinny "if you deem it necessary to prevent trouble after consulting with the agent at San Carlos."[12] Still loath to act, Carr consulted Lieutenant Cruse concerning the attitude of the Apache scout company, for he had heard rumors that their loyalty was now doubtful. Admitting that he expected trouble, Cruse replied that although the scouts wanted to be loyal, in a showdown they would not support the whites for their families were all with Nocadelklinny and they would probably be swept along with them. Carr was astounded. "But the scouts have always been loyal. They have obeyed orders under the most adverse conditions, even shooting some of their own relations when occasion demanded it." He asked for suggestions. Cruse urged that the scouts be sent to Fort Huachuca and replaced by scout Company C from Fort McDowell; it was composed of Yavapais, Hualapais, and Chiricahuas, who did not know the Cibecue band.[13] Interpreter Hurrle agreed with Cruse, for although he insisted that Nocadelklinny himself was peaceful, there were many others who would not hesitate to fight, and Hurrle was sure that certain "bad men" were planning an outbreak.

Carr requested permission to dismiss any scouts who appeared unreliable and asked for two companies of troops from Fort Grant to strengthen his command and make a show of force. Just after the message had been sent however, the telegraph line suffered one of its frequent failures, and melting snow as well as heavy rains made the Gila impassable for couriers. Partly because the telegraph lines were out of action much of the time, Carr received no answer to his request until early September, when it was too late.

Because Tiffany continued to suggest arresting or killing Nocadelklinny, Carr informed him that such action would be more likely to cause trouble than to prevent it. At any rate Carr refused to act merely on Tiffany's suggestion, for he would then be responsible for anything that might happen. "Please state clearly whether you want him arrested and how," he concluded. Tiffany replied that he wanted Nocadelklinny arrested or killed or both—and before the next dance.[14]

Carr still hesitated, but a few days later, on August 28, when the telegraph line was temporarily functioning, Willcox ordered him to arrest the "Indian doctor, who you report as stirring up trouble," as soon as possible. Carr still considered the arrest unwise, but Willcox's order left him no choice. He wired Willcox, nevertheless, that "I wish it to be observed that I did not report the Indian doctor as stirring up hostilities. . . . " He had, he said, merely reported statements and inferences of the interpreter "for what they might be worth."[15]

The situation became even more explosive when a clerk at Fort Apache started a rumor that the Apaches would be moved from Camp Apache because of Nocadelklinny's activities. The rumor spread quickly, adding considerably to the agitation. By August 17, when Carr had learned of it from a respected old chief, Notchiclish, the damage was done. The chief was not worried about Nocadelklin-ny, who had, he said, already been paid more than one hundred animals to raise the dead. He believed that the medicine man would soon possess all that the Apaches owned.

Lieutenant John Bourke, who had heard settlers express their fears of Nocadelklinny and his prophecies while on his way to Fort Apache late in August, found to his surprise equal uneasiness among the army officers at the fort. Carr asked Bourke to visit Pedro's camp, for this would be a subtle reminder of General Crook's Apache campaigns. Bourke, with Lieutenant Carter, complied with this request and found the Apaches drinking tizwin, excited, irrita-ble, and "saucy." Both Bourke and Carter were convinced that trouble was coming. Some Apaches asked Bourke if he had seen any Navajos on their way to Camp Apache, for some were expected—perhaps to take part in an uprising. Bourke continued his journey as the troops were preparing for the march to Cibecue Creek.

Expecting two companies to arrive from Fort Thomas in a day or two to guard Fort Apache, Carr assembled his officers on the after-noon of August 28 and read them the telegram from Willcox order-ing the arrest of the "Indian doctor." All present expressed fears that this might cause the outbreak they hoped to avoid. Carr replied that it was an order and must be obeyed. Captain Edward C. Hentig, who had received orders to report to Jefferson Barracks for recruiting duty, asked permission to accompany the troops, and Carr agreed. Troops D and E, Sixth Cavalry, and the pack train would march in the morning. The only question, Carr said, was whether or not to take the Apache scouts, and he asked Cruse for his opinion. Although he had doubts as to the reliability of the scouts for this particular campaign, Cruse recommended that they be taken. Carr concurred, deciding that they should accompany the cavalry rather than remain at Fort Apache, where there would be only one infantry company under Major Neville A. Cochran until the reinforcements arrived from Camp Thomas. Since the telegraph line to Camp Thomas was out Carr had no way of knowing that high water in the Gila had prevented the troops from crossing and that they had been ordered back to Thomas.

As was customary the troops passed in review before setting out from the fort. The force consisted of seventy-nine troopers, four officers, twenty-four Apache scouts, and six packers under Nat Nobles. The scouts led the way single file, for it was not necessary for them to spread out fan-like to search for enemies. The column had been gone only a short time when Major Cochran noticed unusual excitement among the Apaches around the fort. Later in the day it appeared that many of them, heavily armed, were following Carr's trail. Cochran dispatched a messenger to warn Carr and to inquire when he could expect reinforcements to arrive.

That night, camped at Carrizo Creek, about twenty-five miles from Fort Apache, Carr informed the scouts that he wanted only to talk to Nocadelklinny concerning rumors that whites would soon leave the area. Apache scout Sergeant Mose asked permission to take two scouts and ride ahead to inform Nocadelklinny that the troops would not harm him and to prevent his followers from attacking the troops. If Nocadelklinny had not stated that the whites would soon leave the country, Carr assured Mose, he would be released.

For several weeks the scouts had not been given ammunition because of the suspicion that some were under Nocadelklinny's influence. Now Carr ordered ammunition issued to them, explaining later, "I had to take chances. They were enlisted soldiers of my command; and I could not have found the medicine man without them. I deemed it better also that if they should prove unfaithful it should not occur at the Post."[16]

About 3:00 in the morning of August 30 Sergeant Mose and two other Apache scouts rode ahead toward Nocadelklinny's camp, fol-

Sánchez
Western History Collection, University of Oklahoma

lowed an hour and a half later by Cruse and the scout company, and at daybreak by the main force. Carr reported later that he had learned from Mose that Nocadelklinny's camp was a few miles above the Verde crossing. He suspected that the Apaches might be ready to defend the crossing, so he surprised them by taking a direct route to the Apache camp near Cibecue Creek, arriving in the afternoon. As Cruse approached the camp the renegade Sánchez galloped toward him, painted for war and brandishing a pistol and a Winchester carbine. "What do you want here, *Nantan Eclatten* (Raw, Virgin Lieutenant)?" he asked. Cruse replied that they were not looking for him. Sánchez rode off. More painted Apaches galloped up, but made no threatening gestures. Mose led Cruse to the medicine man, who was lying on a pile of Navajo blankets, apparently exhausted. Nocadelklinny was small, light-skinned, and ascetic looking, Cruse noted. As the cavalry drew up in a line before him, Nocadelklinny welcomed them gravely.

Through the interpreter Carr informed him of the reason for his coming, explained that he would treat him as a friend until the charges had been investigated, and promised that if they were not true he would be released. But, Carr said, the meetings and dances must be stopped for a time. Nocadelklinny listened intently. "Say that I cannot go now," he told the interpreter. "I have matters of importance to settle before leaving this place. Say that if the soldiers will go back to their post I will follow soon—within three or four days." "No," Carr replied, "that will not do. Tell him that he comes with me—now."[17]

Cruse could feel tension rising in the huge crowd of silent Apaches and he was sure an attack was only moments away. Sergeant Mose and other Apache scouts approached Nocadelklinny, reassuring him that he would not be harmed. The crowd relaxed. Carr ordered Sergeants MacDonald of Troop D and Mose of the scouts to take charge of Nocadelklinny. "He is your prisoner," Carr informed MacDonald. "You will permit nobody to harm him. But if he attempts to escape, or if any of his people fire on us, shoot him instantly." The interpreter explained to Nocadelklinny that he was to be escorted by Sergeant MacDonald and that if he tried to escape or if an attempt was made to rescue him he would be killed. Nocadelklinny smiled. No one would try to rescue him, he said. Carr told him that part of his family could accompany him if he wished.

It appeared that the situation was well in hand and that the Apaches would not interfere with the arrest. MacDonald and Mose each took one of Nocadelklinny's arms and moved him out of the shelter. Carr ordered the column to move out at once and to set up camp farther downstream. He rode off, followed by Troop D and the pack train, leaving the rest of the command to escort Nocadelklinny, who had called for someone to bring his horse and asked his wife to bring him certain things for the journey.

Whoever went after the horse was slow in returning, and those waiting anxiously for Nocadelklinny to mount and accompany them felt the tension still rising. They were surrounded by a huge, still growing crowd of Apaches, many painted and stripped to the waist, as if going into battle. Finally Lieutenant Stanton, commander of Troop D, ordered Sergeant MacDonald to bring Nocadelklinny along. There was an ominous rustling in the crowd, a sound that reminded Lieutenant Cruse of a rattlesnake's warning. The Apaches edged closer to the troops. Carr and the others were already half a mile away and still moving, not looking back, and disappearing from sight as they rounded a bend in the trail. As Cruse and the others started off Nocadelklinny's wife ran ahead of them, doing a "queer little dance" and scattering sacred meal. Downstream, Carr stopped his column to set up camp for the night. To Captain Hentig he remarked that he was "rather ashamed to come out with all this force to arrest one poor little Indian."[18]

When Nocadelklinny and his escort reached the place where Carr's column had crossed the creek he asked through Sergeant Mose if they could continue down the creek beyond the cornfields before crossing, in order to avoid trampling the corn. Stanton and Cruse saw no reason to object, for they could cross the creek almost anywhere, and they rode on a short distance beyond where the others were setting up camp on the opposite side. Apache warriors, painted and armed, swarmed about them until they crossed the stream. When the group reported to Carr the colonel ordered Nocadelklinny placed in an enclosure formed by pack saddles and supplies, adding that he was to be warned to sit there quietly. At the court of inquiry held later the court would make much of the separate routes taken by the troops and would find that Carr had made a grave error of judgment in "dividing" his command in the face of the enemy.[19]

Cruse, who was officer of the day, remarked to Carr that "It looked pretty scaly for a while, as we came along. Those Indians . . . " Carr interrupted, demanding that he explain what he meant. Cruse replied that Apaches had kept pouring onto the trail, stripped and painted for fighting. Where are they now? Carr asked.

Cruse pointed toward the creek, where many Apaches were crossing it. Surprised, Carr shouted to Lieutenant Carter, "Here! Those
Indians mustn't come into camp! Direct Troop Commanders to keep
them out!"[20]

Carter relayed this order to the troop commanders and then
showed the Apache scouts where they were to camp. But Dead Shot
objected. "Too much anthills," he said. "Then go beyond the anthills," Carter replied. At the same time Cruse led Nocadelklinny
into the enclosure the packers had made.

In response to Carter's order Captain Hentig walked, unarmed,
toward the Apaches crossing the creek, shouting "U-ka-she! U-
ka-she" (Go away)!" Most of the Indians stopped momentarily. One
of them, Apache scout Dandy Jim, went up to Captain Hentig and
caught him by the arm. He was a soldier, he said. Hentig allowed
him to enter the camp. A moment of silence followed.

Then three or four Apaches, including Sánchez, raised their rifles
and fired and the shooting immediately became general. Dandy Jim
shot Captain Hentig, and a soldier standing near him also fell dead.
The other scouts loaded their rifles and began firing at the troops.
When the firing started Sergeant MacDonald, according to his
orders, shot Nocadelklinny, who was calling to the Apaches to fight,
saying if he were killed, he would come to life again. His wife threw
herself across his body, wailing his death chant. About this time
Sergeant MacDonald fell with a wound in the leg. Apache Sergeant
Mose rushed up to Cruse and asked for protection from the soldiers;
Mose was the only member of the scout company who did not
mutiny. Sergeant Bowman sat on the ground firing rapidly, while
Carr coolly gave orders.

Soon Nocadelklinny's pony came into sight with the medicine
man's son on its back, galloping through the Apaches toward the
soldiers. Without knowing who was charging them the troops shot
him. His mother screamed and ran. As she passed Captain Hentig's
saddle she grabbed his pistol from its hoster and pointed it at a
soldier, who shot her before she could pull the trigger.

Stanton's troop, the last to reach camp, dismounted and charged,
forcing the Apaches to fall back out of range. Sánchez and others
killed the soldiers guarding Troop D's horses and a few pack mules,
stampeding them. From a distance of several hundred yards the
Apaches fired harmlessly into the camp. During the confusion
Nocadelklinny began crawling away, but the trumpeter of Troop D
saw him. Shouting, "Why, he's not dead!" he placed his revolver
against Nocadelklinny's head and fired.

When darkness fell, the firing ceased. Many Apaches, now fearful of the consequences of the largely spontaneous attack, rode rapidly for their reservation camps, boasting to those they met that they had annihilated the troops who came to arrest Nocadelklinny. Their stories were interpreted by troops at Fort Apache to mean that Carr's entire command had been lost and that the hostiles intended to attack the fort. Major Cochran had learned only the previous day that no reinforcements were coming. He sent civilian scout Thomas Owens with urgent dispatches for Camp Thomas, but Owens had gone only a few miles before Apaches killed him.

Similar rumors reached San Carlos. The telegraph line to Fort Apache was not operating, as usual, so agent Tiffany was unable to confirm the story. The line to Camp Thomas had been repaired, however, and he relayed the story there. Soon newspapers all over the country were printing stories of a new "Custer massacre."

Nocadelklinny though badly wounded, made a number of attempts to crawl to safety, only to receive additional wounds. After dark he made one last attempt, when a sergeant finished him with an axe. The sergeant, John A. ("Give-a-damn") Smith of Troop D, also removed from Nocadelklinny's neck the peace medal President Grant had given him on his visit to Washington in 1873. On the medal was printed the legend "On Earth Peace, Good Will Toward Men. 1871."[21]

After the firing had ceased Colonel Carr ordered a large grave dug inside his tent and interred Captain Hentig's body along with those of three of the troopers. He had Taps played over the grave, partly as a farewell and partly to make the Apaches believe that the troops had bedded down for the night. Although the Apaches greatly outnumbered the troops they rarely fought at night unless attacked, and Carr had decided to march toward Fort Apache.

Troop D, which had lost its horses, was mounted on pack mules. At about ten o'clock the march began, guided by Sergeant Mose and Lieutenant Cruse, on foot. At one point Mose tugged at Cruse's sleeve and whispered a warning. Cruse heard a soft rustling in the grass and knew that Apaches were watching the retreat. There were others hiding along the way, but though the night was dark and the command had difficulty finding its way, it reached Fort Apache on the afternoon of August 31.

Colonel Carr immediately prepared to defend Fort Apache, which had no real defensive bulwarks. The expected attack began shortly after noon the next day, for the Apaches had found a dead pack mule with a load of ammunition. There was desultory firing all afternoon, but it ended at dark and was not resumed. Next morning, there were no Apaches in sight.

Pedro and his Coyotero band had withdrawn to Cloverdale Creek near Cooley's Ranch; other peaceful bands had also moved to remote parts of the reservation, to avoid trouble either with hostile Apaches or with troops. Carr sent John Colvig with dispatches for Camp Thomas, but "Cibicu Charley," as Colvig was known thereafter, was stopped by a large party of Apaches and forced to return. Carr then sent Lieutenant Stanton and most of Troop E to carry a message to Camp Thomas. By September 12 Carr had six troops of his own regiment on hand and others continued to arrive from California and New Mexico until there were at least twenty-three troops or companies in addition to those previously stationed at Fort Apache. In the meantime Apaches had killed a number of soldiers and civilians throughout the region around Fort Apache.

General Willcox ordered Carr to round up any hostiles who might still be in the Cibecue area and also to bring in all Apaches found camping at Cooley's Ranch. He suggested that Carr "hang without trial" any prisoners he took. Carr demurred. "I think it would be well not to hang any," he said, "till after all have fully shown their hands, as it would make the rest desperate." If the scouts were guilty only of desertion and had not fired on the troops, he reasoned, they should not be punished as severely as those who had.[22]

General Sherman, annoyed at what appeared to be bungling by senior officers, ordered Brigadier General Ranald S. Mackenzie, a veteran Indian fighter, to take command of field operations in Arizona, a slap at Willcox. Carr may well have rejoiced over his commander's embarrassment, but he soon received equally unwelcome orders that placed him under Major George Sanford and Captain Reuben F. Bernard, First Cavalry, who were in charge at San Carlos. Sherman demanded a "decisive blow" against the Apaches even if it took every available man in the army. In effect he wanted a war of extermination, and he wanted it carried out by troops, not Apache scouts, so that the survivors—if any—would never forget it. "I will approve," he stated, "the most severe measures. . . . I expect Willcox to destroy the renegade Apaches. . . . I only want to hear results, not intentions."[23]

Major Sanford asked Carr to help arrest Sánchez and about fifty warriors who were in one of the camps on the reservation. When the hostiles saw Carr's command in position between them and their escape route and recognized some of the troops who had been in the

Cibecue fight, they hastened to the post to surrender. Nantiotish, a noted White Mountain Apache chief, had escaped with a dozen warriors before Carr's force arrived.

Captain Benjamin Egbert was ordered to investigate the Cibecue affair and to determine, if possible, which individuals were actually involved. Agent Tiffany was certain that Pedro's band was thoroughly implicated, but Carr thought otherwise. Egbert concluded that those mainly involved in killing the couriers, ranchers, and other Anglos were Bonito and George, but that some smaller bands—as well as a few members of Pedro's band, including Alchise and Uclenny—had also been involved. The Apaches who attacked the fort, Egbert decided, were from George's and Pedro's bands, together with a small party of renegades and some of the mutinous scouts. Most active were Sánchez, Nebigjay, a brother of Nocadelklinny, and Nantiotish.

Others believed that misunderstandings because of faulty translations had led to the fighting at Cibecue Creek. The interpreter, Hurrle, was a private who had spent much time among the Apaches. Scout Al Sieber, who was not present, believed that Hurrle had garbled Carr's words, giving the Apaches an erroneous impression of what was intended and exciting them to the point of attacking the troops.

Eight Apache leaders believed to be hostile, including Alchise and Batiatist, had quietly joined the peaceful bands at Camp Apache and at Cooley's Ranch. Carr was ordered to arrest them. Knowing that if one were arrested the others would flee, Carr laid his plans carefully. He sent Captain Tupper and a cavalry detachment to arrest Alchise and Uclenny at Cooley's Ranch. Simultaneously, he took a wagon train and two companies of cavalry to the camp where Batiatist and others were known to be. At a signal two companies of infantry sprang from the wagons, surrounded the camp, and arrested the supposedly hostile chiefs.

Some of the scouts who had mutinied drifted back to their families and were arrested and sent to the guardhouse at Fort Grant. Among them were Sergeants Dead Shot and Dandy Jim, Corporal Skippy, and two privates. They were to be the only Apache scouts punished as a result of the Cibecue Creek mutiny. Others had joined Juh and Nachez in Mexico. On his return to Arizona in 1882 General Crook offered amnesty to all who had been involved in the Cibecue fighting, but for some it was too late.

The final chapter of the Cibecue tragedy was the November 1881 court-martial at Fort Grant of some of the scouts for mutiny. The court found five guilty of the charges of mutiny, desertion, and inciting insurrection—concepts which were beyond any Apache's understanding. The unfortunate five were Dead Shot, Dandy Jim, Corporal Skippy, and the two privates known only by their numbers. The first three were sentenced to be hanged on March 3, 1882. The two privates were sentenced to imprisonment on Alcatraz Island, one for eight years, one for life. Both were paroled in June 1884.

Dead Shot had been popular among both whites and Indians at Fort Apache. The day before the execution he made a dash for freedom, rounding the guardhouse and heading for a canyon, but the sergeant of the guard felled him with shots in the elbow and under the arm. A few days before the execution, the wife of Colonel Gilbert C. Smith had passed by the guardhouse on her way to the post trader's store. Dandy Jim motioned to her from the window and took a red glass and turquoise bead necklace from around his neck. "You take," he said, "me pretty soon hang. . . . "[24]

On the day of the execution Dead Shot's wife hung herself, although suicide was extremely rare among Apaches. Their two sons stayed at their camp, half-starved, until Lieutenant Charles B. Gatewood learned about them and had rations issued to them. Signalman Will C. Barnes gave them a home on his ranch near Fort Apache. The cowboys called the older boy Riley; the younger one was always known by his Apache name of Eskinewah Napas, meaning "boy with a scar on his head."

Many considered the scouts' execution a grave miscarriage of justice, as was the killing of Nocadelklinny. Lieutenant Cruse, writing many years later, commented, "I have always regretted the fate of Dead Shot and Skippy. The former was the sage of the Indian company, the latter the clown and wag. I doubted at the time if they had intentional part in firing upon us. It seemed to me that they were swept into the fight by excitement and force of evil circumstances."[25]

Alchise and the others whom Carr and his troops arrested were confined at Fort Apache then in the guardhouse at Camp Thomas. No charges were filed against them and it did not appear that they would ever be brought to trial or released. A concerned citizen finally hired a Tucson law firm to write the secretary of the interior. Among other things the letter pointed out that the Indians had been arbitrarily imprisoned for an indefinite period on vague and uncertain charges of murder. "These Indians," it continued, "have nothing to fear from a fair trial for they can show by competent and reliable witnesses their whereabouts during the entire time of the recent troubles (Cibicu fight) and establish their innocence of any crime beyond a doubt."[26] This letter initiated government action that eventually, after many more months had passed, resulted in the freeing of the men.

Many citizens demanded hanging for all Apaches who had been at Cibecue, but General McDowell, commander of the Division of the Pacific, viewed the Apaches more sympathetically. From Carr's reports he deduced that the Apaches had been surprised when Carr arrived with most of his command to arrest Nocadelklinny. They had been aroused by false rumors, he said, and were afraid of being attacked by the troops. The fact that they were in their camps planting corn indicated that they were not at that time preparing for war. "I cannot concur, therefore," McDowell concluded, "in denouncing their conduct as treacherous. . . . These Indians simply made war upon the troops in retaliation for the arrest of their leader."[27]

The commissioner of Indian affairs, Hiram Price, also felt that the Apaches were victims of circumstances beyond their control, and he set off part of the reservation by a "peace line." In this way he attempted to protect peaceful Indians without interfering with General Sherman's orders to the troops to ignore reservation boundaries. Some of the hostiles seized this opportunity to seek refuge from the numerous columns that were searching for them and thus prevented Willcox from striking the "decisive blow" Sherman had demanded. But despite the peace line, there were patrols continually crossing and recrossing the reservations, destroying cornfields and killing a number of Indians. According to agent Tiffany many of them were aged and infirm people who had gone out to gather any of their corn the military had failed to destroy. Most of the Apaches were thoroughly awed by the overwhelming show of force.

Apache police arrested fifty or sixty supposed hostiles and allowed seven of the principal chiefs to surrender. George and Bonito also surrendered to subagent Ezra Hoag, who accompanied them to Camp Thomas. Because of an injury George was permitted to return to his camp and Willcox paroled Bonito.

Willcox soon reversed himself, however, and ordered Colonel James Biddle to arrest these same two chiefs and their bands. Biddle and his troops arrived at the subagency on issue day at the end of

September 1881. The chiefs agreed to surrender as soon as the issue was completed, but late in the afternoon they sent Biddle word not to wait for them, saying they would follow with the subagent.

Colonel Biddle replied that they must come at once and marched toward George's camp in what appeared to be a threatening manner. As the two cavalry companies approached the two chiefs fled to the Chiricahua camp, shouting that troops were coming to attack them. Seventy Chiricahuas and Nednhis under Juh, Geronimo, Chato, and Nachez stampeded and dashed from the reservation. When he heard of the exodus Colonel Carr remarked, "I think the great mistake that has been made was by . . . Willcox, in having brought the band of Chiricahua under Whoo [Juh] out of Mexico. They came or were brought out almost as conquerors, not as captives."[28]

Captain R. F. Bernard followed hard on the Chiricahuas' trail with four companies of cavalry. The Indians saw a wagon train approaching Cedar Springs and captured it; the delay enabled the cavalry to overtake them near Mount Graham. The warriors held off the cavalry all day while their women and children sped for the border. After dark the Apaches did not quit fighting. Even more unusual, they charged through the line of soldiers blocking their path and successfully escaped. They left a path of death and destruction as they rode through the ranch country and settlements, passing near Tombstone and evading a posse led by Mayor John P. Clum, the former San Carlos agent. When they joined Nana's small Warm Springs band in the Sierra Madre they brought with them around six hundred head of horses and cattle. They had killed thirteen whites and destroyed a large wagon train during their dash to Mexico.

One of the underlying causes of Apache discontent in Arizona was the graft and mismanagement of San Carlos agent Tiffany, who found some way to profit out of almost every reservation activity. Inspector R. S. Gardner compiled an impressive list of Tiffany's misdeeds and other inspectors corroborated the findings. But by his vigorous denials of wrongdoing as well as collusion with Indian Bureau officials, Tiffany managed to retain his post until his resignation on June 30, 1882.

Tiffany had lost control of the San Carlos Apaches in April of that year when Juh and Geronimo fulfilled their threat to force Loco and his people to join them. Tiffany had ignored the threat and was totally unprepared when Chato and Nachez led sixty renegades to Loco's camp and forced him and several hundred of his unarmed people to accompany them. Sterling and his Apache police followed them in a vain effort to check the exodus. The renegades turned on them, killing Sterling and ten others, and then continued up the Gila to the Clifton region. When they passed near Fort Thomas Colonel George W. Schofield and a cavalry force pursued them briefly.

More serious troubles lay ahead for the Apaches: Colonel George A. Forsyth sent troops from New Mexico to cut them off at Horseshoe Canyon. The warriors fought off the troops all day to give the women and children time to reach a safe refuge across the Mexican border.

The international boundary had often provided temporary relief from pursuit, for the Apaches were aware that both Anglo and Mexican troops usually stopped at the border. There had been a number of minor border violations, as in November 1881 when Lieutenant Thomas Garvey, First Cavalry, crossed into Sonora and was arrested by Mexican authorities. He was released when General José Tiburcio, commander of the army in Sonora, was assured that the matter would be investigated. In January 1882 Lieutenant David N. McDonald, Fourth Cavalry, crossed into Chihuahua and was also arrested. General Mackenzie, who secured McDonald's release, recognized the danger that over-zealous junior officers in pursuit of Apaches might cause serious incidents. He informed Forsyth, whose command was along the border in southern New Mexico, that it was "unwise to leave any discretion to officers about crossing the Mexican boundary line."[29]

Captain Tupper, with two companies of the Sixth Cavalry and one of Apache scouts, followed the flight from Arizona and struck Loco's band near modern-day Cloverdale, New Mexico, killing six and capturing most of the horses. The Apaches fled south into Mexico; Forsyth and Tupper joined forces and kept on their trail. On April 30 they met Colonel Lorenzo García and the Mexican Sixth Infantry Regiment, who protested their presence in Mexico. García explained that the Apaches, in their haste to escape from Forsyth's command, had been sighted and ambushed by his troops, who had killed seventy-eight and captured thirty-three women and children in a five-hour battle. Mexican losses were twenty-one killed.[30]

Jason Betzinez, a cousin of Geronimo, was a boy at the time of the flight, and he retained vivid memories of it. Once the Apaches had crossed the border, he said, they had relaxed, certain that the U.S. troops would not follow them into Mexico. But the cavalry had stayed on their trail and attacked their camp. Those men who had horses rode on ahead into the foothills, leaving the others to escape as best they could. The advance party, according to Betzinez, saw the Mexican troops approaching but were afraid to go back and warn the others. "Some of those men who took part in this disgraceful abandonment of their mission as a security detachment," Betzinez wrote years later, "were subchiefs Chatto and Naiche and one of Nanay's warriors, a man named Kanhtenny [Kaetennae]."[31]

Most of the warriors, following a mile or two behind their women and children to protect them from the American cavalry, were completely unaware of the Mexican troops ahead. The Apaches— women, children, and aged—were strung out in a long line when Mexican troops rushed from a ravine and opened fire. The Apaches scattered, but many women and children were killed, and whole families were decimated. For the most part these were Indians who had never left the reservation voluntarily and who had tried to remain peaceful.

When the firing started the warriors of the rear guard rushed forward to save the women and children. Geronimo demonstrated his noted qualities as a war leader by rallying the warriors to make a stand so that the women and children could escape. About thirty-two warriors responded to his call, and they fought furiously all afternoon. One of the Apaches, because of exhaustion, had dropped a sack containing five hundred cartridges. An old woman offered to retrieve it; she returned with the precious ammunition just as the men were exhausting their supply. This action was typical of the Apaches—old people frequently took on risky missions, for warriors were too few to be lost needlessly.

With Geronimo and Chihuahua directing the defense, the Mexicans charged several times, shouting "Geronimo, this is your last day!"[32] The Mexicans set fire to the grass and the Apaches were caught in an ever-narrowing circle of fire. After dark, however, they crawled out and escaped. Of the seventy-eight Apaches killed in the fight only eleven were men.

The flight continued, but some wounded men and women who could not keep up were left at a spring to recover. Among them were Kay-i-tah [Kieta] and Tso-ay [Tzoe], who would serve as guides for General Crook in 1886. A month later, fully recovered, they rejoined the others at Juh's *netdahe* (or outlaw) camp in the Sierra Madre.[33] In Juh's band were Chiricahuas, Warm Springs, Bedonkohes, Mescaleros, White Mountain, and other Apaches as well as a few Navajos, and Mexicans who had been captured and raised by Apaches.

In the Sierra Madre the Apaches moved camps frequently, breaking up into small parties and reassembling for raids. It was a hard and

U.S. Cavalry and Apache scouts, about 1886
Arizona Historical Society

perilous life, for there were garrisons of Mexican troops in each town
and the Indians were always in danger of being attacked. And
although some Apaches liked to boast that they killed Mexicans with
rocks, the fighting was not that one-sided, for Mexican troops usually gave a good account of themselves.

Because of the revival of Apache troubles General Sherman made
an inspection tour of Apache country in April 1882, a trip that should
have made him better attuned to the problems the troops faced in
campaigns against hostile bands. He did recognize the difficulties
resulting from the division of Apachería between the Departments
of Arizona and New Mexico as well as between Chihuahua and
Sonora on the Mexican side, and he recommended creating a new
Department of the Border which would include southern Arizona
and New Mexico. This plan would be set aside, however, in favor of

returning General Crook to command the Department of Arizona and giving him considerable latitude in New Mexico.

At San Carlos some deserters from the scout company joined the band of renegades headed by Nantiotish and avenged Nocadelklinny's death by raiding the San Carlos agency, ranches, mining camps, and freight trains south of the reservation as well as various settlements in the Tonto Basin. The raiders eluded a dozen cavalry troops for about a year. "Cibicu Charley" Colvig, who replaced Sterling as chief of Apache police at San Carlos, kept on the raiders' trail, hoping to discover their hideout. In July 1882 Nantiotish and his band ambushed the Apache police, killing Colvig and seven or eight others and pursuing the survivors almost to the agency headquarters. They seized a supply of ammunition, rounded up all of the horses and mules in sight, and headed for the Salt River and the Tonto Basin.[34]

A multi-column campaign was immediately launched to put an end to Nantiotish and his raiders. Captain Drew and two troops of Third Cavalry set out from Fort Thomas to follow the trail. Colonel A. W. Evans and four more troops of Third Cavalry set out from Fort Apache, while Captain Adna R. Chaffee marched from Fort McDowell; both were heading for the Tonto Basin in an attempt to intercept Nantiotish. Two other columns marched from Camp Verde along the rim of the Tonto Basin, ready to cut off any attempt to escape to the vast Navajo reservation.

Lieutenant Cruse and his scout company marched with Colonel Evans from Fort Apache to the Salt River near where Roosevelt Dam was later built. The scouts reported that the renegades had camped at the mouth of Tonto Creek not long before and then had taken the trail across the Tonto Basin toward Navajo country. A small raiding party apparently had dashed down to strike the settlements along the Salt, then rejoined the main party. Evans and Cruse pushed on, for the trail was fresh. At dark the scouts reported that a large party, probably cavalry, had entered the trail ahead. Evans sent a patrol to check, and it came upon Captain Chaffee, with Troop I, Sixth Cavalry, and a scout company.

Because Chaffee had found the trail Colonel Evans, who could have assumed command of the whole force because of his rank, generously let Chaffee take charge of the attack. Chaffee's troop was mounted on white horses, as was Captain Converse's—a part of Evans' force. "I'll put Converse at the head of my column," Evans told Chaffee. "So if the Indians do stop to fight, you'll have two 'white horse troops' to throw at them. The rest of my force can be placed wherever seems best for attack. It may confuse the hostiles to face two troops where they're expecting [only] one."[35]

It did. The next day Chaffee found the hostiles camped at Chevelon Fork of Canyon Diablo, ready to fight. The Apaches' position seemed perfect to stage an ambush, for their rifles could cover every part of the narrow trail down into the canyon. Nantiotish had watched Chaffee's troop the previous day and was confident that he could annihilate it. When he saw Converse's troop coming along the trail on white horses he assumed it was Chaffee's, until too late. By then the Apache scouts had run off his pony herd and he was surrounded and trapped by forces on both sides of the canyon. The "Big Dry Wash" or Chevelon Fork battle destroyed Nantiotish and his band, for the survivors fled back to reservation camps.

When Cruse and the command reached Cooley's Showlow ranch on their return to Fort Apache they were astonished to learn that Cooley already knew all about the battle and its outcome. He had been told about it by his Apaches, who learned of it through the mysterious "Apache telegraph."

There were repercussions in the army over the Cibecue affair for several years. Both Willcox and Carr, the protagonists, were given to writing long, plaintive letters to their superiors. As departmental commander Willcox had the upper hand. He had ordered Carr to leave his regimental headquarters at Camp Lowell, near Tucson, and to go temporarily to Fort Apache—a remote and rustic spot where living conditions were much less attractive. Carr requested a return to Lowell; Willcox ordered him to transfer his headquarters to Fort Apache, adding that Lowell, which Carr had built, was now an infantry post.

Carr then wrote to General McDowell in San Francisco; he sent his letter through official channels and dispatched a copy directly to McDowell. Willcox delayed forwarding first Carr's letter and then McDowell's reply, calling Carr's writing to McDowell a grave breach of discipline and demanding a court-martial. Willcox also accused Carr of responsibility for the Cibecue troubles. General McDowell responded by criticizing Willcox for ordering Nocadelklinny's arrest in the first place.

When Willcox' demand for a court-martial was forwarded to the War Department President Chester A. Arthur rejected it. He was not, however, satisfied with the state of affairs in the Department of Arizona and instructed General of the Army Sherman to admonish Carr for disrespect and insubordination. Carr was outraged and demanded a court of inquiry so insistently that one was finally granted in August 1882. The court found that Carr had exposed his column to attack by allowing the two troops to become separated on leaving the Apache camp, although this had nothing to do with the fight that ensued. The court praised Carr for his "gallant" conduct during the battle and said that he was guilty only of "errors of judgment."

Carr was almost completely vindicated by the court; his headquarters were transferred back to Camp Lowell; and a short time later Willcox was relieved of command of the Department of Arizona. Carr was, nevertheless, infuriated by the charge of "errors of judgment" and tried unsuccessfully to have this blot removed from his record. He and Willcox exchanged charges and countercharges for another year, but the president had heard enough.

On July 29, 1882 the governments of Mexico and the United States signed an agreement stating that "the regular federal troops of the two Republics may reciprocally cross the boundary line of the two countries, when they are in close pursuit of a band of savage Indians." Crossings should be made only in "the unpopulated or desert parts of said boundary line," and the commander of the troops should, at the time of crossing or before, notify the nearest military commander or civil authority of the country he was entering. The pursuing force should retire from the country as soon as it had fought the Indians or lost their trail. Since the Apaches usually chose to cross the border in "unpopulated or desert parts" anyway, the convention now made effective pursuit possible.[36]

General George Crook resumed command of the Department of Arizona in September 1882. As before the Apaches would soon feel his presence and Apache affairs would take a turn for the better. The "Apache problem," however, was still far from solution as long as the Nednhis and Chiricahuas retained a base in the Sierra Madre for raids into Arizona, New Mexico, Chihuahua, and Sonora. Crook's task was by no means simple, for he had first to restore peace among the reservation Apaches and then to deal with the large band of irreconcilables in their impregnable Sierra Madre retreats.

XII
Crook and Geronimo

TAKING COMMAND IN ARIZONA for the second time in September 1882 Crook (who was given police control of the entire reservation as well as supervision of ration issues) lost no time in learning what the discontented Apaches had to say. He went at once to Camp Apache, but there were few Apaches to be seen except the very old and the very young; most of the able-bodied warriors were hiding in the mountains. There had been a number of clashes with troops, and prospects for peace seemed slim. Many people, however, maintained that the Apaches were not to blame for the troubles, and Crook agreed, offering amnesty to all who had participated in the Cibecue fighting. "If the Indians had been in earnest," he said, "not one of our soldiers could have gotten away from there alive."[1]

Crook sent a message to those in hiding that he was coming to see them; if no whites were killed in the meantime, the troops would not fire on them. He took with him C. E. Cooley as interpreter, Captain Bourke, and scout Al Sieber, followed by a pack train escorted by a company of the Sixth Cavalry. Crook was able to confer with old Pedro, Cut-Mouth, Moses, Alchise, Uclenny, and about forty others. He told them he wanted to know everything that had happened to bring on the trouble, and he wanted what they told him put down on paper.

When Crook left them, seven years ago, Alchise replied, there had been no "bad" Indians off the reservation and all were content. But the officers the general had put in charge had been removed. The agent didn't give them rations, Alchise said, then the San Carlos agent (Clum) had forced them to move there. Alchise explained that he and Uclenny had been doing all they could to help the whites, but the agent put them both in the guardhouse. Alchise told how he had served as a scout against the Yavapais, Tontos, Pinaleños, and even his own people. Old Pedro confirmed what Alchise had recounted

259

and added a bit more concerning the absurdity of arresting Nocadelklinny.

Severiano, a Mexican who had been captured and raised by Apaches, informed Crook that what they had told him about white civilians and soldiers stealing their cattle and horses and destroying their fields was true. Although he served as interpreter, his own cattle had been taken. The reason for these thefts, according to Captain Bourke, was that the "Tucson ring" was determined to prevent the Apaches from becoming self-supporting, so that they would not lose lucrative contracts. As a result the White Mountain Apaches, who were at least partly self-supporting in their own country, were herded down to the "malaria-reeking flats of San Carlos."[2] The assurances given them by Vincent Colyer and General Howard and to old Pedro by President Grant during his visit to Washington had all been swept away. Any time conspirators reported that the Apaches were restless the government would send ten regiments, but not one honest man to inquire if the Apaches had a story.[3]

The conference also revealed that agents were quick to imprison Indians on trivial or baseless charges—the innocent as well as the guilty were imprisoned for long periods. In October 1882, because of the widespread reports of unjust arrests and imprisonments, a grand jury investigated the administration of the San Carlos reservation and looked into the matter of Apaches sent to Tucson for trial. Agent Tiffany had released the guilty ones and held eleven innocent ones in confinement for fourteen months without presenting any charges against them. During that time they were given insufficient food and clothing.

The grand jury investigation exposed Tiffany's colossal mismanagement, "a disgrace to the civilization of the age. . . . " They felt it their duty, jury members stated, "as honest American citizens, to express our abhorrence of the conduct of Agent Tiffany and that class of reverend peculators who have cursed Arizona as Indian officials, and who have caused more misery and loss of life than all other causes combined." The grand jury investigation also revealed that the Apaches had "unbounded confidence" in General Crook. In addition the jury verified what had been charged elsewhere: "With the immense power wielded by the Indian agent almost any crime is possible. There seems to be no check upon his conduct."[4] Despite all the evidence presented, however, Tiffany was never convicted.

Other Apaches told Crook similar stories of thefts of Indian supplies by the agents; they no longer even knew what they were supposed to receive. Clothing, blankets, and other items intended for the Indians were sold to traders in the town of Globe. Corn and melon fields were destroyed to compel the Indians to depend on the agent, yet he never issued them adequate rations. The reports of arbitrary punishments were numerous, and the reservation had been whittled down five times in order to exclude mineral deposits, bearing out the old saying that the worst calamity for Indians was the discovery of mines on their lands. On one occasion the agent had assembled twenty chiefs and headmen and offered each $100 for signing a paper agreeing to give up the southern part of the reservation, where the agent and his friends believed there were silver deposits. If the chiefs refused to sign the agent told them, soldiers would be sent to kill them.

One of the Apaches' most consistent complaints was of hunger; twenty people were expected to live for a week on one small shoulder of beef and twenty cups of flour. "We eat all the meat from the hoofs to the horns, and the insides, too," one chief declared, adding that when they needed rawhide for moccasins they had to buy it from the agent.[5] Tiffany had refused to issue passes so they could hunt off the reservation. An Apache who spoke English was given the unwelcome duty of asking the agent about the wagonloads of supplies leaving the agency each night. For his temerity he was rewarded with six months in the guardhouse. Idleness, too, bred discontent, for men who had wandered freely over vast areas were forced to sit idly on one small tract of desert they despised. Another complaint was that the interpreters insisted on the Apaches paying them for their services.

Surprised to learn of the Apaches' great distrust of the army as well as civil officials, Crook issued his General Order No. 43 on October 5. In it he stated that "Officers and soldiers serving in this department are reminded that one of the fundamental principles of the military character is justice to all—Indians as well as white men . . . . In their dealings with the Indians," Crook continued, "officers must be careful not only to observe the strictest fidelity, but to make no promises not in their power to carry out. . . . Grievances, however petty, if permitted to accumulate, will be like embers that smoulder and eventually burst into flames." In conclusion he reminded the officers that he was holding each one strictly responsible for his conduct.[6]

Crook rode all over the Department of Arizona, visiting all of the Indians he might have to deal with later. He also reorganized the pack trains and Indian scout companies under the command of

Captain Emmett Crawford, Third Cavalry. From the commander of the Division of the Pacific he requested and received permission to double the number of scouts enlisted to a total of 250, explaining that "The great difficulty in the solution of the Apache problem is in catching the Indians, which, if done at all, must be mainly through their own people. . . . "[7] "Nothing," he added later, "breaks them up like turning their own people against them. They don't fear the white soldiers, whom they easily surpass in the peculiar style of warfare which they force upon us, but put upon their trail an enemy of their own blood, an enemy as tireless, as foxy, and as stealthy and familiar with the country as they themselves, and it breaks them all up. It is not merely a question of catching them better with Indians, but of a broader and more enduring aim—their disintegration."[8]

Crook next turned his attention to the reservations, so that when he began a campaign into Mexico he would have a secure base behind him, with no danger of outbreaks to join the hostiles. Within a week after he arrived Crook stationed a cavalry unit at San Carlos, where no troops had served since Clum had had them removed in 1875. Crook also ordered the expulsion of all unauthorized persons from Apache lands, and troops escorted the miners and squatters to the reservation boundaries. He vigorously opposed any further reduction of the reservations as well as all proposals to move the Apaches to Indian Territory. He also provided work for the reservation Apaches, work for which they were paid in cash.

For some of these actions Crook was roundly damned; there were still many people whose profits would suffer if theApaches became self-supporting. Crook explained his position to U.S. District Attorney Zabriskie: "I believe that it is of far greater importance to prevent outbreaks than to attempt the difficult and sometimes hopeless task of quelling them after they do occur. . . . Bad as Indians often are, I have never yet seen one so demoralized that he was not an example in honor and nobility to the wretches who enrich themselves by plundering him of the little our Government appropriates for him."[9]

Commenting that the Apaches had shown "remarkable forbearance" in remaining at peace Crook explained to them that their troubles were caused by evil white men who wanted them to go to war so they would have an excuse to seize their lands. Since it was necessary to distinguish between Indians who were peaceful and those who were not, he reintroduced metal identification tags and frequent roll calls for all adult males.

Agency rules had required the Apaches to camp near the headquarters where rations were issued. This made it impossible for them to settle at distant places where there was fertile land for farming. In November 1882 Crook informed the Apaches they no longer had to be counted and were free to live anywhere on the reservation. They remained accountable to Captain Emmett Crawford at San Carlos and Lieutenant Charles B. Gatewood at Camp Apache. Crook insisted that they govern themselves as far as possible through revived Apache courts and police. The boredom of reservation life, when combined with alcohol, Crook knew, was certain to produce violence. The brewing of tizwin was still, therefore, forbidden, as were wife-beating and mutilation.

Captain Crawford had served briefly in Arizona in 1870 and 1871 before the Third Cavalry had been transferred to the northern plains to campaign against the Sioux. In mid-May 1882 most of the regiment had returned to Arizona, where Crawford was immediately involved in frequent and strenuous expeditions against Apaches. When Crook returned to Arizona he immediately placed Crawford on detached duty as military commandant at San Carlos. He was to cooperate with the civilian agent in maintaining peace and making the Apaches self-supporting; an added duty was enlisting and training Apache scouts.

Lieutenant Britton Davis, Third Cavalry, was ordered to report to San Carlos as Crawford's assistant. He and Crawford and several other officers camped there temporarily and were initiated into life on the Arizona desert. The first morning Davis, who was not long out of West Point, discovered a ten-inch centipede in his bedroll and protested jokingly to Crawford. "You were lucky," Crawford informed him, "I found a young rattler in mine." Another officer had discovered an enormous tarantula as his sleeping companion. Although Fort Thomas was generally regarded as the worst army post in the West, "San Carlos won unanimously our designation of it as 'Hell's Forty Acres,'" Davis wryly commented. It was hot, dry, and dusty, with summer temperatures as high as 110°. At all times of the year San Carlos swarmed with flies, gnats, and other flying or crawling pests. It was no surprise that the Apaches detested it, for they were mountain people.

On every side there were naked, hungry, and frightened children, who hid at the sight of an officer. "Everywhere," Davis wrote, "the sullen, stolid, hopeless, suspicious faces of the older Indians challenging you. You felt the challenge in your marrow—that unspoken challenge to prove yourself anything else than one more liar and thief, differing but little from the procession of liars and thieves who had preceded you." The Apaches' main activity was gathering at the agency once a week for ration issue.[10]

Of the four officers in charge of the two reservations—Captain Crawford and Lieutenants Charles B. Gatewood, Britton Davis, and Hamilton Roach—only Gatewood knew much about Apaches. Two years after graduating from West Point he had taken part in the Victorio campaigns and thereafter had been almost continuously involved in campaigning or scouting after them. "In the four years of Apache trouble that followed," Davis wrote later of Gatewood, "no man accomplished more, got less credit for it, or suffered such injustice as fell to his lot."[11]

The San Carlos agent, F. P. P. Wilcox of Denver, was a political appointee who had taken the position, he admitted, because he could find nothing better. He detested Indians and vowed he would spend as little time on the reservation as possible. He agreed to cooperate with the military, but he was away from the agency much of the time. Most of the agent's work was done by his chief clerk, an ex-Civil War officer, Colonel Beaumont, a "fine old gentleman" who cooperated with the military and who saw to it that the Apaches were not cheated.

While he was making his home base secure against inroads of the hostiles among reservation Indians Crook also completed the reorganization of the pack trains and scout companies. For the latter he secured the services of several veteran chiefs of scouts including Al Sieber, Archie McIntosh, and Sam Bowman. Five companies of scouts were enlisted, each with a first and second sergeant, two corporals, and twenty-six privates. Captain Crawford chose the sergeants and corporals from among the chiefs and headmen. The scouts in each company were from the same bands. There were also "secret scouts" who kept the officers informed about any suspicious activity on the reservations. These spies were both men and women, and none knew about the others. Most of them communicated through interpreters or through Sieber, McIntosh, or Mickey Free. Those who knew a little Spanish preferred to talk directly to Lieutenant Davis, however, for they distrusted Free and suspected that he translated what they told him in a way he knew would please the officers. They also feared that he would betray them to their own people. Mickey Free was the Ward boy whose capture by Apaches in 1860 had led to the so-called Bascom affair at Apache Pass. He lived like an Apache and was married to an Apache woman, but few of her people trusted him. To what degree he deserved their distrust is difficult to ascertain, but, according to Lieutenant Davis, Sieber's

Apache scouts
Arizona Historical Society

opinion of Free was unprintable and the Warm Springs Apaches
detested him.[12]

The army officers in charge of the reservation continually discovered additional reasons for Apache discontent. Since the Apaches
were not allowed to leave the reservations, they were at the mercy of
the Indian trader for all purchases and he could charge any price that
suited him. After Captain Crawford had a serious talk with the trader
at San Carlos, however, he did reduce prices by about 50 per cent.

Because there had been a great many complaints Davis checked
on all aspects of the beef issue. After testing the scales he discovered
that the beef contractor was being paid for fifteen hundred pounds of
beef each week that was not delivered. The contractor grazed his

herd across the river from agency headquarters; animals to be delivered were held without water for a day and then driven through the river, so that the government paid for half a barrel of Gila water delivered with each animal. Some of the cattle were so thin that Davis accused the herders of carrying them to the slaughter pens on their ponies. They denied it, insisting that each animal had walked there. The contractor was dismissed and a new contract was issued to H. C. Hooker, a prominent cattleman with a ranch west of Camp Grant. Thereafter, there were no complaints about the beef issues.

As before Crook was eager to see the Apaches earn money by working or farming. Some had been doing a little farming, but they had been discouraged by agents who cooperated with contractors selling supplies to the agency. There were no tools available, and the irrigation ditches had become clogged. It is hardly surprising that most of the Apaches had simply given up the effort or that most of them were restless, discontented, and apprehensive about the future.

The White Mountain and Cibecue bands who had been allowed to remain at Camp Apache when Clum moved the others to San Carlos were much more fortunate. They were, in fact, nearly self-supporting, for they raised grain and also cut hay and wood which they sold to the post at Fort Apache. The same practice was now introduced at San Carlos. The women and children cut the gramma grass with butcher knives and delivered it in bundles of from fifteen to forty pounds, for which they were paid one cent per pound. Hay purchasing became the afternoon diversion at San Carlos, for the women tried all manner of schemes to increase the weight of their bundles, such as slipping rocks or pieces of mesquite into them. When Davis removed these the women called him various graphic names they had learned from Anglo soldiers and Mexican packers, for the Apaches' own language was deficient in oaths.

Although hay gathering was largely the work of women and children the men took an active part in bringing wood to the post to sell. Once these programs were begun Davis noted a marked change taking place among the Apaches: children no longer fled at the sight of an officer or soldier; the women dressed in clean clothes; and there was much laughing and joking.

Crook's insistence that the Apaches take the responsibility for punishing their own offenders led to complications at San Carlos when a man killed his wife. Crawford reminded the chiefs of Crook's orders; they arrested the man, tried him, found him guilty, and sentenced him to death. According to Apache custom the dead woman's relatives were expected to kill him, but Crawford refused to turn the man over to the Apaches to execute. The Captain could not face that gruesome task himself, but fortunately he had an assistant of inferior rank—Lieutenant Britton Davis. He ordered Davis to carry out the execution, but he did not want to be told anything about it. Davis and Al Sieber and a few others secretly took the man out one night in a buckboard, and while he was sleeping Sieber shot him and then helped bury him.[13]

In order to impress reservation Apaches with the white men's numbers and power Crook sent a delegation to Washington in 1882, a trip that had awed other tribes in the past. One man decided to count all the people he saw along the way, then only the dwellings. Overwhelmed by numbers, he switched to counting towns, but finally gave up. The trip failed, nevertheless, for when the delegates returned no one would believe their stories.

Late in October, when preliminary arrangements for a Mexican campaign had been completed, Crook sent Captain Crawford with three companies of Apache scouts to patrol the border and try to locate the hostiles in Mexico. In March 1883 Crook began final preparations for his expedition to Mexico, knowing that sooner or later the hostiles would conduct raids across the border into Arizona and New Mexico and that he would then have the opportunity to pursue them under the convention with Mexico.

While Crook was organizing the expedition a party of barroom Indian fighters who called themselves the "Tombstone Rangers" and who were well fortified with bottled spirits, patriotically set out for San Carlos to massacre all of the reservation Apaches. Before they reached the southern edge of the reservation, however, they ran out of both whiskey and courage. They continued on their way with diminished enthusiasm until they saw an old Apache man out gathering mescal. Fortunately for them he was unarmed; fortunately for him, when they shot at him they missed. He fled north while the Tombstone Rangers dashed in the opposite direction, having completed one of the least bloody "massacres" of the Apache wars.[14] The organization, Bourke noted, "expired of thirst."[15]

The expected raid from the Sierra Madre hostiles came during the last week of March. Chato and Bonito led twenty-six warriors on a lightning foray across southern Arizona and New Mexico to obtain ammunition, while Geronimo led a raid into Sonora for livestock. In six days the raiders traveled between two hundred and four hundred miles, stealing fresh horses from ranches and moving so rapidly that none of the dozens of cavalry troops sent after them ever saw them.

Tzoe or Penaltishn (known as "Peaches" to whites), the scout who
guided General Crook to the Chiricahua hideout in the Sierra Madre
Arizona Historical Society

The renegades killed twenty-six people, including Judge H. C. McComas and his wife, of Silver City, New Mexico, and carried off their six-year-old son Charlie. One warrior died and Tzoe or Penaltishn (The Coyote Saw Him) left them and returned to the reservation. Tzoe, who was known to the soldiers as "Peaches" because of his complexion, was a White Mountain Apache who had been married to Chiricahua women killed in the battle with Colonel Lorenzo García's troops during the flight of Loco's band. Lieutenant Davis arrested him and sent him to Crook; Tzoe apparently had been forced to accompany his wives' people against his will and he agreed to guide Crook to the Chiricahua refuges in the Sierra Madre. He told Crook that the hostiles had seventy warriors and fifty boys of fighting age; they were well supplied with 16-shot rifles, he said, but they were short of ammunition.

Chato's raid gave Crook the opportunity he had waited for. He sent telegrams to the various Mexican field commanders in Sonora and Chihuahua, but lacking accurate addresses for them he received no reply. He went by rail to Guaymas and Hermosillo over the new line opened the previous October to confer with Sonora officials and then took a train to Chihuahua City. At each meeting he found Mexican officials cooperative and willing to take a broad view of the border-crossing agreement, but they recommended that the Apache scouts wear something, such as red headbands, to distinguish them from hostiles. Crook's instructions from General Sherman were to follow the Apaches without regard to departmental or national boundaries, but the secretary of war instructed Crook to abide strictly by the terms of the agreement with Mexico.

The Apache scouts, as usual, were excited and ready for adventure. The night before the march began they held a night-long war dance. In the morning when Lieutenant Gatewood said "Go!" they trotted off, each moving according to his own inclinations, without any order, in groups of two or three. Their faces were painted with red ochre or other materials, partly for ornamentation and partly to protect against sun and wind. Each wore a scarlet headband for identification, a loose-fitting shirt, loose cotton drawers, moccasins of buckskin hanging in folds below the knees, and a cartridge belt containing fifty rounds. Most had small buckskin bags of *hoddentin*, a sacred powder made of pollen, with which to offer morning and evening sacrifices. Some also carried amulets to ward off arrows and bullets. "The Apache is an eminently religious person," Bourke remarked, "and the more deviltry he plans the more pronounced does his piety become."[16]

The scouts, traveling on foot, moved at a speed not quite fast enough to make a horse trot and covered thirty-five to forty miles a day no matter how hot the sun or difficult the terrain. They were ideal scouts, sharp-eyed, ever-alert, and untiring. They knew the country perfectly and could take care of themselves under any circumstances. They knew the meaning of every track or mark in the grass and could tell almost to the hour when it had been made. They were obedient to authority but they could not tolerate restraints. For that reason they were allowed to set their own pace. "The nearer an Indian approaches to the savage state," Crook wrote, "the more likely he will prove valuable as a soldier." Because of this the scouts he chose were "the wildest I could get."[17] And although the sufferings of white troopers were often vividly described the hardships of the Apache scouts were rarely mentioned. "I pity our poorly clad Indian scouts," Lieutenant John Bigelow wrote. "It is only, I suppose, by thoroughly exhausting themselves that they are enabled to sleep through these freezing cold nights with their scant covering. Most of them, having no trousers, wear nothing on their legs but a pair of drawers. Several of them go barefoot."[18] The scouts told Crook they were anxious to end the Apache war so that whites and Apaches could work together.

Before crossing the border they assembled at San Bernardino Springs, where Crawford and 100 more scouts joined them. Crook notified Mexican authorities that he would cross the border on May 1 as agreed. Each man was allowed to take one blanket, 40 rounds of ammunition, and the clothes he wore. The five pack trains of 266 mules and seventy-six civilian packers carried 160 more rounds of ammunition for each man as well as rations of hard bread, bacon, and coffee for sixty days. There were, in all, six officers, forty-two men of Company I, Sixth Cavalry, and 193 scouts under Captain Crawford and Lieutenants Gatewood and Mackay. The chiefs of scouts and interpreters were Al Sieber, Archie McIntosh, Severiano, and Mickey Free. The Apache scouts included Chiricahuas, White Mountain Apaches, Tontos, Hualapais, and Yavapais. It was an auspicious beginning, for the medicine men predicted a great success—one was so confident that he backed up

The theater of operations of the Sierra Madre expedition
Reproduced from Dan L. Thrapp, *General Crook and the Sierra Madre Adventure* (Norman, University of Oklahoma Press, 1972).

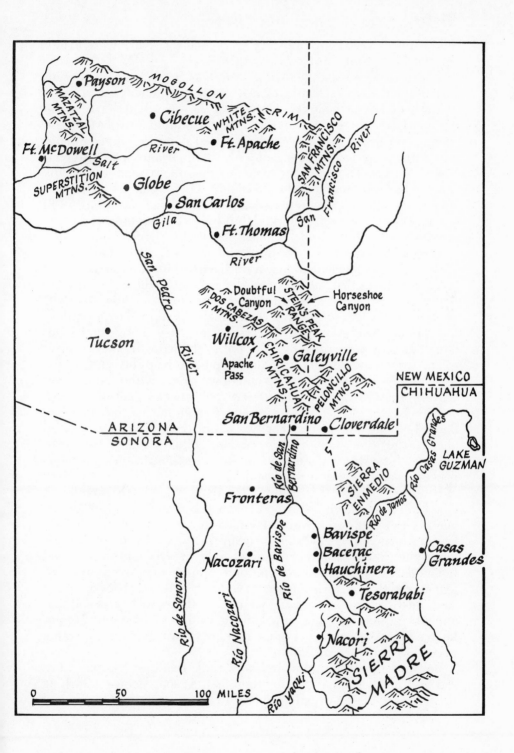

Payson

MOGOLLON

MAZATZAL MTNS.

Cibecue

WHITE MTNS. RIM

Ft. Apache

SAN FRANCISCO MTNS.

San Francisco River

Ft. McDowell

River

Salt

SUPERSTITION MTNS.

Globe

San Carlos

Ft. Thomas

San

Gila

River

San Pedro

Doubtful Canyon

STEIN'S PEAK RANGE

Horseshoe Canyon

DOS CABEZAS MTNS.

Tucson

Willcox

Apache Pass

CHIRICAHUA MTNS.

Galeyville

PELONCILLO MTNS

NEW MEXICO

CHIHUAHUA

River

San Bernardino

Cloverdale

ARIZONA
SONORA

LAKE GUZMAN

Río de San Bernardino

SIERRA ENMEDIO

Río de Casas Grandes

Fronteras

Río de Janos

Nacozari

Río de Bavispe

Bavispe

Bacerac

Hauchinera

Casas Grandes

Río de Sonora

Río Nacozari

Tesorababi

Nacori

SIERRA

MADRE

Río Yaqui

0   50   100 MILES

his prophecy with a forty dollar wager—and the scouts were in high spirits, for fighting surely lay ahead.

The expedition marched down the San Bernardino Valley into that of the Bavispe, a fertile, attractive region that was a total desert because of Apache hostility. The farther they marched the worse the devastation became. They entered the forbidding Sierra Madre on May 7, and although the scouts had trotted along without complaint and with many a jest they suddenly stopped and solemnly confronted Crook. They pointed to an owl that photographer A. Frank Randall had caught and tied to his sadde. They would go no farther, they said, unless it was released, for the owl (bu) was a bird of ill omen. They could expect nothing but misfortune as long as the owl was with them. It was quickly released and the march continued.[19]

They followed a trail made by the hundreds of cattle, horses, and mules the Apaches had stolen, a trail marked by the carcasses and bones of animals that had not been able to keep up the pace. The trail led up one rough mountain range and down the other side, with falls of hundreds of feet for any man or animal that slipped or stumbled. The heavily packed mules had especially hard going, and sure-footed as they were, five of them fell to their death.

The troops and officers struggled step by step up the rough trails, while the Apache scouts ran up and down ridges without difficulty. On one occasion a scout gave a low cry, half whisper, half whistle. All were instantly alert, for by some indefinable means the news had flashed among the scouts that two Chiricahuas had been spotted ahead. The scouts stripped for action, sending ten or twelve in pursuit. But it was a false alarm; the supposed Chiricahuas were two packers searching for strayed mules.

It was soon clear that troops slowed the pace of the march, so Crook sent Crawford, Gatewood, and Mackay ahead with 150 scouts and assurances from the medicine men that in two days they would find the Chiricahuas and kill a "heap" of them. As the others followed they found a number of horses and mules the Chiricahuas had left in places where grass was plentiful. A messenger from Crawford announced that a Chiricahua camp was not far ahead. The command soon heard firing; at dark Crawford and the scouts returned and announced that they had attacked the camp of Chato and Bonito, killing nine and capturing five—two boys, two girls, and a young woman, a daughter of Bonito.

Bonito's daughter admitted to Crook that her people were shocked and dismayed when they saw Apache scouts attacking them. Most of the warriors were away on raids in Sonora and

Chiricahua chief Chato, photographed in 1927
on the Mescalero Reservation
Arizona Historical Society

Chihuahua, she said, and she was sure that they would give up without more fighting. Loco and Chihuahua, she knew, would willingly live on the reservation if properly treated, but she was not sure about Chato and Geronimo. Juh probably would never surrender, she added, but he had few warriors left.

In the camp just destroyed, she continued, was a little white boy named Charlie, who had been captured by Chato. This was undoubtedly Charlie McComas, whose parents had been killed by Chato's raiders. Although there was great interest in finding the boy he was never seen, and his fate remained a mystery until Jason Betzinez revealed it half a century later. When the scouts attacked Chato's camp they had killed the mother of one of the Chiricahua warriors. Out of anger this man had killed the white boy. The Chiricahuas disapproved of his act but they said nothing about it for fear the warrior would be killed.[20]

The young woman offered to bring in the whole band in two day's time, so Crook sent her and the oldest boy on this mission. Two women, sisters of scout Tô-Klani (Plenty Water), came into Crook's camp saying they had suffered heavy losses in the attack. Six more women, one the sister of Chihuahua, also surrendered. She said that Chihuahua, too, wanted to surrender and was gathering up his scattered band for that purpose. But if they wanted to talk to him, the troops were told, they must return his white horse with its Mexican saddle and bridle. The horse and gear were located and given her. When Chihuahua later rode into the camp on the white horse he charged through the scouts, who had to leap out of his way. "If you wanted me for a friend," he said to Crook, "why did you kill that old woman, my aunt?" He referred to a woman the San Carlos scouts had shot when attacking the camp.[21]

Day after day men, women, and children straggled into the camp. Like Chihuahua most of them expressed a desire for peace, for they were tired of constant warfare. By May 20, 121 Apaches had surrendered, 60 of them women and girls, the rest old men, young men, and boys. Chato and Geronimo, however, were still away on a raid.

Soon armed warriors were sighted on the crags overlooking the camp, indicating that the raiders had returned. Two days earlier Geronimo had suddenly exclaimed to his men that the people they had left in camp were now in the hands of U.S. troops and asked, "What shall we do?" All wanted to return to camp immediately. A day later Geronimo told them, "Tomorrow afternoon as we march along the north side of the mountains we will see a man standing on a hill to our left. He will howl to us and tell us the troops have captured our base camp." In mid-afternoon the next day they heard a howl from a hilltop, and a warrior reported that the scouts with General Crook had captured the main camp. These were examples of Geronimo's mysterious ability to know what was happening elsewhere. Jason Betzinez was with him and observed it, but was never able to explain it.[22] It was, however, one of Geronimo's sources of power as a leader.

The Chiricahua and Warm Springs chiefs warily entered the camp, a few from one direction, a few from another. Crook told them bluntly that Mexican troops were closing in from all sides and that Geronimo could decide whether he wanted war or peace. Geronimo declared that he was willing to surrender. Later a story was spread to the effect that Crook had been captured by the hostiles and forced to accept their terms. Since the Chiricahuas with Geronimo did not come to the border for nearly nine months, the story was widely believed for there were many people in Arizona who opposed Crook's policies and were delighted at any opportunity to discredit him.

Soon after Geronimo had surrendered, Kaetennae and his band of thirty-eight young warriors arrived with a herd of stolen cattle. Five Mexican women straggled into camp about the same time; they were wives of soldiers stationed in Chihuahua. Geronimo had captured the women to exchange for Apaches seized during a supposed fiesta in Casas Grandes, when the visiting Apaches had been plied with mescal and then attacked. On the return trip north Crook turned the women over to Mexican authorities.

By May 23 there were 220 Chiricahuas and other Apaches in the camp, and the food supply was running low. Crook informed Geronimo that if he was willing to settle down, surrender his weapons, and take up farming, he could return to the reservation. Geronimo was willing but said that he needed more time to round up stragglers and their livestock. He promised to come to the border in "two moons," which, it turned out, did not mean two months, but some vague time in the future. Crook accepted his promise and headed for San Carlos with 52 men and 273 women and children, mostly of the Warm Springs band. About two hundred Apaches, mainly Chiricahuas under Nachez, Chato, Zele, and Geronimo, remained in Mexico; among them were most of the warriors. The reason they gave for remaining behind was to gather their people who lived in remote and isolated camps, but their real purpose was to raid for horses, mules, and cattle to trade with the San Carlos Apaches. Among the fighting men who did accompany Crook were

Mangus, son of chief Mangas Coloradas. He succeeded Victorio as chief
of the Warm Springs Apaches.
Western History Collection, University of Oklahoma

old Nana, Loco, subchief Bonito, and Kaetennae, the rising war leader of the Warm Springs band. Kaetennae had never been on a reservation before and he was restless and suspicious, making no pretense of concealing his intense hatred of the white eyes. He had a personal following of 32 fierce young warriors, and he was regarded as a potential trouble-maker who must be carefully watched.

Mangus, son of Mangas Coloradas, became chief of the Warm Springs band after the death of Victorio, but both Nana and Loco were more influential than he. Nachez was the son of Cochise and nominally head chief of the Chiricahuas, but like Mangus he was not warlike enough to satisfy his people and had been pushed aside— first by Juh, then by Geromino, who arose as war leader after Juh had drowned in the autumn of 1883.

While Crook's expedition was in Mexico for nearly two months Lieutenant Britton Davis was left with the responsibility of controlling five thousand restless and turbulent reservation Apaches, with only Sam Bowman as an assistant and Lieutenant West and his cavalry troop for military support. There was, however, only one incident, and it did not prove serious. Davis learned that a white man was selling whiskey to the Apaches and had sworn to "shoot the hell out of any damned army officer who attempted to arrest him." The next morning, accompanied by two Apache scouts, Davis entered the man's cabin. "Bin expecting you," he said, inviting Davis to share his breakfast. When told he would be taken to Tucson for trial the man laughed, saying they would do nothing to him. When Davis turned his prisoner over to the U.S. marshal and the district attorney in Tucson, they appeared enthusiastic about the arrest. The prisoner, however, told Davis he would join him in the hotel for a drink in half an hour; he kept the appointment, and that was the last Davis heard of the case.[23]

On the way to Tucson with his prisoner Davis had passed the farms of Eskiminzin and a few other Arivaipa Apache families. When Clum had resigned "Skimmy" had said, "I will go down on the San Pedro and take up some land and live like a white man—then they will not blame me for what happens on the reservation." The Arivaipas had farmed there for ten years, drawing rations only the first three years. Eskiminzin insisted that Davis join him for dinner, letting Bowman and the scouts continue with the prisoner.

The little colony of half a dozen families appeared quite prosperous, with neat adobe houses, well-tilled and fenced fields, farming equipment, cattle, and teams of horses. All of them dressed after the fashion of Mexican Americans in Arizona. Davis enjoyed a substantial meal with Eskiminzin and his family, then a young man with a team and buggy drove him to Bowman's camp. The next morning Eskiminzin drove up and insisted that Davis ride with him to Tucson, where they visited merchants with whom he regularly did business. These men told Davis that Eskiminzin's credit was good for up to $5000, at that time a substantial sum.

When Crook returned to Arizona in 1882 he asked Eskiminzin how he was getting along with the whites with whom he came into contact. "When first go San Pedro," Eskiminzin replied, "white man pass by, look back over shoulders. Say 'There go ol' Skimmy.' Now white man pass by, raise hat, say 'good morning Mr. Skimotzin.' "[24]

During the early 1880s there were rumors of rich coal deposits on the southern edge of the San Carlos reservation, and loud demands arose for excluding this land—as well as the fertile land Eskiminzin and the others were farming—from the reservation limits. As long as Crook remained in charge of the Department of Arizona he prevented any dirty work against Eskiminzin, but as soon as General Nelson A. Miles succeeded him in 1886, Eskiminzin and his people lost everything.

While the Crawford expedition was in Mexico agent Wilcox became apprehensive about receiving the Sierra Madre renegades at San Carlos. He wired Secretary of the Interior Teller that a number of chiefs on the reservation had requested that the hostiles be sent elsewhere. Teller informed Secretary of War Robert T. Lincoln that the hostiles would not be allowed to return to San Carlos. Lincoln, in turn, ordered Crook to keep them away from other Apaches until a decision had been reached on the matter.

Surprised and angered by this order Crook replied that Wilcox had understood from the start that the Chiricahuas and Warm Springs Apaches would return to San Carlos. To send them elsewhere would be a breach of faith by the government, and the renegades still in the Sierra Madre would never surrender. If the Interior Department refused to receive them, he added, he could not be responsible for their actions.

In June Lincoln ordered Crook to Washington for a meeting on affairs at San Carlos. Before Crook left Captain Crawford reached San Carlos with 325 Apaches who were allowed to camp near the agency and to mingle freely with others.

Present at the Washington conference were Teller and Commissioner of Indian Affairs Hiram Price as well as Crook and Lincoln. On July 7, 1883 the two secretaries officially settled on a division of responsibility on the reservation and agreed that the renegades who had surrendered (or would in the future) were to be under the exclusive control of the War Department. The army would have police control of the reservation and would protect the agent in the discharge of his ordinary duties, which included everything except "keeping the peace, administering justice, and punishing refractory Indians." The dual administration would result in constant friction between Crawford and Wilcox, for Crawford interpreted the agreement as limiting the agent to issuing rations, nothing more.[25]

The "two moons" Geronimo had promised now stretched into many months. Crook was anxious to get the hostiles settled safely on the reservation, for he had been soundly criticized in the press for bringing "renegades" back to Arizona, and he knew they were in danger the moment they crossed the border. He sent Lieutenant Britton Davis to the border with a company of scouts to hurry the stragglers on to San Carlos and to protect them from citizens once they entered Arizona. During the fall Nachez and Zele arrived with their people; Davis escorted them rapidly to San Carlos and then returned to the border. By the end of November there were more than 400 Warm Springs and Chiricahua Apaches on the reservation. In February 1884 Chato's and Mangus's bands arrived and were also taken quickly to San Carlos, to avoid trouble with authorities or citizens. Once more on the border Davis waited impatiently for six weeks, with no sign of Geronimo. He asked a Yavapai medicine man where Geronimo was and when he would arrive. The medicine man, who disliked Chiricahuas, meditated all day and into the night. Finally he emerged and walked through the camp twirling a piece of flat wood around his head. He threw some pungent powder into the scouts' campfire, waved his arms, and suddenly ceased. He was bathed in sweat and appeared exhausted, but he announced that he had "found Geronimo." Entering the circle of scouts mumbling incantations, he declared that Geronimo was three days away, riding a white mule and bringing a herd of horses.[26]

Four or five days later one of the scout patrols came upon Geronimo and his party. Geronimo was riding a white pony and was accompanied by fifteen or sixteen men and seventy or more women and children. He rode up to Davis until his pony bumped into Davis' mule and angrily demanded to know why he was to have an escort. He had made peace, he said, and he had no need for an escort. Davis replied that there were bad Americans who might make trouble; since the scouts were soldiers, anyone who interfered with them would be in trouble with the government.

Following Geronimo and his party were some of his warriors with a herd of 350 cattle stolen from Mexican ranches. This posed a new problem for Davis; he had avoided trouble earlier by pushing the Apache bands to cover forty or fifty miles a day over the most direct route so that no citizens could overtake them. But the cattle could travel only twelve to fifteen miles a day at best and required a route that was easy to travel and had frequent waterholes or springs. It would take at least two weeks to reach San Carlos, and Geronimo's party would be constantly exposed to danger, for a herd of cattle raised a cloud of dust that could be seen for miles.

Geronimo had pushed the cattle hard to evade Mexican pursuers and he now demanded that they be allowed to rest for three days. Davis refused and insisted that they start for San Carlos the next afternoon, reminding Geronimo that under the government's agreement Mexicans had the right to cross the border in pursuit of Apaches. Added to the prospect of troubles with Anglo authorities and civilians was the likelihood of fighting among the scouts and Chiricahuas, for a few of the scouts were Tontos, who hated Chiricahuas. One night his fears were nearly realized, for he heard wild yells and the sound of rifle-shots. He found a drunken Tonto scout walking back and forth cursing the Chiricahuas and daring them to send out a man to fight him. Davis had the Tonto disarmed and tied to a tree, and the next day he was both sober and remorseful. [27]

The route taken passed within thirty miles of Fort Bowie. Among the officers stationed there was a fellow Texan and West Point friend of Davis, Lieutenant J. Y. F. ("Bo") Blake. Davis sent him a message that he would camp at Sulphur Springs Ranch in a few days. They were pushing the cattle eighteen or twenty miles a day, and Geronimo angrily protested that they were "running all the fat off the cattle and they would not be fit for trading" when they reached San Carlos. [28]

The night before they reached Sulphur Springs Ranch they stopped at an old Apache camp ground where there was good water and plenty of grass. Geronimo informed Davis that the lieutenant, the scouts, and the pack train could go on, but that he and his people were going to stay there several days to rest their cattle. Davis reminded him that they were still close to the border. To Geronimo this was a meaningless excuse. His women, he said, could whip the Mexicans. Davis compromised and agreed to stop for one day.

When they reached Sulphur Springs Ranch two civilians came out of the ranch house. They asked a multitude of questions about the number of Apaches, who they were, and so forth. Then one turned back the lapel of his coat and showed Davis the badge of U.S. marshal of the Southern District of Arizona, saying that he had warrants for the arrest of Geronimo and others for murder. His companion was the collector of customs from Nogales, who intended to sequester the cattle and ponies as contraband. Their plan was to arrest the Chiricahuas and take them and their smuggled stock to Tucson, where the Indians would stand trial.

Davis protested that he could not obey such an order unless it came from General Crook. The marshal then wrote out a subpoena for Davis as a citizen to aid in the arrest of the Indians. This was a legal federal order that could not be ignored. The marshal planned to do the same with the packers and the cowboys at the ranch. If they refused, he said, he would go to the town of Willcox and raise a posse.

Attempting to arrest Geronimo and his people would be suicidal, Davis explained. Of the thirty-three scouts in the company all but eight or ten were Chiricahuas, who would certainly aid their people against Anglos. There were eleven packers, but most of them were Mexicans who were not obliged to obey his order, and only four were armed. Even with a posse from Willcox they would be out-numbered three to one—very poor odds in a battle with Chiricahuas.

The marshal was stubborn and unyielding. It was his duty to make the arrest, he said, and make it he would regardless of the conse-quences. Davis was a citizen under his orders and would be a law-breaker if he refused to obey. Davis knew he was in a serious predicament, for Fort Bowie was too far to send for help or instruc-tions, and Geronimo was already in an ugly mood. General Crook, furthermore, had ordered Davis to escort Geronimo and his people safely to San Carlos, and Crook was not interested in explanations or excuses from subordinates who failed to carry out his orders.

At this dark moment Davis' friend "Bo" Blake arrived from Fort Bowie for a visit. Blake had graduated from West Point a year ahead of Davis and so was his senior in rank. He immediately took com-mand of the situation, ordering Davis to remain, subject to the marshal's instructions. Blake had brought a quart of whiskey with him, which he generously shared with the marshal and the customs collector that night, until they staggered off to bed.

Calling his scout first sergeant, Davis explained that they must move at once, and together they approached Geronimo, who flatly refused to move. The first sergeant took over the argument at this point, and the words flew so fast that Davis had no idea what was being said. All he could tell was that the sergeant's advice was effective, for Geronimo's demeanor changed.

At this point Davis cunningly suggested that Geronimo's people were not smart enough to get away from the ranch without the Anglo officials knowing it. His people, Geronimo haughtily informed Davis, could leave while he was standing there, and he would not even know they had gone. Davis replied that it would be a good joke on the officials at the ranch to wake up in the morning and find the Apaches, cattle, and horses all gone. Geronimo almost smiled, and the battle was won.

Awakening his pack master Davis explained the situation. The packers carried the aparejos a safe distance from the ranch house before packing the mules. They silenced the bell of the bell-horse, but like most bell-horses it was white and the mules followed it without difficulty.

The two officials slept late in the morning. When they arose they looked everywhere for the Apaches and their cattle, scanning the country from the roof of the ranch house with field glasses, but there was no tell-tale cloud of dust to be seen in any direction. Since there were many routes the Apaches might have taken and cattle tracks everywhere, the two officials simply gave up, releasing Davis from his duties with a few profane comments.

After two days of hard riding, Davis overtook Blake and Geronimo near the reservation and soon delivered his charges to Captain Crawford. The stolen cattle were sold and the proceeds sent to Mexico to reimburse the owners according to the brands. Geronimo never forgot or forgave this affront, and it apparently was a factor in his outbreak the following year.

Most of the Chiricahuas were settled under Davis' charge at Turkey Creek, about seventeen miles southwest of Fort Apache. Davis and Crawford were well aware that the Apaches were more suited to a pastoral life than to farming and recommended that they be given sheep and cattle. The Indian Bureau was in charge once more, however, and it was still under the influence of the Friends of the Indian, who insisted that all Indians become imitation white farmers—even if they starved to death in the process. Instead of livestock, therefore, the bureau sent the Apaches a dozen light wagons, plows, sets of harness, picks, shovels, and a few sacks of corn and wheat for seed. All of this was not totally wasted, as might have been the case, for hitching ponies to wagons and plows produced hilarious entertainment. The former renegades made little

Loco, Mimbreño Apache chief, photographed in 1886
Western History Collection, University of Oklahoma

attempt to farm except, perhaps, to raise some corn for brewing tizwin.

At Turkey Creek the more intractable of the Chiricahuas and Warm Springs Apaches—Mangus, Chihuahua, Geronimo, and their bands—set up camps several miles from Davis' tent. Kaetennae's followers also camped at a distance, but his own wickiup was on a ridge overlooking Davis' tent, so that he could observe all that went on.

Living alone with the Chiricahua and Warm Springs Apaches, Davis grew to admire them, especially his first sergeant, Chato, whom he trusted absolutely. He also saw Loco frequently and established friendly relations with him. As a result, when the next outbreak occurred Loco and his people did not take part. Davis became well acquainted with subchiefs Bonito and Zele, who visited him frequently, and with the witty scout called "Dutchy" because he looked German. Geronimo, Nachez, and Kaetennae remained aloof, avoiding contact with Davis. Chihuahua came to see him occasionally to complain against the ban on making tizwin, which he said was not part of the agreement. Davis was especially concerned about Kaetennae, for he and his band were openly antagonistic and seemed ready to cause trouble at the first opportunity.

The Apaches, Davis learned, were not resentful over their past treatment, only confused by it. Why had the government done this or that to them? "And above all," Davis wrote, "they wondered if they would be allowed to live at peace. Poor devils! Their fears were realized. In two years they were prisoners in Florida; four hundred innocent people, men, women and children, who had kept the faith with us, punished for the guilt of barely one-fourth who had been led to and frightened into leaving the reservation by Geronimo, Chihuahua, and two or three other malcontents!"[29] To Davis the most striking characteristic of the Apaches was their utter disregard for the consequences when excited or enraged.[30]

During the summer of 1884 Crook wrote to Herbert Welsh of the Indian Rights Association concerning the Apaches. Once the fiercest of Indians, he said, the Apaches were now at peace. "Opinion may differ as to the place in the scale of intelligence the Apache should occupy," he wrote. "Speaking for myself, after a somewhat extended experience of over 32 years duration . . . I do not hesitate to put the Apache at the very head for natural intelligence and discernment . . . ." In the past, he concluded, the Apaches had been "systematically and outrageously plundered by a gang of sharks thinly disguised as Indian Agents and others."[31]

On one occasion Lieutenant West sent word that he was coming for a visit and a wild turkey dinner. Davis obligingly set out to shoot a wild turkey. He hunted along the creek, then started up a trail to the top of a mesa. Hearing a turkey gobble along the creek, he turned back and shot one.

That night he heard pebbles thrown against the top of his tent, the signal that one of his secret scouts had come to report. The secret agent was a woman, who asked him why he had turned back from the mesa top that morning. When he told her he had heard a turkey call near the creek, she said, "That was the good spirit of one of your ancestors in that gobbler." She explained that when he started up the trail Kaetennae and his band were drinking tizwin on the mesa. They saw him and assumed he was coming to arrest them. They ran for their Winchesters and were lying in wait, for they had decided to defy Crook's order against drinking tizwin, vowing to kill anyone who interfered. Realizing how close he had come to death Davis prayed that the turkey he shot was not the one that had saved his life. [32]

To prevent the violence that seemed inevitable if Kaetennae had his way Davis decided to arrest him and send him to San Carlos for Crawford to deal with. It would be a risky business, for Kaetennae's followers were as eager as he for a fight, and the memory of the Cibecue arrest three years before was still fresh. But Davis knew that Kaetennae was opposed by Chato, Bonito, Loco, Mangus, and Zele, and he counted on the help—or at least the neutrality—of these chiefs.

When Lieutenant West left that night Davis asked him to send four troops of cavalry from Fort Apache; they were to arrive at sunrise the next day and to stop a few hundred years behind his tent. At daybreak he sent the scouts to call all chiefs to his tent. They came armed, for the "Indian telegraph" had informed them that troops had left the fort and were coming toward Turkey Creek. They seemed worried and wanted to know why he had sent for them. He would tell them, Davis replied, when Kaetennae arrived.

Last to arrive was Kaetennae, who came with his armed followers and angrily asked why Davis had sent for him. Because he was going to send him to San Carlos, Davis replied. Kaetennae demanded to know who was accusing him of making trouble, then spun and started back to his own men. They spread out in a line with rifles ready, stepping forward to meet him. As Kaetennae started, scouts Dutchy and Charley quickly followed him, with cocked and leveled rifles in their hands.

Chiricahua chief Bonito after his surrender to General Crook in 1883
Western History Collection, University of Oklahoma

Kaetennae met his men, then returned to Davis. Two hundred yards behind the tent the four troops of cavalry dismounted and came forward in a skirmish line, carbines raised. Kaetennae's men stopped, while he again approached Davis, shaking with anger and once more demanding to know his accuser. Davis, relieved to see that Kaetennae had decided against a fight, unbuckled the warrior's cartridge belt with its holster and pistol and slung it over his arm, informing Kaetennae that he was under arrest and would be sent to San Carlos. Kaetennae seemed suddenly to wilt.

Bonito now approached Davis, offering himself and Charley as hostages for Kaetennae's safe arrival at San Carlos if Davis would return his gun to him and permit him to go as a warrior. Without hesitation Davis handed Bonito the belt and pistol and informed the officer in command of the cavalry that he and his men could return to Fort Apache.

The Apache court at San Carlos found Kaetennae guilty and Crawford sentenced him to three years at Alcatraz. General Crook, who was convinced that Kaetennae was not irreconcilable, kept informed about his behavior and pardoned him after eighteen months. "His authority among his people for good or for harm," Crook said, "is very considerable."[33] Kaetennae's attitude was completely changed by his experience at Alcatraz; on his return he was good-natured and amiable and willingly accepted Crook's invitation to enlist as a scout.

Wilcox resigned as agent in August 1884 to be replaced by Charles D. Ford in December. Soon there was serious friction between the new San Carlos agent and Captain Crawford. A modest man who invariably gave all credit to his subordinates, Crawford was determined that the Apaches should receive fair treatment, and he took a firm stand on every issue regarding them. Earlier he had informed agent Wilcox that "no man save my commanding officer will come between me and my Indians."[34] As a result Crawford had frequent clashes with agents as well as with private interests who attempted to exploit the Apaches. Ford, who was equally determined to help the Apaches in any way possible, and also to exercise his rightful authority as agent, resented Crawford's organization of the irrigation system. He appointed a new chief of Apache police and a head farmer who ordered work stopped on the irrigation ditches. To enforce this order Ford had his police seize the picks and shovels.

Another source of friction was the issuing of annuity goods to the Chiricahuas and Warm Springs Apaches at Turkey Creek, who were badly in need of clothing. Ford distributed the annuity goods at San

Carlos soon after his arrival and offered to go to Fort Apache to make the distribution there, for bureau regulations required him to be present at such issues and to take receipts. Crawford refused, however, to allow any communication between Ford and the former renegades. He sent two pack trains from Fort Apache with the demand that the agent hand over the annuity goods forthwith. Ford replied that he could not comply because of regulations. Crawford ordered the pack trains to return to Fort Apache. He reported that the Interior Department wanted to create dissatisfaction among the former hostiles and cause an outbreak—an inaccurate assessment. As a result of Crawford's stubbornness the Chiricahuas and Warm Springs Apaches received no clothing, although the winter was unusually severe.[35]

The Apaches quickly perceived the civil-military friction and exploited it for their own advantage. Defiance of authority quickly spread from San Carlos to the remote camps, and soon Davis received frequent reports of tizwin bouts and wife-beatings. When he arrested one man for brewing tizwin and another for wife-beating and sent them to San Carlos, Nachez and Chihuahua, accompanied by other chiefs, angrily demanded that both men be released. When Mangus joined the protesters it was clear that insubordination had spread widely, for he had been one of the most cooperative chiefs, on occasion joining Loco in support of Davis. But one of Mangus' wives had been returned by Mexican officials, and because she was an expert tizwin-maker Mangus wanted her to be able to ply her trade. Another point of contention was the right of Apaches to beat their wives and mutilate them for committing adultery.

Affairs at San Carlos steadily worsened, for although the interdepartmental agreement giving the military police control of the reservation Indians remained in effect Indian Bureau officials were determined to limit the army's authority to such control. The territorial newspapers, taking the side of those who opposed helping the Apaches become self-supporting, launched an unrestrained attack on Crawford and Crook. The attacks on Crawford, together with the intense friction between himself and agent Ford, induced him to call for a board of inquiry. The board sustained Crawford in everything, but seeing no hope of continuing constructive work among the Apaches, he asked to be returned to his regiment. He was replaced by Captain Francis C. Pierce, First Infantry, who unfortunately had no acquaintance with Apaches. This change at so critical a time proved disastrous.

Before dawn on May 15, 1885, Lieutenant Davis found all of the chiefs, subchiefs, and about fifty others assembled in front of his tent. As he looked about Davis noted that there was not a single woman or child to be seen, an ominous sign. Even more menacing was the presence of several armed warriors on a nearby hilltop from which they could observe any movement of troops in or out of Fort Apache. Except for Chato, who remained outside with the scout company, the chiefs and subchiefs entered the tent and squatted in a half-circle facing Davis. Loco began a slow, halting harangue.

Springing to his feet Chihuahua impatiently interrupted Loco. "What I have to say can be said in a few words," he said. "Then Loco can take all the rest of the day to talk if he wants to do so." He repeated the earlier arguments concerning tizwin-making and wife-beating. They had agreed to remain at peace with Americans, Mexicans, and other Indians, he said, but they had not agreed on anything concerning their conduct among themselves. They weren't children to be taught how to live with their women or what to eat or drink, Chihuahua complained. How they treated their wives was their own business, he continued, and anyway women weren't mistreated when they behaved.

Davis reminded them of Crook's reasons for prohibiting the drinking of tizwin. Old Nana, who was especially irked by the ban on wife-beating, said something and then stalked out of the tent. Interpreter Mickey Free was silent. Davis insisted tht he translate what Nana had said. Reluctantly Free told him: "Tell the *Nantan Enchan* (Stout Chief) that he can't advise me how to treat my women. He is only a boy. I killed *men* before he was born." Chihuahua, who was also in an angry mood, went directly to the purpose of the visit. "We all drank tizwin last night," he stated defiantly, "all of us in the tent and outside, except the scouts, and many more. What are you going to do about it? Are you going to put us all in jail? You have no jail big enough even if you could put us all in jail."[36]

What to do about the tizwin drunk, Davis replied, was too serious a matter for him to decide. He would send a telegram to Crook for instructions and let them know as soon as he had heard from the general.

The Apaches had seen nothing of Crook since returning to the reservation, and some of them, especially Geronimo, had frequently asked Davis if *Nantan Lupan* was still in charge of them. Crook was the man they feared most but he was also the one they relied on for protection against rapacious Anglos. The fact that Crawford, Elliott, agent Wilcox, and Colonel Beaumont—men they all knew—were gone made them suspect that Crook had also left Arizona. Because of the repeated questions concerning Crook, Davis knew that they were not satisfied with his answers. He and the Apaches waited anxiously for Crook's reply. It never came.

According to military regulations telegrams Davis sent were to be channeled through Captain Pierce, his immediate superior. Pierce could forward them with approval, disapproval, or comments. From San Carlos telegrams went to Willcox station, to be relayed over the military line to Crook's headquarters at Whipple Barracks. Because there were frequent leaks which newspapers were eager to publish, especially if they contained sensational news detrimental to Crook's reputation, the general had ordered that all messages be limited to a bare statement of the facts. He was so well informed on every phase of reservation activity and knew at once what action to take that no comments or recommendations were necessary. In his telegram to Crook, therefore, Davis stated the facts simply.

Captain Pierce had been at San Carlos only two months; aware that his knowledge of Apaches was limited, he relied on scout Al Sieber for advice. When the telegram arrived, therefore, Pierce awakened Sieber, who had been gambling and drinking all night and whose mind was far from clear. Sieber glanced at the telegram through bleary eyes. "It's nothing but a tizwin drunk," he replied. "Don't pay any attention to it. Davis will handle it." He fell back and continued sleeping.[37] Pierce filed the telegram instead of forwarding it to Crook and thereby triggered calamity.[38]

Four months later, when Davis reported to him after a campaign in Mexico, Crook mentioned that the newspapers were making much of a telegram they claimed Davis had sent. He had not received it and thus assumed none had been sent. Davis told him about the message and obtained a copy from Pierce. Later Crook stated that if he had received the message the outbreak probably could have been prevented, and at any rate he would have intercepted the Apaches before they reached Mexico. If Crawford had been in charge at San Carlos he would have recognized the urgency implied in the message and taken the proper action.

At Camp Apache, meanwhile, Davis and the Apaches waited with mounting anxiety for Crook's reply. On Sunday afternoon, three days after sending the wire, Davis was called on to umpire a baseball game between two post teams. During the game Chato and Mickey Free reported that a number of Apaches had left their camps on

Turkey Creek and were on their way to Mexico. Davis immediately tried to send a telegram to Pierce, but the line was out. Next Davis assembled the scouts, taking the precaution of having his trusted scouts Chato, Charley, and Dutchy by his side with rifles ready and orders to shoot anyone who raised his gun from the ground. Second Sergeant Perico, Geronimo's half-brother, and two other scouts slipped out of line and disappeared into the brush. Geronimo had ordered them to kill Davis and Chato, but, unable to catch either off-guard, the three fled south after the others. The Apaches had cut the reservation telegraph wire where it passed through the fork of a tree and tied the ends together with buckskin thongs. By the time the cut was found next day the fugitives were one hundred miles away, traveling rapidly. Geronimo and his party had such a head start that there was no hope of overtaking the fugitives immediately. Davis ordered a count of the Chiricahua and Warm Springs bands and found that thirty-five men, eight boys old enough to fight, and ten women and children were missing. The leaders of the outbreak were Geronimo, Chihuahua, Nachez, Mangus, and Nana. Bonito Zele, Loco, and most of the members of the two bands, had refused to be stampeded into flight.

Captain Pierce set out after Geronimo, leaving agent Ford with no force for controlling the reservation, as the Apache police had been disbanded. Ford requested and received permission to organize a new agency police force. When Lieutenant John B. McDonald, Tenth Cavalry, who was temporarily stationed at San Carlos, tried to arrest one of the Apache police, Ford interfered. On learning of this conflict Secretary of the Interior Lucius Q. C. Lamar ordered Ford to surrender the Apache policeman, suspended Ford from office, and asked Secretary of War William C. Endicott to name an officer to take over the agency temporarily. Endicott named Captain Pierce, and the army had finally won the contest for jurisdiction over San Carlos; the army retained control of the reservation for sixteen years.[39]

There soon was dissension among the Apache fugitives, for Nachez and Chihuahua accused Mangus and Geronimo of lying to them, telling them that Davis and Chato had been killed and that troops were coming to arrest them. They threatened to kill Geronimo, but split up instead. Chihuahua and his people hid in the Mogollón Mountains northeast of Morenci, trying to decide if it was safe to return to Camp Apache. Before they reached a decision, however, Davis and his scouts attacked them. Chihuahua and his people fled, traveling ninety miles without stopping and crossing the Mexican border before they made camp. At Skeleton Canyon they found the supply camp of Troop D, Fourth Cavalry, guarded by a sergeant and seven men. They surprised the camp, killing the sergeant and two others and capturing a supply of ammunition and provisions as well as a herd of horses and mules.

General Sheridan immediately authorized Crook to send another expedition to Mexico and transferred the New Mexico posts to the Department of Arizona to simplify command problems. Knowing that the renegades would need to raid north of the border to obtain ammunition for their American-made guns, Crook placed a troop of cavalry at every spring or waterhole along the border from the Patagonia Mountains of Arizona to the Río Grande.[40] He hastily recalled Captain Crawford to Arizona and sent him into Mexico in June with a large force of Apache scouts. Another force consisting of two troops of the Fourth Cavalry under Captain Wirt Davis and a company of White Mountain Apache scouts under Lieutenant Gatewood, followed in July. Davis came upon the Apache rear guard crossing a steep canyon, but they gave him a hard fight and escaped.[41]

North of Skeleton Canyon Lieutenant Davis joined forces with Crawford, and together they crossed into Mexico with one troop of cavalry and 130 scouts. North of Oputo they found the hostiles' trail. Knowing that it was useless to follow Apaches with cavalry Crawford sent 30 scouts under Chato and Big Dave, a White Mountain Apache sergeant, to follow the trail.

The scouts returned the next day with fifteen women and children they had captured as well as fifty-four of the cavalry horses taken by the renegades from the supply camp. In the fighting Big Dave had been shot through the elbow. As the army surgeon prepared to amputate his arm the Apache scouts stopped him—they would cure the wound themselves. They made two small circles of green twigs wrapped with narrow strips of cloth, placing one over each hole the bullet had made. They placed poultices of green sprigs of snakeroot over the wounds, changing them every few days. To the surprise of the surgeon, no water was allowed to touch the wounds. He was certain that the arm would be stiff and useless, but Big Dave recovered the use of it.

On a visit to Nacori Lieutenant Davis learned first hand the cost of Apache hostility in Sonora. The town had been reduced to a population of 313, including only 15 adult males. Every family had lost at least one member killed or captured by Apaches.

Before taking up Geronimo's trail Lieutenant Davis learned that

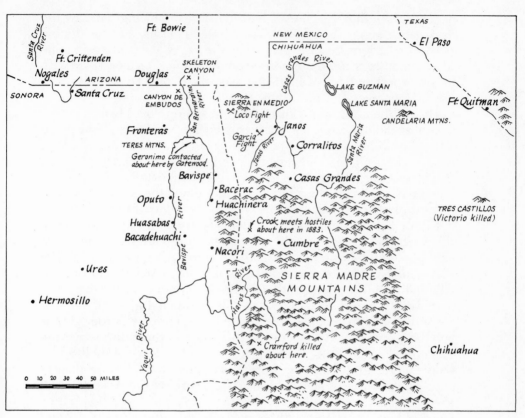

The Mexican theater of war
Reproduced from Thrapp, *The Conquest of Apachería.*

Lieutenant Elliott with five scouts and two packers had been killed
or captured by Mexican troops stationed in the town of El Valle. At
night in a heavy thunderstorm Davis mounted his mule and started
for the town in search of Elliott. On the way he met four mounted
men who asked in Spanish who he was. He replied that he was an
American army officer and learned that they were two officers of the
Mexican command with two soldiers as escort. They assured him
that Elliott and his men were in El Valle, unharmed. While they
were talking there was a flash of lightning and a cry of terror from one
of the soldiers. In the light Davis saw that they were surrounded by a

dozen naked men, black eyes flashing, faces scowling. He saw the dark bands about their heads, their breech cloths, and the double belts of cartridges each wore, then the sky was black again. The Mexican officers and their men sat on their horses as if petrified with fright. Another flash of lightning followed, and Davis recognized Chato and several of his scouts.

They did not intend to let Davis ride alone into a Mexican town, Chato explained later, for they trusted no Mexicans. If he were killed, his killers would pay a heavy price. They had slipped out of camp unnoticed and had stayed close to him. Davis assured Chato that he was safe and sent two scouts to the camp to tell Sieber to meet him in El Valle in the morning. Chato and the scouts insisted, nevertheless, on accompanying him to the edge of town.

Elliott and his men who had been held by the Mexicans were released, but it was noon the next day before Davis and his scouts could take up Geronimo's trail. It led across a mountain range the Mexicans considered impassable to any but Apaches and on into Chihuahua. Only once did they sight Geronimo's party, which had just raided the Terrazas' Santa Clara ranch for fresh horses. Geronimo and his people now headed north for the border. Davis and the scouts stayed doggedly on their trail for three days, covering 125 miles in that time; they were were out of food, and all of the scouts were barefooted, for there was no time to make new moccasins. They learned that Mexican troops were on the Apaches' trail ahead of them, and under terms of the agreement with Mexico they were obliged to abandon their pursuit and return to the United States.

The nearest point in the United States was El Paso, 100 miles to the northeast. Hoping to ride the Mexican Central train from San José station 40 miles to the east, they marched there. But the station agent refused to believe that the ragged, hungry group was part of the U.S. Army; he was convinced, in fact, that they planned to rob the train. They were forced to walk along the tracks to El Paso, covering the remaining 75 miles in two days without food.

The Mexican commanding officer at the Río Grande also refused to believe that the bearded, ragged Davis was an army officer. When he asked Davis how he had gotten into Chihuahua and learned that he had crossed the mountains just north of the Río Aros, the commander was certain he was lying, for the Mexican army had been unable to cross the mountains in that area. He threatened to throw Davis in the guardhouse and to shoot his men if they were Apaches. Davis replied that his men were forty of the best Apache fighters, and that they were going to cross the river. The colonel reluctantly gave him a pass. [42] In twenty-four days they had marched more than five hundred miles through mountainous country, in rain and mud. In El Paso Davis resigned his commission to become manager of the Corralitos Ranch and its mining operations in Chihuahua. Al Sieber returned with the scouts to San Carlos.

In September 1885 a party of twenty warriors raided into Arizona. Crawford's scouts were soon on their trail, as were troops of the Fourth and Tenth Cavalries, pursuing them hotly into the Dragoon Mountains. The San Simon Valley cattlemen at this time were in White Tail Canyon, preparing for the fall round up. Warned that Apaches were in the area, they tied their best horses to the ranch house where they slept for the night.

At dark the troops were closing in on the Apaches and were confident of overtaking them in the morning, for the raiders' horses had given out. But by the time the pursuit was resumed at dawn the Apaches were far away, mounted on some of the best horses in Arizona, unwittingly provided them by the San Simon Valley cattlemen. Crawford returned to Fort Apache, for the scouts' enlistments were about to expire. All that could be claimed after four months of the most arduous campaigning imaginable by the two columns was the killing of three women and the capture of thirty others along with some ponies and camp equipment.

Early in November Chihuahua sent his younger brother, Josanie, with a dozen warriors into Arizona on one of the most spectacular raids of the Apache wars. The party was sighted near Fort Apache and scouts were sent in pursuit. The raiders cut the telegraph line and struck the Camp Apache reservation, killing any Apache they saw except for a few women they carried off, and stealing Bonito's horses. Their purpose apparently was revenge against those Apaches who had remained peacefully on the reservation and particularly against the families of scouts. Josanie's little party headed into the Mogollón Mountains with a troop of cavalry and Navajo scouts on their trail. Crook sent another scout company into the mountains to ambush them; the scouts struck the raiders' camp, capturing their horses and camp equipment. The next day, however, the fast-moving raiders struck a ranch on the middle fork of the Gila, killed two men, secured horses, and vanished. Ten days later they ambushed the cavalry troop. When, after four weeks, they finally returned to Mexico, Josanie and his men had ridden upwards of twelve hundred miles, killed thirty-eight people, and stolen and worn out 250 horses—all with the loss of only one man.

While this raid was taking place General Sheridan arrived at Fort Bowie, sent by the secretary of war to investigate and solve the Apache problem. There was a growing belief among Washington officials that the Apache difficulties would remain until all Chiricahuas and Warm Springs Apaches were removed far from the Southwest. Crook was strongly opposed to the removal, arguing that the newly organized scout companies contained many Chiricahuas and that their performance of duties would surely be adversely affected. To Sheridan, who thoroughly disapproved of using Apaches to fight Apaches, this was a hollow argument.[43]

In December Captain Crawford re-entered Mexico with a large force of Apache scouts and the usual pack trains, assisted by Lieutenant Marion Maus in place of Britton Davis and accompanied by Lieutenant Shipp. Tom Horn was chief of scouts in place of Al Sieber. Early in January 1886 they surprised the hostiles' camp on the Río Aros above its junction with the Bavispe and captured all of the ponies, camp equipment, and provisions. Demoralized by finding Chiricahuas now fighting on the side of the scouts, Geronimo, Nachez, and Chihuahua opened negotiations, agreeing to meet Crawford the next day.

At daybreak next morning a force of Mexican irregulars commanded by a well-known scalp hunter, opened fire on Crawford's camp. The captain called out in Spanish that they were American soldiers, and the firing ceased. Crawford then climbed onto a boulder to speak to the Mexican commander but fell, shot through the head. The furious Apache scouts now opened fire for the first time, killing the Mexican commander, his second in command, and perhaps a dozen more before Lieutenant Maus could stop the shooting. He went among the Mexicans, who demanded mules and rations before they would release him. Even after he had complied they did not let him go until his scouts made the mountains echo with their blood-chilling war cries. Geronimo and his party watched the whole affair in silence.

Crawford died five days later. In the meantime Maus resumed negotiations with the hostiles, who agreed to meet Crook at Cañon de los Embudos near the border in the usual "two moons." The Apaches reached the rendezvous on March 25, suspicious and wary of a trap. Mangus and thirteen others were not with them. As Crook informed Sheridan, the renegades remained about five hundred yards from Maus' camp. "I found them very independent," he wrote, "and as fierce as so many tigers. . . . After my talk with them it seemed as if it would be impossible to get any hold on them except

The meeting between General Crook and Geronimo in 1886.
Left to right: Captain Roberts, Geronimo, Nana, Lieutenant Maus,
three interpreters, Captain Bourke, and General Crook.
Western History Collection, University of Oklahoma

on condition that they be allowed to return to the reservation on their old status."[44]

It was the hostiles, not Crook, who set the conditions for their surrender. They gave him three choices: they would go East to join their families for two years; they would return to the reservation as before; or they would continue the war. Crook chose the first and informed Sheridan of the surrender terms.

Sheridan bluntly rejected the agreement. "The President," he wrote, "cannot assent to the surrender of the hostiles on the terms of their imprisonment in the East for two years, with the understanding of their return to the reservation. He instructs you to enter again into negotiations on the terms of their unconditional surrender, sparing only their lives."[45] "Take every precaution against the escape of the hostiles," Sheridan instructed Crook, in obtaining unconditional surrender. Unless these terms were accepted Crook was to "insure against further hostilities by completing the destruction of the hostiles. . . . "[46]

What this meant was that Crook, who above all others had been punctilious in keeping his word to Apaches, was expected to resort to what he considered sheer treachery. It may be that the famed "Apache telegraph" again mysteriously alerted the Apaches to impending troubles. At any rate, the night after Crook left their camp an American named Tribolet began selling mescal and rotgut whiskey to the hostiles, telling them that all who surrendered would be tried and hanged by the territorial authorities. Lieutenant Maus sent Lieutenant Shipp and some troops to destroy whatever liquor they could find in Tribolet's camp, but too late. Geronimo, Nachez, and a dozen others were already drunk. During the night twenty men, thirteen women, and six children accompanied the two chiefs back to the Sierra Madre, although two of the warriors changed their minds and returned.[47]

Crook wired the bad news to Sheridan, who replied on March 31: "Your dispatch of yesterday received. It has occasioned great disappointment. It seems strange that Geronimo and party could have escaped without the knowledge of the scouts."[48]

Angered at this slur on his trusted scouts, Crook declared "There can be no question that the scouts were thoroughly loyal, and would have prevented the hostiles leaving had it been possible." He pointed out that the hostiles had scattered their camps so as to make it impossible to surround or surprise them or even to keep close track of them.[49]

Sheridan replied that there was nothing to be done except to concentrate the troops and protect the people. Crook disagreed. As long as there were hostiles in the Sierra Madre the troops must be constantly ready, he said. Also, the hostiles provided a refuge for discontented Indians from all reservations. "I believe that the plan upon which I have conducted operations is the one most likely to prove successful in the end. It may be, however, that I am too much wedded to my own views in this matter," Crook continued, "and as I have spent nearly eight years in the hardest work of my life in this department, I respectfully request that I may be now relieved from its command."[50]

Sheridan immediately accepted Crook's request and the following day ordered General Nelson A. Miles to relieve him. In his orders to

Miles Sheridan repeated his belief that Indian scouts were unreliable and advised Miles to make "active and prominent use of the Regular troops. . . . " Sheridan was convinced that Crook's policies must be discredited.

In the meantime Chihuahua, Nana, and about sixty other Chiricahuas accompanied Lieutenant Maus to Fort Bowie; a few days later they were loaded on trains at Bowie Station and shipped—"removed"—to Fort Marion in St. Augustine, Florida. Crook would fight Apaches no more, but his efforts to aid them would be unceasing for the remaining four years of his life.

XIII
The Apache
Prisoners of War

As DISTRICT COMMANDER General Miles was given five thousand troops, about one-fourth of the entire U.S. Army; following Sheridan's suggestion he dismissed all but a few of the Apache scouts. He divided the border into districts, each with its garrisons, and established a series of heliograph stations on mountain tops for rapid communications. This was the army's answer to the Apaches' system of smoke signals. Once the stations were in operation, the troops, using a system of mirror signals, could send a twenty-five-word message four hundred miles and receive an answer in four hours. To pursue the hostiles into Mexico, Miles also organized a mobile striking force of one hundred troops and twenty San Carlos and White Mountain Apache scouts under Captain Henry W. Lawton of the Fourth Cavalry, a veteran of the Mackenzie campaigns. On Lawton's staff were Lieutenant Stanton and surgeon Leonard Wood; this force was based at Fort Bowie.

Before Miles' preparations were completed Geronimo and Nachez struck the Santa Cruz Valley, scattering into small parties and raiding as far north as the Fort Apache region. Scores of cavalry columns pursued them in vain. Early in May 1886 Captain Lebo of the Tenth Cavalry cut their trail and overtook them in northern Sonora, but found them too strongly entrenched to attack. Captain C. A. P. Hatfield of the Fourth Cavalry found the hostiles' trail in northern Mexico and captured all of their horses and camp equipment. He started for the border, but the Apaches ambushed his command in a narrow canyon and recovered their horses. They immediately launched another raid into Arizona, leaving a wounded warrior, Kieta, at Camp Apache. Losing horses and camp equipment meant little to the Apache hostiles; it had happened to them seven times in fifteen months, and on each occasion they had re-equipped themselves within a week by raiding ranches and Mexican

300

towns.[1] Miles would learn what Crook and Crawford had learned earlier, that it was simply impossible to wear Apaches down with regular troops. Only Apache scouts, unhampered by troops and pack trains, could keep up with the hostiles in the mountains.

Lawton's troops pursued the hostiles for four months, following them from one impenetrable mountain range to another, covering nearly fourteen hundred miles. For all their hardships, however, they had little to show for it. As surgeon Leonard Wood commented,

> One who does not know this country cannot realize what this kind of service means—marching every day in the intense heat, the rocks and earth being so torrid that the feet are blistered and rifle-barrels and everything metallic being so hot that the hand cannot touch them without getting burnt. It is a country rough beyond description, covered everywhere with cactus and full of rattlesnakes and other undesirable companions of that sort. The rain, when it does come, comes as a tropic tempest, transforming the dry cañons into raging torrents in an instant. . . . We had no tents and little or no baggage of any kind except rations and ammunition.[2]

All were obliged to walk, for the horses broke down within a week. Only one-third of the enlisted men endured the whole campaign, and the officers were replaced twice. But all of this effort and perseverance accomplished little.

General Miles learned of Kieta's presence at Camp Apache and sent for him. Kieta himself wanted no more fighting and said the others were also becoming weary of the constant fighting and running. If two or three men the hostiles knew and trusted visited them, Kieta declared, all might be persuaded to surrender. Miles swallowed his pride and decided to send Chiricahuas Kieta and Martine to negotiate with Geronimo, along with an officer whom Geronimo and Nachez knew and trusted. Since Captain Crawford was dead and Lieutenant Britton Davis had resigned, Gatewood was the only one remaining in the department who met the qualifications. He had already been detached from Fort Apache to rejoin his regiment, and although he was in ill-health he agreed to undertake the strenuous and perilous assignment.

Gatewood left for Mexico with Kieta and Martine, under orders to obtain a twenty-five man escort at Fort Bowie and not to go near the hostiles without it for fear of capture and ransom. Colonel Beaumont, commander at Bowie, could not furnish any troops, however, because his command was scattered on patrols. Gatewood obtained only an interpreter, George Wratten, a packer, and a courier. Beaumont sent Gatewood to Cloverdale, a temporary post near the border, to secure an escort.

At Cloverdale Gatewood found only a few squads of infantry and no animals, but a column of cavlary under Lieutenant James Parker escorted him to Lawton's camp on the Río Aros, two hundred miles below the border. Lawton had no information about the hostiles, but in mid-August Gatewood learned that they were near Fronteras, trying to negotiate a peace treaty with Mexican officials there.

With his small party Gatewood hurried to Fronteras, where he was told that two Apache women had been in town buying supplies and asking for a peace treaty. From Lieutenant Wilder Gatewood borrowed two extra interpreters, Tom Horn and José María, and then followed the tracks of the two women for three days. Martine and Kieta traveled well in advance and discovered the hostiles' camp on a peak of the Torres Mountains above a bend in the Bavispe River. Geronimo held Kieta as a hostage and sent Martine back to tell Gatewood he was willing to talk.

That night Lieutenant Brown and thirty scouts arrived from Lawton's command, but when they attempted to accompany Gatewood in the morning they met three armed Chiricahuas who told them to return to camp and remain there. Only Gatewood and a few others could continue.

The meeting place was a little glade on the banks of the Bavispe. As Gatewood recalled, "By squads the hostiles came in, unsaddled and turned out their ponies to graze. Among the last was Geronimo. He laid his rifle down twenty feet away and came and shook hands, remarking [on] my apparent bad health and asking what was the matter." Gatewood passed tobacco around as they sat in a semicircle. Geronimo sat close to Gatewood and announced that they were there to hear General Miles' message.[3]

Miles' terms were brief: Surrender and you will be sent to Florida to rejoin your families; after two years you will return to the reservation. "Accept these terms or fight it out to the bitter end." There was a long silence, while all looked intently at Gatewood. Geronimo, passing his hand across his eyes, explained that they had been on a three-day mescal drunk and asked if Gatewood had any whiskey. Gatewood had none.

Geronimo's initial reaction to Miles' demands was to reject them outright. He insisted on returning to the reservation, where they would have farms and receive ration issues as before. All day the discussions continued, with Geronimo repeating at intervals, "Take

Geronimo's camp in the 1880s. The sentinel has his rifle cocked
ready to shoot.
Western History Collection, University of Oklahoma

us to the reservation or fight." But before the talks broke up for the
day Nachez inquired after his mother and daughter. They were with
Chihuahua's band in Florida, Gatewood told him.

This news made the hostiles more willing to listen when the talks
resumed the next day, for like Nachez they were concerned about
their families. Seeing that he was rapidly losing ground, Geronimo
suddenly asked what sort of man Miles was. "We want your advice,"
he told Gatewood later. "Consider yourself not a white man but one
of us. Remember all that has been said today and tell us what we
should do." Gatewood's reply was well-intentioned, however ill-
advised it may have been: "Trust General Miles and surrender to
him."

The next morning the Chiricahuas called for Baychendaysan
(Long Nose), their name for Gatewood. Geronimo, Nachez, and
others told him they had decided to take his advice and surrender.[4]
Knowing there were other troops looking for them, the Apaches

announced they would retain their guns until they had talked to
Miles. They insisted that Gatewood remain with them during the
entire return trip and that Lawton's column march near them for
protection. They set out for the border on August 26.

On the second day of the return trip the commander of the
Mexican garrison at Fronteras approached with two hundred troops.
Gatewood and the Apaches, with only twenty-four men and fourteen women and children, dashed north while Lawton delayed the
Mexican troops. After a short time a messenger from Lawton informed them that he had agreed to a meeting between the Apaches
and the Mexican commander, so that he could convince himself that
Geronimo had indeed surrendered. When the commander arrived
Geronimo informed him that he was surrendering to the Americans
because he could trust them. The Mexican commander replied that
he would accompany the party and observe the surrender actually
taking place.

To this Geronimo reacted violently. With his hand on his pistol,
he shouted "No! You are going south and I am going north." As a
compromise solution, a Mexican soldier was allowed to go with
Lawton's command and return with Miles' official confirmation of
the surrender, so that the Mexicans could be satisfied that it was
genuine.[5]

The month before, while Gatewood and Lawton were still in
Mexico, Secretary of the Interior L. Q. C. Lamar had sent his son to
report on the Arizona Apaches. In only a year or two the Apaches at
both San Carlos and Camp Apache had made excellent progress in
farming and stock-raising; their herd of cattle had already increased
to four thousand. Lamar, Jr., who was accompanied by Miles on his
inspection of the reservations, urged prompt support of the program
Crook had begun, but he agreed with Miles that the presence of the
Chiricahuas in Arizona was a threat to peace.

Also in July Miles had requested permission to send a delegation
of Chiricahua and Warm Springs chiefs and headmen to Washington
to discuss the removal of all of their people from Arizona. Sheridan
was opposed to the wholesale transfer, pointing out that uprooting
tribes in the past had led to war. He did not object, however, to a
delegation coming to Washington. Thirteen Apaches (including
Chato, Kaetennae, and some women) accompanied by Captain
Dorst arrived in Washington for a visit with Secretary Lamar. Chato
was given a silver peace medal stamped with the likeness of President Arthur.

Captain Bourke, who knew the Apaches well, visited them and

entertained them. Dressed in cheap suits and straw hats, they accompanied him around the city and were especially pleased that he took them to hear a Mexican orchestra. When a woman vocalist performed they could not control their laughter: to them nothing was funnier than a woman singing.

On July 31 the fate of the Chiricahua and Warm Springs bands was discussed at a White House cabinet meeting. President Cleveland inquired about the feasibility of sending all Chiricahuas to Fort Marion, Florida, and wanted to know whether the present delegation could be sent to Florida instead of returning to Arizona. Captain Bourke, who had been invited to attend the meeting, vigorously opposed the removal as unwarranted, for the Chiricahuas were behaving well and applying themselves to farming and stock-raising. Other Apaches would resent their removal as unfair to them, he said. Captain Dorst took the opposite view. The other Apaches hated the Chiricahuas, he declared, and would be relieved to be rid of them. Bourke soon realized that arguments and expert information were useless, for Cleveland had already made up his mind and refused to listen to other views. He seemed convinced that regardless of promises, the hostiles should be "punished" for their "crimes."

General Miles, whose efforts to run down the hostiles with cavalry were proving fruitless, was sure that if all of the Chiricahuas and Warm Springs Apaches were removed to Indian Territory, Geronimo and the others would be willing to follow. He objected to sending them to Florida for two years, for that had been Crook's plan; Cleveland, furthermore, talked in terms of permanent exile.

The Apache delegation posed the most immediate problem, for Sheridan had promised them that they would be returned to the reservation. He feared, however, that once back they would frighten the others into flight. He ordered Dorst to delay them for five days at Carlisle Indian School in Pennsylvania before starting back to Arizona. Once they reached the reservation Sheridan's promise would have been kept; then the army could arrest them before they had an opportunity to panic the others. But Miles did not want them to return to Arizona at all, for he was sure that their presence would complicate the rounding up and removal of the others. By the time Miles had convinced his superiors of his views, Dorst and the Apaches were already crossing Kansas. Dorst received orders by telegraph to take the Apaches to Fort Leavenworth, where they were held for a month, constantly assured that all was well.

Next Miles called Dorst to Albuquerque for a conference and informed him that the people of Arizona and New Mexico wanted to try Chato and others for past crimes. Dorst was to warn the Apaches of this danger and then present Miles' plan to relocate them elsewhere. Dorst dutifully conveyed Miles' promise of a sixty-square-mile reservation, farming equipment, and livestock; and each member of the Indian delegation obligingly made his mark on Miles' "treaty."

In the meantime the secretary of war had inquired of Colonel Langdon, who was in charge of Chihuahua's band at Fort Marion, if he could make room for four or five hundred more Chiricahua and Warm Springs Apaches. It was a needless inquiry, for although Langdon replied that room could be made for perhaps seventy-five more, conditions were already crowded. President Cleveland and the secretaries of war and of the interior ordered the Apaches sent there anyway. Miles instructed various cavalry units to march to Fort Apache to be ready to help in the removal.

In an article about the end of the Apache troubles Brigadier James Parker recalled meeting General Miles at Fort Huachuca early in June 1886, and seizing the opportunity to make a suggestion.

> I have recently come from Fort Apache where the Chiricahuas not with Geronimo are located. Whenever there is news of a raid, the Chiricahuas, in order not to become involved in the fighing, go to the post and are quartered in the quartermaster corral.
>
> I would suggest a false report of a raid be spread and when the Indians are in the corral, they be surrounded by the troops, disarmed, taken to the railroad and shipped east as prisoners of war. Geronimo's band in the field will then be isolated, will no longer receive aid and comfort, as heretofore, and will surrender."

To this suggestion Miles replied with shocked sensibilities, "Why that would be treachery. I could never do that."[6] A month or two later, however, Miles had overcome his reluctance to engage in treachery.

Meanwhile Gatewood and thirty-eight hostiles, accompanied at a distance by Lawton's detachment, reached Skeleton Canyon, where Geronimo and Nachez had agreed to surrender to Miles. Miles' insistence that the Apaches surrender to Lawton almost shattered the precarious peace with Gatewood. Knowing that the Apaches were nervous and wary and likely to stampede at any moment, Lawton had sent a multitude of messages to Miles, urging him to meet with them. Miles used every excuse he could think of to avoid the meeting, even suggesting that Lawton and other officers catch Geronimo off guard and murder him. Lawton refused, and Miles reluctantly went to Skeleton Canyon on September 3.

After two days of talks, in which he offered conditions he knew would not be honored, Miles persuaded the Apaches to surrender and accompany him to Fort Bowie, although he could not convince them to give up their guns. Miles now misled General Oliver Howard, commander of the Division of the Pacific, into believing that the Apaches had surrendered unconditionally, and Howard happily relayed this good news to the War Department, asking at the same time what should be done with them. From President Cleveland came instructions to hold the Apaches as prisoners until they could be tried for their "crimes."

Miles deluged the War Department with telegrams and suggestions, but to no avail, for on September 8 Cleveland ordered the hostiles to be taken to the nearest fort or prison and held there. The telegram arrived as Miles was preparing to ship the Apaches off to Florida. One of his officers, however, Captain William Thompson, intercepted and pocketed it until the hostiles were disarmed and hauled away in wagons to Bowie Station, while the Fourth Cavalry band from Fort Huachuca sardonically played "Auld Lang Syne." Kieta and Martine, who had risked their lives to find and enter the hostiles' camp, were invited to see them off at the train. Once the Apaches were on board and the train was ready to move, Kieta and Martine were treacherously seized and thrown in with the Florida-bound prisoners of war.

Miles had knowingly ignored two presidential orders—first, by giving terms to the hostiles and, second, by sending them to Florida instead of incarcerating them at the nearest fort or prison. He now informed General Howard that the Apaches had surrendered with the understanding they would be sent out of the Southwest. Next he tried to convince the War Department that he had sent the Apaches to the nearest place of confinement, for though they were on a train bound for Florida Miles feared they might be stopped at Fort Sam Houston, Texas, or sent to Fort Leavenworth, Kansas. The War Department did order the train stopped at San Antonio, and the Apaches were taken to Fort Sam Houston. There they languished for six weeks while their fate was debated.

While Geronimo and his party waited hopelessly at San Antonio, Chato and the delegation being held at Fort Leavenworth were sent to Florida instead of Arizona as promised, arriving at Fort Marion on September 17. Three days later 381 reservation Chiricahua and

Warm Springs Apaches also arrived at Fort Marion; 382 had boarded the trained at Holbrook, but one had escaped in Missouri.

Meanwhile General Howard and the War Department searched vainly for copies of the messages from the War Department that Miles implied had authorized him to offer terms to the hostiles and to send them to Florida. The telegrams were not found, for they had not been sent. In Arizona there were many who demanded that Geronimo and his band of hostiles be returned to the territory for trial and punishment. Without knowledge of the surrender terms, however, officials in Washington could take no action other than to demand of Howard and Miles the "exact" conditions made. But Miles was traveling around Arizona and New Mexico, enjoying his hero's welcome everywhere, blithely ignoring repeated orders. When President Cleveland peremptorily demanded all information concerning the Apaches' surrender, Miles blandly requested permission to report to him in person. With growing irritation Cleveland denied the request and repeated his demand. Miles cheerfully led a parade, was feted at various ceremonies as the "conqueror of Geronimo," and three days later sent Cleveland a most uninformative and unsatisfactory reply. There was nothing left for the administration but to turn to the humiliating recourse of questioning Nachez and Geronimo separately as to their understanding of the surrender terms. Their stories agreed: Miles had promised them protection, reunion with their families, and a large, well-stocked reservation.

The dilemma was discussed at length in Washington before President Cleveland made his decision. The Apache men were to be held at Fort Pickens on Santa Rosa Island in Pensacola Bay; the women and children were to be sent to Fort Marion. Late in October the protesting Apaches were sent on their way from San Antonio. Cleveland considered the Apache problem settled at last, but there were certain aspects of the solution that would soon embarrass the government. The separating of families, for example, was difficult to justify; even less defensible was the incarceration at Fort Marion of seventeen Apache scouts who had served the army loyally and well. There was also Miles' promise of a large reservation.

After Nachez and Geronimo had surrendered only Mangus and a dozen of his band and a few other isolated families remained at large. In October, Mangus' people ran off a herd of mules from the Corralitos Ranch managed by Britton Davis, who followed them to the border and then wired Miles. Captain Charles L. Cooper and a detachment of Tenth Cavalry found them in an open area near the

A group of captive Apaches at Fort Bowie, 1886. Their moccasins
are worn from their flight. The woman on the left hides her nose
where the soft part has been sliced off, the customary Apache
punishment for a wife's infidelity.
Western History Collection, University of Oklahoma

Black Mountains and captured the whole party—the only time
armed Apache men were captured during the whole campaign.[7]
With Mangus were three men, three women, two half-grown boys,
and four children. On November 1, 1886 the captives were placed
on a train in Holbrook; Mangus and the warriors were sent to Fort
Pickens, while the others went on to Fort Marion. There were still a
few families of Apaches in the Sierra Madre, and although they stole
some horses and cattle from time to time, they posed no threat to
Mexico or Arizona. Survivors of these small groups lingered in the

Sierra Madre for nearly half a century, long after the Apache wars were forgotten. As late as 1900 some of them attacked Mormon settlers in Chihuahua.

One of these renegades was Massai, a Warm Springs Apache who had served as a scout in the 1880 campaign against Victorio. Two years later he and other scouts were returning to Arizona by train from Texas when he learned that Loco's Warm Springs band had been forced to leave San Carlos and was on its way to Arizona. Massai slipped off the train and somehow rejoined his family in the Sierra Madre. Thereafter he and his family left the renegades and returned to San Carlos. In 1885 he fled with Geronimo but soon returned to Turkey Creek, where he lived with his family until all of the Chiricahuas and Warm Springs Apaches were rounded up for exile in Florida.

According to Jason Betzinez, Massai tried to stir up a revolt on the way to Holbrook but no one cared to join so futile a venture. Before the train reached St. Louis, however, Massai escaped and made his way through unfamiliar country back to the Warm Springs region. He went secretly to Mescalero and stole a young woman, remaining in hiding with her for a quarter of a century. Part of the time he was with the Apache Kid and other irreconcilables, mainly Chiricahuas.

The most famous of the Apache renegades who remained at large after Geronimo's surrender was the former scout known as the Apache Kid. He was probably a White Mountain or San Carlos Apache. He had served well as a scout against the Chiricahuas and had risen to first sergeant of Company A, Indian Scouts. He was married to a daughter of Arivaipa chief Eskiminzin. His troubles began in the summer of 1887 when he avenged the killing of his father by shooting an Apache named Rip.

The Apache Kid and the scouts with him returned to San Carlos after the killing. Captain Pierce, now Indian agent at San Carlos, ordered the scouts to hand over their rifles and ammunition belts, and all of them complied. Then the interpreter, Antonio Díaz, apparently told them they would be sent to Florida, alarming other Apaches who were within hearing. Some mounted warriors rode up, and one of them opened fire at Pierce and Al Sieber. The Apache Kid and the scouts with him fled, most of them unarmed.

General Miles, at his headquarters in Los Angeles, declared, on the basis of inadequate information, that "The Indians have been well treated, and the [San Carlos] affair is the result of the innate deviltry of the Indian character, excited by very bad liquor."[8] Soon after this Miles traveled to San Carlos, where he received a message

The Apache Kid with friends in front of a wickiup, 1880
Western History Collection, University of Oklahoma

from the Apache Kid saying that he wanted to return there but couldn't with troops pressing him so closely. Miles called off the pursuit, and the scouts came to San Carlos to surrender.

Despite their admission that they did not understand the charges against them, Miles ordered the Apaches court-martialed "as if they had been white soldiers." One member of the court asked to be excused because of "bias and prejudice." Others admitted to the same handicap, but asserted that they could "arrive at a judgment on the basis of the evidence presented."[9] The fact was that they had already reached a decision; after going through all of the formalities, they sentenced the Apache Kid and four other scouts to death by a firing squad.

Miles objected to the harsh sentence on the grounds that Antonio Díaz' statement had excited others and that the "mutiny" was not premeditated. He ordered the court to reconsider its verdict. The court dutifully met again in August and sentenced the scouts to life in prison. Miles reduced the sentence to ten years and sent them under guard to Alcatraz.

The courts now decided that the army did not have jurisdiction in such cases, and the prisoners were returned to San Carlos and released, only to be rearrested by civil authorities and taken to Globe to stand trial in October 1889. Largely on Sieber's testimony they were again found guilty. Edward Arhelger, who was present, wrote that "All were promptly found guilty, which I think myself was wrong, but the sentiment was such that a good Indian was a dead Indian."[10]

The Apache Kid and his companions were sentenced to serve seven years in the territorial prison at Yuma. Sheriff Glen Reynolds and one deputy took the shackled prisoners in a stagecoach to Casa Grande en route to Yuma, having rejected Sieber's offer to provide an escort of scouts. On the second day they came to a steep hill; the sheriff and his deputy unloaded those prisoners who were shackled in pairs to lighten the load. The Apache Kid and Say-es, who were handcuffed separately, were left in the coach. The others pinioned the sheriff and his deputy, seized their guns, and killed both. They shot the driver and left him for dead, though he survived.

Troops and scouts were soon on their trail, killing two and capturing two, but the Apache Kid and several others were still free. Apparently the Kid and Massai joined forces for a time, and although they were blamed for numerous killings far and wide, neither was ever caught. Because the Apache Kid was his son-in-law, Eskiminzin was suspected of giving him supplies and information concerning troop movements; for this the chief was shipped off to Mount Vernon Barracks in Alabama, to be held with other prisoners of the Apache war.

In 1890 Mexican rurales killed three Apaches, recovering from one of them Sheriff Reynolds' watch and pistol. Four years later Walapai Ed Clark saw moccasin tracks near his cabin in the Galiuro Mountains and hid to watch. After dark he saw two forms approaching his horses and opened fire. The next day he and a posse found a dead Apache woman and tracks made by a wounded man, but the trail soon disappeared. If the wounded man was the Apache Kid, as was generally believed, he was not known to be in Arizona again. Later that same year an Apache woman came out of the Sierra Madre and reported that she had left him dying, apparently of tuberculosis. In 1911 or shortly before, Massai's wife returned to Mescalero with their four children, after Massai apparently had been killed. A few Apache families remained in the Sierra Madre and stole cattle and horses occasionally in the 1920s and 1930s. During the winter of 1935 Sonora ranchers killed all of the members of one band.[11] Jason Betzinez believed that there were still a few Apaches living in the Sierra Madre as late as the 1950s.

Among the Apache prisoners crowded into Fort Marion malaria and other diseases made heavy inroads. Although most visitors to the fort were attracted by curiosity to see the dreaded "savages" who had caused such terror and havoc in the Southwest, a few men and women were moved by a desire to help the Apaches out of their miserable situation. Education was a particular concern to many, and after much discussion the War and Interior Departments decided to send those Apaches between ages twelve and twenty-two to the U.S. Industrial School at Carlisle Barracks, Pennsylvania. In November 1886 twenty-four boys and fifteen girls were sent to Carlisle, and others soon followed. To the Apaches separation from their children was the cruelest blow yet.

The younger children were to be educated by the Sisters of Charity of the Convent of St. Joseph in St. Augustine, Florida—a decision that aroused the ire of local Protestant ministers. Their efforts to supersede the sisters were futile, however, for neither Interior nor War Department officials were willing to become embroiled in a religious controversy. The ministers were informed that "nothing could be done."

Despite some public interest in the Apaches' welfare their situation steadily worsened as winter came on and no clothing was provided; many of them were half-naked. Under public pressure the War Department requisitioned clothing for them, but the shipment failed to arrive during the winter, leaving the Apaches to suffer from exposure and disease. By early 1887 the growing number of complaints was brought to the attention of Herbert Welsh of the Indian Rights Association, who enlisted the aid of Captain John Bourke. It was March before the secretary of war reluctantly allowed the two to visit the Apaches at Fort Marion.

They found the Apaches extremely crowded, exposed to inclement weather, and suffering from injustice. Welsh carefully assembled information concerning the Apaches and began rallying support for their cause. As the War Department began to feel the growing public pressure some officials suggested moving the

Apaches from Fort Marion to Fort Pickens. There, on Santa Rosa Island, the public could be excluded and kept from causing trouble. Welsh, forewarned by Bourke, had this shameful scheme scotched.

By mid-April President Cleveland agreed that the Apaches should be moved. He sent Bourke secretly to inspect Mount Vernon Barracks, a former arsenal about thirty miles north of Mobile, Alabama. It seemed to Bourke a great improvement over Fort Marion. Late in April, therefore, most of the Apaches were moved from Fort Marion to Mount Vernon Barracks; the families of warriors held at Fort Pickens were sent to Fort Pickens.

At about this same time Welsh's report entitled *The Apache Prisoners in Fort Marion, St. Augustine, Florida* was published. In it he pointed out the various injustices done to individuals such as Chato, but his main purpose was to provide a happier and more useful future for all of the Apache prisoners. Bourke and Crook encouraged Welsh in his project. Crook was convinced that the "Apache business" would provide better material for a novel than chronicles of the mistreatment of the mission Indians in California. A novel like *Ramona* on the Apaches, he believed, would help their cause more than factual accounts.

In his *Resume of Operations Against Apache Indians, 1882–1886* General Crook had already protested bitterly the dishonorable treatment of the former scouts, asserting that they were "of more value in hunting down and compelling the surrender of the renegades, than all other troops engaged in operations against them, combined. . . . During the entire course of operations against them . . . the only hostiles killed or captured were in encounters with the scouts alone, except for two men. . . ." Every successful encounter with the hostiles, Crook continued, was "due exclusively to the exertions of Indian scouts." It was "the unanimous testimony of officers commanding scout companies, that the Chiricahuas were the most subordinate, energetic, untiring and, by odds, the most efficient of their command."[12]

Moving the Apache prisoners to Mount Vernon Barracks was simply an empty gesture made in response to public pressure. As Bourke reported, the Apaches were simply "dumped" there, and the War Department did nothing more for them. Interpreter Sam Bowman wrote that they were idle, for the land was too sandy for successful farming, and there was little else for them to do. Both the post surgeon and the commanding officer, Major William Sinclair, frequently informed General Howard that the Apaches were not receiving enough to eat, but it was not until November 1887 that the army took steps to remedy the situation.[13] Even worse, disease was spreading, and within six months after their arrival ten had died— most of tuberculosis. Lozen, Victorio's sister, who had accompanied Geronimo on his last outbreak, was one of those who died there. And although Major Sinclair manfully tried to provide work for them building log cabins and repairing roads, few men were strong enough for labor.

By the end of January 1888 it was generally agreed that Mount Vernon Barracks was unsuitable as a permanent home for the Apaches, but the various interest groups could not agree on a new location. As the quarrels among these groups intensified Secretary of War Endicott simply took no action. The Apaches, too, began fighting among themselves, and at both Mount Vernon and Fort Pickens unscrupulous citizens aggravated the situation by secretly selling them whiskey. In May the Apaches at Fort Pickens were also transferred to the inadequate facilities at Mount Vernon Barracks.

After conferring with General Crook, who recommended giving Apaches individual farms at Fort Sill, Indian Territory, Welsh tried to convince Endicott of the need for such a change. But the secretary had not forgiven Welsh for the public attack on him the previous year and refused to listen to anything Welsh had to say. Crook urged Welsh to intensify his efforts; the general was convinced that unless strong influence was brought to bear on the administration it would continue to ignore the Apaches' plight.

In March 1889 the Republican administration of Benjamin Harrison took office, and the new secretary of war, Redfield Proctor, was willing to consider various other sites, for he had not been party to the earlier arguments. The deplorable situation of the Apaches at Mount Vernon was made even sadder by the return of seven children from Carlisle Indian School, all of them dying of tuberculosis. Lack of anything worthwhile to occupy most of the men remained a serious problem, and Colonel Robert Hughes asserted that life at Mount Vernon Barracks could produce nothing but vagabonds and thieves.

In June Captain Bourke and Charles C. Painter, a Congregationalist minister who represented the Indian Rights Association in Washington, visited the Apaches and interviewed the leading men. Painter asked for their views about leaving Mount Vernon in order to support themselves. They would need, Chato replied, fertile land, pastures, and livestock. Others reminded Painter that they had farmed successfully in Arizona, adding that they wanted to live near a river and in a place where it snowed.

Bourke and Painter inspected the region around Asheville, North Carolina, but the Cherokee reservation in the Great Smoky Mountains seemed particularly attractive. The Cherokees, they learned, would be willing to sell twelve thousand of their one hundred thousand acres and would welcome the Apaches. The two commissioners also inspected other sites, particularly an eight-hundred-acre farm near Hampton Institute in Virginia. In his report Bourke recommended the Cherokee land as the most suitable for the Apaches, adding that the War Department should continue to look after them when they were resettled. Secretary of War Proctor approved Bourke's suggestions and proposed that he take some of the Apache headmen to confer with the Cherokees. But when Bourke's report was published, opposition to the plan unexpectedly arose in western North Carolina.

Meanwhile at Mount Vernon a dozen more Apache children returned from Carlisle, all of them dying of tuberculosis. Major Charles Witherell, who had replaced Sinclair, reopened the school at Mount Vernon and encouraged the teachers in everything they undertook. A new teacher, Miss Sophie Shepard, looked forward with anticipation to the day her students would be able to march around the Christmas tree singing "Onward Christian Soldiers" in unison. [14] While the missionary teachers viewed such achievements as significant and rewarding, their contribution toward eventual Apache self-sufficiency was greatly overrated. A similar attitude toward Indian education in general would persist for another seventy or eighty years.

Late in December 1889 Secretary of War Proctor sent General Crook to inspect the Cherokee lands and to confer with the Apaches in Alabama. Crook agreed that the Cherokee country was similar to the mountainous terrain the Apaches had known, but he was sure there was not enough arable land on the site to support them.

In January Crook visited the Apaches at Mount Vernon Barracks. As soon as word spread that *Nantan Lupan* had arrived, Chihuahua, Kaetennae, and others met him and took him to their log cabins, where Chato embraced him warmly. Soon a conference with chiefs and headmen was arranged, but when Geronimo tried to take his place at the meeting, Crook called him a liar and sent him away; he never forgave Geronimo for his flight after surrendering. The talk went on all day as the Apaches detailed the wrongs done them. At the conclusion Chihuahua expressed the feelings of all when he said they wanted to go where they could see great distances.

In Washington Crook's press conferences attracted widespread attention; as one reporter wrote, he aroused both sympathy for a suffering people and indignation against the authors of a "perfidious and heartless wrong." Crook especially emphasized the fact that the hostiles would never have surrendered except for the help of the Apache scouts who were now imprisoned along with those they had helped capture. They were, Crook concluded, "innocent victims of a great outrage."[15]

To the secretary of war Crook pointed out that "The most ordinary justice would seem to demand a different course of procedure with men not only innocent of offense against the Government, but to whom the Government is largely indebted for services of the very greatest value, and which they alone could have rendered."[16] The present administration could make partial recompense, Crook concluded, by giving the Apaches farms in Indian Territory and permitting them to keep their children at home.

The secretary of war recommended that the Apaches be moved from Alabama, adding that Indian Territory was a more preferable home for them than North Carolina. Although a law of 1879 prohibited Indians from Arizona or New Mexico from living in Indian Territory, Proctor announced that they could remain at Fort Sill until Congress granted them a permanent reservation there. Senator Henry Dawes immediately went into action, but in the House Committee on Indian Affairs an obstacle arose. General Howard had instructed his son to enlist Herbert Welsh's support for the North Carolina plan; as commander of the Division of the Atlantic, Howard would have control of the Apaches in North Carolina.

Opposition to the Fort Sill site was quickly voiced by newspapers of the Southwest, and they were strongly supported by General Miles, who had previously urged sending the Apaches to Fort Sill. Now that it was Crook's suggestion and no longer his own, however, Miles could see absolutely no merit in the proposal. Fort Sill was too close to Arizona and New Mexico, he now cautioned, and the Apaches might once more terrorize the people of those territories.

Some newspaper editors claimed that Crook had been misled by the Apaches on his visit to Alabama. He denied the charge, saying that there was no probability that the Apaches would turn "like snakes upon the Government. The Apaches are broken in spirit and humbled to the dust."[17]

Once more the Apache issue brought forth a deluge of opinion, most of it unfavorable to the Fort Sill proposal. When it was pointed out that there was no favorable location for the Apaches east of the

Mississippi River, the Arizona delegate to Congress declared that the people of the Southwest would gladly purchase land for them in Vermont, adding snidely that the people of Arizona preferred to listen to Miles, who had captured the Apaches, than to Crook, who had failed. On March 21, while the controversy was raging with no sign of abatement, General Crook died of a heart attack, and the Fort Sill plan lost its most influential supporter. There was great mourning among the Apaches.

When it appeared that the North Carolina project was certain to succeed Lieutenant Howard, the general's son, who had shifted his support to Crook, suggested that something be done to help the Apaches right away, while a new home for them was being selected. The House Committee on Indian Affairs happily accepted this suggestion as an excuse to put off further discussion of the controversial removal issue. Herbert Welsh, who was still dedicated to the North Carolina proposal, tried in vain to revive it.

In June 1890 Lieutenant William Wallace Wotherspoon was placed in command of the Apaches at Mount Vernon Barracks, as part of the War Department's program for helping the Apaches. Wotherspoon had already served in several administrative positions in a well-designed career that would carry him to head of the Army War College and to the post of chief of staff of the army. Captain Bourke was no admirer of Wotherspoon, whom he considered to be "self-seeking and willing to let everything go for a little present, personal advantage. . . . " Wotherspoon would, Bourke asserted, make "show Indians" out of the Apaches as long as they were where he and his wife could live comfortably, but he would never go to North Carolina or anywhere he might have to "rough it."[18]

When he arrived at Mount Vernon Barracks Wotherspoon seemed certain that the Apaches would remain there indefinitely and that their troubles had aroused widespread public concern. And since General Howard and other high-ranking officers were hoping to solve the "Apache problem" to their own credit, Wotherspoon was in an ideal position to enhance his own future. He immediately insisted that the Apaches forget about leaving and start working like "white men." He would find them work at thirty-five cents a day, and they could freely spend half of what they earned. He soon had some of them cutting wood at the post and others working for local farmers. The problem of drunkenness continued, however, for there were too many people around the post who were willing to sell whiskey to the Apaches. But after fourteen men were arrested and tried for selling whiskey to Indians and eleven were convicted, the liquor problem was drastically reduced if not totally solved.

Secretary of War Proctor, on a tour of military establishments in the South, visited Mount Vernon in March 1891. His solution to the Indian problem, he informed Wotherspoon, was to integrate Indians fully into American life. This meant military service as well as other activities, and he had decided to recruit fifteen hundred Indians for infantry and artillery companies. The first Apaches were enlisted in Company I, Ninth Infantry, at San Carlos in mid-May 1891. They were sent to Whipple Barracks for training under Lieutenant Charles Dodge, Jr., who informed Proctor that they were "as fine a set of young men as were ever recruited for the Army."[19]

Shortly after this Company I, Twelfth Infantry, was recruited at Mount Vernon Barracks among the prisoners of war; forty-six enlisted. The company was brought up to full strength by twenty-nine Apaches from San Carlos, and it became the largest Indian troop unit. By October the Apache company was able to join white units for drills and parades. In addition to military activities the Indian soldiers had daily instruction in English and mathematics as well as training in carpentry, blacksmithing, and similar crafts, and played baseball and football. Wotherspoon called them "the most intelligent of our [nation's] Indians." Their only problem was their weakness for alcohol, which was apparently equal to—but not greater than—that of white soldiers.

Another company was recruited at Fort Apache. Their commander, Lieutenant Zebulon B. Vance, Jr., found them proud and intelligent, with an exceedingly clear concept of justice but unforgiving of anyone who offended them. They clung to their traditional ways and resented routine duties as "women's work."[20]

At Mount Vernon Barracks two ex-renegades and two Carlisle-educated Apaches became sergeants. They assumed a large share of responsibilities and, in the opinion of officers who observed them, nowhere in the army were there "brighter, more reliable sergeants taking more interest in their profession." Although the War Department considered the experiment successful, there was much prejudice against the use of Indians as soldiers. Furthermore, except at Mount Vernon Barracks the re-enlistment rate was low.[21]

By the fall of 1893 Wotherspoon reported that the Apaches had progressed as far as they could at Mount Vernon Barracks and that it was time to decide on their permanent location, which apparently

Apache scouts photographed on the San Carlos Reservation, about 1893
Arizona Historical Society

meant he could see no further advantage in maintaining charge of them. He recommended that they be moved to the Cherokee lands and given individual farms; after that it would be up to them to provide for themselves. In December he and Captain Pratt visited the Cherokee country, which had already been thoroughly inspected numerous times. Wotherspoon now decided, as Crook had earlier, that there was not enough land suitable for cultivation, an opinion the Indian Rights Association did not appreciate.

In 1894 the "Apache problem" was again the cause of much discussion. Grover Cleveland had returned to the presidency in March of the previous year, but neither he nor Secretary of War Daniel Lamont gave the Apaches high priority. Bourke and Welsh still favored the North Carolina site, and John Clum, now in the Post Office Department in Washington, also took an interest in the Apache prisoners and their fate.

On a visit to Mount Vernon Barracks Clum was surprised to see his old friend Eskiminzin there. "Skimmy" had been blamed for everything that occurred on the San Carlos reservation, for some Anglos were determined to have the prosperous farms and herds he and his people had developed. In 1888 the commander at San Carlos sent a detachment to warn him that Anglos were coming to kill him or drive him away, and the timely warning had saved him. The men arrived the next day, drove off his family, and took everything he owned. At San Carlos Eskiminzin had selected farm land and had it nearly fenced when, because he was suspected of aiding his son-in-

law, the Apache Kid, he was sent to Mount Vernon Barracks as a
"military precaution." Although Clum was unable to interest Herbert Welsh in the injustice done Eskiminzin, the old chief was
quietly allowed to return to San Carlos, where he died a short time
later. [22]

In August 1894, after a spring and summer during which a
number of Mount Vernon Apaches were involved in killings, Congress appropriated money to send them to military reservations
throughout the country. The disgraceful plan was to scatter them
widely and allow them to disappear quietly, a plan even General
Miles opposed as cruel and unjust. Reversing himself once more he
proposed sending the Apaches to Fort Sill in Indian Territory (evidently the fact that this was originally Crook's recommendation had
been forgotten). In September the War Department ordered the
removal, and a month later the prisoners of war and the Apache
troops boarded a train for Fort Sill. The last part of the trip was across
open country in wagons; when the Apaches first heard coyotes
howling in the distance the women began to wail, for they had not
heard that welcome sound for eight years.

In the meantime two of the three remaining Apache companies
failed to re-enlist. Forty-six Apache soldiers from Arizona were
merged with twenty-three Comanches in Troop L, Seventh Cavalry, until their enlistments expired the following year. By the summer of 1895 the Indian soldier experiment was down to the sixty-
seven Apaches who were at Fort Sill. Captain Hugh L. Scott, who
commanded this last Indian unit, had praise for the Apaches: they
were excellent in drill, reliable on guard details, able to maintain
order in the Apache camps and to keep illegal Anglo cattlemen and
traders off the reservation. Much of their time was spent learning
various crafts. In his program for gradual adoption of the white man's
occupations Scott found Chihuahua, Chato, Loco, and Nachez completely cooperative.

Because of their good conduct Judge Advocate General G. Norman Lieber ruled that all Apache soldiers would be free men when
discharged, even if they had been prisoners of war when they
enlisted. In practice, however, they remained prisoners of war until
1913, when all were freed.

In May 1897 the Indian company held its last drill. Twelve of the
Apaches were able to re-enlist as scouts, but few of the others could
find any employment near the post and were soon starving. The
army neither helped them nor allowed them to leave Fort Sill to find
work. There were still officers who were strongly biased against

Indians, and the Apaches' six years of excellent service had not changed these attitudes. General Howard commented that the experiment was resisted by men who resented the fact that they might in the future have to take orders from Indian sergeants.[23]

When the Apaches arrived at Rush Springs, about thirty miles from Fort Sill, delegations of Comanches and Kiowas were there to greet them. The newcomers were unable to converse in the sign language used by Plains tribes, and so each group put forward a few Carlisle Indian school graduates to serve as interpreters. There was ample room for the Apaches on the lands the Kiowas and Comanches gave them, with good pasture and water.

The Apaches were divided into village groups, each under a head man, who received the pay and uniform of an Indian scout. Among these were Chato, Geronimo, Martine, Perico, Chihuahua, Kaetennae, Mangus, and Nachez. They built cabins on the ten acres each family received for growing food. When they were given cattle they had to fence the huge tract and to dig stock tanks. Having no horses at first, they were obliged to do everything on foot— including handling cattle on the open range, round ups, and branding.

Under the guidance of several officers who had charge of them over the years the Apaches built up a tribal fund by cutting and selling hay and by raising cattle. As more and more Anglos moved onto land around the reservation after it was opened to settlement in 1901, the sale of liquor became a serious problem. Some Apaches would trade their horses or saddles for whiskey. Major George W. Goode, who was in charge of them at the time, handled such cases sternly and kept the whiskey peddlers off the reservation, which eased the problem.

In 1900 or the following year the Apache prisoners opened discussions on the possibility of returning to their former lands in Arizona and New Mexico, to live as they had before. Differences soon arose, however, for some men, such as Jason Betzinez, were successful at farming and ranching and had no desire to move and start over again.

Geronimo at Fort Sill in 1898, photographed by Tom Burdick,
a civil engineer with the U.S. Medical Department.
He is not wearing Apache dress.
Courtesy of Cecil Tendick,
Jacksonville Journal Courier, Jacksonville, Ill.

When Chato and Toclanny went to Washington to discuss removal with officials, Betzinez accompanied them to present a minority view. Chato and Toclanny informed Secretary of War William H. Taft that they wanted to return to their old Warm Springs reservation. "How long," Taft asked, "since you have seen that reservation?" Forty years, they replied. He suggested that they revisit the site and report to him and their own people on the condition of the land. Then if they still wanted to go there, he would try to arrange it.[24]

Jason Betzinez spoke up and informed Taft that he and a few others preferred to remain in Oklahoma. The Kiowas and Comanches had given them enough land to provide an allotment of 160 acres for every family, he said, but no allotments had ever been made.

In October 1911 a delegation of six Apaches and two officers went to New Mexico to select a site. The Mescaleros welcomed them, for they were under pressure from Anglos trying to usurp reservation lands and felt that additional numbers would help their cause. The delegation continued on to Monticello and the old Warm Springs agency. The land they remembered as fertile and green was now barren, the valleys and pastures were filled with gravel washed down from the hills, possibly as a result of mining. The Warm Springs had disappeared without a trace. Now that the Warm Springs Apaches at last had the opportunity to return to their favorite land it was no longer attractive—ruined, no doubt, by Anglos. As a result 127 adults, including most of the surviving chiefs and warriors—Nachez, Chato, Martine, Kieta, Kaetennae, Noche, and Toclanny—chose to settle at Mescalero. Chihuahua, Nana, and Geronimo had all died at Fort Sill. In the spring of 1913 the Apaches were finally released as prisoners of war, and in April they moved to Mescalero. Eighty-seven adults remained in Oklahoma.

A month after the move was made the Apaches' herd of ten thousand cattle was sold at auction, and buyers came from neighboring states to bid on them. Those Apaches remaining in Oklahoma kept a few horses and cattle and began building homes on their allotments. For them, at least, the "Apache problem" was finally settled, and they were on their own, to survive or fail.

XIV
The Eagles Caged

ONCE ALL INDIANS were finally settled on reservations all were sub-jected to the same laws and pressures. Before examining the impact of these laws and pressures on the Apaches it is necessary to sum-marize briefly the relevant events for reservation Indians from that time to the present.

Because of the success of John Clum and a few other agents in organizing and employing Indians as reservation police, the com-missioner of Indian affairs in 1878 instructed all agents to organize similar forces wherever possible. In 1883 Secretary of the Interior Henry M. Teller also authorized the creation of courts of Indian offenses, to deal with minor "crimes." It would be a delusion, however, to suppose that either institution was established to pro-vide Indians with an increasing measure of self-government. The underlying if not explicit purpose was exploitative: to use Indians to control their own people and especially to destroy tribal government and leadership. Secretary Teller, a former senator from Colorado, admitted that he established the courts because he was determined to eliminate certain "heathenish dances" as well as other customs and to break the power of the medicine men. He decreed that the three top officers of the Indian police at each reservation should serve as judges and added, out of a delicate sense of concern for the American taxpayer, that they should serve without pay.[1] In 1885 Congress extended federal criminal jurisdiction over the reserva-tions.

Most of the "offenses" with which the court dealt involved drunk-enness and family problems, participation in native ceremonies, bigamy, and so forth. Reservation Indians especially hated the bans on ceremonies, plural marriages, and medicine men which forced them into clandestine meetings in order to preserve even the mem-ory of their traditional ways.

From the beginning of the reservation system government policy was to "assimilate" all Indians until they lost their identity, which meant reshaping the Indians' concept of life and system of values, particularly as reflected in their attitude toward land. Officials based this policy on the undying belief that if Indians owned land as individuals rather than collectively as members of a tribe they would develop the stalwart characteristics of the small farmer. It was the accepted wisdom from the time of Thomas Jefferson that the yeoman farmer was the salt of the earth, the backbone of the nation, and the repository of all civic virtues.

Based on this faith, a land-in-severalty bill was proposed in 1880 which Senator Henry L. Dawes of Massachusetts ultimately pushed through as the General Allotment (Dawes) Act of 1887. It was undoubtedly the most destructive legislation ever devised for the "welfare" of Indians. When the act was first introduced Senator Teller called it "a bill to despoil the Indians of their lands and to make them vagabonds on the face of the earth," adding, "I want to put upon the record my prophecy in this matter, that when thirty or forty years will have passed and these Indians shall have parted with their title, they will curse the hand that was raised professedly in their defense. . . . "[2] "It is part of the Indian's religion not to divide his land," Teller stated another time. "Do you suppose that when Indians have those religious ideas that you can violate their moral sentiments and compel them to live on land and own it in severalty?"[3]

Captain Richard Henry Pratt of Carlisle Indian School also opposed the act, but not out of sympathy for Indians. "I would blow the reservations to pieces," he declared. "I would not give the Indian an acre of land. When he strikes bottom, he will get up."[4] Theodore Roosevelt later called the Dawes Act "a mighty pulverizing engine to break up the tribal mores."[5] And as secretary of the interior, Teller would encourage land grabs against the Teton Sioux and others, thereby assuring that his prophecy would be quickly fulfilled.

The most articulate indictment of the land-in-severalty bill was the minority report of the House Committee on Indian Affairs, which pointed out that "it does not make a farmer out of an Indian to give him a quarter section of land." The training and traditions of the Indian predisposed him against this scheme for his improvement "devised by those who judge him exclusively from *their* standpoint instead of from *his*." The bill, the report continued, assumed that the Indian is, like other men, able to take care of himself, then "turns round upon itself and, assuming that the Indian *is not* and *will not be* able to take care of himself . . . proceeds to hedge him around with provisions. . . . " If he was able to take care of himself the precautions were unnecessary, the report stated; if he was not it was illogical to make him try.

Brushing aside the platitudes about the welfare of the Indians, the minority members concluded that "The provisions for the apparent benefit of the Indian are but the pretext to get at his lands and occupy them—a development that would surely pave the way for his extinction.

> If this were done in the name of Greed, it would be bad enough, but to do it in the name of Humanity . . . is infinitely worse. Of all the attempts to encroach upon the Indian, this attempt to manufacture him into a white man by act of Congress and the grace of the Secretary of the Interior is the baldest, the boldest, and the most unjustifiable.
>
> Whatever civilization has been reached by the Indian tribes has been attained under the tribal system. . . . Gradually, under that system, they are working out their own deliverance, which will come in their own good time if we but leave them alone and perform our part of the many contracts we have made with them. But that we have never yet done, and it seems from this bill we will never yet do. We want their lands, and we are bound to have them.[6]

The Dawes Act called for allotment of 80 acres of farm land or 160 of grazing land to each family head. The government would retain title to the land for twenty-five years or longer if the president considered it desirable; after that the land would go on the tax rolls and could be retained, leased, or sold by the allottee, who became a citizen upon receiving the title. Lands remaining after the allotments were distributed were to be considered "surplus" and sold to the public; in practice, however, "surplus" lands were sometimes sold before any allotments had been made. The law was later amended to allow the secretary of the interior to give title without waiting twenty-five years—land-hungry whites regarded that as an unreasonably long waiting period to get their hands on allotted lands. The result was that between 1917 and 1921 twenty thousand titles or fee patents were issued, more than twice the number issued before 1917. Many of the new landowners were quickly relieved of their land. Fortunately for the Apaches, the allotment policy played only a minor role in Arizona reservations, and although part of the Jicarilla reservation in New Mexico was allotted, the remainder was not sold.

When the Dawes Act was passed Indian reservations comprised some 138,000,000 acres. Forty-seven years later, when the allotment system was abolished in 1934, the reservations retained only 48,000,000 acres, mostly eroded, desert, or otherwise useless land, and at least ninety thousand Indians were landless. The act had been bitterly opposed by the few Indians who were aware of it, but Congress blatantly disregarded the principle of mutual agreement in the enactment of laws concerning Indians, thereby creating a pattern for bypassing tribal organizations in the future. Tribal government atrophied as a consequence, while federal supervision and control were asserted with increasing insistence. The allotment system, carried to its logical conclusion, would have lifted the burden of assimilation from government agencies and deposited it squarely on helpless individual Indians. One of the most paradoxical aspects of this calamitous legislation was that Senator Dawes, noted Friend of the Indian, was motivated by the delusion that he was providing a happy future for the Indians. The land-grabbers, more realistic as to the actual beneficiaries, looked on Dawes as their benefactor.

During the era of the Dawes Act the federal government began to assume responsibility for Indian education, another calamity for reservation dwellers. In treaty after treaty Congress had promised to provide schools for the various tribes, but before the 1880s no serious effort was made to keep these promises other than allowing some church groups to establish mission schools on reservations. But as was pointed out many times, missionaries too often were more interested in making converts than in educating Indians. It brought tears to the eyes of devout folk in the home congregations to hear forlorn Indian children singing familiar hymns in their native tongues, and it probably helped loosen purse strings. Marching around a Christmas tree singing "Onward Christian Soldiers" hardly prepared Indian children to cope with reservation life as adults.

During the late nineteenth century, Indians—totally isolated on reservations except for a few inept, prejudiced, and underpaid Bureau of Indian Affairs (BIA) employees—were expected, in some miraculous fashion, to become thoroughly assimilated into white society. To aid this impossible cause the commissioner ordered in 1887 that all instruction in Indian schools must be in English—thereafter Indian children were punished for using their own language even at play. No one realized that English should have been taught as a second language, one not used in the home. Teachers expected Indian children to have the same background and preparation as Anglo children. And of course few had. In 1892 Congress authorized the commissioner to make school attendance compulsory, and the following year it allowed him to refuse rations to families who stubbornly kept their children out of school. Even the Friends of the Indian considered starvation proper punishment for willful Indians who refused to recognize "what was good for them."

Anglo officials and reformers tried persistently to make Indians acquire private property on the assumption that pride in individual ownership was the greatest "civilizing" agent available. They could never grasp the fact that private ownership of land was an immoral concept to Indians. They believed the land had been placed there for all to use and enjoy and that it was sacrilegious to monopolize it. To BIA officials and pious reformers alike this attitude smacked of un-Americanism which they were determined to root out and replace with acquisitiveness and greed, the virtues of civilized men. In their frustration officials pecked away at anything the Indians did differently. In 1896 another order was issued to hasten the assimilation process; this inspired edict decreed that henceforth Indian men must wear their hair short. Since in many tribes cutting the hair was a sign of deep mourning, perhaps this order was unintentionally appropriate.

Education, however, became the chief instrument for remaking the Indians, and in the effort unfortunate, inappropriate policies were pursued tenaciously despite the unfavorable results they invariably produced. In 1879 Captain Richard Henry Pratt had inaugurated the federal educational program by establishing the Indian Industrial School in the old cavalry barracks at Carlisle, Pennsylvania. Over the years hundreds of frightened and homesick children were exiled there from western reservations, to die of disease or to return home totally unfitted for life on the reservation or off it. Ridiculed by their own people, most of them simply went "back to the blanket" and tried to forget the whole unhappy experience.

As he made clear, Pratt was committed to absolute assimilation. "A great general has said that the only good Indian is a dead one," he declared in 1892. "In a sense I agree with the sentiment, but only in this: that all the Indian there is in the race should be dead. Kill the Indian in him, and save the man."[7] "The school at Carlisle," he said later, "has always planted treason to the tribe and loyalty to the nation at large."[8]

One of the Apaches who was converted by Pratt's methods was Jason Betzinez, a nephew of Geronimo and one of the Apache prisoners of war. Pratt took him along with others from Fort Marion in 1887 when Betzinez was already twenty-seven years old. Although resentful at first he remained at Carlisle for nine years, becoming assimilated and a great admirer of Pratt in the process. Betzinez was also converted to Christianity and thereafter regarded his people's traditional beliefs as "superstitions."

One of Pratt's methods was to place Indian children with Pennsylvania farm families during the summers, to acquaint them thoroughly with the whites' way of living. Betzinez, for example, worked summers for a Quaker farmer and his family. After leaving Carlisle he worked in a steel mill for several years before rejoining his people at Fort Sill.

Convinced by Pratt's "success" that Indians could indeed be "educated," the BIA established off-reservation boarding schools at Albuquerque in 1884 and at Santa Fe and Phoenix in 1890; by 1900 there were twenty-six of them as well as several day or boarding schools on reservations. In 1898 the superintendent of Indian schools succinctly expressed the bureau's educational aims. "In our efforts to humanize, christianize and educate the Indian," he wrote, "we should endeavor to divorce him from his primitive habits and customs . . . we must recreate him, and make him a new personality. . . ."[9] "Educating" Indians seems to have brought out in American officials and reformers a latent desire to play the deity.

In formulating its educational policies the BIA consistently disregarded the existence of the Bureau of American Ethnology (BAE), which had been established in Washington to obtain information on the different tribes so that government bureaus and agencies could deal sympathetically and intelligently with the Indians. It was not until John Collier became commissioner of Indian affairs in the 1930s, however, that the BIA ever opened communications with the BAE. In 1935 when the Indian school at Chilocco, Oklahoma, sought material for a course on Indian history and lore, the BIA still had little to offer.[10]

The dual policies of education and land allotment almost destroyed several tribes. When reformers at last began during the 1920s to look seriously at the condition of the Indians—the "vanishing race" that had refused to vanish—they found Indians generally weakened by hunger and disease, in grave danger of losing the small amount of good land they had left, and scourged by an educational program that fostered intense hatred of the white man's ways. Led by John Collier, Oliver LaFarge, and others, reformers began demanding sweeping changes in federal Indian policy.

In 1926 Secretary of the Interior Hubert Work engaged a private research institution to investigate the BIA, its policies, and their effect on Indians. Dr. Lewis Meriam directed the study and in 1928 published the findings as *The Problem of Indian Administration*, generally called the Meriam Report. It criticized past policies, especially the destructive allotment system and boarding schools, and was hailed as a "stinging reproach to a niggardly and exploiting government."[11] Meriam's work revealed that boarding school children were cruelly starved on a diet costing nine cents a day per child, had almost no medical care, and were overcrowded and mercilessly overworked. Because of low pay, qualified teachers and staff could not be hired. Discipline, which was left to the director of each school, was usually severe. Oliver LaFarge condemned the boarding schools as "penal institutions—where little children were sentenced to hard labor for a term of years to expiate the crime of being born of their mothers."[12]

Until the 1930s, LaFarge said, the office of commissioner of Indian affairs had been a "political plum to be handed to a good party member too dumb or compliant to be entrusted with a job the public watched. . . . " The role was simple—when whites wanted part of a reservation, the commissioner saw that they got it. President Herbert Hoover, however, violated tradition in 1930 by appointing two dedicated reformers, Charles J. Rhoads and Henry Scattergood, as commissioner and assistant commissioner. They laid the foundation for new policies by bringing in experts and qualified personnel. For the first time Indian education was directed by a trained educator. For the first time, too, children in the boarding schools were given enough food and their hours of drudgery were reduced.[13]

John Collier, who served as commissioner from 1933 to 1945, stated his goals as "economic rehabilitation of the Indians, principally on the land; organization of the Indian tribes for managing their own affairs; and civil and cultural freedom for the Indians."[14] Half a century later these goals have yet to be realized.

The first major steps of the "Indian New Deal" were the 1934 Johnson-O'Malley and the Indian Reorganization (or Wheeler-Howard) Acts. The former enabled the secretary of the interior to negotiate contracts with the various states for education, agricultural assistance, and social welfare for Indians. Through it many public school districts were reimbursed for Indian students in their schools, although the districts were under no obligation to provide special programs for Indian children or even to apply the federal funds to their education. Nor would public school officials brook any interference from BIA officials, who justifiably feared that the Indians might be short-changed. Consequently, most school districts simply added the funds to the general school budgets and permitted the Indian students to stay or drop out. Johnson-O'Malley funds are still being used, but as usual, when laws or appropriations were passed for Indian education, the Indians were the last to be informed. It was not until the late 1960s, in fact, that Indians discovered that the act provided funds for special educational programs for their children. Only then did the Johnson-O'Malley Act become anything more than financial assistance to schools that happened to have some ignored and neglected Indian students enrolled.[15]

The Indian Reorganization Act (IRA) prohibited further allotment of Indian land and authorized the use of federal appropriations to enable tribes to buy back lands lost earlier or to purchase other land. But when the BIA used IRA funds to acquire some land for Acoma Pueblo Reservation in New Mexico, Congress immediately banned the use of IRA money to buy land for reservations in Arizona or New Mexico. The act charged the secretary of the interior with preventing the erosion, overgrazing, and deforestation of Indian lands, with establishing a revolving fund to provide credit, and with facilitating the adoption of tribal constitutions and business charters. A unique feature of the bill gave individual tribes the choice of accepting or rejecting its provisions.

Although passage of the IRA marked the beginning of many needed changes in Indian policy, the tribal "self-government" it authorized was an illusion. Tribal constitutions contained a painful reminder that whatever they authorized was "subject to the approval of the Secretary of the Interior." The government retained a veto power which the Indians could not override. Clarence Wesley, chairman of the San Carlos Apache Tribal Council, commented that "With the new changes taking place and the new tribal business committee . . . lacking knowledge in their various undertakings, the beginning of tribal government was not easy. In fact, Superintendent Kitch was still the boss."[16]

The IRA also made Indians eligible for BIA positions without regard to Civil Service requirements. Under Collier, who called the Indian Service "by intention a regimented operation through bureaucratized robots," the BIA ceased to be an "employment agency for self-seeking whites," and Indians were given preference in hiring.

The loan fund established by the IRA proved to be one of its most beneficial features, and Indians on many reservations used it to inaugurate new economic projects. The first general appropriation to provide reservation Indians with credit had been passed in 1911, when the modest sum of $30,000 was made available; additional sums were later provided. Under the regulations for the IRA loan program, however, government officials purchased the livestock or machinery and then resold it to the Indians—as usual Indians had no say concerning the type or quality.[17]

Many New Deal emergency measures were applicable to reservations, and a branch of the Civilian Conservation Corps, called the Indian Emergency Work Program, was created for Indians. One result of these programs was the introduction of many projects to improve the economic conditions on reservations; another was that many Indians began working for wages and acquired valuable vocational training that could lead to future employment.

In education many community day schools were opened, and some boarding schools were closed or converted. Curriculum changes were introduced to eliminate the bureau's stifling Uniform Course of Study as well as to reduce the overwhelming emphasis on white society. One of Collier's directives attempted to check the incessant assault on Indian religious beliefs and practices: he ordered that there would be no more "interference with Indian religious life or ceremonial expression."[18] Because of bureaucratic inertia and fossilized attitudes, however, such reversals of policy were by no means universally observed or effective throughout the Indian Service. And many tribes had already forgotten most of their religious ceremonies.

World War II had a profound impact on Indians, for a large number served in the armed forces and many others found employment in off-reservation industries. The development of reservation resources, begun during the 1930s, was temporarily neglected. When war veterans returned to the reservations and found that their status had not improved they no longer accepted discrimination and second-class citizenship passively. The veterans who returned to Arizona and New Mexico played a major role in forcing both states to extend voting rights to Indians in 1948. The seeds of Indian self-determination thus were sown.

From 1883 to 1946 Indians could not bring claims against the government except by special act of Congress, a situation that had intensified their feeling of futility and despair. In 1946, however, Congress passed the Indian Claims Commission Act which replaced the law of 1883 forbidding Indians to sue in the U.S. Court of Claims. Under the new act the government acknowledged that such claims existed and gave the commission jurisdiction over them.

During the postwar years government policy shifted from an emphasis on reservation development to "relocation" (moving Indians from reservations to urban areas) and then to "termination" (abolishing reservations altogether). Arrangements were made to train reservation Indians for various urban jobs, relocate them and their families in certain selected cities, and help them find jobs and living quarters. But there seldom was adequate preparation for such sudden and drastic changes, and there was no continuing attention to help the Indians overcome the problems that inevitably arose. Some Indians made the transition successfully, but many either returned, defeated, to the reservations or joined the winos in the gutters of Skid Row. Relocation revived BIA interest in off-reservation boarding schools, for these were again seen as way stations on the road to assimilation, places where Indians could be trained for urban employment.

In 1944 a new force had appeared in Indian affairs, the National Congress of American Indians, organized in Denver that November. It was almost immediately confronted with the termination issue, which was already gathering strength in Congress through use of the same deceitful or misguided arguments concerning the "betterment" of the Indians, arguments that had led in 1887 to the passage of the Dawes Act. The battle against termination was an invigorating training ground for Indian leaders. In the first place, it pushed tribal rivalries into the background before they could exercise a divisive effect; such rivalries had no place in a fight for survival. The struggle was also an education in political realities, for Indian leaders learned for the first time where the centers of power were located and the value of nationwide publicity in dealing with them. Previously they had appealed to the commissioner of Indian affairs; now they realized that the real power over Indian affairs lay in congressional committees, not with the BIA. This proved a most valuable lesson, for it paved the way to achieving educational self-determination.

In 1953 Congress issued a new statement on Indian policy—House Concurrent Resolution 108—which sent a wave of fear through all reservations. The resolution declared that it was the intention of Congress to make Indians subject to the same laws as other citizens and to "free" them of federal supervision and control. Implicit in this "freeing" of the Indians was the termination of their special relationship with the federal government and of the government's responsibilities to them based on treaties by which the Indians had surrendered their lands. The resolution soon resulted in the termination of the special federal relationship with about a dozen Indian groups in the 1950s, abruptly casting them adrift without adequate preparation and with disastrous results. Senator Arthur V. Watkins of Utah, the most dedicated champion of termination, exclaimed that "Approximately ten thousand Indians were thus set on the road to complete citizenship rights and responsibilities." For most of the Indians involved termination was ruinous. Even though the resolution was no longer applied by the 1960s, and although President Lyndon B. Johnson favored Indian self-determination over termination, Congress did not repeal the termination resolution. Even today fear that the policy may be revived at any time still looms over reservation Indians and is a constant inducement to tribal leaders to keep their people on the reservations if possible.

Congress struck another blow at reservation Indians in 1953 with the passage of Public Law 280, which authorized states to extend civil and criminal jurisdiction over reservations within their boundaries. In signing the bill, President Dwight D. Eisenhower noted that it did not require consent of the Indians, and he urged Congress to add such a requirement. Amendments to PL 280 requiring Indians' consent were submitted in Congress, but none was enthusiastically supported. The BIA, in fact, opposed them, preferring instead an amendment that required only "consultation" with the Indians. Since that was little better than no amendment at all, the issue died. No one even questioned the possible violation of treaty obligations. It was not until passage of the Civil Rights Act of 1968, fifteen years later, that PL 280 was modified to require a state to obtain tribal consent before extending its civil and criminal jurisdiction over a reservation.

In 1953 Congress took yet another action regarding Indian rights by legalizing local option concerning the sale of liquor on reservations, allowing the indivual tribes the choice of permitting or prohibiting it. There seems to have been a note of unintentional sardonic humor in this last action. With House Concurrent Resolution 108 and PL 280 Congress had prepared the way for the Indians' ultimate and thorough ruin. By lifting the ban on the sale of liquor to Indians it gave them the opportunity to wash away their pain and sorrow in a flood of cheap whiskey.

Eisenhower took a more positive step in 1955 when he transferred the responsibility for providing medical services to Indians from the BIA to the Public Health Service, which had far greater resources for building and staffing health facilities on reservations. Since then the Indian Health Service has made considerable progress in providing needed medical facilities as well as sanitation measures, safe drinking water, and adequate housing.

After pushing relocation of Indians in several large cities during the 1950s and 1960s, government policy has shifted once more to promoting the establishment of industries and employment opportunities on reservations. Recent legislation has extended many federal programs to Indians, who were previously ineligible for the benefits. The major trend of recent years had been toward decentralization of responsibility for administering Indian affairs, decreasing federal control in order to generate greater Indian participation in decision-making. The BIA has plans for contracting many of its present services to tribes or to private organizations.

Early in 1961 President John F. Kennedy's Task Force on Indian Affairs began a study of Indian conditions. The task force reported that the BIA still emphasized termination more than economic development for Indians. It found Indians apprehensive that they would be "terminated" before they were prepared for so drastic a step. For this reason the task force urged maximum development of Indian self-sufficiency, insisting that Indians who lived off the reservations should receive the same rights and privileges as other citizens of the region.[19]

The political experience gained in the battle against termination enabled Indian organizations and leaders to conduct a promising campaign for self-determination in educating their children. The number of intertribal national organizations has been increasing substantially, and these special interest groups have provided an avenue for exchanging ideas at regional and national meetings. In 1969 the National Indian Education Association held its first meeting; it subsequently provided Congress with its members' reactions to legislation concerning Indian education and cooperated with congressmen in preparing bills on the same subject.

The 1965 Elementary and Secondary Education Act was intended to meet the special educational needs of low-income families, a category which included almost all Indians. Like Johnson-O'Malley funds, however, much of the money allocated to public schools serving Indian students went into general school district budgets—in some cases, with less benefit to Indians than to other children. The early fears of BIA officials that state school systems would be more eager to acquire federal funds than to provide adequate education for Indian children had, from the beginning of the Johnson-O'Malley program, proved well-founded.

Following custom and precedent those government officials involved in the programs never considered consulting Indians. During the late 1960s, however, Indian leaders anxious to improve the quality and effectiveness of the education their children received, concentrated their attack on federal funding for public schools. In some states intertribal groups won the right to review Johnson-O'Malley budgets before their final approval. In New Mexico and Arizona, furthermore, programs were offered to inform parents of Indian children in public schools of their rights and the steps necessary to obtain them.

In 1969 a special Senate subcommittee published *Indian Education: A National Tragedy—A National Challenge.* Known informally as the Kennedy Report, it protested that education for Indians had not improved significantly since the publication of the Meriam Report in 1928. One by-product of the Kennedy Report was passage of the Indian Education Act of 1972. Although it was concerned only with Indian education in public schools, it applied to two-thirds of all Indian students.

The new law, the most important one concerning Indian education that Congress had ever enacted, went a long way toward assuring Indian control of Indian education. One of its provisions made parental and community participation in the direction of impact-aid programs mandatory by requiring that parents of Indian children constitute at least half of the parent advisory committees called for in the act. These committees were to formulate the plans, draw up budgets, and monitor and evaluate the programs. For the first time urban, "terminated" Indians had a voice in the education of their children. Until the parent advisory committees approved a project, a school district could not apply for federal funds. The act also created a National Advisory Council to consult with and advise the U.S. Office of Education. Even after the act was passed and appropriations were voted, however, Indian pressure was necessary to force the government to release the funds. Another significant step was the establishment in 1972 of the Office of Indian Education within the U.S. Office of Education.

It was against this backdrop that the Apaches had to make their way. In 1882 the Jicarilla and Mescalero agencies were combined, but the plan to move the Mescaleros was abandoned, and in the following year 721 Jicarillas were moved to Mescalero. Neither band had been consulted, and neither was happy with the arrangement. A few years later groups of Jicarillas began leaving the reservation and returning to their own country, many of them starving. Finally in

1887 they were given a permanent reservation of their own in north central New Mexico. At first it encompassed about 415,000 acres, but in 1908 more than 300,000 acres were added to the southern part of the reservation as a grazing area for sheep.

The much-neglected Jicarillas were in a deplorable condition, but owing to apathy and despair their condition worsened steadily for the next thirty years. Their folk hero, Monster Slayer, had given them lands in northeastern New Mexico and southeastern Colorado, warning them they must live there always or perish. When placed on a reservation outside their traditional lands, the belief that they would surely die virtually paralyzed them. A healthy people before their reservation life began, they deteriorated rapidly. By 1914 nearly 90 per cent of them had tuberculosis, and their death rate was so high that it was confidently predicted they would be extinct within twenty years.

In the 1920s the agency superintendent secured permission to sell reservation timber to buy sheep for the Jicarillas. It was difficult to persuade them to accept these animals, but those who did were conscientious in looking after them. This small step marked the beginning of slow progress toward recovery. In 1920 the boarding school was converted into a sanitorium and a special medical program was established to check the inroads of tuberculosis. The Jicarillas began to revive. By 1942 the process could be reversed, and the boarding school was reopened. Although the northern part of the reservation had been allotted, in 1934, thanks to the Indian Reorganization Act, the allotted lands were returned to the tribe. In 1937 the Jicarillas accepted a constitution and established a tribal council. The council labored to devise ways to use the reservation's limited resources more effectively, for the population began increasing.[20] The tribal council established a $1 million scholarship fund for Jicarillas who go to college, and all children of one-quarter or more Jicarilla ancestry living on the reservation were accepted as tribal members. In addition to timber, minerals, and livestock, the Jicarillas have developed a profitable tourist-recreation complex at Dulce Lake. They own the trading post, and they have a group of professional forest-fire fighters modeled after the Red Hats of the Mescaleros.

The Mescaleros, too, had trouble adjusting to the unfamiliar confinement of a reservation, even though it contained half a million acres as well as some of their favorite mountains. The frequent changes of agents, each introducing new policies, brought instability. For example, one agent, dissatisfied with the small number of children in the reservation boarding school, ordered Apache police to the scattered camps to seize children of school age and deliver them to the school. Admitting that this proceeding was "unusual," he was not disturbed to find the men "sullen and muttering, the women loud in their lamentations, and the children almost out of their wits with fright."[21]

From time to time the Mescaleros were plagued by agents who were unusually determined to remake them instantly into imitation white men. In 1895 V. E. Stottler set out to force them to alter their family structure, make the men cut their hair short and dress like whites, cease brewing and drinking tizwin, and abandon most of their ceremonial dances. He abolished the court of Indian offenses, induced some of the men to work in a saw mill, and tried to force every family to build a wooden house. On orders from the commissioner he purchased five thousand sheep—ten for each Mescalero—and imported some expert Navajo weavers to instruct the women. Some fortunate Mescaleros were employed hauling supplies from Las Cruces, a task which afforded them a taste of their former mobility. Stottler also introduced the planting of potatoes, garden vegetables, and oats in his efforts to push them toward a cash economy. Some were induced to trade ponies for additional sheep, and others sold enough agricultural products to purchase goats. The Mescalero population had, by the late 1890s, shrunk to 450. All of the changes made were over their opposition. And even though they began playing baseball in 1899, this evidence of cultural change so dear to Anglos was far more symbolic than genuine.

Under agent J. A. Carroll, who served for ten years beginning in 1901, the Mescaleros were pushed even further along the white man's road by the agent's determined use of his virtually dictatorial powers over them. In 1902, despite the fact that the Mescaleros lived in abysmal poverty, BIA officials declared them to be self-supporting and ended ration issues except to the elderly and incapacitated. At the same time the agent began paying men for their labor, using tribal income derived from leasing grazing lands to Anglo cattlemen.

During Carroll's regime the Mescaleros began receiving income from wool and livestock, from agricultural produce such as oats, and also from the sale of handicrafts. The population nevertheless continued to decline. In 1905 the arrival of thirty-seven Lipan Apaches, the pitiful remnants of that once-powerful Texas band, gave the population a slight boost.

The Mescalero reservation, like those of the Arizona Apaches, was surrounded by Anglos eager to obtain Indian lands by fair means or foul. In 1909 President Theodore Roosevelt was persuaded to incorporate the reservation in the newly created Alamo National Forest, which meant that land use thereafter would be determined by the secretary of agriculture. Although President William H. Taft restored the reservation to its former status outside the national forest in 1912, the Mescaleros' land troubles were not over. New Mexico became a state the same year, and hunger for Indian land was an incurable malaise.

Senator Albert B. Fall, a prominent rancher whose range bordered the western edge of the reservation, introduced a bill to create a national park out of the Mescalero holdings. Although the bill did not pass Fall continued to resubmit it to Congress session after session. The Mescaleros, knowing that Anglo land-hunger was insatiable and that "permanent" guarantees in treaties were actually temporary, worried constantly. Their fears discouraged any serious effort to develop their reservation economy.

In 1913 the Mescaleros welcomed 187 Chiricahua and Warm Springs Apaches from Fort Sill, the former prisoners of war. In their struggle to preserve their reservation intact the Mescaleros hoped that these additions to their own declining numbers would help their cause. Soon after the arrival of the former prisoners of war the BIA used part of the income from grazing leases to purchase a tribal cattle herd. Cattle-raising would become an important Mescalero activity, but this action, like so many others directly affecting the Apaches and all other reservation Indians, was taken without consulting them. The agents' powers over their wards were so complete that they forgot they were dealing with human beings.

At the end of World War I the Mescaleros organized a tribal business committee and endeavored to become part of the decision-making process concerning the reservation's economy. But because Congress had decided to use reservation income to pay BIA employees and to purchase equipment the Mescalero Business Committee could not even sell timber or use part of the grazing-lease money without congressional authorization, and that authorization was not forthcoming. The president of the business committee became virtually head chief of the Mescaleros, but he and his committee could decide only minor matters.

In 1922, as demands increased for reforms in the management of Indian affairs, Congress belatedly confirmed the Mescaleros' title to their reservation. In 1924, in a sweeping action, Congress made citizens of all Indian people whether or not they wished citizenship.

This action affected only those living on reservations, for the others were already citizens.

Two years after the Indian Reorganization Act was passed in 1934 the Mescaleros adopted a constitution and made the business committee their tribal government. They also took advantage of the IRA revolving fund to purchase farming equipment and distributed the tribal herd among the individual families. They ended all leases to Anglo cattlemen and established a Cattle Growers' Association to manage all herds on the reservation. In three years the income from cattle rose from $18,000 to $100,000, and the value of their agricultural products increased similarly. By 1942 every Mescalero family had a wooden house built of lumber cut and sawed on the reservation. It has been suggested that the Mescaleros benefitted more from the "Indian New Deal" than any others. [22]

Shortly after the end of World War II, a war in which many Apaches served in the armed forces or worked in wartime industries, Congress passed the Indian Claims Commission Act. The Mescaleros and other Apaches entered suits for compensation for the loss of their lands by treaty violations. In 1967 the Mescaleros received an award of $8.5 million, most of which was invested by their business committee.

In 1948 the forest ranger called for volunteers to help fight a forest fire, and the Mescaleros' famous Red Hats—a group of parachuting forest-fire fighters—was born. Eventually the Red Hats grew to a total of two hundred men organized into effective teams. Word of their prowess spread beyond New Mexico and they have frequently been called on to fight forest fires in the Pacific coast states.

When government policy shifted to relocation, the Mescaleros, whose increasing population had far outgrown reservation resources, accepted the program, and many families moved to Los Angeles or San Francisco. They were ill-prepared for the conditions they found, and nearly all returned to the reservation.

The Mescalero Business Committee undertook the development of reservation industries and activities that could support the growing population. During the 1950s young Mescaleros began seeking university educations to prepare them for various occupations previously closed to them. In 1956, when the Apache Summit tourist center was opened on a mountain pass near the highway between Ruidoso and Mescalero, tourism began to provide a new source of reservation income. The center included a motel, restaurant, craft shops, and trailer park—all built with tribal funds. In 1962 the business committee borrowed $1.5 million from the government to purchase a ski run on the north slope of Sierra Blanca, and it proved a profitable investment.

A new constitution, adopted in 1964, made all Indians on the reservation members of the Mescalero Apache Tribe and provided that children of one Mescalero parent would be considered members and shareholders. It also replaced the business committee with a tribal council of eight elected members.

In the early 1970s tribal council president Wendell Chino, a college graduate who had gained widespread recognition in national Indian organizations, contracted for the construction of an earth dam to create a lake as part of a new recreation complex that would also include a hotel, golf course, dude ranch, and hunting lodge. By these various diversified activities the Mescaleros have provided increasing opportunities for those living on the reservation, although many are still unemployed or underemployed. The tribal council also invested $600,000 of the claims money to endow a scholarship fund for Mescaleros who wish to attend college.

For most Mescaleros the high point of the year is the annual "Feast" or ceremony of girls' puberty rites held during the first week of July. It is the occasion for identity renewal, and most Mescaleros living off the reservation make a determined effort to attend. Because of the rigid control by Stottler and other agents this ceremony is the only one of their old religious practices that many Mescaleros remember.[23]

Among both Mescaleros and Jicarillas the younger generation is in danger of losing touch with the old ways of their people without replacing them by Anglo cultural ways. The old ties that held the extended family together are gradually being forgotten.[24] Another problem is the continual battle against alcoholism; many Apaches regard this as their primary health problem.[25] The Mescaleros do not allow the sale or possession of liquor on the reservation, but they do not have to travel far off the reservation to obtain it.

The Apache reservations in Arizona—San Carlos and the Fort Apache or White Mountain reservation—suffered from the same problems that plagued those in New Mexico. The San Carlos Apaches had begun raising cattle early, but during the 1880s cattle ranches spread around the reservation and many Apaches worked as cowboys for Anglo ranchers. In 1892, as cattle prices fell, the Apaches lost interest in cattle and worked on the railroads, especially on the branch line from Globe to Bylas. In 1902, when rations were issued for the last time, most of the Apaches supported themselves by off-reservation jobs. As farming profits declined and the

Apaches showed little interest in reviving cattle-raising, the BIA began leasing grazing rights on both reservations to Anglo ranchers. Some Apaches continued working for these ranchers, both on and off the reservations. As agent Hall commented in 1878, "They are almost without exception willing to work, and could constant employment be found for them they would easily be made self-supporting."[26]

Little was done to educate the San Carlos Apaches, but in 1890 the Dutch Reformed Church opened a school there. Two years later Commissioner of Indian Affairs Thomas J. Morgan demanded the use of force to compel all Indian children to attend schools. "At San Carlos," he said,

> are the Apaches, who are regarded as the most vicious of the Indians with whom we have to deal. They are held virtually as prisoners, the San Carlos Agency being under the control of the military. For years there has been a military officer in command, supported by two or three companies of colored soldiers. The conditions on that reservation are simply deplorable. . . . These people decline to send their children to school; but I have within the last twelve months taken from that reservation about two hundred of them. They are to-day well fed and properly clothed, are happy and contented, and making good progress.[27]

Most Indian children taken forcibly from their homes, however, were far from "happy and contented." Whether they were "well fed" or not and what they were making "good progress" toward are, of course, other questions.

The BIA took over the church school at San Carlos and converted it into a boarding school. Attendance was compulsory, and boys and girls were segregated for all activities. Since discipline was severe and punishments excessive, many children fled, and most developed an intense hatred for the white man's ways.[28]

In 1936 both the San Carlos and White Mountain Apaches organized under constitutions and established tribal councils to administer the affairs of the whole group as well as all tribally owned property and enterprises. Although neither band had ever been organized on a tribal basis before, this innovation was successful. The Apaches took a strong interest in the council and its affairs; women as well as men were active, and women have been elected to the council.

One of the most profitable enterprises under the councils' supervision at both reservations has been the cattle industry. The BIA

The Sunrise Ceremony, White River Fair Ground, September, 1951
Arizona Historical Society

provided breeding stock on several occasions, and in 1934 the
bureau procured purebred animals to upgrade the reservation
herds. When Anglo grazing leases expired they were not renewed,
and the Apaches quickly established valuable private and tribal
herds. The San Carlos Tribal Council maintains a herd of registered
Herefords for breeding stock as well as an "old folks" herd to support
the tribal welfare program. Five livestock associations handle about
twelve thousand head of cattle which produce an annual income of
about $1 million. All who own cattle must belong to one of the cattle
growers' associations which control separate range areas assigned to

them. Only about one-third of the San Carlos families own cattle, however, and about two-thirds of them receive less than $1000 a year from sales. Some Apaches have no other source of income except irregular off-reservation jobs.

Because reservation grazing land at Fort Apache is limited, no individual may own more than seventy cows for breeding. When an association member dies, furthermore, his cattle are sold and the proceeds distributed among his heirs. This practice makes it possible for another individual, who had been on a waiting list, to enter the cattle business. The association lends him twenty head of breeding stock. During the next seven to ten years he must repay that number and two additional animals as interest on his loan.[29]

In 1953 the Fort Apache Tribal Council established the White Mountain Enterprises to develop recreational areas for the tourist trade. They built a winter sports area—Sunrise Park—then added Sunrise Lake for fishing and to make it a year-round resort. One of the major reservation industries is the Fort Apache Timber Company, organized to exploit the excellent stands of timber. The company operates a large sawmill at Whiteriver.

The San Carlos reservation today covers more than a million and a half acres, about half its original size, and much of it lacking fertile soil or water. San Carlos Lake was created long after the reservation was established. Most of the San Carlos Apaches who live on the reservation are located in San Carlos, Bylas, or Peridot. Unemployment is chronic, and since few of the San Carlos Apaches have attended college, there are few successful and educated elders for younger members to emulate. Even many tribal leaders have had to rely more on native intelligence than on formal education or training. Because of the widespread poverty it has been difficult to overcome apathy and indifference toward education, for its advantages have not been made explicit.

San Carlos Apache students who attend public schools near the reservation have lacked adequate preparation, and few have received encouragement either from teachers or from parents. As Edward A. Parmee commented in 1968, after an intensive study of educational problems at San Carlos, "The orientation of the entire program . . . was towards the assimilation of Apaches into the Anglo culture, an aim which was diametrically opposed to the desires of most Apaches. . . . " There was, he continued, little effort to mesh the goals and operation of the local educational program with the needs and desires of the Apache people.[30]

The Apaches' relationship to the state of Arizona is complex.

Apaches are not supported by the government, as some people believe, although they do receive free medical services and education by treaty guarantees. Until the Public Health Service took over medical facilities in the 1950s, however, medical care was often inadequate because the BIA had insufficient funds. Although the land within the reservation boundaries is not taxed by the state and Apaches do not pay state income taxes, they do pay federal income taxes and state sales taxes, and those living off the reservations are taxed the same as other citizens. Apaches on and off the reservations are eligible to vote in both state and federal elections, although Arizona delayed as long as possible—until 1948—before extending voting privileges.

After Arizona did legalize voting for the state's Indians, however, few Apaches saw any reason to register. Fort Apache and San Carlos leaders, increasingly aware of the value of political power, launched a drive to register all eligible voters. Since many families lived in clan groups scattered in remote and inaccessible parts of the reservations, the drive took a number of years to be effective. Tribal leaders then began inviting candidates to appear before the tribal council, after which they endorsed certain candidates and urged Apaches to vote as a bloc. The results were gratifying.[31]

Because of the emphasis within the federal government on termination, in 1952 the University of Arizona established the Bureau of Ethnic Research. Its purpose was to study social and economic problems of the state's Indian peoples in case the state should have to assume responsibility for services previously provided by the federal government. Two years later Arizona created a Commission of Indian Affairs to study conditions among the Indians and to provide them with a more direct means of communications with state government. The commission is composed of five Indians and two non-Indians, all appointed by the governor. During the same decade Arizona State University at Tempe inagurated a special program in Indian education; the University of Arizona established an Indian Studies program; and Northern Arizona University at Flagstaff began a teacher corps training program designed especially for Indians.

Apaches, like many other Indian people, are not at all eager for assimilation into white society and cling desperately to their old ways. Their desire for a better life, a material standard of living more nearly equal to that of whites, is by no means the same as wanting to adopt the white man's values or his cultural heritage. They understand clearly today that education is the key to living standards above the poverty level, but they do not intend to sacrifice their basic beliefs for decent housing or for a chance to escape chronic malnutrition and a life expectancy at least one-third less than that of other Americans. Herein lies the basis for much of the conflict between Apaches and Anglos, for Anglos regard education as the avenue to "assimilation"—meaning the total adoption of white ways.

Some officials have been convinced that Apache children should be placed in integrated public schools as far as possible, to hasten their assimilation, although the high dropout rate and other evidence of difficulty in such schools should have suggested caution. Many Apache parents prefer community day schools near their homes, where their children will not be overexposed to alien white cultural values. Such diametrically opposing views have caused real problems and fundamental misunderstandings; as a result Apache parents have been unfairly accused of being indifferent to their children's education.

In the public schools Apache children only rarely receive necessary special attention, for teachers and administrators are unfamiliar with their problems and unaware of their needs. Even teachers who are sympathetic and who make an effort to aid Apache students know so little about them that they cannot communicate effectively. The problem is less one of language than of cultural ideals and values. There has been no understanding between Apache parents and students, on one side, and teachers and administrators, on the other. The latter simply have not understood that Apaches are opposed not to education but to the manner in which it has been imposed on their children.[32]

One of the most fundamental differences between Indian and white attitudes concerns the notion of time. "To white culture," Robert L. Faherty wrote, "time is a regularized object whose symbol is the clock"; and white society virtually lives by the clock. "Set off against this," he continued, "is natural time, a fluid continuum that is geared to the rising and setting of the sun and to the changes in seasons." Indians, he added, joke among themselves about operating on "Indian time," saying that a community meeting "will start this evening sharp." Another important cultural difference is that lines of authority among whites are vertical, while among Indians they are horizontal.[33] These different outlooks are effective obstacles to complete understanding.

The San Carlos reservation has been unable to provide expanding employment for its growing population. During the 1960s, 75 per cent of Apaches of working age—more than twelve hundred—were unemployed. They and their families lived in deplorable poverty, and their children who were in school were waiting hopelessly for the ordeal to end.

The shift to a cash and wage economy caused the head of the extended family to ignore other families, whereas formerly he would have felt responsible for them and their needs. Government paternalism in providing education as well as welfare and public health programs has largely eliminated the family head's responsibility for the children and for the sick and aged. As family structures change and new stresses appear, new social problems also arise. In the case of the Apaches in both Arizona and New Mexico these are alcohol addiction, abandonment of children, gambling, and prostitution. All of these indicate a changing culture under serious tensions. Together these pervasive problems discourage young Apaches from making the effort to acquire an education.

The problems of San Carlos have been more acute than at other Apache reservations. The tribal council, composed of men with little education or training, tried its best to increase opportunities for employment on the reservation, but in 1964 there were still only eighty Apaches with full-time jobs there. Half worked on tribal enterprises such as cattle-raising; only five worked at farming; the rest were employed by the BIA or other federal agencies.

Only during the late 1960s did conditions begin to improve at San Carlos with the introduction of specialized training for teachers along with reading laboratories and new, more appropriate testing methods. Also during this period some Apaches were elected to off-reservation school boards, and many parents took a renewed interest in their children's education. Head Start programs at the San Carlos and Fort Apache reservations helped children prepare for the public schools; adult education and vocational training programs, such as the one at Whiteriver, near Fort Apache, raised hopes for increased employment. Today all civil service jobs on both reservations are held by Apaches.

In 1968 an office of educational coordinator was set up at Fort Apache to provide an effective link between the BIA and the schools. The Apaches, too, match BIA grants for education with equal amounts from tribal funds.[34] The culture center at Fort Apache, which teaches both Apache lore and language, has proved popular with young Apaches.

Urban Indians comprise one of the least visible and most neglected groups in Arizona, for they share many of the problems of reservation dwellers but lack the agencies to help meet their needs. Unlike other urban minority groups Indians hesitate to seek the health, education, and welfare services available to them as citizens. One partial solution for young urban Indians is the Pan-Indian movement, which enables them to retain a sense of identity as Indians. Where such organizations exist, urban Indians are able to avoid some of the apparent hostility or indifference of white society as well as the limitations of identification with a particular tribe. But tribal rivalries, unfortunately, are all too likely to survive in cities.

Reservations provide the support and security of family ties that most people need. Many Indians are torn between the lure of urban economic opportunities and the temptation to remain with family and friends in familiar surroundings. For many the only attractive solution is to develop their reservations so that those who receive education and training will not have to leave to find appropriate employment. Because House Concurrent Resolution 108 has never been repealed, the threat of termination of reservation trusteeships and federal services continues to hang over all reservation Indians. This danger is obviously increased by any exodus from a reservation, and that is one reason why tribal councils are striving to provide employment opportunities. Failure to provide such opportunities will tempt or force young educated Apaches to leave the reservations; without them and their skills any plans for economic development are seriously jeopardized. This is the dilemma all reservation Apaches face today.

Coupled with the desire to keep the young people on the reservations is the fear that federal funds will be shifted from declining reservation populations to the growing number of urban Indians. These fears came to the fore in 1971 when, at a meeting of the National Indian Manpower Task Force, tribal leaders flatly refused to share available funds with urban Indians, insisting that separate allocations be made for them:[35]

Although off-reservation Indians retain the same property rights as those on the reservations, their physical separation means they have virtually no voice in what is done with their property. Most who go to the cities, therefore, do so on a temporary basis, out of a serious need for employment. They return to the reservations as frequently as possible—to retain their eligibility for ceremonial roles, to maintain family ties, and to renew their "Indianness." The Indian centers at Phoenix and Tucson are almost the only Arizona service organizations for Indian people that are run by Indians.

Their role is to help with the immediate problems of Indians when they arrive in the cities.

Although most Indians have much to lose by cutting their ties with the reservations permanently, some who go through the training programs established by the BIA and other agencies do leave the reservations for good. These are the "invisible" Indians whose problems, often serious, remain largely unknown to whites and reservation Indians alike. The urban Indian is "the man of two worlds, yet unseen and ignored by both."[36] But because the Indian population is growing rapidly and because efforts to create employment opportunities on reservations are quite recent, many Indians have little choice but to seek off-reservation jobs.

At both Fort Apache and San Carlos more than half of the labor force is unemployed today. Many of the families—more than 60 per cent at both reservations—lack access to adequate transportation, a situation that aggravates their employment problems.

Even after years of exposure to the profit motive Apaches are still geared to a subsistence level economy, and this tradition is a significant limitation on the economic potential of Apache wage labor. They have no feeling against such work, but most prefer to live with a minimum of contact with or dependence on Anglos. In order to meet all social and ritual obligations, furthermore, Apaches prefer to work within a radius of seventy-five miles from the reservation.

When working away from the reservation Apaches invariably live in a clan-local group of related families, and they rarely remain away for more than a year. Most reject off-reservation employment that would require separation from their families. Many off-reservation jobs go unfilled "because," as an Apache state employment officer put it, "everybody wants to stay home." Yet in 1970 the labor force over sixteen years of age at San Carlos numbered 2200; of these only 640 had jobs. Clearly, the desire to remain Apache outweighs the wish to enjoy more of the material comforts of modern society. The historical and cultural factors that produced this situation are still present, perhaps even more strongly felt today than at any time since reservations such as San Carlos were established.[37]

The future of the Apaches is no longer as bleak as it seemed for many years. Given opportunity and encouragement, their inherent intelligence and ability will enable them to improve their lives substantially without forsaking their own cultural values. As General Crook wrote long ago, in reply to those who opposed his plan to give Apaches the right to vote: "I wish to say most emphatically that the

American Indian is the intellectual peer of most, if not all, the various nationalities we have assimilated to our laws, customs and language. He is fully able to protect himself, if the ballot be given and the courts of law not closed against him. [38]

What happens to the Apaches during the rest of this century depends in part on their success in overcoming the attitude of hopelessness engendered by a century of total domination and in part on the continuation and expansion of enlightened policies by government agencies and officials. One can only hope that the disturbing and discouraging fluctuations of governmental policy toward Indians is behind us, and that the future will see Apaches and other Indians attaining genuine control over the decisions that affect their lives. Only then can Crook's appraisal of their abilities be fairly tested.

Notes

Introduction

1. During the colonial period what is now Chihuahua was usually called Nueva Vizcaya; to avoid confusion, Chihuahua is used throughout.
2. Goodwin 1942, p. 123.
3. *Ibid.*, p. 124.
4. Opler 1936, p. 90.
5. Goodwin 1942, pp. 459–62.
6. Carroll and Haggard 1942, p. 200.
7. Opler 1941, pp. 229–31, 472, 473; Opler 1936, pp. 84–88, 93, 94.

Chapter I

1. See Thomas 1935.
2. Forbes 1957, pp. 320–22.
3. Fernández de Jáuregui 1964, p. 112.
4. Goodwin 1971, pp. 18, 19.
5. "Mandamiento para que el governador de la nueva méxico conforme al número de gente de armas . . . que acuda al remedio de los daños que hacen los yndios apaches de guerra a los amigos y cavallada de Spañoles, 6 março, 1608." A.G.I. 58-3-16. Bancroft Library University of California, Berkeley transcript. Also, *Auto* de Velasco II and the Audiencia of México, September 28, 1609. *Ibid.*
6. Benavides 1630, pp. 39, 40; Worcester 1941.
7. Marqués del Guadalcázar, A.G.I. 58-3-18 Bancroft Library transcript; Worcester 1951.
8. Hackett and Shelby 1942, 2: 299.
9. Clark 1963, pp. 241–47.

10. Bolton 1916, p. 451.
11. See Bolton 1936.
12. Hernández Sánchez-Barba 1957, p. 41.
13. Wyllys 1931, p. 138.
14. Kessell 1970, p. 76.
15. See Ewing 1938.
16. Hackett 1926–37, 3: 478; Worcester 1945.
17. Pfefferkorn 1949, p. 143.
18. Kinnaird 1958, pp. 214–16; see also Thomas 1940, pp. 195–98, and Moorhead 1975a.
19. See Brinckerhoff and Faulk 1965, and Moorhead 1975a.
20. Kessell 1964, p. 308.
21. Thomas 1932, pp. 10, 11, 367; Moorhead 1975a, pp. 71, 72.
22. Quoted in Spicer 1962, p. 319.
23. See Moorhead 1968.
24. Archer 1973, pp. 376, 377.
25. Gálvez 1786.

Chapter II

1. Moorhead 1968, pp. 187–96.
2. *Ibid.*, pp. 135–38.
3. *Ibid.*, pp. 141, 274, 281, 286.
4. *Ibid.*, pp. 186, 187.
5. *Ibid.*, pp. 191, 192.
6. Moorhead 1975a, pp. 260–65.
7. Archer 1973, pp. 377–85; see also Moorhead 1975b.
8. Thomas 1932, pp. 266–68.
9. Matson and Schroeder 1957, p. 350.
10. *Ibid.*, p. 351.
11. *Ibid.*, pp. 348, 349.
12. Pike 1925, pp. 166, 167.

13. Park 1962, pp. 342, 343.
14. Goodwin 1942, p. 86; see also, Moorhead 1975a, p. 265.
15. Bloom 1928, pp. 268–72.
16. Carroll and Haggard 1942, p. 200.
17. Acuña 1974, p. 7.
18. Gregg, 1954, pp. 203, 204.
19. Smith 1964, p. 11; Smith 1962.
20. Smith 1963b; Smith 1965.
21. Keleher 1952, p. 487 n. 28.
22. Senate *Executive Document* No. 18, 31st Cong., 1st sess.; Keleher 1952, p. 71.
23. Abel 1915.
24. Rippy 1919, p. 374.
25. Cooke 1878, p. 180.
26. Acuña 1974, p. 8.
27. McCall 1968, pp. 98, 99.
28. *Ibid.*, pp. 103–105.
29. *Ibid.*, p. 108.

Chapter III

1. Bartlett 1854, 2: 386.
2. *Ibid.*, p. 390.
3. Cremony 1868, pp. 86, 87.
4. *Ibid.*, p. 243; Ball 1972, p. 11.
5. Bartlett 1854, 2: 329.
6. Abel 1915, p. 263.
7. *Ibid.*, p. 350.
8. Steck Papers, Box 2, Folder 7; Murphy 1972, p. 103.
9. Horn 1963, p. 25.
10. "Report of the Secretary of War for 1851," p. 133.
11. Abel 1915, p. 485.
12. Bennett 1947, p. 89.
13. Abel 1915, p. 485.
14. "Report of the Secretary of the Interior for 1854," p. 133.
15. *Ibid.*, pp. 376–78.
16. *Ibid.*, p. 379.
17. Keleher 1952, p. 88.
18. "Report of the Secretary of the Interior for 1854," p. 389.
19. *Ibid.*, p. 390.
20. *Ibid.*, p. 391.
21. Keleher 1952, p. 77.
22. "Report of the Secretary of War for 1854," p. 34.
23. "Report of the Secretary of the Interior for 1855," p. 512.
24. "Notes and Documents" 1946a, pp. 261–65.
25. "Report of the Secretary of War for 1855," pp. 56–62.
26. *Ibid.*, p. 69.
27. "Notes and Documents" 1947, p. 103.
28. "Report of the Secretary of the Interior for 1856," p. 732; "Report of the Commissioner of Indian Affairs for 1857," p. 576.
29. "Report of the Secretary of the Interior for 1857," pp. 576, 577.
30. *Ibid.*, pp. 565, 566.
31. "Notes and Documents" 1947, pp. 99, 100.
32. "Report of the Secretary of the Interior for 1857," p. 481.
33. Steck Papers, Box 2, Folder 7.
34. Keleher 1952, p. 138 n. 94.
35. Colyer 1871, p. 40.
36. "Report of the Secretary of War for 1858," pp. 284–89, 291.

Chapter IV

1. "Report of the Secretary of the Interior for 1858," pp. 554–57.
2. *Ibid.*, p. 724.
3. Procter 1964, pp. 47–65.
4. Poston 1963, pp. 66, 67.
5. Bancroft 1889, p. 517 n. 39.
6. "Report of the Secretary of the Interior for 1857," p. 587.
7. Pumpelly 1965, p. 68.
8. "Report of the Secretary of the Interior for 1859," pp. 549, 714, 715.
9. Park 1961, p. 40.
10. "Report of the Secretary of War for 1859," p. 545.
11. *Ibid.*, pp. 309–25.
12. Sacks 1962, p. 267; Sacks found two of Bascom's reports of the Apache Pass incident, which provided vital missing evidence.
13. Pumpelly 1918, 1: 203.
14. *Arizona Weekly Star* (Tucson), June 28, July 5, 1877.
15. Irwin 1928.
16. *Ibid.*, p. 7; Pumpelly 1965, pp. 152, 153;

Sacks 1962, pp. 276, 277.

17. Browne 1950, p. 269.

Chapter V

1. Hall 1974, p. 144.
2. Keleher 1952, p. 325; *The War of the Rebellion*, Series I, Vol. 50, Pt. 1, p. 942.
3. Cremony 1868, p. 197.
4. Sabin 1935, 2: 846, 847.
5. Keleher 1952, p. 414.
6. Keleher 1952, pp. 410–13; "Report of Commissioner of Indian Affairs for 1863," pp. 105–109.
7. Sabin 1935, 2: 847, 848.
8. *Ibid.*, p. 705; Opler and Opler 1950, p. 15; Cremony 1868, p. 201.
9. "Report of Commissioner of Indian Affairs for 1867," p. 102; Opler and Opler 1950, p. 16.
10. Cremony 1868, pp. 290, 291.
11. Keleher 1952, p. 288.
12. Conner 1950, pp. 34–39 n.
13. *Condition of the Indian Tribes* 1867, p. 105.
14. Keleher 1952, p. 295.
15. *Condition of the Indian Tribes* 1867, p. 220.
16. Opler and Opler 1950, pp. 16, 17.
17. October 31, 1864, quoted in Keleher 1952, p. 433 n.
18. Sonnichsen 1958, p. 110.
19. *Ibid.*, p. 112.
20. *Condition of the Indian Tribes* 1867, pp. 306, 307.
21. *Ibid.*, p. 438; Keleher 1952, pp. 356–76.
22. Keleher 1952, pp. 474, 475.
23. *Condition of the Indian Tribes* 1867, p. 97.
24. *Ibid.*, p. 328.
25. *Ibid.*, p. 329.
26. *The War of the Rebellion*, Series I, Vol. 43, Pt. 2, pp. 1150, 1151.
27. *Ibid.*
28. Keleher 1952, pp. 353–58.

Chapter VI

1. *Army and Navy Journal*, June 6, 1868, quoted in Utley 1973, p. 178.

2. These natural waterholes were called *tinajas* in Spanish; Anglos corrupted this to "tanks."
3. Lockwood 1938, p. 150; Woody 1962, pp. 159–64.
4. Bancroft 1889, p. 518 n.
5. Ogle 1970, p. 248.
6. Browne 1950, pp. 162, 163.
7. Lockwood 1938, p. 152.
8. Keleher 1952, p. 496 n.
9. Lockwood 1938, p. 156.
10. *Ibid.*, pp. 159, 160.
11. Thrapp 1967, pp. 39–45.
12. Ogle 1970, p. 64.
13. Lockwood 1938, pp. 165–69.
14. Ogle 1970, p. 73.
15. Lockwood 1938, p. 171.
16. *Ibid.*, pp. 171, 172; Ogle 1970, pp. 74, 75.
17. Lockwood 1938, p. 177.
18. *Ibid.*, p. 178; see also Lummis 1966, pp. 15–17.
19. Lockwood 1938, p. 172.
20. *Ibid.*, p. 173.
21. Captain Bernard was the former cavalry sergeant who presumably had been courtmartialed for insubordination during the Bascom affair at Apache Pass.
22. Ogle 1970, p. 73.

Chapter VII

1. Bourke 1891, pp. 29, 30.
2. Hastings 1959, p. 150.
3. *Ibid.*, p. 151.
4. Colyer 1871, p. 34.
5. Hastings 1959, p. 152.
6. Schellie 1968, pp. 161, 162.
7. Mardock 1971, p. 34.
8. Reeve 1952, p. 232.
9. Schellie 1968, p. 189.
10. Murphy 1972, p. 179.
11. Colyer 1871, p. 8.
12. *Ibid.*
13. Bancroft 1889, p. 563 n.
14. Colyer 1871, p. 23.
15. *Ibid.*, p. 47.
16. *Ibid.*, p. 25.
17. *Ibid.*, p. 27.
18. Ogle 1970, pp. 94, 95.

19. *Ibid.*, p. 97.
20. Hastings 1959, p. 156.
21. *Ibid.*, p. 158.
22. Ogle 1970, p. 100.
23. Thrapp 1967, p. 110.
24. Hastings 1959, p. 159.
25. Thrapp 1967, p. 110.
26. Howard 1907, pp. 175, 176; see also Lummis 1966, pp. 128–36.
27. *Ibid.*, pp. 187, 188.
28. *Ibid.*, pp. 203, 204.
29. *Ibid.*, p. 207.
30. *Ibid.*
31. Opler and Opler 1950, p. 25.
32. Lummis 1966, p. 17, quoting Crook: "To polish a diamond there is nothing like its own dust."

Chapter VIII

1. King 1967, p. 335.
2. *Ibid.*, p. 336.
3. Dunn 1969, pp. 616, 617.
4. Thrapp 1964, p. 104.
5. Bourke 1891, p. 181.
6. Thrapp 1964, p. 174.
7. Bourke 1891, pp. 150–53; Corbusier 1971, pp. 18, 19.
8. Bourke 1891, p. 195.
9. *Ibid.*, pp. 195–200.
10. *Ibid.*, pp. 201–203.
11. Thrapp 1964, p. 69.
12. Bourke 1891, pp. 161, 162.
13. Ogle 1970, p. 120; Thrapp 1967, p. 143.
14. Bourke 1891, p. 233.
15. *Ibid.*, p. 218; see also Lummis 1966, p. 17.
16. Bourke 1891, p. 221.
17. Ogle 1970, p. 119.
18. Thrapp 1967, pp. 147, 148.
19. *Ibid.*, p. 148.
20. Ogle 1970, pp. 140, 141.
21. Bourke 1891, p. 217.
22. Thrapp 1964, p. 120.
23. Corbusier 1971, pp. 249, 250.
24. Thrapp 1964, p. 120.
25. *Ibid.*, p. 146.
26. Corbusier 1971, p. 85.
27. Thrapp 1964, p. 147.
28. Dunn 1969, p. 621.
29. Thrapp 1964, p. 156.
30. Corbusier 1971, p. 271.
31. *Ibid.*, pp. 263, 267.
32. *Ibid.*, p. 276.
33. Thrapp 1964, p. 160.
34. Cruse 1941, pp. 57, 58.

Chapter IX

1. Ogle 1970, p. 145.
2. *Ibid.*, pp. 151, 152.
3. *Ibid.*, p. 153 n.
4. *Ibid.*, pp. 155, 156.
5. Clum 1936, pp. 166–79.
6. *Ibid.*, pp. 180, 181.
7. Ogle 1970, p. 167 n; see also Cochise 1971, pp. 4–8.
8. Clum 1936, pp. 185–200.
9. *Ibid.*, pp. 209–12.
10. *Ibid.*, p. 218.
11. *Ibid.*, pp. 219–25.
12. Thrapp 1974, p. 193.
13. *Ibid.*, p. 190.

Chapter X

1. Thrapp 1974, p. 159.
2. *Ibid.*, p. 167.
3. *Ibid.*, p. 170.
4. Cruse 1941, p. 31.
5. Ball 1970, pp. 25, 26.
6. *Ibid.*, p. 35.
7. *Ibid.*, p. 57.
8. Thrapp 1974, p. 209.
9. *Ibid.*, p. 210.
10. *Ibid.*, p. 220.
11. *Ibid.*, p. 237.
12. Ball 1970, pp. 11, 16.
13. *Ibid.*, p. 21.
14. *Ibid.*, p. xiii.
15. Cruse 1941, pp. 54, 55.
16. *Ibid.*, p. 66.
17. *Ibid.*, p. 81.
18. Thrapp 1967, p. 185.
19. Thrapp 1974, p. 250.
20. Thrapp 1967, p. 187.
21. Ball 1970, p. 12.
22. *Ibid.*, pp. 18, 19.
23. Dunn 1969, p. 628.
24. Thrapp 1974, p. 218.

25. Dunn 1969, p. 629.
26. *Ibid.*, pp. 629, 630.
27. *Ibid.*, p. 634.
28. Thrapp 1974, p. 314.
29. Dunn 1969, p. 630.
30. *Ibid.*, pp. 630, 631.
31. *Ibid.*, p. 631; Thrapp 1974, p. 259.
32. Thrapp 1974, pp. 257–59.
33. *Ibid.*, pp. 260, 261.
34. March 27, June 7, 1880. In Ellis, 1972, 276, 277.
35. Thrapp 1974, p. 265.
36. Sonnichsen 1958, p. 179.
37. Thrapp 1974, pp. 272, 273.
38. Sonnichsen 1958, p. 183.
39. Cruse 1941, p. 80.
40. *Ibid.*, p. 82.
41. Thrapp 1967, p. 201.
42. Ball 1970, p. 102; Thrapp 1974, p. 308.
43. Thrapp 1967, p. 209.
44. Ball 1970, p. 107.
45. "Report of the Secretary of War for 1881," pp. 117, 118; Sonnichsen 1958, p. 195.

Chapter XI

1. Lynn 1966, p. 117.
2. Ogle 1970, pp. 195–97.
3. *Ibid.*, p. 203.
4. "Report on Coyotero Apaches," January 11, 1875 (ms. in Bancroft Library), quoted in Thrapp 1972, p. 4.
5. Cruse 1941, p. 95.
6. *Ibid.*, p. 96.
7. *Ibid.*
8. Wharfield 1971, pp. 21, 22; King 1963, pp. 197, 198.
9. King 1963, pp. 198, 199.
10. Cruse 1941, p. 98.
11. *Ibid.*, p. 99.
12. Wharfield 1971, p. 22.
13. Cruse 1941, pp. 100, 101.
14. Wharfield 1971, p. 23.
15. *Ibid.*, pp. 23, 24.
16. *Ibid.*, p. 32.
17. Cruse 1941, p. 106.
18. King 1963, p. 209.
19. Cruse 1941, pp. 108, 109.
20. *Ibid.*, p. 110.

21. Wharfield 1971, pp. 43–44; the medal is now in the Arizona Historical Society, Tucson.
22. Thrapp 1972, pp. 40, 41.
23. *Ibid.*, p. 40.
24. Wharfield 1971, pp. 91, 92.
25. *Ibid.*, p. 91.
26. *Ibid.*, pp. 56, 57.
27. McDowell, Annual Report, 1881, pp. 140, 141; in Thrapp 1972, p. 23.
28. Thrapp 1972, p. 51.
29. *Ibid.*, pp. 60, 61.
30. *Record of Engagements*, 1882, p. 101.
31. Betzinez 1959, p. 70.
32. *Ibid.*, p. 74.
33. *Ibid.*, p. 75.
34. Cruse 1941, p. 158.
35. *Ibid.*, p. 161.
36. Thrapp 1967, p. 275.

Chapter XII

1. Thrapp 1972, p. 107.
2. Bourke 1891, pp. 435–37.
3. *Ibid.*, p. 438.
4. *Ibid.*, p. 439; see also Harte 1975.
5. Harte 1973, p. 32.
6. Bourke 1891, p. 443.
7. Thrapp 1972, pp. 103, 104.
8. Utley 1973, p. 55.
9. Bourke 1891, p. 445.
10. Davis 1929, pp. 30, 31.
11. *Ibid.*, p. 32.
12. *Ibid.*; Ball 1970, p. 166; Griffith 1969.
13. Davis 1929, pp. 48, 49.
14. *Ibid.*, p. 56.
15. Bourke 1958, p. 30. Early in 1889 someone belatedly pointed out that sixteen of the Apache prisoners were Mescaleros from New Mexico, who were being improperly held. But when Lieutenant George Chase arrived to escort them to Mescalero, only twelve were allowed to leave.
16. *Ibid.*, pp. 38–42.
17. Utley 1973, p. 388.
18. Bigelow 1968, p. 114.
19. Bourke 1958, p. 74.
20. Betzinez 1959, p. 118.
21. Thrapp 1972, p. 152.

22. Betzinez 1959, pp. 113–15.
23. Davis 1929, p. 60.
24. *Ibid.*, pp. 62–64.
25. Harte 1973, pp. 37–40.
26. Davis 1929, p. 83.
27. *Ibid.*, pp. 85, 86.
28. *Ibid.*, p. 87.
29. *Ibid.*, p. 114.
30. *Ibid.*, p. 52.
31. Thrapp 1972, p. 177.
32. Davis 1929, pp. 124, 125.
33. Thrapp 1967, p. 308.
34. Nalty and Strobridge 1964, p. 34.
35. Harte 1973, p. 41.
36. Davis 1929, pp. 144–46.
37. *Ibid.*, p. 148.
38. Crook 1960, p. 253.
39. Harte 1973, pp. 43, 44.
40. Crook 1960, p. 255.
41. Cruse 1941, pp. 208, 209.
42. Davis 1929, pp. 190–93.
43. Utley 1973, pp. 393, 394.
44. Davis 1929, p. 198.
45. Bigelow 1968, p. 19.
46. Utley 1973, p. 396.
47. Lummis 1966, p. 16.
48. Davis 1929, pp. 213, 214.
49. *Ibid.*, p. 217.
50. *Ibid.*, pp. 214–17.

Chapter XIII

1. Davis 1929, p. 221.
2. Utley 1973, p. 398.
3. Davis 1929, p. 225.
4. *Ibid.*, p. 227.
5. Cruse 1941, p. 232.
6. Davis 1929, pp. 236, 237.
7. *Ibid.*, p. 232.
8. *Arizona Star* (Tucson), June 7, 1887.
9. Miles 1896, p. 536; Thrapp 1964, p. 329.
10. Thrapp 1964, p. 337.
11. Bailey 1966, pp. 59–68; see also Cochise 1971, and Opler 1973, pp. 48, 56.
12. Crook 1887, pp. 22, 23.
13. Goodman 1968, p. 121.
14. *Ibid.*, p. 168.
15. *Ibid.*, pp. 177, 178.
16. *Ibid.*
17. *Ibid.*, p. 180.

18. *Ibid.*, p. 195.
19. Tate 1974, p. 349.
20. *Ibid.*, p. 356.
21. *Ibid.*, pp. 357–59.
22. Clum 1928b, pp. 22–26.
23. Betzinez 1959, p. 191.
24. *Ibid.*, p. 191.

Chapter XIV

1. Washburn 1971, pp. 68–70; Prucha 1973, pp. 295–99.
2. Fey and McNickle 1970, p. 82; Prucha 1973, pp. 134, 137.
4. Prucha 1973, p. 134.
4. *Ibid.*, p. 276.
5. Fontana 1974b, pp. 38–41.
6. Prucha 1973, pp. 125–29.
7. *Ibid.*, p. 261.
8. *Ibid.*, pp. 269.
9. Szasz 1974, p. 45.
10. *Ibid.*, p. 67.
11. *Ibid.*, p. 46.
12. *Ibid.*, pp. 22–23.
13. LaFarge 1935, pp. 232, 233.
14. Zimmerman 1957, p. 32.
15. Antell 1974, p. 269.
16. Fontana 1974c, pp. 48, 49.
17. Washburn 1971, pp. 79, 80.
18. Szasz 1974, p. 67.
19. Forbes 1964, pp. 127–29.
20. Gunnerson 1974, pp. 149, 150.
21. Opler and Opler 1950, p. 34.
22. Dobyns 1973, p. 83.
23. Curley 1967, p. 118.
24. Parmee 1968, pp. 25, 26.
25. Curley 1967, p. 118.
26. Adams and Krutz 1971, p. 118.
27. Prucha 1973, p. 254.
28. Spicer 1962, p. 257.
29. Baldwin 1965, p. 129.
30. Parmee 1968, pp. 7, 8.
31. Steiner 1968, pp. 244, 245.
32. Parmee 1968, pp. 47–49.
33. Faherty 1974, p. 244.
34. Burlison 1973, pp. 147–49.
35. Weaver and Gartell 1974, pp. 72–82.
36. *Ibid.*, p. 84.
37. Adams and Krutz 1971, p. 132.
38. Crook 1960, pp. 269, 270.

Bibliography

Abel, Annie Heloise.
1915 *The Official Correspondence of James S. Calhoun while Indian Agent at Santa Fe and Superintendent of Indian Affairs in New Mexico.* Washington. (Editor.)
1941 "Indian Affairs in New Mexico under the Administration of William Carr Lane." *New Mexico Historical Review* 16 (April); 206–32; 16 (July): 328–58.
Acuña, Rodolfo F.
1970 "Ignacio Pesqueira: Sonoran Caudillo." *Arizona and the West* 12 (Summer): 139–72.
1974 *Sonoran Strongman: Ignacio Pesqueira and His Times.* Tucson.
Adams, Alexander B.
1971 *Geronimo, A Biography.* New York.
Adams, William Y., and Gordon V. Krutz.
1971 "Wage Labor and the San Carlos Apache." In *Apachean Culture History and Ethnology,* edited by Keith H. Basso and Morris E. Opler. Tucson.
Antell, Will.
1974 "Education of the American Indians." *Current History* 67 (December): 267–70, 279.
Archer, Christon I.
1973 "The Deportation of Barbarian Indians from the Internal Provinces of New Spain, 1789–1810." *The Americas* 29 (January): 376–85.
Bailey, L. R.
1966 *Indian Slave Trade in the Southwest.* Los Angeles.
Baldwin, Gordon C.
1965 *The Warrior Apaches: A Story of the Chiricahua and Western Apache.* Tucson.
1973 *Indians of the Southwest.* New York.
Ball, Eve.
1965 "The Apache Scouts: A Chiricahua Appraisal." *Arizona and the West* 7 (Winter): 315–28.

1970   *Recollections of a Warm Springs Apache: James Kaywaykla, nanata*. Tucson.

1974   "Juh's Stronghold in Mexico." *The Journal of Arizona History* 15 (Spring): 73–84.

Bancroft, Hubert Howe.

1884   *History of the North Mexican States and Texas*. 2 vols. San Francisco.

1889   *History of Arizona and New Mexico, 1530–1888*. San Francisco.

Bartlett, John Russell.

1854   *Personal Narrative of Explorations and Incidents in Texas, New Mexico, California, Sonora, and Chihuahua*. 2 vols. (Glorieta, N.M., 1965.)

Basehart, Harry W.

1971   "Mescalero Apache Band Organization and Leadership." In *Apachean Culture History and Ethnology*, edited by Keith H. Basso and Morris E. Opler. Tucson, 1971.

Basso, Keith H.

1971   "To Give Up on Words: Silence in Western Apache Culture." In *Apachean Culture History and Ethnology*, edited by Keith H. Basso and Morris E. Opler. Tucson, 1971.

Basso, Keith H., and Morris E. Opler, eds.

1971   *Apachean Culture History and Ethnology*. Tucson.

Benavides, Alonso de.

1630   *The Memorial of Fray Alonso de Benavides, 1630*. Translated and edited by Mrs. Edward E. Ayer. Albuquerque, 1965.

Bender, A. B.

1934   "Frontier Defenses in the Territory of New Mexico, 1846–1853." *New Mexico Historical Review* 9 (October): 219–72.

Betzinez, Jason.

1959   *I Fought with Geronimo*. Edited by W. S. Nye. New York.

Bigelow, John, Jr.

1968   *On the Bloody Trail of Geronimo*. New York.

Bloom, Lansing B., ed.

1928   "Barreiro's *Ojeada sobre Nuevo Mexico*." *New Mexico Historical Review* 3 (January): 73–96; 3 (April): 148–78.

Bolton, Herbert E.

1916   *Spanish Exploration in the Southwest, 1542–1706*. New York. (Editor.)

1936   *Rim of Christendom: A Biography of Eusebio Francisco Kino, Pacific Coast Pioneer*. New York. (New ed., 1960.)

1939   *Outpost of Empire*. New York.

1948   *Kino's Historical Memoir of Pimería Alta*. 2 vols. Berkeley, Calif. (Editor.)

Bourke, John G.

1891   *On the Border with Crook*. New York. (New ed., Glorieta, N.M.,

1971)
1958   *An Apache Campaign in the Sierra Madre*. New York.
Brinckerhoff, Sidney B.
1967   "The Last Years of Spanish Arizona, 1786–1821." *Arizona and the West* 9 (Spring): 5–20.
Brinckerhoff, Sidney B., and Odie B. Faulk.
1965   *Lancers for the King*. Phoenix.
Brodhead, Michael J.
1973   "Elliott Coues and the Apaches." *Journal of Arizona History* 14 (Summer): 87–94.
Brooks, Clinton E., and Frank D. Reeve, eds.
1947   "James A. Bennett: A Dragoon in New Mexico, 1850–1856." *New Mexico Historical Review* 22 (January): 51–97; 22 (April): 140–76.
Brophy, William A., and Sophie D. Aberle, et al.
1966   *The Indian: America's Unfinished Business; Report of the Commission on the Rights, Liberties, and Reponsibilities of the American Indian*. Norman, Okla.
Browne, J. Ross.
1871   *Adventures in Apache Country: A Tour Through Arizona*. New York (New ed., Tucson, 1974)
1950   *A Tour Through Arizona, 1864; or Adventures in Apache Country*. Tucson.
Burlison, Irene.
1973   *Yesterday and Today in the Life of the Apaches*. Philadelphia.
Cargill, Andrew Hays.
1936   "The Camp Grant Massacre." *Arizona Historical Review* 7 (July): 73–79.
Carroll, H. Bailey, and J. Villasana Haggard, trans.
1942   *Three New Mexico Chronicles*. Albuquerque.
Carson, G. B., ed.
1964   "William Carr Lane Diary." *New Mexico Historical Review* 39 (July): 181–234; 39 (October): 274–332.
Carter, William Giles Harding.
1900   *From Yorktown to Santiago with the Sixth U.S. Cavalry*. Baltimore.
Chamberlain, Sue Abbey.
1975   "The Fort McDowell Indian Reservation: Water Rights and Indian Removal." *Journal of the West* 14 (October): 27–34.
Chapel, William L.
1973   "Camp Rucker: Outpost in Apacheria." *Journal of Arizona History* 14 (Summer): 95–112.
Clark, LaVerne Harrell.
1963   "Early Horse Trappings of the Navajo and Apache Indians." *Arizona and the West* 5 (Autumn): 233–48.
Clendenen, Clarence C.

1955 "General James Henry Carleton." *New Mexico Historical Review* 30 (January): 23–43.

Clum, John P.
1928a "Es-kim-in-zin." *New Mexico Historical Review* 3 (October): 399–420; 4 (January): 1–27.
1928b "Geronimo." *New Mexico Historical Review* 3 (January): 1–40; 3 (April): 121–44; 3 (July): 217–64.
1929 "The San Carlos Apache Police." *New Mexico Historical Review* 4 (July): 203–19; 5 (January): 67–92.
1930 "Apache Misrule: A Bungling Agent Sets the Military Arm in Motion." *New Mexico Historical Review* 5 (April): 138–53; 5 (July): 221–39.

Clum, Woodworth.
1936 *Apache Agent: The Story of John P. Clum.* Boston.

Cochise, Ciyé "Niño."
1971 *The First Hundred Years of Niño Cochise: The Untold Story of an Apache Indian Chief.* As told to A. Kinney Griffith. London, New York.

Colyer, Vincent.
1871 *Peace with the Apaches of New Mexico and Arizona.* Washington (reprinted, Freeport, N.Y., 1971).

Condition of the Indian Tribes: Report of the Joint Special Committee Appointed under Joint Resolution of March 3, 1865. Washington, D.C. 1867.

Conner, Daniel Ellis.
1956 *Joseph Reddeford Walker and the Arizona Adventure.* Ed. by Donald Berthrong and Odessa Davenport. Norman, Okla.

Conrad, David E.
1969 "The Whipple Expedition in Arizona, 1853–1854." *Arizona and the West* 11 (Summer): 147–78.

Cooke, Philip St. George.
1878 *The Conquest of New Mexico and California: An Historical and Personal Narrative.* New York (New ed., Glorieta, N.M., 1964.)

Corbusier, William T.
1971 *Verde to San Carlos: Recollections of a Famous Army Surgeon and His Observant Family on the Western Frontier, 1869–1886.* Tucson.

Cozzens, Samuel Woodworth.
1874 *The Marvellous Country, or, Three Years in Arizona and New Mexico.* Boston.

Cremony, John C.
1868 *Life Among the Apaches.* San Francisco. (Reprinted, Glorieta, N.M., 1968.)

Crook, General George.
1887 *Resumé of Operations Against Apache Indians, 1882–1886.*

Washington, D.C.
1960 *General George Crook, His Autobiography*. Ed. by Martin F. Schmitt.

Cruse, Thomas.
1941 *Apache Days and After*. Caldwell, Idaho.

Curley, Richard T.
1967 "Drinking Patterns of the Mescalero Apache." *Quarterly Journal of Studies on Alcohol* 28: 116–31.

Daly, W. H.
1917 *Manual of Pack Transportation*. Washington, D.C.

Davis, Britton.
1929 *The Truth About Geronimo*. Edited by Milo Milton Quaife. New Haven, Conn.

Debo, Angie.
1976 *Geronimo: The Man, His Time, His Place*. Norman, Okla.

Deloria, Vince, Jr.
1974 "Religion and the Modern American Indian." *Current History* 67 (December): 250–53.

DiPeso, Charles.
1953 *The Sobaípuri Indians of the Upper San Pedro River Valley, Southeastern Arizona*. Dragoon, Ariz.

Dobyns, Henry F.
1963 "Indian Extinction in the Middle Santa Cruz Valley, Arizona." *New Mexico Historical Review* 38 (April): 163–81.
1971 *The Apache People*. Phoenix.
1972 *The Pápago People*. Phoenix.
1973 *The Mescalero Apache People*. Phoenix.
1976 *Spanish Colonial Tucson*. Tucson.

Donohue, J. Augustine.
1960 "The Unlucky Jesuit Mission of Bac." *Arizona and the West* 2 (Summer): 127–39.

Downey, Fairfax, and Jacques Noel Jacobsen, Jr.
1973 *The Red Bluecoats*. Ft. Collins, Colo.

Dunn, J. P. Jr.
1969 *Massacres of the Mountains: A History of the Indian Wars of the Far West*. New York.

Ellis, Richard N.
1969 "The Humanitarian Soldiers." *Journal of Arizona History* 10 (Summer): 53–66.
1972 "The Apache Chronicle," *New Mexico Historical Review* 47 (July): 275—82.

Emory, W. H.
1951 *Lieutenant Emory Reports: A Reprint of W. H. Emory's Notes of a Military Reconnaissance*. Albuquerque.

Evans, George W. B.

1945 *Mexican Gold Trail: The Journal of a Forty-Niner*. Edited by Glenn S. Dumke, San Marino, Calif.

Ewing, Russell C.
1938 "The Pima Outbreak in November, 1751." *New Mexico Historical Review* 13 (October): 337–46.

Faherty, Robert L.
1974 "The American Indian: An Overview." *Current History* 67 (December): 241–44, 274.

Farish, Thomas Edwin.
1915–18 *History of Arizona*. 8 vols. San Francisco.

Feather, Adlai.
1964 "The Territories of Arizona." *New Mexico Historical Review* 39 (January): 16–31.

Fernández de Jáuregui Urrutia, Josseph Antonio.
1964 *Description of Nuevo León, México (1735–1740)*. Edited by Malcolm D. McLean. Monterrey, Mexico.

Faulk, Odie B.
1969 *The Geronimo Campaign*. New York.

Ferris, Robert G., ed.
1971 *Soldier and Brave: Historic Places Associated with Indian Affairs and the Indian Wars in the Trans-Mississippi West*. 2nd. ed., Washington, D.C.

Fey, Harold E., and D'Arcy McNickle.
1970 *Indians and Other Americans—Two Ways of Life Meet*. Rev. ed., New York.

Fontana, Bernard L.
1974a "Contemporary Indians." In *The Indians of Arizona: A Contemporary Perspective*, edited by Thomas Weaver. Tucson, 1974.
1974b Historical Foundations." In *The Indians of Arizona: A Contemporary Perspective*, edited by Thomas Weaver. Tucson, 1974.
1974c "Twentieth Century Legislation." In *The Indians of Arizona: A Contemporary Perspective*, edited by Thomas Weaver. Tucson, 1974.

Forbes, Jack D.
1957 "The Janos, Jocomes, Mansos and Sumas Indians." *New Mexico Historical Review* 32 (October): 319–34.
1960 *Apache, Navaho, and Spaniard*. Norman, Okla.
1964 *The Indian in America's Past*. Englewood Cliffs, N.J.

Forrest, Earle R.
1947 *Lone War Trail of Apache Kid*. Pasadena, Calif.

Frazer, Robert W.
1968 "Fort Butler: The Fort that Almost Was." *New Mexico Historical Review* 43 (October): 253–70.

Gálvez, Bernardo de.
1786 *Instructions for Governing the Interior Provinces of New Spain,*

1786. Translated and edited by Donald E. Worcester. Berkeley.

Gardner, Hamilton.
1953 "Philip St. George Cooke and the Apache, 1854." *New Mexico Historical Review* 28 (April): 115–32.

Goodman, David Michael.
1968 "Apaches as Prisoners of War." Ph.D. dissertation, Texas Christian University.

Goodwin, Grenville.
1936 "Experiences of an Indian Scout." *Arizona Historical Review* 7 (January): 31–68.
1942 *The Social Organization of the Western Apache*. Chicago.
1971 *Western Apache Raiding and Warfare*. Edited by Keith H. Basso. Tucson.

Gregg, Josiah.
1954 *Commerce of the Prairies*. Edited by Max L. Moorhead. Norman, Okla.

Griffin, P. Bion, Mark P. Leone, and Keith H. Basso.
1971 "Western Apache Ecology: From Horticulture to Agriculture." In *Apachean Culture History and Ethnology*, edited by Keith H. Basso and Morris E. Opler. Tucson.

Griffith, A. Kinney.
1969 *Mickey Free, Manhunter*. Caldwell, Idaho.

Gunnerson, Dolores A.
1974 *The Jicarilla Apaches: A Study in Survival*. DeKalb, Ill.

Haas, Theodore H.
1957 "The Legal Aspects of Indian Affairs from 1887 to 1957." *The Annals of the American Academy of Political and Social Science* 311 (May): 12–22.

Hackett, Charles Wilson, ed.
1926–37 *Historical Documents Relating to New Mexico, Nueva Vizcaya, and Approaches Thereto, to 1773*. 3 vols. Washington, D.C.

Hackett, Charles Wilson, and Charmion Shelby, eds.
1942 *Revolt of the Pueblo Indians of New Mexico and Otermín's Attempted Reconquest, 1680–1682*. 2 vols. Albuquerque.

Hageman, E. R., ed.
1969 *Fighting Rebels and Redskins: Experiences in Army Life of Colonel George B. Sanford, 1861–1892*. Norman, Okla.
1970 "Surgeon Smart and the Indians: An 1866 Apache Word-List." *Journal of Arizona History* 11 (Summer): 126–40.

Hall, Martin Hardwick.
1974 "Captain Thomas J. Mastin's Arizona Guards, C. S. A." *New Mexico Historical Review* 49 (April): 143–51.

Hammond, George Peter.
1929 "The Camp Grant Massacre: A Chapter in Apache History." *Proceedings* of the Pacific Coast Branch of the American Histori-

cal Association.

1931 "The Zúñiga Journal, Tucson to Santa Fe; The Opening of a Spanish Trade Route, 1788–1795." *New Mexico Historical Review* 6 (January): 40–65.

Harte, John Bret.

1973 "Conflict at San Carlos: The Civilian-Military Struggle for Control, 1882–1885." *Arizona and the West* 15 (Spring): 27–44.

1975 "The Strange Case of Joseph C. Tiffany: Indian Agent in Disgrace." *Journal of Arizona History* 16 (Winter): 383–404.

Hastings, James R.

1959 "The Tragedy at Camp Grant in 1871." *Arizona and the West* 1 (Summer): 146–60.

Hernández Sánchez-Barba, Mario.

1957 *La última expansión española en América.* Madrid.

Hodge, Frederick Webb, ed.

1907–10 *Handbook of American Indians North of Mexico.* 2 vols. Washington, D.C.

Hoopes, Alban W.

1932 *Indian Affairs and Their Administration, with Special Reference to the Far West, 1849–1860.* Philadelphia.

Horn, Calvin.

1963 *New Mexico's Troubled Years.* Albuquerque.

Howard, Oliver O.

1907 *My Life and Experiences among Our Hostile Indians.* Hartford, Conn.

Irwin, Dr. B. J. D.

1928 "The Fight at Apache Pass." *Infantry Journal* 32 (April).

John, Elizabeth.

1975 *Storms Brewed in Other Men's Worlds.* College Station, Texas.

Jones, Oakah L.

1966 *Pueblo Warriors and Spanish Conquest.* Norman, Okla.

Josephy, Alvin, Jr.

1971 *Red Power: The American Indians' Fight for Freedom.* New York.

Keleher, William A.

1952 *Turmoil in New Mexico, 1846–1868.* Santa Fe.

Kenner, Charles L.

1969 *A History of New Mexico—Plains Indian Relations.* Norman, Okla.

Kessell, John L.

1964 "San José de Tumacácori—1773: A Franciscan Reports from Arizona." *Arizona and the West* 6 (Winter): 303–12. (Editor.)

1966 "The Puzzling Presidio: San Phelipe de Guevavi, Alias Terrenate." *New Mexico Historical Review* 41 (January): 21–46.

1968 "Anza, Indian Fighter: The Spring Campaign of 1776." *Journal of*

Arizona History 9 (Autumn): 155-63. (Editor.)

1970 *Mission of Sorrows: Jesuit Guevavi and the Pimas, 1691–1767.* Tucson.

King, James T.
1963 *War Eagle: A Life of General Eugene A. Carr.* Lincoln, Neb.
1967 "George Crook: Indian Fighter and Humanitarian." *Arizona and the West* 9 (Winter): 333–48.

Kinnaird, Lawrence, tr. and ed.
1958 *The Frontiers of New Spain: Nicolás de la Fora's Description, 1766–1768.* Berkeley, Calif.

LaFarge, Oliver.
1935 "Revolution With Reservations." *New Republic* 84 (October 9): 232–34.
1957 "Termination of Federal Supervision: Disintegration and the American Indians." *The Annals of the American Academy of Political and Social Science* 311 (May): 41–46.

Lockwood, Frank.
1938 *The Apache Indians.* New York.

Loyola, Sister Mary.
1939 "The American Occupation of New Mexico, 1821–1852." *New Mexico Historical Review* 14 (January): 34–75; 14 (April): 143–99; 14 (July): 230–86.

Lummis, Charles F.
1966 *General Crook and the Apache Wars.* Edited by Turbesé Lummis Fiske. Flagstaff, Ariz.

Lurie, Nancy Oestreich.
1957 "The Indian Claims Commission Act." *The Annals of the American Academy of Political and Social Science* 311 (May): 56–70.

Lynn, Juana Fraser.
1966 "Archie McIntosh, the Scottish Indian Scout." *Journal of Arizona History* 7 (Autumn): 203–22.

Mansfield, Joseph King Fenno.
1963 *Mansfield on the Condition of the Western Forts, 1853–54.* Edited by Robert Frazer. Norman, Okla.

Manypenny, George W.
1880 *Our Indian Wards.* Cincinnati.

Mardock, Robert Winston.
1971 *The Reformers and the American Indian.* Columbia, Mo.

Mason, Joyce Evelyn.
1970 "The Use of Indian Scouts in the Apache Wars, 1870–1886." Ph.D. dissertation, Indiana University.

Matson, Daniel S., and Albert H. Schroeder, eds.
1957 "Cordero's Description of the Apache—1776." *New Mexico Historical Review* 32 (October): 335–56.

Mattison, Ray H.

1946 "Early Spanish and Mexican Settlements in Arizona." *New Mexico Historical Review* 21 (October): 273–327.

McCall, George Archibald.
1968 *New Mexico in 1850: A Military View.* Edited by Robert W. Frazer. Norman, Okla.

McCord, T., Jr.,
1946 "An Economic History of the Mescalero Apache Indians." M.A. thesis, University of New Mexico.

McNitt, Frank.
1970 "Fort Sumner: A Study in Origins." *New Mexico Historical Review* 45 (April): 101–18.

1972 *Navajo Wars: Military Campaigns, Slave Raids and Reprisals.* Albuquerque.

Merrill, James M.
1966 *Spurs to Glory: The Story of the United States Cavalry.* New York.

Miles, Nelson A.
1896 *Personal Recollections.* Chicago.

Moody, Marshall D.
1953 "Kit Carson, Agent to the Indians of New Mexico, 1853–1861." *New Mexico Historical Review* 28 (January): 1–20.

Moore, Mary Lu, and Delmar L. Beene, eds.
1971 "The Interior Provinces of New Spain: The Report of Hugo O'Conor, January 30, 1776." *Arizona and the West* 13 (Autumn): 265–82.

Moorhead, Max L.
1958 *New Mexico's Royal Road: Trade and Travel on the Chihuahua Trail.* Norman, Okla.

1968 *The Apache Frontier: Jacobo Ugarte and Spanish-Indian Relations in Northern New Spain, 1769–1791.* Norman, Okla.

1975a *The Presidio: Bastion of the Spanish Borderlands.* Norman, Okla.

1975b "The Spanish Deportation of Hostile Apaches: The Policy and the Practice." *Arizona and the West* 17 (Autumn): 205–20.

Mowry, Sylvester.
1859 *The Geography and Resources of Arizona and Sonora.* New York (New ed., San Francisco and New York, 1863.)

Murphy, Lawrence R.
1972 *Frontier Crusader—William F. M. Arny.* Tucson.

Myers, Lee.
1966 "Fort Webster on the Mimbres River." *New Mexico Historical Review* 41 (January): 47–57.

Nagel, Gerald S.
1974 "Economics of the Reservation." *Current History* 67 (December): 245–49, 278.

Nalty, Bernard C., and Truman R. Strobridge.
   1964   "Captain Emmet Crawford, Commander of Apache Scouts, 1882–1886." *Arizona and the West* 6 (Spring): 30–40.
"Notes and Documents."
   1946a *New Mexico Historical Review* 21 (July): 257–65.
   1946b *New Mexico Historical Review* 21 (October): 350–57.
   1947   *New Mexico Historical Review* 22 (January): 98–103.
Ogle, Ralph Hedrick.
   1970   *Federal Control of the Western Apaches, 1848–1886.* Albuquerque.
Opler, Morris E.
   1936   "An Interpretation of Ambivalence of Two American Indian Tribes." *The Journal of Social Psychology* 7: 82–116.
   1938   "A Chiricahua Apache's Account of the Geronimo Campaign of 1886." *New Mexico Historical Review* 13 (October): 360–86.
   1941   *An Apache Life-Way: The Economic, Social, and Religious Institutions of the Chiricahua Indians.* Chicago.
   1942   "Adolescence Rite of the Jicarilla." *El Palacio* 49 (February): 25–38.
   1955   "An Outline of Chiricahua Apache Social Organization." In *Social Anthropology of North American Tribes*, edited by Fred Eggan. Chicago, 1955.
   1961   "Cultural Evolution of the Southern Athapaskans, and Chronology in Theory." *Southwestern Journal of Anthropology* 17 (Spring): 1–20.
   1973   *Grenville Goodwin among the Western Apache: Letters from the Field.* Tucson.
Opler, Morris E., and Harry Hoijer.
   1940   "The Raid and War-Path Language of the Chiricahua Apache." *American Anthropologist* 42 (October–December): 617–34.
Opler, Morris E., and Catherine H. Opler.
   1950   "Mescalero Apache History in the Southwest." *New Mexico Historical Review* 25 (January): 1–36.
Oury, William S.
   1877   "A True History of the Outbreak of the Noted Chieftain Cochise in the Year 1861." *Arizona Weekly Star* (Tucson), June 28, July 5.
Park, Joseph F.
   1961   "The Apaches in Mexican-American Relations, 1848–1861: A Footnote to the Gadsden Treaty." *Arizona and the West* 3 (Summer): 129–46.
   1962   "Spanish Indian Policy in Northern Mexico, 1765–1810." *Arizona and the West* 4 (Winter): 325–44.
Parmee, Edward A.
   1968   *Formal Education and Culture Change: A Modern Apache Community and Government Education Programs.* Tucson.

Pattie, James Ohio.
  1905 *Pattie's Personal Narrative of a Voyage to the Pacific and Mexico,
        January 1824–August 1830*. Vol. 18 of *Early Western Travels,
        1748–1846*. Edited by Reuben Gold Thwaites. Cleveland.
Pfefferkorn, Ignaz.
  1949 *Sonora, A Description of the Province*. Translated by Theodore
        E. Treutlein. Albuquerque.
Pike, Zebulon Montgomery.
  1925 *The Southwestern Expedition of Zebulon Montgomery Pike*.
        Edited by Milo Milton Quaife. Chicago.
Poston, Charles D.
  1963 *Building a State in Apache Land*. Tempe, Ariz.
Priest, Loring Benson.
  1972 *Uncle Sam's Stepchildren: The Reformation of United States
        Indian Policy, 1865–1887*. 2d ed. New York.
Procter, Gil.
  1964 *The Trails of Pete Kitchen*. Tucson.
Prucha, Paul Frances, ed.
  1973 *Americanizing the American Indians: Writings by the "Friends of
        the Indian," 1880–1900*. Cambridge, Mass.
Pumpelly, Raphael.
  1918 *My Reminiscences*. 2 vols. New York.
  1965 *Pumpelly's Arizona: An Excerpt from "Across America and Asia"
        by Raphael Pumpelly, Comprising Those Chapters Which Con-
        cern the Southwest*. Edited by Andrew Wallace. Tucson.
*Record of Engagements with Hostile Indians Within the Military Divi-
        sion of the Missouri from 1868 to 1882, Lieutenant General P. H.
        Sheridan Commanding*. Washington, D.C., 1882.
Reeve, Frank D.
  1948 "Puritan and Apache: A Diary." *New Mexico Historical Review* 23
        (October): 269–301; 24 (January 1949): 12–53. (Editor.)
  1952 "Albert Franklin Banta: Arizona Pioneer." *New Mexico Historical
        Review*, 27 (April): 81–106; 27 (July): 200–52; 27 (October): 315–
        47; 28 (January 1953): 52–67; 28 (April): 133–47. (Editor.)
  1957 "Seventeenth Century Navaho-Spanish Relations." *New Mexico
        Historical Review* 32 (January): 36–52.
Reid, John Coleman.
  1858 *Reid's Tramp, or a Journal of the Incidents of Ten Months Travel
        Through Texas, New Mexico, Arizona, Sonora, and California*.
        Selma, Ala. (New ed., Austin, Tex., 1935.)
"Report of the Commissioner of Indian Affairs," various years.
"Report of the Secretary of the Interior," various years.
"Report of the Secretary of War," various years.
Rippy, J. Fred.
  1919 "The Indians of the Southwest in the Diplomacy of the United

States and Mexico, 1848–1853." *Hispanic American Historical Review* 2 (August): 364–96.

Rue, Norman L.
1971 "Pesh-Bi-Yalti Speaks: White Man's Talking Wire in Arizona." *Journal of Arizona History* 12 (Winter): 229–62.

Ruxton, George Frederick Augustus.
1951 *Life in the Far West.* Edited by Leroy R. Hafen. Norman, Okla.

Sabin, Edwin Legrand.
1935 *Kit Carson Days, 1809–1868.* 2 vols. New York.

Sacks, Benjamin H.
1962 "New Evidence on the Bascom Affair." *Arizona and the West* 4 (Autumn): 261–78.

Salzman, M., Jr.
1967 "Geronimo, The Napoleon of the Indians." *Journal of Arizona History* 8 (Winter): 215–47.

Schellie, Don.
1968 *Vast Domain of Blood.* Los Angeles.

Scholes, France.
1937–41 "Troublous Times in New Mexico, 1659–1670." *New Mexico Historical Review* 12 (April): 134–74; 12(October): 380–452; 13 (January): 63–84; 15 (July): 249–68; 15 (October): 369–417; 16 (January): 15–40; 16 (April): 184–205; 16 (July): 313–27.

Schroeder, Albert H.
1952 "Documentary Evidence Pertaining to the Early Historic Period of Southern Arizona." *New Mexico Historical Review* 27 (April): 137–67.

1955 "Fray Marcos de Niza, Coronado and the Yavapai." *New Mexico Historical Review* 30 (October): 265–96.

1963 "Report by Albert H. Schroeder for Western Apache Docket Number 22-D Before the Indian Claims Commission." 6 vols. Typescript. Santa Fe. University of New Mexico Library.

1968 "Shifting for Survival in the Spanish Southwest." *New Mexico Historical Review* 43 (October): 291–310.

Scott, Richard B.
1959 "Acculturation Among Mescalero Apache High School Students." M.A. thesis, University of New Mexico.

Smart, Captain Charles.
1867 "Notes on the 'Tonto' Apaches." *Smithsonian Institution Annual Report.* Washington, D.C.

Smith, Ralph A.
1962 "Apache Plunder Trails Southward, 1831–1840." *New Mexico Historical Review* 37 (January): 20–42.

1963a "Indians in American-Mexican Relations Before the War of 1846." *Hispanic American Historical Review* 43 (February): 34–64.

1963b "The 'King of New Mexico' and the Doniphan Expedition." *New Mexico Historical Review* 38 (January): 29–55.

1964 "The Scalp Hunter in the Borderlands, 1835–1850." *Arizona and the West* 5 (Spring): 5–22.

1965 "The Scalp Hunt in Chihuahua—1849." *New Mexico Historical Review* 40 (April): 117–40.

Sonnichsen, C. L.

1958 *The Mescalero Apaches*. Norman, Okla.

Spicer, Edward H.

1962 *Cycles of Conquest: The Impact of Spain, Mexico, and the United States on the Indians of the Southwest, 1533–1960*. Tucson.

Stanley, F.

1962 *The Apaches of New Mexico, 1540–1940*. Pampa, Tex.

Starnes, Gary B.

1971 "Juan de Ugalde (1729–1816) and the Provincias Internas of Coahuila and Texas." Ph.D. dissertation, Texas Christian University.

Steck, Dr. Michael.

Dr. Michael Steck Papers, University of New Mexico Library, Albuquerque, N.M.

Steiner, Stan.

1968 *The New Indians*. Evanston.

Stevens, Robert C.

1964 "The Apache Menace in Sonora, 1831–1849." *Arizona and the West* 5 (Autumn): 211–22.

Stout, Joseph A., Jr.

1974 *Apache Lightning: The Last Great Battles of the Ojo Calientes*. New York.

Szasz, Margaret.

1974 *Education and the American Indian: The Road to Self-Determination, 1928–1973*. Albuquerque.

Tate, Michael L.

1974 "Soldiers of the Line: Apache Companies in the U.S. Army, 1891–1897." *Arizona and the West* 16 (Winter): 343–64.

Taylor, Morris F.

1969 "Campaigns Against the Jicarilla Apache, 1854." *New Mexico Historical Review* 44 (October): 269–92.

1970 "Campaigns Against the Jicarilla Apache, 1855." *New Mexico Historical Review* 45 (April): 119–36.

Taylor, Theodore W.

1974 "American Indians and Their Government." *Current History*, 67 (December): 254–58, 275.

Thomas, Alfred Barnaby. ed. and tr. [all of them].

1931 "Governor Mendinueta's Proposals for the Defense of New Mexico, 1772–1778." *New Mexico Historical Review* 6 (January):

21–39.

1932   *Forgotten Frontiers: A Study of the Spanish Indian Policy of Juan Bautista de Anza, Governor of New Mexico, 1777–1787.* Norman, Okla.

1935   *After Coronado: Spanish Exploration Northeast of New Mexico, 1696–1727.* Norman, Okla.

1940   *The Plains Indians and New Mexico, 1751–1778.* Albuquerque.

1941   *Teodoro de Croix and the Northern Frontier of New Spain, 1776–1783.* Norman, Okla.

Thrapp, Dan L.

1964   *Al Sieber, Chief of Scouts.* Norman, Okla.

1967   *The Conquest of Apachería.* Norman, Okla.

1972   *General Crook and the Sierra Madre Adventure.* Norman, Okla.

1973   *Juh, An Incredible Indian.* El Paso, Tex.

1974   *Victorio and the Mimbres Apaches.* Norman, Okla.

Turcheneske, John A., Jr.

1973a   "The Arizona Press and Geronimo's Surrender." *Journal of Arizona History* 14 (Summer): 133–48.

1973b   "Arizonians and the Apache Prisoners at Mount Vernon Barracks, Alabama: 'They Do Not Die Fast Enough!' " *Military History of Texas and the Southwest* 11 (Nov. 3): 197–226.

Turner, Katherine C.

1951   *Red Men Calling on the Great White Father.* Norman, Okla.

Twitchell, Ralph Emerson.

1911–12   *Leading Facts of New Mexican History.* 2 vols. Cedar Rapids, Iowa.

Underhill, Ruth Murray.

1971   *Red Man's America: A History of Indians in the United States.* Rev. ed. Chicago.

Unrau, William E.

1972   "The Civilian as Indian Agent: Villain or Victim?" *Western Historical Quarterly* 3 (October): 405–20.

Utley, Robert M.

1961   "The Bascom Affair: A Reconstruction." *Arizona and the West* 3 (Spring): 59–67.

1973   *Frontier Regulars: The United States Army and the Indian, 1866–1891.* New York.

Valputic, Marian E., and Harold H. Longfellow, eds.

1971   "The Fight at Chiricahua Pass in 1869 as Described by L. L. Dorr, M.D." *Arizona and the West* 13 (Winter): 369–78.

Walker, Henry P., ed.

1971   "Soldier in the California Column: The Diary of John W. Teal." *Arizona and the West* 13 (Spring): 33–82.

Waltmann, Henry G.

1971   "Circumstantial Reformer: President Grant and the Indian Problem." *Arizona and the West* 13 (Winter): 323–42.

The War of the Rebellion: A Compilation of the Official Records of the Union and Confederate Armies. 70 vols. Washington, D.C., 1880–90.

Washburn, Wilcomb E.
1971   *Red Man's Land/White Man's Law: A Study of the Past and Present Status of the American Indian*. New York.

Watkins, Arthur V.
1957   "Termination of Federal Supervision: The Removal of Restrictions Over Indian Property and Person." *The Annals of the American Academy of Political and Social Science* 311 (May): 47–55.

Weaver, John M.
1947   "The History of Fort Lowell" M.A. thesis, University of Arizona.

Weaver, Thomas, ed.
1974   *The Indians of Arizona: A Contemporary Perspective*. Tucson.

Weaver, Thomas, and Ruth Hughes Gartell.
1974   "The Urban Indian: Man of Two Worlds." In *The Indians of Arizona: A Contemporary Perspective*, edited by Thomas Weaver. Tucson, 1974.

Welsh, Herbert.
1887   *The Apache Prisoners in Fort Marion, St. Augustine, Florida*. Philadelphia.

Westerman, Joann.
1974   "The Urban Indian." *Current History* 67 (December): 259–62, 275.

Wharfield, Colonel H. B.
1914   *Apache Indian Scouts*. El Cajon, Calif.
1965   *With Scouts and Cavalry at Fort Apache*. Tucson.
1971   *Cibicu Creek Fight in Arizona: 1881*. El Cajon, Calif.

Woody, Clara T., ed.
1962   "The Woolsey Expeditions of 1864." *Arizona and the West* 4 (Summer): 157–76.

Worcester, Donald E.
1941   "The Beginnings of the Apache Menace in the Southwest." *New Mexico Historical Review* 16 (January): 1–14.
1944   "The Spread of Spanish Horses in the Southwest." *New Mexico Historical Review* 19 (July): 225–32.
1945   "The Spread of Spanish Horses in the Southwest, 1700–1800." *New Mexico Historical Review* 20 (January): 1–13.
1951   "The Navaho During the Spanish Regime in New Mexico." *New Mexico Historical Review* 26 (April): 106–18.
1975   "Apaches in the History of the Southwest." *New Mexico Historical Review* 50 (January): 25–44.

Wyllys, Rufus K.

1931   "Padre Luis Velarde's Relación of Pimería Alta, 1716." *New Mexico Historical Review* 6 (April): 111–57.

Zimmerman, William, Jr.
   1957   "The Role of the Bureau of Indian Affairs Since 1933." *The Annals of the American Academy of Political and Social Science* 311 (May): 31–46.

Index

377